THE IMPACT OF TELEVISION ADVERTISING ON CHILDREN

NAMITA UNNIKRISHNAN
SHAILAJA BAJPAI

Sage Publications
New Delhi ▪ Thousand Oaks ▪ London

First published in 1996 by
Sage Publications India Pvt Ltd
M 32 Greater Kailash Market I
New Delhi 110 048

Sage Publications Inc
2455 Teller Road
Thousand Oaks, California 91320

Sage Publications Ltd
6 Bonhill Street
London EC2A 4PU

Published by Tejeshwar Singh for Sage Publications India Pvt Ltd, phototypeset by Pagewell Photosetters, Pondicherry, and printed at Chaman Enterprises, Delhi.

Library of Congress Cataloging-in-Publication Data

Unnikrishnan, Namita.
    The impact of television advertising on children / Namita Unnikrishnan, Shailaja Bajpai.
        p.   cm.
    Includes bibliographical references and index.
    1. Television advertising and children—India. 2. Television and children—India. I. Bajpai, Shailaja. II. Title.
    HQ784.T4U54   1995   302.23'4'083—dc20   95–20736

ISBN: 0–8039–9242–4 (US-HB)   81–7036–471–X (India-HB)
          0–8039–9243–2 (US-PB)   81–7036–472–8 (India-PB)

Sage Production Editors: Sarita Vellani ▪ Indiver Nagpal

To Ami who ensured that there was never a dull moment and to all the children who made this study a fascinating and enriching experience.

To our families for all their support.

To Vik and Jo forever, and after.

CONTENTS

List of Tables	**9**
List of Illustrations and Plates	**10**
List of Figures	**11**
Acknowledgements	**13**
Preface	**14**

PART I
TELEVISION

Introduction		**17**
1.	Television—The Magic Box	**35**
2.	Television: Ownership and Exposure	**42**
3.	Children and Television	**49**
4.	Is TV Altering Family Life?	**61**
5.	The World of Television	**78**
6.	Cable and Satellite TV	**94**
7.	The Future	**109**
Notes to Part I		**116**

PART II
ADVERTISING

Introduction		**123**
8.	Advertising and Television	**137**
9.	TV Commercials and Children	**146**
10.	Understanding Advertisements	**159**
11.	Elements of Advertising	**169**
12.	The Child in Advertising	**190**

13. TV Advertising in India   196
Notes to Part II   217

PART III
CONSUMERISM

Introduction   223
14. What TV Advertising Sells   234
15. Responses to Advertising   239
16. Children's Advertising   252
17. Toyland   278
18. Money, Money, Money   293
19. Dominant Images   301
20. Images and Attitudes   328
21. Changing Values   336
Notes to Part III   345

Conclusion and Recommendations   347
Annexures   371
Bibliography   413
Index   419

LIST OF TABLES

Tables

5.1 Programme Preference by Class — 80
5.2 Programme Preference by Sex — 84
11.1 Type of Music Used in Indian Advertising — 173
12.1 Type of Appeal Used in Indian Advertising — 191
14.1 Kinds of Commercials and Product Categories Advertised — 235
15.1 Preference for Advertised Goods by Class — 246
16.1 Favourite Cold Drink Ads by Class (in Order of Preference) — 261
16.2 Overall Soft Drink Consumption — 266
19.1 Languages Used in Advertising on Doordarshan — 306
19.2 Elements of Culture in Advertising — 311
19.3 Ranking of Ads by Children of Different Classes — 313
19.4 Classification of Indian Ads by Class — 318
19.5 The Top Ten Preferred Professions — 322
19.6 Ambitions of Children by Social Grouping — 324

LIST OF ILLUSTRATIONS AND PLATES

Illustrations

I.1 Dreams on Sale Everywhere . . . 23
3.1 Television: The Constant Companion 57
4.1 T.V.: Home Alone 63
7.1 All the Time, TV Time 111
8.1 Children: Hooked Up and Easy Prey 141
11.1 *Mein Bhi Madonna*: Aping the Michael Jacksons and
the Madonnas 174
16.1 Rebels without a Cause 273
19.1 Image Building: A Unifying Experience 303
19.2 India? But Mom I've Been Down this Street before 310
C.1 Drinking in a Vision of the World 349
C.2 Looking beyond the Tube of Plenty 365

Plates

11.1 Images to Live Up to 185
12.1 Children: A Good Bait for Customers 194
13.1 *Raga Desh*: Socially Relevant Advertising—Rejoicing in
the Maestros to Promote National Integration 214
13.2 Children Hold Up the Light of Freedom 216
16.1 Frooti: Tough Battle against the Fizzies 260
16.2 Buy a Ticket to Freedom 274
17.1 G.I. Joe: Big Names, Big Claims 280
17.2 Barbie: The Best Ambassador from the West 286
18.1 We are Going to Look Right 298
C.1 Advertising: Creating Problems, Offering Solutions 363

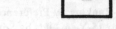

LIST OF FIGURES

Figures

I.1 Children, Television and Advertising (CTA) Study: Age/Class Profile of Total Sample — 21

2.1 TV, VCR Ownership — 44

2.2 Cable, VCR by Families Owning Colour/Black and White TV Sets — 45

3.1 Frequency of TV Viewing in Age Group 8 to 15 Years and above — 51

3.2 Frequency of TV Viewing by Age and Sex — 52

4.1 TV Viewing Pattern of 8 to 15-Year Olds — 67

5.1 Family Preferences for Doordarshan, Local Cable and Satellite TV — 79

5.2 Programme Preferences of 5 to 8-Year Olds — 82

5.3 Favourite DD Programmes: Age Group 8–15 Years — 83

6.1 Installation of Cable TV — 99

6.2 Channel Preference in Families of 8 to 15-Year Olds — 103

6.3 Favourite Satellite Channels by Cable Viewers — 105

9.1 Responses to the Question 'Do You Like TV Ads' by Age, Sex and Class — 148

9.2 Responses to the Proposition 'Ads are Better than Programmes' by Age, Class — 149

12.1 Advertising Appeal — 192

13.1 Weekly Pattern of Advertising on DD, 20 April–3 May 1992: CTA Study — 198

15.1 Preferences of 5 to 15-Year Olds for Household Durables — 248

16.1 Demand for Advertised Products — 256

16.2 Favourite Chocolate Ads: 5 to 15-Year Olds — 257

16.3 Children and Soft Drinks: 5 to 15-Year — 262

16.4 Responses to Soft Drink Ads of 5 to 15-Year Olds — 263

16.5 Soft Drink Consumption Patterns: 5 to 15-Year Olds — 267

16.6 Favourite Cycle Ads: 5 to 15-Year Olds — 272

17.1 Children's Desire to Own Toys/Games   288
18.1 What Children Want to Do with Rs 150   295
19.1 Culture: Impact of Ads by Class   314
19.2 Culture: Impact of Ads—Ranking by Preference and Sex   315
19.3 Future Aspirations of 5 to 15-Year Olds by Sex   326
19.4 Future Aspirations of 5 to 15-Year Olds by Class   327

ACKNOWLEDGEMENTS

We wish to thank the children, parents and teachers who made our research possible.

The International Development Research Centre deserves our very special thanks not only because it supported our research but because it constantly encouraged us. Dr Mira Aghi and Ms S. Thukral guided and helped us and reposed an unquestioned trust in our work.

We also wish to thank Jagriti, Mobile Creches and all the educational institutions which permitted us to interact with children and welcomed us during fieldwork.

Sushma Kapoor, who would have been part of the project had she been in India.

The Institute of Scientific Research and Communications.

Tripta Batra and Suneet Verma who contributed enormously as members of our Research Team, helping to organise and conduct research in different parts of the city.

Praveen Krishnamurthy who designed data analysis programmes for us.

To Sumita Sarkar for her assistance with taping and classifying TV ads.

Dr. S. Sheshadari of Nimhans for his valuable inputs and guidance.

Jaya Thankappan for her support and involvement throughout the project and for typing the manuscript.

The advertisers, professionals, media persons, experts and officials who shared their knowledge, experience, time and opinions with us.

Lola and P.C. Chatterjee who went out of their way to read and evaluate the manuscript.

The Delhi Science Forum for their help in July 1992.

Finally, Sage Publications: our editors Primila Lewis, Harsh Sethi, Sarita Vellani and Indiver Nagpal, with whom it was a pleasure to work.

PREFACE

The idea to conduct research on TV, advertising and children first took shape in 1990. It was not until 1992 that the project got underway. The final draft of the book was completed by May 1994 and the text is based primarily upon fieldwork conducted during the project. However, since then several changes have occurred in the world of television. An effort has been made to update information during editing of the manuscript. It is hoped that the observations and findings of the study will be of use to many different kinds of people including parents, teachers and older children.

May 1995   NAMITA UNNIKRISHNAN
                                                          SHAILAJA BAJPAI

1

TELEVISION

■

INTRODUCTION

TELEVISION

This book is the result of a growing sense of unease at what has been happening in the world of television and the manner in which ideas conveyed by television, particularly TV advertising, are beginning to shape our consciousness.[1]

Just a few years ago, before Pepsi, Adidas and a plethora of other consumer goods began to overwhelm the public mind, a visit to a village in Haryana offered a glimpse into the world of children newly entranced by television. At the time, there was only one household with a TV set in the village and the child of the house was the uncrowned king of the entire population of children. He strutted about bare-bottomed, well aware of the crowd of hopefuls of every conceivable size, that trailed behind him.

We struck up a conversation. Shyly the children attempted to articulate their passion for TV, giggling at memories of luxurious bathrooms and bathing women, screen images that amused them no end. They knew and loved the TV advertisements best of all, even though they acknowledged that they did not always understand them. The Amul chocolate advertisement seemed to have especially captured their imagination.

Not one of the 20-odd children who clearly remembered the ad and the product it sold had ever tasted a chocolate although they lived on the outskirts of Delhi, the capital of this huge country, close enough to a womb that was quietly nurturing an explosive consumer revolution.

The ad had conveyed to them that chocolate belonged to a category that could be labelled 'irresistible', especially to children. It had also given them something else to yearn for—a warm, comfortable and cosy family environment, a promise of loving indulgence that was different, perhaps more intimate than the kind familiar with. The language barrier (the ad they saw appeared in English) and the unfamiliar cultural milieu did not prevent their appreciation of these sentiments.

The chocolate dream as recounted by those children was arresting, particularly in the context of their lives. In their village, which was struggling to cope with a crippling lack of electricity, the priority at the time was to somehow sustain agricultural production. Village elders expressed an acute embarrassment at having jumped the gun to invest in modern mechanised agricultural methods that required electricity which, though promised, was so irregular as to threaten their agricultural operations. Typically too, lack of schooling facilities, inadequate health care, improper drainage and unsafe water remained problems that needed to be resolved. But the children were looking far beyond these realities at alternatives vested in the material world.

In the city, consumerism had already begun to spin its web. Children of the more affluent strata were moving very fast towards a consumption-oriented lifestyle, travelling further afield and luxuriating in conspicuous consumption—feasting on junk foods, revelling in video fare and longing to acquire a wide range of personal products. They seemed frantic to transform themselves into miniature adults capable of fitting into standardised international images.

Consumption patterns had begun to change visibly. Families travelling by train were now opting for tetrapack drinks and their children were devouring potato chips out of colourful packets instead of an array of home-made snacks, fruit and other small eats which were once the norm.

When the visit to the village in Haryana took place, television was of no great consequence. Although this was the era of *Buniyaad* and *Nukkad*, whether these serials would be harbingers of quality programming was still a question mark. What these serials did do was to extend television viewing, on a regular basis, from movie time, especially on Sundays, and from when *Chitrahaar* was aired, to another form of programming.

Television advertising told a different story. It begun to reveal its potential, standing head and shoulders above all other programming. How much more superior it was to become we could not have anticipated. After all, the Indian marketplace was still to throw off its defiant resistance to change and open its doors to multinational giants anxious to step in.

The conversation with the children about chocolates evoked an interest which continued to grow and fascinate as both TV and the advertising on it underwent transformation. Soon people began to marvel at the finesse of Indian TV commercials and admitted that they were as good, if not better, than ads made by the most developed nations of the world.

Our research on the impact of TV advertising on children was conducted with the understanding that of all segments of the television audience, children deserve special attention because they are most likely to accept and orient their view of life to the one TV and TV advertising promote, especially as television was becoming a major source of information and ideas.

There are, therefore, two main components and areas of study that this book incorporates—inextricably linked to each other. First, that advertising in *itself* is worth looking at (more so in its most sophisticated and advanced form, i.e. advertising on television). Such advertising appears innocuously between programming and is hard to get away from. Thus, sooner or later the TV viewer gets to see virtually every advertisement broadcast on the air and these leave an indelible mark on the mind of the individual.

Second, that television as a technology has changed the complexion and manner of conveying ideas to people and therefore, there is a need to examine the individual's relationship with the TV set. In our study, both aspects have been looked at from the standpoint of the child (with the age group extending from 5 to 15 years and the selection of respondents and families including children from all strata of society).[2]

Our study revealed that consumerism is the new religion of the day and that its most devout followers are children. This is not to say that the adult world is above the dictates of this new ethos. The difference is that the vision of the good life being drilled into viewers' minds by TV advertising is, in some ways, better internalised by children than the older generation. The latter's experience and identity spring largely from a more direct knowledge of the world rather than from a television set which provides a wide but artificial and selective exposure to the world.

Television advertising, we feel, suggests to children across the board that their redemption lies in high levels of consumption and that happiness is defined by the products that are now becoming available.

Our findings showed that almost every child in Delhi is a regular television viewer; that children spend a good deal of their free time in front of the TV set; that most Indian children watch adult programming; that TV viewing is adversely affecting their reading, writing and concentration skills; and that it is bringing about a major change in familial relationships by creating greater segregation between generations and individuals. Children are more aware today of products and brands in the marketplace and are reorienting their priorities to keep abreast with the changing economic environment. They are looking to a well-equipped future home (they cannot envisage life without a TV set), clothes have become more important than ever before and levels of dissatisfaction with what they have are now noticeably high.

Culturally, we found that TV advertising is imposing an image of life that is completely alien to the vast majority of Indian children. Many children are beginning to believe that the India and the Indians they see in TV ads are the only ones worth emulating and learning from. In other words, all other Indians and Indian lifestyles are either retrograde or passé—maybe even both.

Unfortunately, few attempts are being made to draw children, or adults for that matter, into a critical debate on the values and lifestyles that television and the advertising on it advocate. As a result, material aspirations are reaching unrealistic heights. Development has never appeared so disjointed. While consumerism is spreading like wildfire, access to the basics of life remains a serious problem for many.

In this context advertising, we believe, does have an ideological function in that it seeks to create an environment conducive to a particular interest group—that of manufacturers and marketers—by altering people's perceptions of themselves and of reality in order to be able to orient the large Indian market to their products.

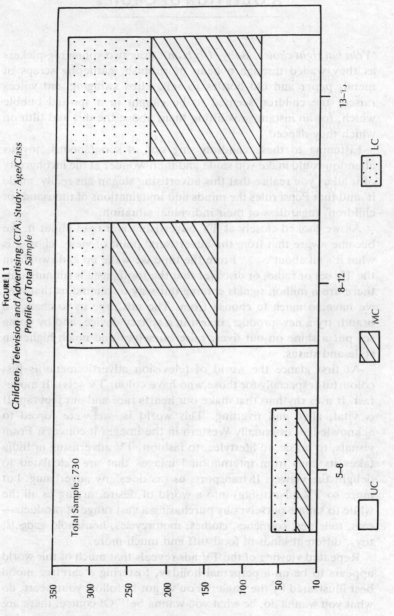

FIGURE 1 1

Children, Television and Advertising (CTA): Study: Age/Class
Profile of Total Sample

A QUESTION OF CHOICE

'*Yehi hai right choice, Baby. Un Huh*'! sang two young rag-pickers as they waded through a heap of rubbish, gathering scraps of metal, paper and old bottles to sell. Hips swinging and voices raised, the children seemed to be caught in a spirited bubble which, for an instant, was lifting them above the dirt and filth on which they danced.

Listening to these children sing out in spontaneous, joyous abandon could make you smile and then wonder at the incongruity of it all as you realise that this advertising slogan has really 'made it' and that Pepsi rules the minds and imaginations of thousands of children, regardless of their individual situation.

As we looked closely at TV advertising and read about it, we became aware that from the advertisers' point of view, 'choice' is what it's all about . . . . From the time we wake up and switch on the TV set or radio, or discover that the toothpaste is running out, there are a million signals coming our way to remind us that now we have so much to choose from. The ads urge us to change a brand, try a new product, invest in a snazzy device, and by doing so, put a shine on our lives, raise ourselves one notch higher in style and status.

At first glance the world of television advertisements is just colourful (especially for those who have colour TV sets). It moves fast. It uses rhythms that make our hearts race and our feet tap. It is vital, alive and rivetting. This world is, we were forced to acknowledge, essentially Western in the images it conveys. From visuals, to music, to lifestyles, to fashion, TV advertising in India takes its cues from international images that are calculated to delight the viewer. It transports us (as does any advertising, but more so TV advertising) into a world of desire, urging us all the while to satiate ourselves by purchasing a vast range of products—cars, toiletries, cosmetics, clothes, motorcycles, household gadgets, toys, different kinds of foodstuff and much more.

Repeated viewing of the TV ads reveals that much of this world appears to be on a perpetual holiday, fostering a carefree mood best illustrated by the jingle: 'You've got to follow your heart, do what you wanna do, be what you wanna be!!' Of course, there are

People who are strangers speak to them in the intimacy of their homes, making them both spectators to and participants in the situations being enacted. As George Gerbner, Dean Emeritus, Annenberg School of Communication, University of Pennsylvania has stated:

> I care about trying to characterise accurately this new age into which our children are born . . . . They are born into homes in which the TV set is on for several hours a day. They start viewing as infants. Most of the stories they hear are not told by parents, the school, the church or neighbours. They are told by a handful of conglomerates who have something to sell. That has a powerful affect.[4]

Gerbner's comment reflects the concern of many media experts in Western countries who continue to be deeply anxious about the commercial context of television programming and the impact of television advertising on society, particularly children. The focus on television advertising is not without reason.

Many ads broadcast on television are masterpieces. They are the creations of brilliant minds and wonderfully talented people who have but one mission in life: to persuade us to buy, buy and buy. Consumption, advertisers say, is limitless and always exciting. They even suggest, and perhaps believe, that consumption may hold the key to happiness and success, which we all strive for in life. All these messages get across, especially to children.

Most advertisers argue that the individual consumer has an independent mind. The business of persuading the consumer must, therefore, be seen as 'innocent' because it cannot force or push anyone into inconsequential buying. While this may or may not be true for the adult consumer, the primary concern of this study is children, who form a large section of the TV audience. Even the most hardcore advertisers are uncomfortable when it comes to discussing children in the context of advertising. Just what sort of influence does TV advertising have on the minds of the young? Does it set a future agenda and reorient their attitudes and aspirations by constantly telling them that consumption is essential to modern-day life?

The various influences television has on children have been studied extensively in a number of countries, particularly the U.S., where watching TV is a major activity. Children are considered 'vulnerable' and 'susceptible' to its influences. Television advertising being brief, repetitive and catchy has a lasting impact on them. Many researchers have suggested that advertising is unfair to children since they do not have the skills and experience required to process advertising messages in the context of their reality and needs.[5]

In this study we have concentrated upon the impact of TV advertising on children. Some of the questions that needed addressing were: Does TV advertising make children want to look and live in a certain way? If so, does it suggest how they can achieve that image and lifestyle? Does it enforce a sense of social responsibility? Does it create a true and acceptable picture of the adult world? In other words, does it influence the child's values, attitudes and aspirations? Or are children, at least those above eight years of age, discerning enough to recognise the commercial intent of advertising and therefore cautious of any distortions that it may present?[6]

Any study of the impact of TV advertising on children, we feel, must take into account the relationship between the child and television which, in India, is still evolving. After all, the success of advertisements shown on TV depends upon who watches them (the audience), how often they are watched (how much TV the child watches) and whether their messages are indeed absorbed and internalised sufficiently to induce the audience to eventually purchase a product.

Over the last decade television in India has undergone a complete transformation, moving from a single channel, government-controlled service to multi-channel, multi-optioned, transnational programming. In this process, advertising on television has blossomed and become fragmented, adapting itself to the dictates of the various avenues now open to it. For example while banner ads appear exclusively on films and programmes shown by the local cable channels, satellite TV permits liquor and jewellery ads prohibited on Doordarshan.

Right now, the novelty of seeing our single-source television network explode into a multi-choice one is making us hold our breath with excitement. Just owning a TV set and accessing newly available programming options has transformed TV into the cheapest and most varied form of entertainment.

This television explosion was experienced by the West almost 30 years ago. In studying the contribution of television—positive and negative—what has emerged is an acknowledgement of:

- How powerful a medium television is;
- How it can be used as an effective teaching tool;
- How it can serve to bring worlds, peoples and cultures together.

However, there is a large body of concerns related to television which have been addressed at the micro level—individual, parent, teacher, group, community—as well as at the macro level—national, policy, legal. Attention has been drawn to the fact that:

- The more TV a child watches, the greater the influence it has on the child;
- Watching TV for long hours adversely affects reading and writing skills;
- Television promotes violent and/or aggressive behaviour;
- Television as a passive activity takes children away from other, more direct, experiences;
- The passivity induced by watching too much TV can lead to obesity;
- Television may encourage and influence early sexual activity, drug and alcohol abuse;
- The world as TV represents it, is not always true to reality but children who grow up with such representations tend to believe and know the world as picturised on TV.[7]

We feel that as a nation on the threshold of a whole new spectrum of broadcasting in the nineties, we are greatly advantaged in that we can be guided by the experience of nations where television 'happened' much earlier.

We also need to assess the meaning and impact of current and future developments in TV technology (digital compression, interactive services et al.) and the unlimited access international media conglomerates have to the Indian sky. Television clearly represents one form of communication which is tied up with a world-view that promotes a material culture, the basis, relevance and future of which needs to be debated.[8]

If we choose to, we can learn about the beneficial and harmful effects of television, exploit its positive potential and prevent, insofar as is possible, the damage it can do to the growth and mental development of our children. We should not have to wait for 15 years to look at the impact of TV and the manner in which it is influencing our children, before desperately seeking a cure. By then the damage would already have been done.

This book seeks to reach out to individuals—parents, teachers, policy makers and even children—in the hope that it may initiate a debate on television and advertising which, in turn, may help us to determine the future of television in this country. It is, therefore, only a beginning. We would like to make clear the limitations we faced and explain the perspective from which we have looked at certain issues:

- Access in India to studies and information on the subject we were dealing with is still limited. However, we have used as much background material as we could in order to provide a broad perspective;
- Television as a mass media has been viewed by us, theoretically, as one means by which it is possible to produce and distribute symbolic forms/representations (which are invested with meanings) for eventual consumption by large audiences. Undoubtedly, these semiotic structures originate from within society and will change in accordance with social processes. Therefore, we believe that TV influences, and is influenced by, social, cultural and political forces and developments.
- It is not possible or within the scope of the present study to examine all of these processes. TV and TV advertising touch many aspects of our lives. This is reflected by the views of many people interviewed by us but the answers to some of their fears and anxieties can only emerge when the debate within society takes note of these.

    For instance, after reading this book a reader might well ask: 'Whose responsibility is it to protect the child from the impact of TV and TV advertising?' Clearly there is a collective responsibility and a response should be forthcoming from parents and educationists as well as advertisers, businessmen, the government and society at large.

However, we hope more research on television, advertising and children will start from where we have left off.

■ Due to the limited time available for research and the fact that the subject was so broad, we have presented an analysis of the major aspects of the impact of TV and TV advertising which our interaction with children in Delhi drew attention to.

■ Since the purpose of this study was to initiate a debate involving as wide an audience as possible, we have adopted a style which makes for easy reading. We have deliberately stayed away from theoretical and academic discourse, although a variety of views have been woven into the text.

■ The question of culture and society and the role of television and TV advertising in this context, is a very complex one. We understand culture as a reflective process which is a part of all personal, social, economic and political practices and interactions. Culture then, is constantly in a state of flux, containing and mirroring meanings and values that originate and evolve distinctively within these for different social groups and classes.

■ Terms such as 'Westernisation' have been used widely throughout the text for want of a better, more appropriate definition. The term is not meant to be pejorative but rather to indicate how the dominance of Western ideologies have created a culture, a whole way of being, thinking and feeling in societies such as ours.

The process of Westernisation is associated with giving us a particular kind of administrative framework, introducing industrialisation, constructing the infrastructure it required—communications, railways, etc.—and equipping us with the means for mass production in agriculture, industry and technology.

Westernisation has also meant an economy dominated by market forces and consumerism. In turn, the latter has spawned a world of services and goods which we today identify as off-shoots of Western culture: potato chips and colas, tomato ketchup and pizzas, jeans and MTV . . . . These products of the Western way of life are beginning to dominate and overwhelm other social and cultural customs, especially in countries which have been neither politically or economically strong enough to withstand their onslaught.

Since Indian advertising, by this criterion, reflects a heavily Westernised ethos, we have had to repeatedly deal with the process of Westernisation, its impact, meaning and consequences, throughout the book.

NOTES

1. *Terminology*
   For the purpose of this book the definition we have followed for the term 'TV' is: *TV is anything and everything that comes through a TV screen from any source: terrestrial TV (Doordarshan), cable networks, satellite networks and even video cassette players.*
   Programming vs. advertising: The menu on television comprises a main course—programming. Programming is interspersed with, or interrupted by, advertisements.

METHODOLOGY

The contents of this book are based on 15 months of research and study in Delhi (1992–93). The relationship between the child and television, as it is evolving in a large, metropolitan city like Delhi, is likely to be similar to the experience of children in other parts of India, especially in urban areas. Since the TV advertisements that the children in our sample responded to are those that are broadcast to the whole nation via Doordarshan's National Network, they will be familiar to the majority of Indian viewers.

After analysing TV advertising appearing on Doordarshan, we evolved a questionnaire and methodology which we discussed with child psychiatrists and psychologists in Delhi and Bangalore. They gave us several useful insights into the world of children and made suggestions on how we should approach children. They pointed out that although children are basically honest, dominant behaviour in the group could indicate the kind of peer group pressure that might steer some children into putting forward views other than their own. They also warned us that children sometimes attempt to provide the 'right answers' rather than to state openly how they feel about the issues raised.

We included group discussions as a follow-up to the formal questionnaires hoping that these would help reveal the way children felt most deeply about television and advertising. Our intention was to gather information both formally and informally. One questionnaire was designed so that children in the 8 + age group could respond to it themselves and another to be used by us during interactions with children under 8 years of age, and their families.

All interviews with 5 to 8-year olds were conducted at their homes with the permission and participation of elders. Most of the older children were contacted at their schools and interviews/group discussions held with the concurrence of school authorities. We used Hindi and English to communicate with them.

The questionnaires sought qualitative and quantitative responses on the following:

(a) Exposure: Did the child have a TV set at home? A VCR/VCP? Cable? Satellite? How many TV sets?

(b) Relationship with TV: How much TV did they watch? When and what? Who usually took decisions on what should be watched? Who at home switched the TV on/off? Did children discuss what they saw on TV with anyone?

(c) Viewing habits: What do children like watching on TV? Options exercised on cable, satellite and Doordarshan and, more specifically, the programmes they enjoyed watching.

(d) Reaction to advertising: Did children like watching ads? What did they like about the ads? Which cold drink, sweet, chocolate, ice cream, toy ads did they like best? Which were their favourite ads? Did they desire, need and demand products advertised on TV? How much pocket money did they receive?

(e) Aspirations: What were their aspirations? What would they like to be when they grow up? What durable commodities would they like to have in their own homes?

It must be remembered that we were going to talk to hundreds of children who lived very different lives from one another. Some were very privileged—they had everything a child could desire, including the advantages of a good education, books to read and every conceivable material comfort. Others had almost nothing, not even two square meals a day. Their vision of the world, their experiences, their hopes and needs were all radically different.

At every interaction, although we used the same questionnaire (the one for 5 to 8-year olds was shorter), we painstakingly explained each question to the children, cleared any doubts they had (to some we had to explain what a TV advertisement was) and encouraged them to answer as truthfully and honestly as possible. There were no right and wrong answers, we told them.

The group discussions were a delight. Children soon warmed up and debated various issues including 'What is an ad? What do ads do? Are they honest? What sort of view of India do you see in advertisements?' We used a couple of ads to test recall and understanding.

Some members of the research team were acutely sensitive to the environment in which they met children. They were embarrassed at having to ask consumption-related questions when the child seemed to have so little.

This is a tragedy—one that we simply cannot ignore. So many children are being urged, just as we are, to live by the standards of the rich. This message pervades their thinking, however irrelevant it may be to their lives. Some of them can acknowledge the new consumption ethic that is developing around them. Others cannot. They are confused, diffident and unhappy. In the chapters that follow we have spoken out on behalf of the deprived child who is oppressed by the ways of our world.

Lastly, we have used the terms upper, middle and lower classes to differentiate broadly between different social segments to which the children we met belong. But the criterion for defining these groups was not income-related. (We could not solicit accurate information on family income directly from children.)

By and large we have defined the school rather than the family. Each school caters predominantly to children of a broad social class. A look at the professions of parents who send their children to the different institutions covered by the study confirms this.

These terms have also been used from a consumer standpoint. In this context we see the three social groupings as bearing the following characteristics:

(i) The upper class: This comprises families with a relatively high educational level which are affluent in terms of material and non-material things (they have the best exposure to ideas, culture and information and are, therefore, in a position to make choices that others cannot. It is, by and large, this section that sees itself, and its lifestyle, reflected in many advertisements. This group can afford not to watch television, and has the wherewithal to enhance the quality of life of its children beyond material necessities most of which they can take for granted.

(ii) The middle class: This is seen as the social grouping where consumerism has made the greatest impact. This class seeks to maximise on material goods and looks to them for status and security. TV viewing is consequently a major activity, and the influence of TV is the greatest here.

(iii) The lower class: This social group includes families which are just about managing to keep their heads above water and those who live frugally under harsh conditions. The trickle-down effect which is initially generated by consumerism is visible amongst these families. Many more have acquired TV sets although their quality of life has not improved significantly and it is hard to see television as a priority when the basics of food, water, shelter, education and family health have still to be acquired.

2. For a breakdown of the research sample which included 730 children and in many cases their teachers and families as well, please see Graph 1 entitled 'Sample'.

3. In their book *Social Communication and Advertising* (see bibliography) these authors describe the setting for advertising in the following way:

We may think of marketing as the host, and advertising as the master of ceremonies and conductor. Their staging for the spectacle of consumption often is brilliant, so much so that it can distract us from our duty to ensure that we do not sacrifice or neglect other important values and goals just because we have become enraptured by the dance.

They see advertising as one of the most important social, economic and cultural institutions in society—'a communications activity through which social change is mediated'.

While the authors suggest that there is nothing intrinsically manipulative about the 'masks' designed by advertising, other writers like Vance Packard are unrestrained in their critique of advertising which uses the 'depth approach' to manipulate people's minds.

4. George Gerbner's statement is quoted from a debate on TV violence in which Peggy Charen (President, Action for Children's Television), Deborah Prothrow-Smith (Harvard School of Public Health), Rosalyn Weinman (Vice President of Broadcast Standards and Practices, NBC), Dick Wolf (television producer), Ronald Slaby (senior scientist, The Education Development Centre and lecturer, Harvard University) and John Leonard (TV critic) also participated.

In the course of the debate, the discussion veered around to whether certain representations on TV should be banned or censored by strict policies, or whether in a democracy such a move would be viewed as a curtailment of the freedom of expression. To us, in the context of the Indian situation, an important first step is to create awareness regarding the use of media. In the end, it is the viewer who counts and it is the viewer who must exercise the right to accept or reject various kinds of programming.

5. There are two dominant views on the relationship of TV advertising with the child audience. From the advertisers point of view it makes eminent sense to spend vast amounts of money on commercials aimed at children if the end result is higher current and future day sales. The popularity of advertisements put out on TV makes this proposition attractive to ad agencies, producers/sponsors, and to those who control the mass media. This group argues that it would be a mistake to harp on the vulnerability of the child viewer. They feel that very young children who find it difficult to distinguish between ads and programmes are in any case too young to buy any of the products advertised. Older children on the other hand have an equal right to be informed by honest advertising and it is up to their parents to decide what information their children should receive. Scott Ward, Daniel Wackman and Ellen Wartella's study, *Children Learning to Buy: The Development of Consumer Information Processing Skills* (1975) is sometimes quoted to prove that children aged 7 and above are conversant with the selling intent of commercials on TV.

On the other hand those who favour a policy to restrict TV advertising aimed at children, including parents and consumer groups, claim that it is unfair to young children because they do not have the cognitive ability or enough real life experience to handle the messages and suggestions made to them by TV commercials and that this can encourage children to desire inappropriate products and lead to unwanted parent–child conflict.

The American Federal Trade Commission's 1981 report clearly argues that advertising to young children is inherently unfair. Aimee Dorr in her book *Television and Children. A Special Medium for a Special Audience* (1986), discusses how children, until they are between 7 and 9 years of age, cannot really identify the persuasive selling intent of commercials and, because they have less knowledge and experience of the physical and social world, this could 'lead them to misunderstand, misevaluate and wrongly learn from television'.

6. Eric Barnouw in his book *The Sponsor. Notes on a Modern Potentate* (1978, p. 98) writes: 'Commercials have worked with success—toward revision of many traditional tenets of our society . . . reverence for nature has been replaced by

a determination to process it. Thrift has been replaced by the duty to buy. The work ethic has been replaced by the consumption ethic.'

7. These observations are based on research and campaigns conducted by a number of organisations and institutes which have studied the impact of television on children. In the United States, the American Academy of Pediatricians produced a task force report in 1984 on 'Children and Television' which raised some of these issues. Action for Children's Television (ACT), also based in the U.S. and one of the oldest and most visible citizens' action groups, has similarly drawn attention to the positive and negative aspects of television viewing by children. Consumer societies such as the Penang Consumer Society, Malaysia, have conducted independent research which reflects the very same concerns.

8. Eric Barnouw in *The Sponsor* draws attention to the dangers of squandering resources:

> The consumption binge which television has done so much to push has been fouling air, water, roads, streets, fields, and forests . . . American television is not only American, but multinational. Sending its programmes, mythology, and salesmanship into more than a hundred countries, it offers its salvation-through-consumption message—welcomed by many groups and creating enclaves of high consumption even within wastelands of poverty. In poor societies the drive to divert scarce resources and funds into the unnecessary-made-necessary naturally meets resistance and even indignation—and yet presses on. If it should achieve success comparable to that on the home front, it could quickly push the planet to catastrophe.

This view is gaining greater acceptability especially amongst those concerned with what production (of the kind that advertising promotes) is doing to the earth. It is suggested that the theory that the developing world can, if it tries hard enough, 'catch up' with the nations of the North, conveniently side-steps the real issue. Currently 20 per cent of the world's population is using up to 80 per cent of the world's resources and if similar levels of affluence are to be enjoyed by more and more people outside the North, either their levels of consumption would have to be curtailed, or the earth's resources would be consumed so rapidly as to endanger its survival.

1

TELEVISION

THE MAGIC BOX

'My six-year-old son was going to see a film at a cinema hall for the first time in his life. I was amused at his excitement and pleased that I had proposed the outing.

At the hall, we bought tickets and took our seats. My son gazed around. Then the lights dimmed and the film rolled. Unable to believe his eyes he whispered urgently, "*Amma*, I have never seen a TV screen this big!" '

—*A mother in New Delhi*

AN OVERVIEW

How times have changed! Today, children born into 'television families' regard television as a permanent fixture in their lives. The TV set is as familiar to them as the faces of family members— sometimes even more so. Unlike human beings, the TV set is always there, to entertain and to keep children company, especially when no one else is in the mood to play, chat or interact with them. Little children love the way a television set responds instant- aneously to the press of a button; they enjoy feeling they can control it and make it do what they want.[1]

For the child of the nineties, television has come to represent a state of complete bliss or *nirvana*. As one teenage girl in Delhi put it:

When I come home from school there's nothing I like better than to kick off my shoes, get into some comfortable clothes, and switch on the TV. There's always something to watch. You don't have to concentrate, you don't have to think. You can relax completely, get away from school and from studying. You never really feel bored.

This remark mirrors fairly accurately the opinion of many of the children we met in the course of our fieldwork in Delhi. As such, it indicates a complete break with the past—a change in the attitudes, perceptions and lifestyle of the Indian child.

Even until a decade ago, children growing up in metropolitan India lived by an entirely different agenda—certainly television formed no part of it. For entertainment, for an escape from the routine drudgery of life, children did what the rest of India was doing: they went to the movies.

Television in India played second fiddle to the silver screen—cinema. We boasted then, and still do, of the largest film industry in the world. Every movie hall was packed and people waited with baited breath for new releases, planning, plotting, scheming to somehow wangle tickets for a show. It was from films, and film stars that little children and teenagers alike acquired role models, mannerisms, attitudes and even figures of speech. From Dev Anand's cocky air and Rajesh Khanna's romantic smile to Amitabh Bachchan's angry young man image; from Sharmila Tagore's coquettish looks and Rekha's sultry beauty to Sridevi's impish charm—there were so many superstars to admire and imitate.

Although cinema continues to dominate public taste, its visual arena has shrunk from a panoramic screen to a 12-inch one and today, fewer and fewer people venture out to cinema halls to satiate their hunger for Hindi or other language films.

And why should they? The latest films are now just an arm's length away—on TV. With an investment of between Rs. 10,000 and Rs. 1,50,000 or more (depending on how sophisticated the consumer can afford to be), it is possible to partake of a veritable technological feast. On offer are television sets, video cassette players, dish antennas, and cable and satellite connections. Together, this range of products and services is designed to keep you entertained for every waking moment of the day (and night) with an endless treat of films, serials, documentaries, news broadcasts, advertisements, and other entertainment/information programmes.

In India, the evolution of television into a medium of consequence (dealt with in greater detail further on) has been painfully slow and has been characterised by long periods of stagnation and sudden flurries of activity. But while our nation may have adopted a ponderous pace with regard to the use of this very powerful technology, elsewhere in the world amazing changes have been and are still taking place, altering the manner and speed at which information can be transmitted across the globe.

Silently and unobtrusively, the world has shrunk until it is possible to communicate over huge distances in a fraction of the time that it used to take. Transnationalisation of the media is swiftly unifying the world by beaming the same programmes to people of different nationalities, races and cultures and is, thereby, also skipping over political, social and economic hurdles that once etched boundaries between one country and another. For instance, the satellite TV service, STAR TV is beamed to 53 nations across Asia, West Asia and South-East Asia.

Since 1991, India has been rapidly moving towards an integration with the world market. One consequence of liberalisation is that the country has had to open its doors to new information technologies. Computers, video machines, electronic telephone exchanges, fax machines, and satellite connections have crept up on us and we have absorbed them without much ado.

However, for the average consumer, the most telling change has come about in the use of television, which is now not only widely accessible but is also multifaceted, offering as it does a wide range of programme choices in many different languages.

It is useful to remember that in 1991, the majority of Indian viewers had access to only one TV channel with limited broadcast hours. The national, state-owned and controlled TV network, Doordarshan, offered a single national/regional service which usually ran (with substantial breaks in-between) from 7 a.m. to 11 p.m. Programming was almost wholly indigenous and dominated by Hindi films. Unlike many developing countries in South-East Asia and elsewhere, India's reliance on and use of imported programming was negligible.

From the mid-eighties onwards, audiences in the four metropolitan cities of Delhi, Bombay, Madras and Calcutta were offered a second local channel which broadcast only during the evenings.

The schedule included local language talk shows, plays or skits and a few foreign serials.

In the nineties, within the span of just three years, the entire spectrum changed irrevocably. Today, viewers throughout the country have access to double digit channel options. The advent of transnational satellite TV, in one fell swoop, altered and broadened our choices: we now have additional Doordarshan channels beamed by satellite, privately owned Indian language satellite channels and, of course, foreign language channels. Many of these, including all the STAR TV channels, are 24-hour services.

In some areas of Delhi today, cable networks are luring viewers with a 40–60 channel offer and the urban viewer is suddenly innundated with a bewildering choice of programmes. It is possible now to spend hours watching programmes designed and executed not here, in the familiar Doordarshan studios, but in the United States, Hong Kong and Britain.

In a manner of speaking, we have leap-frogged several phases of the television experience and, some might say, of development. Overnight, we moved from a single-channel world into a multi-channel one. We have never really known the meaning of multi-network terrestrial TV (for example, in Britain this meant access to BBC 1, BBC 2, ITV and, more recently, Channel 4. In the United States network TV was the staple till the late seventies: ABC, NBC and CBS dominated the small screen). Similarly, cable TV (as a separate entity from satellite TV) did not exist long enough to be recognised as an independent option in India.

Instead, we have shifted dramatically from a low-key and limited relationship with television to one that now provides so much variety that we could well suffer from visual indigestion; variety moreover, that represents a major turning point in terms of programme content, offering as it does so many different kinds of programme types: soap operas, police serials, situation comedies, talk shows, game shows, films, cartoons, news, current affairs, documentaries and so on with the accent on foreign programming growing immeasurably.

The effect all this will have upon us is still incalculable. For example, our children are growing up with a sophisticated knowledge of TV, a visual literacy their parents never knew. In fact, many of them will be visually literate but still unable to read or write. What influence will this have on them? Future research will need to concentrate on subjects such as this.

As we look at the television experience and children's relationship with TV, the rapidity of change they have been exposed to should be kept in view.

THE TV EXPERIENCE

Many writers focus on TV as an experience unlike any other in the history of mankind. They appreciate the fact that TV is a 'window to the world': it brings real life drama, action and happenings into the home of the viewer who can, sitting comfortably and even alone, participate in real and imagined events without having to stir, talk, share or even explore. Many of them believe that the very technology of television determines the nature and impact of its influence on the individual viewer.[2]

Television is exciting. Its potential as a mass media is unquestioned. Sitting in Delhi, you can witness a war in the Gulf and feel that you are watching history unfold.

The sports lover no longer needs to jostle for tickets to a good match or sit out in the heat amidst crowds in a stadium. The TV camera provides a better view of every exciting moment and carries the crowds' cheers right into the home, office or schoolroom. Meanwhile, the voice of the commentator reassuringly explains what is happening on the field.

The nature lover, the student of geography, biology or natural history can also succumb blissfully to programmes designed to transport him into the mountains, under the rush of sea water, or into tiny crevices where the secrets of worlds, not easily accessible, are revealed by the hidden camera.

The affluent find a comforting reflection of themselves in the elegant dramatisation of the lives of the rich and the famous who live by a code that television presents as a model to be emulated. The average viewer hungers to be 'like them' and may even feel a thrill at being able to peek into lives (and homes) which, before TV, were hidden from the public eye.

If you need advice, TV brings you a host of business, current affairs and news programmes to keep you abreast with events in the world that may affect your professional and other interests. Then there are talk show hosts, beauticians, and gym instructors to help you fulfill more personal needs.

And so it goes on. There is information, excitement, entertainment, music and dance, travel and fun. And there are advertisements.

The question is: Does TV alter our lives in any way? Is the act of watching TV one of those things modern people do just because TV is there? Has it become a necessity or can we envisage life without it?

LIFE BEFORE AND AFTER

Before television, people had to rely on their own resources, their friends and families and the communities they belonged to, to fill in leisure time. People organised activities, played or went out with their children, read, learnt to create things with their hands, developed talents like music or sports. They went on voyages of discovery—learning about life and the world around them from direct experience. At home they ate together, facing one another, found time to talk, share and sort out problems.

Television is rapidly changing all this. Without people realising just how, TV has forever altered the complexion of their relationships. This, more so, in a country like ours where television has come to represent 'freedom' from many of the things we believe we suffer from.

Many urban Indians see television as a feast of inexpensive entertainment. Families calculate that they would, on an average, spend anywhere between Rs. 150 and Rs. 300 or more if a couple were to take two children to a movie show. For others it is a welcome sign that we have been accepted into the large international family of television viewers and can today watch what they watch, and have **our** programming beamed to other nations. The effect all this is having on Indian television is also viewed as a cause for celebration. At a seminar held in Delhi during the winter

of 1993, some participants discussing popular culture felt strongly
that STAR TV was at least forcing Doordarshan, the national TV
service, to improve the quality of its programming.

Television has captured the popular imagination.

Certainly every discussion initiated on television during the
course of our study with groups of adults provided and evoked
very interesting responses. Some people love TV and cannot imagine
life without it; a few despise it and see it as a dangerous form of
mental manipulation; most others simply accept it as a given and
live with it. Very few reject it.

Perhaps the best barometer of the transformation TV has wrought
and its impact on our lives, is the younger generation. For children,
in their relationship with the television set and what it transmits,
reflect the enormity of the change we have witnessed in the span of
a few short years.

In the following chapters, we will examine the nature of this
relationship in terms of ownership of TV sets, exposure to the
media (i.e. through TV, VCR or via cable), the role of television
in family life, the child's viewing patterns and how far parents
intervene or regulate their children's TV habits.

$$\boxed{2}$$

TELEVISION

OWNERSHIP AND EXPOSURE

In an attempt to assess the impact of television, and particularly that of television advertising on children in Delhi, we interviewed more than 730 children and, in many cases, their families and teachers. These children represented a cross-section of Delhi's population. Our interaction with them was conducted either in their schools or at their homes in slums, middle class residential colonies and the affluent areas of the capital.

Of the 730 children and families covered by this study, 95 per cent had TV sets at home. Of these TV-owning families, 69 per cent had already acquired colour television sets, more than 40 per cent owned black and white sets and about 55 per cent—*or more than five out of 10 families*—had VCRs. Close to a third of the children in the 8 to 15 years age group told us that their families had gone all the way, and possessed colour TVs, VCRs and cable/satellite connections. These figures suggest, quite obviously, that the television set has become one of the most important household commodities.[3]

The Audience Research Unit at Doordarshan (DART), the state-controlled television network in India, points out that the broadcast of popular serials like the *Ramayana* and *Mahabharata* towards the end of the eighties helped boost the sales of TV sets across the country. Regular TV viewing became an addiction with these epic TV dramas establishing themselves as a Sunday morning ritual.

By Doordarshan's own estimates, there were 20,95,537 (over two million) TV sets in 1982. Exactly a decade later—between the time the TV network went truly commercial with the launch of its sponsored programme scheme and satellite television established its hold (at least on urban India)—the number of TV sets had gone up to 3,48,58,000 (almost 35 million). This put the TV audience at close to 125 million. According to latest market research estimates, TV viewership figures were up to almost 200 million in the year 1992–93, while the figure for TV owning households is estimated to now exceed 40 million.[4]

The fact that 95 per cent of the children interviewed during this study in Delhi had a TV set at home is remarkable in itself (or have we become so accustomed to the new consumer ethic which dominates life in urban India, that we are no longer surprised at this shift in priorities?). Certainly at one time, we considered ourselves a nation sensitive to the extreme inequalities amongst people in the country. We were constantly reminding ourselves of just how many Indians were deprived of even such basics as adequate food, clothing and shelter.

In that scenario words such as 'luxury' and 'opulence' were frowned upon and the sermons delivered to the poor always urged them to focus on improving their lives by investing in health, education and nutrition. Spending lavishly on ceremony and marriage, having large families and paying insufficient attention to family health were considered unwise. The poor were blamed for perpetuating their misery by indulging in such wastefulness.

The economic conditions under which most Indians live today have not altered significantly. In the cities, the quality of life is, perhaps, deteriorating for the poor, who now live in the most congested and filthy environments with bare minimum facilities. Yet, judging from our visits to several slums, a television set is no longer treated as an indulgence—it rates higher than regular water, electricity and decent food.

In one of the poorest areas of Delhi, a *basti* in Paharganj, where unemployed men sleep out in the crowded *galis* or on sidewalks during the day while out-of-school children amuse themselves, the sheer volume of crooked antennas loosely wired to low-roofed tenements left us bewildered.[5] Every family we met had a long list of justifications for having acquired a TV set: for them it is an essential part of their lives; they treat it as their teacher—that faceless link with the rest of their country and the world from which they feel oddly isolated; their baby-sitter on call, and most significantly, the entertainer they turn to for deliverance from the harshness of their environment. Despite rampant unemployment and irregular incomes, the residents in this area had found the

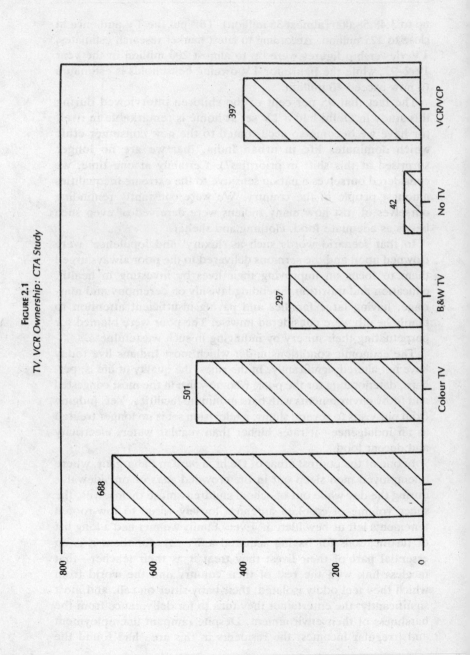

FIGURE 2.1
TV, VCR Ownership: CTA Study

FIGURE 2.2

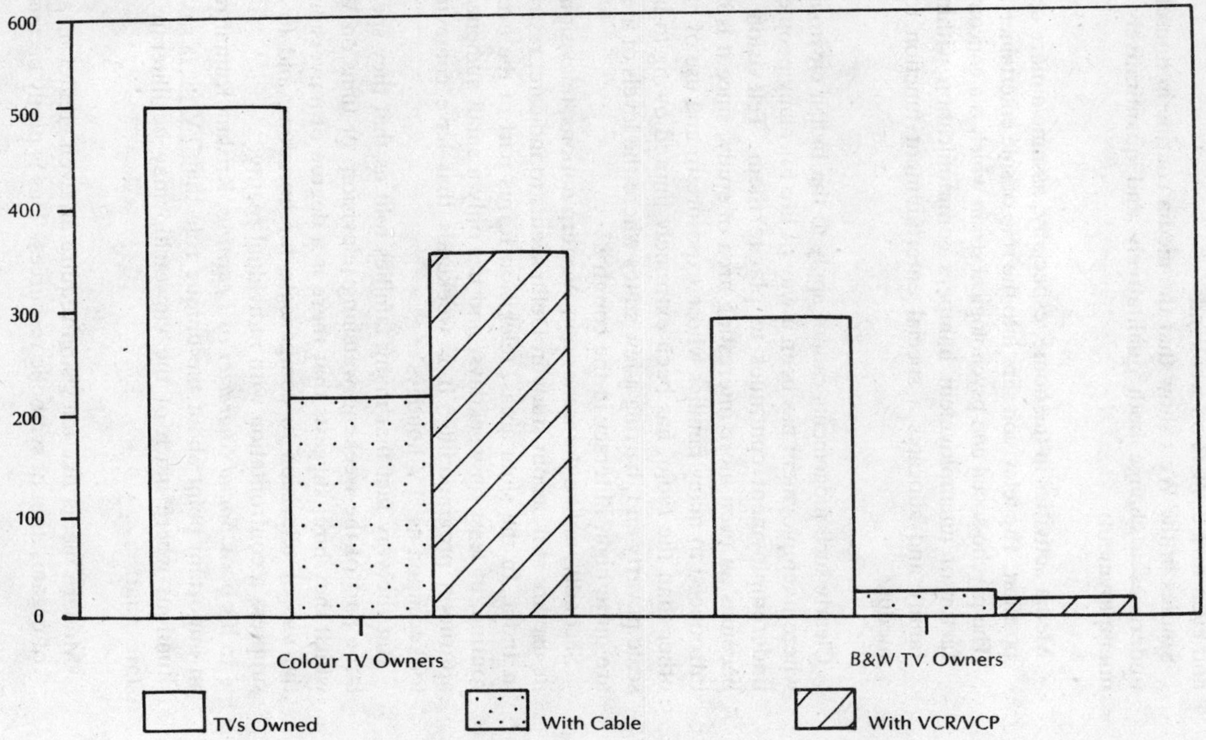

Cable, VCR by Families Owning Colour/Black and White TV Sets

means to purchase a TV set, rig up illegal electricity connections and even hire a VCR on weekends.

Studies in the West show that the media routine in households undergoes a change both qualitatively and quantitatively with unemployment:

> Media activities in the home, especially, assume a more central position. The television slips into the role of sole entertainer . . . . The psycho-social and psychological strain which is a concomitant factor of unemployment hampers communication within the family and allocates a special entertainment function to the media.[6]

Clearly such judgements cannot apply to the Indian environment where unemployment has been a way of life for many people and underemployment continues to plague them. Television then becomes an even more interesting area of study, since it is being introduced to many families whose exposure to and use of media other than the radio, has been extremely limited owing to large-scale poverty and, barring a few states where the levels of literacy are quite high, illiteracy in the country.[7]

Secondly, unlike the scenario in Western nations, television and its use are still, as our study in Delhi seems to indicate, restricted in India. In the slum areas, television forms part of the evening routine, at least on weekdays, and has only a small audience for afternoon programming. It is weekends that have come to be looked upon as 'TV holidays'.

But the very fact that many families told us that they spend a large part of the weekend watching television, or films on VCPs which they hire, suggests that there is a degree of universality in the use of television to compensate for boredom, and to help suppress a confrontation with individual reality.

In his book *Social Character of Learning*, Krishna Kumar raises an important point about the unique role that TV plays even in situations where much of the viewership may be illiterate. He states that:

> Modern media like television require an even greater measure of organisation of symbolic resources. This is partly because of

the extraordinary reach of these media, and the fact that their reach is not dependent upon prerequisites such as literacy or education. The potential audience of each programme prepared for television is many times larger than that of a successful literary text. This is one reason why the preparation of television texts is fraught with extra caution exercised by those involved in text preparation in response to the demands and conditions imposed on them by the owners of telecasting technology.[8]

As our case study of Delhi shows, television reaches everybody, irrespective of their socio–economic status, but may, as our data reveals, mean different things to different groups of viewers. James Lull, commenting on television in India, similarly notes that:

> The roles and meanings of television in families also depend on the level of socio-economic class within countries, not just on the overall level of national development. India offers such clear examples. For the urban elite in India, television now is just part of the mixture of modern appliances that surrounds them. For the poor, however, television assumes great import-ance, taking them from 'dark to light' . . . . Television can empower audience members, giving them access to information and entertainment they didn't have before—as in the case of India and China most recently. Ownership of a television set, especially a colour model, is a source of status in these countries, too, just as it had been in the more developed countries years earlier.[9]

In outer Delhi, residents of an up-market slum told us that social pressures had placed owning a TV set above many other family priorities. A woman with a 15-year old son, a drop-out from school, now famous for his talent for break dancing, said her son had built himself a career as a popular dancer performing at marriages and youth festivals, largely owing to TV. She said:

> It's hard to resist the popular wave. Suddenly everyone feels that they must not only own a TV, but a colour one; they must also now have VCRs and cable connections. Families that don't fall in line, feel marginalised and inferior. Besides, these days,

almost anything is available on easy instalments. People have bought VCRs, two-in-ones, colour TVs and even motorcycles which they pay for in small amounts over a longish period.

Sure enough, we were soon ushered into a six-by-four-foot treasure house. On display were two TV sets, a two-in-one, a VCR, a VCP, a radio. More equipment lay concealed under a thick cloth. This display of electronic gadgetry, we realised, represented more than just a case of keeping up with social trends. The family had not only recovered its extensive investment in these machines but was earning well by hiring out TV sets and VCPs to friends and folks in the colony for a nightly fee of Rs. 50. The money would keep coming in, they told us, as the demand was unlikely to wane. Almost as a regular practice families around them were spending weekends and holidays incessantly watching films. Some *basti* children said they sat up watching films all night long to get their money's worth!

PERSONAL TVs

If a single TV set seems a luxury in such settings, imagine our surprise when we met a middle class child who told us that for a joint family of 15 members there were six TV sets at home. We became conscious of the trend towards multi-TV homes when 21 out of 34 children (from obviously affluent backgrounds) in a sixth standard class raised their hands when asked if any of them had private TV sets in their bedrooms!

According to our data, while less than 5 per cent of our research sample did *not* own a TV set, nearly 60 per cent possessed at least one TV set and 35 per cent owned two or more. Just under 10 per cent of our respondents—almost all of them from the middle class—said their families had three television sets. Households with four to nine TV sets were identified as largely upper to middle class in social ranking. One child, also from a joint family, made the unbelievable claim that there were 16 TV sets in his house!

3

CHILDREN AND TELEVISION

The growth in the pattern of TV set ownership and the level of exposure to the medium suggest that more families are watching television for longer periods of time but not necessarily together. This was confirmed by our study: on an average, children in Delhi watch approximately 17 hours of TV every week (which means that at least 50 per cent of them watch significantly more than that since this is an average figure). By their own estimates a number of children are spending more time now in front of the small screen than on reading, creative hobbies and activities, homework and even meals.

A quick calculation based upon this response indicates that the average 8-year old would, over the next 10 years, have spent about 68 hours every month, 30 days (of 24 hours each) every year, and *one entire year out of 10 exclusively on watching television*. This figure is likely to increase further as more families take to viewing the new options being offered on Doordarshan as well as other cable and satellite channels.

What effect does watching so much television, so regularly, have on children? Researchers insist that it must be considered as a significant developmental experience. 'The experience pool that each child builds is affected by what the child is exposed to and influenced by, and television increasingly is contributing more to this pool and such traditional institutions as the home and school are contributing less.'[10]

Furthermore, the television set, by occupying a central and almost permanent position in our homes, is like a member of the family. As an experience, therefore, it has an enormous impact on children, especially on those under six years of age.[11]

According to Ellen Wartella:

. . . research on children's understanding of the purpose of commercials has relied on children's abilities to articulate the persuasive aspect of advertising. Typically, children have been asked open ended questions such as 'What is a TV commercial?' and 'What do commercials want you to do?' Results of the various survey studies seem to indicate that below age 6 the vast majority of children cannot articulate the selling intent of advertising.[12]

The advertising aspect of the TV experience is not, as many of us would like to believe, especially for our children, purely entertainment related. elevision, as the most influential of all media, also educates. It has the task of holding viewer attention, a task determined by its profit-orientation which distinguishes it from public education systems geared to transmitting and upholding social values.

Joli Jensen writes that, in fact, most people do not realise how they are being shaped by television and in whose interest:

This blindness to media blandishments is deemed to be especially true of children, who are seen as the most vulnerable and susceptible to mediated imagery. Apparently they have not yet had the kind of 'protective' education and experience, or developed the appropriate critical capacities or theoretical sophistication that would enable them to elude seclusion.[13]

Jerry Mander, a former advertising executive in the United States is one person who would like to see television buried. He warns that television is destroying the human fabric, and along with other critics of television, points out that television is a passive activity: you sit, you watch, you listen:

With television, the artificial information-field is brought inside our darkened rooms, inside our stilled minds, and shot by cathode guns through our unmoving eyes into our brains, and recorded. By focussing people on events well outside their lives, television encourages passivity and inaction, discourages self-awareness and the ability to cope personally . . . .[14]

During our study we observed and discussed how passivity can be induced by television, especially amongst very young children. In answer to a question on what their children usually did while the TV was on, several mothers of 5 to 8-year olds said that mostly

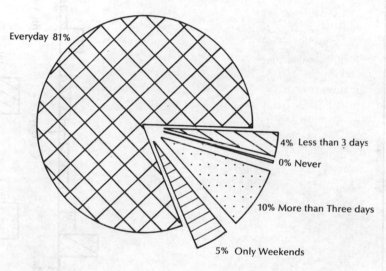

FIGURE 3. 1
Frequency of TV Viewing in Age Group 8 to 15 Years and Above
Total Respondents: 669

Everyday 81%

4% Less than 3 days

0% Never

10% More than Three days

5% Only Weekends

their children would just 'lie down' and 'be still'. The image of a 5 or 6-year old lying inert for any length of time in front of the small screen—absorbed, virtually hypnotised by the moving pictures—seemed to us a cause for concern, particularly since at this age very young children are full of curiosity and always eager to play, explore and interact. These discussions suggested that very young children easily tend to become passive viewers and often, we as adults, are not conscious of how addictive 'just lying there' can be.

Television can induce passivity for several reasons: it does not demand any reaction, response, mental or physical exertion. Sometimes children, particularly those who tend to be regarded as naughty and in the way, learn from the experience that when they are watching television there is relative peace in the house and they

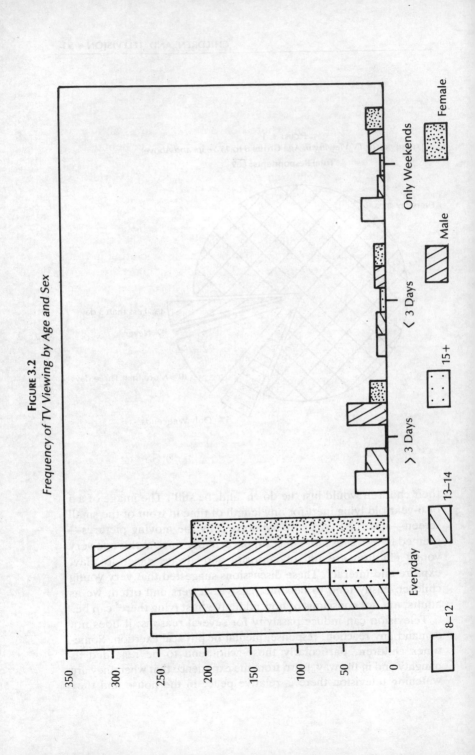

FIGURE 3.2
Frequency of TV Viewing by Age and Sex

are less likely to be reprimanded by their parents, elders or even the maid.

Although their concentration span may be small, the constantly changing pictures on the screen retain their attention and lull them into a state that lies somewhere between wakefulness and sleep, with no one and nothing making any mental or other demands on them.

What happens to children who become passive TV viewers? According to Patricia Marks Greenfield:

> In California there is a group called the Couch Potatoes, who consider themselves 'the true televisionaries'. They take the name from their favourite position—that of vegetating in front of the TV set, and from a vegetable with many eyes. An advertisement to recruit members for the group goes like this: 'Do you enjoy excessive amounts of TV viewing? Were some of the most enjoyable times of your life experienced in front of your set? Were your formative years nurtured by the 'electronic baby-sitter'? Are you annoyed by cry-baby intellectuals who claim that TV viewing is counter-productive and a waste of time? Like to do most of your living on the couch?'
>
> Asked by a reporter to comment on a two-way cable TV system that allows viewers to talk back to the television, one of the Couch Potatoes responded: 'Why watch TV if you have to think and respond? As far as I am concerned, the main point of watching TV is that it lets you avoid having to do that. To put it another way, if you're going to have to respond to your TV, you might as well go out and cultivate friendships or read a book or something'.[15]

According to Jensen, the idea of children sitting silently in front of a television for hours on end, passively absorbing whatever the set dishes out, distills the 'media as education' image to its most disturbing essence.[16]

The Couch Potatoes, according to Greenfield's account, are quite content leading a life twice-removed from reality. This, Mander suggests, is an effect that TV definitely has, and one that viewers should beware of. Television, he argues, replaces direct experience with indirect experience. Our knowledge of the world comes to be derived from secondary images brought to us by television and the people who control it. They decide the agenda for television. They choose, alter and package information, visuals, music, moods and feed them to millions of passive viewers. Viewers in turn, tend to believe whatever those who govern television choose to show them. It's a one-way traffic of ideas: from those who control television, and who make television programmes and advertisements, through the screen right into the viewer's mind.

In this context, Eric Barnouw writes:

> The luminous screen in the home carries fantastic authority. Viewers everywhere tend to accept it as a window on the world, and to watch it for hours each day. Viewers feel they understand, from television alone, what is going on in the world. They consciously look to it for guidance as to what is important, good, desirable, and what is not.[17]

David Littlejohn, in *Communicating Ideas by Television*, describes this experience eloquently:

> TV has become reality for many people, because it is more tolerable than any other. 'Real' reality is too impossibly complex to deal with. Television, which has helped to make both real reality and our perception of it so painful (by exaggerating our needs, by displaying to us more of the world's treasures and evils than we can cope with), provides answers and palliatives. Television we can bear.[18]

Some scholars in India may argue that the average television viewer has still not arrived at the juncture described by Littlejohn and that the commercialisation of television and the extension of viewing options, being relatively new phenomena, have still to impact on the Indian viewer in such a way as to re-order their lives and thinking patterns.

Our own research reveals that for the urban household, television is a social force that is beginning to take the place of other experiences. As the subsequent chapters will show, children are now inordinately concerned with the world of television and TV serial characters, be they of the *Hum Log* variety or the *Santa Barbara* kind. This, in essence, reflects the tendency pointed out by Littlejohn's observations.

After all, guided as they are by their openness to learning, children are quick to absorb television messages. According to Aimee Dorr: '. . . Children of all ages are to some extent different from adults in the ways in which they attend to, process, remember, and use television content.' They are, she argues, 'especially open to influence'. But as television viewers, they do not possess the skills to select what is important for them.[19]

TELEVISION AND THE CHILD'S ATTENTION

During our fieldwork in Delhi, parents repeatedly drew our attention to the fact that their children, especially the very young, begin to recognise programmes, title tunes, TV characters, actors and, of course, learn commercial jingles much in the same way as they learn their first nursery rhymes and children's songs. A great deal of their recall and association, we noticed, is helped along by an adult, someone who keeps up a running commentary; a parent who, while flitting in and out of the room points out something; a maid or baby-sitter who calls attention to images, songs and verbal messages on the television . . . . Of course some things are absorbed purely because they are watched repeatedly.

Since the focus of this book is the impact that TV ads have on children (and parents are often reassured by the way their children can memorise and repeat advertisement jingles), we examined TV advertising from the point of view of the child's attention span.

Today, the television commercial has been condensed and refined into a 10-second spot which is expected to grab your attention, hold it and simultaneously embed a seed of desire in your mind. This is not a simple task. An advertiser in Bombay lamented the heightened pressure on the advertiser whose job it is to successfully package all the elements of advertising strategy into such a brief spot. The advertiser is placed in an unenviable position by these constraints. Yet, against all odds and perhaps because of them, the advertising world has created an audio–visual product which is close to perfection.

The 10-second spot corresponds best to the attention and memory span of the young child—which is one reason why kids love advertisements as much as they do. Aimee Dorr says of children: 'Their attention and memory spans are short', adding that the manner in which children process TV content improves and changes with age. Researchers in Western countries have been particularly concerned with the effect that television, and advertising in particular, have on the child's powers of retention, concentration and attentiveness. Some claim that television, with its high dose of commercials, has an adverse impact which parents and teachers should be wary of.

One argument put forward is that unlike the print medium, television, which is often 'rapidly paced and always in continuous movement', does not provide the viewer with enough time to reflect. 'These qualities,' points out Patricia Marks Greenfield, 'have led to speculation that television leads to an impulsive rather than reflective style of thought and to a lack of persistence in intellectual tasks.' She quotes a study conducted in the United States which concluded that heavy television viewing was associated with a higher degree of impatience and restlessness.[20]

Parental reports received during our study in Delhi seem to echo this tendency. Many parents told us that their youngest children are most excited by and concentrate solely on TV ads, losing interest in television once they are over. In fact, unlike the experience of many Western countries where studies suggest that children begin to distinguish ads from programming and sometimes even react negatively to advertising quite early on, we found that a large number of children covered by our study focused on and enjoyed ads more than programming. This could be explained by the fact that consumerism in urban India is still in its first spring and the novelty of slick advertising has not worn off, or that there is such a dearth of good programming for children on television that ads are more attractive to them.

The cognitive skills required to comprehend, absorb and assess the complexities of the television text develop gradually. While both reading and direct experience are believed to enhance these skills, passive dependence on television and the one-way traffic of ideas it provides does not necessarily do so. The principal of a public school in old Delhi complained that television had replaced reading, affected his students' attention span and that the resulting restlessness amongst the children was hard to cope with.

Let us follow the progress of a young child who, at three or four years of age, avidly watches the 10-second commercial. Trained by this viewing pattern to concentrate for but a brief span, the child grows up into the multi-channelled, remote-controlled world of TV and finds it difficult to stay with programmes of longer duration.

Many frustrated parents who participated in this study observed that their children flit from programme to programme and channel to channel in search of something interesting. This was confirmed by several children in the 10-plus age group who told us how they loved to 'zap', or switch channels to 'check out' the 'action' on alternative programmes.

Psychologists in Bangalore voiced their concern over the particular form of advertising now common on Indian film video cassettes. The continuous band of computerised, graphic commercials which occupy up to 40 per cent of the screen from the bottom were, they said, harmful because viewers are *forced* to watch the advertisements which run alongside the film. The screen is split into two unrelated visual experiences providing two separate and discrete forms of mental stimuli which, they felt, might divide viewer attention and affect concentration ability.[21]

ILLUSTRATION 3.1
Television: The Constant Companion

In his book, *Four Arguments for the Elimination of Television*, Mander quotes a 1975 report on television prepared by researchers from the Australian National University's Centre for Continuing Education:

The evidence is that television not only destroys the capacity of the viewer to attend, it also, by taking over a complex of direct and indirect neural pathways, decreases vigilance—the general state of arousal which prepares the organism for action should its attention be drawn to specific stimulus.

Meanwhile, Marie Winn and others have quoted numerous studies to suggest TV children are showing a decline in recallable memory and that TV is affecting their reading and writing skills.[22]

These claims are discounted by researchers who argue that there is insufficient evidence to substantiate them. Daniel R. Anderson, who undertook a review of relevant scientific literature and wrote a paper entitled 'The Influence of Television on Children's Attentional Abilities', states that television viewing may affect attentional abilities in children both positively and negatively. The paper, commissioned by Action For Children's Television which produced Sesame Street, investigated the impact of the serial as against the impact of commercial television and Anderson drew the conclusion that not all TV programmes have a negative impact.[23]

If current-day television and more so the advertising on it can contribute to reducing our abilities to concentrate, then the future is even more frightening. In *The Hidden Persuaders* Vance Packard says:

> . . . at one of the world's largest advertising agencies, J. Walter Thomson, technicians have made a film depicting what commercials will be like a decade from now. It forecasts that TV messages will be coming at us in two- and three-second bursts that combine words, symbols and other imagery. According to the agency forecast, the messages will be 'almost subliminal'.[24]

TV: THE SIDE EFFECTS

Passivity and shorter concentration spans are two harmful side effects that may result from watching television for long periods of time over many years. However, as became apparent to us after talking to more and more children, there were other repercussions as well.

Television, we found, was not only accessible to children irrespective of their backgrounds but, to an extent, its images and messages were being absorbed by them indiscriminately. Children, particularly those from poor families, seemed perplexed by the many questions on TV and advertising that we put to them during fieldwork. A child at a construction site in West Delhi said: 'I never think about TV, I just watch it.' Another respondent told us: 'They show so many things on TV and we don't understand everything but we watch all the same. My sister pesters my mother because she wants to look like those fair-skinned women we see on TV.' When asked who they thought decides what to present on TV, they turned to us blankly and were embarrassed and confused. We found that they had no idea how the medium works but had decided that it gave them valuable information about the 'world outside' their own. Not their world. Someone else's.

Mander draws attention to a number of fears linked to the effect of television and its technology on the mind. To list just a few:

- Television is in itself a commodity and an expensive one too. Unlike any other inanimate object, it is an active player. 'Television literally enters inside human beings; inside our homes, our minds, our bodies . . . .'
- Television as an experience is one that is available to virtually everyone at the same time. It aids commercial efficiency because it gradually models millions of people into thinking, behaving and desiring the same sort of things. It replaces the natural curiosity of the human being to learn and discover through real experience the wonders of the world. It tricks viewers into thinking that they have travelled far afield and seen it all by just sitting in a room and watching the sights and sounds on television.[25]

Many people might object to the negativity of these claims. One woman who lives on her own in Delhi says she has to thank television for making lonely evenings so much easier to cope with. A father of two young boys extolled the virtues of television to us saying that it had opened up the world to his children, provided them information which they otherwise could not have accessed. He said he was keen that his sons go abroad to work and study and

TV not only familiarised them with life outside India but also improved their general knowledge.

Other people also argue that television is a positive rather than negative force in a country like ours. A former advertiser in Delhi believed that our only hope for the future lay in television. Being such a powerful conveyer of new ideas and information, it is the only instrument for bringing about rapid change in Indian society.

Certainly, a number of parents we spoke to felt very positive about a lot of TV programming, though the larger, intangible experience of television is becoming an issue they debate—at school and at home. One group of parents said that at a parent–teacher meeting, parents were ranged on either side of a strong divide. Some felt that exposure to television had broadened their children's horizons, added to their general knowledge and made them curious about a number of things. 'My son's geography has definitely improved, he now has a sense of "the world"', said one mother. Another complained that she was scared to leave her children at home without strict supervision because there was so much explicit violence and sex on channels like STAR Plus and MTV.

We accept that television, like most aspects of life, can be a beneficial and worthwhile experience if it is handled with caution and is moderated. However, there is a need to acknowledge the potential dangers inherent in an overdependence on or an uncritical acceptance of television. Children, more than adults, are susceptible to the insidious, subliminal influences of this medium and it is important, therefore, that we try to guard against its impact. There is no better place to begin such vigilance than where the child usually watches television: at home.

4

IS TV ALTERING FAMILY LIFE?

Every viewer has a very private and personal relationship with the television set, even when he is watching it as part of a group. After all, each individual has unique feelings, responds differently to and absorbs the messages of television in a distinctive manner. We might, therefore, be watching the same programme but our reactions to it could be diametrically opposite.

What we are currently experiencing is a drawing-room revolution of almost contradictory dimensions. Television is changing relationships within the family and even outside it. On the one hand, the trend, mentioned earlier, of families owning more than one television set and acquiring more viewing options suggests that people living in the same house are getting increasingly isolated from one another.

Simultaneously, our study found that people believe that television has the power to unite people and help them share similar experiences: it is commonplace, nowadays, to discover an entire family sitting and watching TV together either in companionable silence or talking all the while.

Television has also become the focus of social interaction on a larger canvas. Many of the mothers we spoke to, rather shame-facedly admitted that if they were invited out to dinner on a weekday, they did not leave the house till 9.30 p.m.—much to their husbands' annoyance—because they wanted to watch their favourite soap opera. Someone should have told them that they could have watched it along with their hosts! The father of a three-year old told us that he had decided not to opt for satellite TV

> because everywhere you go in the evenings people are so busy watching TV that they have no time for you. We've been invited to people's homes only to find ourselves sitting in silence

watching *Santa Barbara* or something. Is that what we're meeting for? Might as well stay home and watch it. (At the time of
this study *Santa Barbara* and *The Bold and the Beautiful* were
aired from 8 p.m. to 9.30 p.m.)

Also, coming home to find everyone engrossed in *The Bold
and the Beautiful* is not my idea of family life. Besides, if people
can get so involved in what's happening in the lives of a handful
of TV characters who are not even Indian, why can't they show
more interest in what's happening in the lives of people around
them?

Television's ability to simultaneously unite and separate people
worries many observers. Jerry Mander, for one, describes rather
eloquently how TV isolates human beings:

> Television encourages separation: people from community,
> people from each other, people from themselves . . . . It becomes
> everyone's intimate advisor, teacher and guide to appropriate
> behaviour and awareness. Thereby, it becomes its own feedback
> system, furthering its own growth and accelerating the trans-
> formation of everything and everyone into artificial form. This
> enables a handful of people to obtain a unique degree of power.[26]

Mander's observations could just as well be about the modern
urban Indian home. A young working mother, who is away from
home between 9 a.m. and 7 p.m., outlined her normal evening
routine:

> I get back, have my bath, then begin to help in the kitchen. We
> now have two TVs and are thinking to getting a third. You see,
> the men want to watch sports, while my mother-in-law and I
> want to watch serials like *The Bold and the Beautiful*. My 5-year
> old daughter gets irritated if we switch channels from MTV and
> Hindi film song programmes which she enjoys. Instead of having
> to listen to her constantly say, 'why aren't you letting me watch?',
> we may as well invest in another TV.

Many people we spoke to, said they would do anything to keep
the peace at home. Even if it means spending another Rs. 12,000
or more to buy yet another television set for a 5-year old.

cable) tend to watch TV in the afternoons and early evenings—when more programming is directed at them. Television serves to fill in their leisure time, and parents then feel free to take over viewing in the evenings with an untroubled conscience![29]

Early morning viewing, we found, has everything to do with children's access to satellite TV. In 1992–93 STAR TV was offering a series of cartoon films for children between 5.30 a.m. and 8 a.m. In fact, some teachers from a reputed South Delhi school expressed grave concern at the growing tendency amongst children to watch early morning television before setting out for school. They mentioned that they had noticed many more children lining up outside the toilets during school hours because they had not had enough time at home. The children were, they felt, groggy and inattentive during classes. They complained that things were being turned topsy-turvy at school and said that they planned to discuss this issue with parents. Since then TNT's cartoon network has extended the daily listings of animated films for children.

With over 50 per cent of the children covered by our study saying that they watch television in the evening with other people— a term which includes all/any members of the immediate family, extended family, neighbours and even the household help—most children still perceive watching TV as a collective affair. As for afternoon television, many of them said they watched TV with their mothers and other elders—or the maid.

Most children seemed embarrassed to admit that they were the most avid TV watchers at home. Only 40.54 per cent, after much thought, admitted that they watched more TV at home than their siblings or elders. The rest claimed that their brothers, sisters, cousins and other children at home were the ones most hooked on to TV.

However, the children's responses made one thing abundantly clear: if the child audience within a home was considered as a single entity, then 80 per cent of our respondents were telling us that children watch more TV than all the adults (parents, grand-parents etc.) put together.

Mealtime is TV Time

Our earlier observation that dinner was a popular accompaniment to TV watching was confirmed when more than 50 per cent of our respondents (the figure rises to almost 60 per cent in the 8 to 15 years age group) said that mealtimes were synonymous with TV time. This figure drops to just under 20 per cent in the case of the 5 to 8-year olds largely because this age group eats early and presumably goes to bed early too.

The eating-as-you-watch-TV syndrome, our research showed, was most pronounced amongst affluent families and least pronounced in families that are less privileged. Children in the 8 to 15-year age group from middle class and affluent homes said that watching TV, particularly over dinner, has become the norm. Parents admitted that they found TV the best mealtime babysitter, especially for children who are fussy about their food. Describing their evening routine, several adults said that dinner is increasingly becoming a casual affair. It is not always the collective, on-the-table or on-the-floor family event it used to be.

TV watching does not, however, dominate mealtimes in lower class families where eating is not a leisurely pastime. Many children (mostly girls) told us that they are actively involved with household chores throughout the evening. They help to cook, wash, serve and clean; TV time is, therefore, restricted and generally something they indulge in after their chores are over. In families such as these, dinner is a one-time affair, being cooked and served hot as it comes off the stove.

What else do children do while watching TV? Well, when they're not eating they tend to talk. More than 40 per cent of the children in our study, claimed that they chatted to one another or others, repeated things they heard or saw on the picture-tube and even enacted some of the scenes. Sometimes, they admitted, they even enjoyed a good fight!

FIGURE 4.1
TV Viewing Pattern of 8 to 15-Year Olds

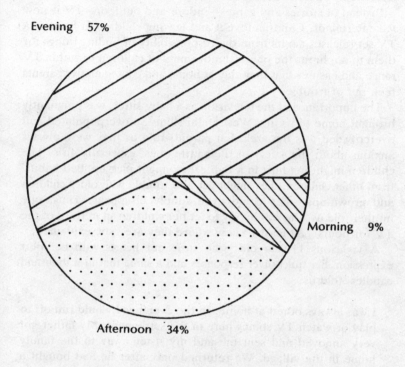

Evening   57%

Morning   9%

Afternoon   34%

THE BABY-SITTER

In India the baby-sitter has traditionally been either the mother who stays at home or an elderly female member of the family. In most affluent households, parents depend more and more on an *ayah* (maid) to take charge of their children when they are out. In middle and lower class families, it is a relative or the older siblings who are left in charge of the younger ones.

However, like so much else within the family unit, the task of baby-sitting is now changing hands. Television, with the variety of viewing options it offers since 1991, is increasingly becoming the child's best friend and favourite baby-sitter—often with the active connivance of the 'caretakers' like the *ayah* or grandmother who divested of her responsibilities doesn't mind watching a bit of television as part of her duties!

Instead of stories and games—indoor and outdoor—TV is now *the* entertainer. Children love it and leaving children in front of a TV set releases adults from the responsibility of finding things for them to do, limits the physical movement of children to within TV range and ensures that they stay at home and consequently, parents feel, out of trouble.

The importance of the television as a baby-sitter, was poignantly brought home to us in a West Delhi slum. So overpopulated and overcrowded was the area that parents told us they were always anxious about the safety of their little ones, especially girls. The children might get hurt in a fight, they might pick up 'bad habits' from other children, they might get into trouble with older children and grown-ups—they could even simply disappear. Thus, one mother told us, she was happy to let her children sit in front of the TV for hours: 'At least I know where they are,' she explained.

A vivacious 11-year old, who stole our hearts with her pert expression, her quicksilver responses and a smile that lit a thousand candles, told us:

> I was always bored at home. In the evenings I would run off to play or watch TV somewhere in the settlement. My father got very annoyed and sent me and my sister away to the family home in the village. We returned only after he had bought a TV. Now we stay at home in the evenings.

For slightly different reasons, the middle and upper classes also see television as a good, safe option for their children. Urbanisation has created its own set of problems for such families. Social and economic pressures keep families on their toes and more mothers work now than ever before (25 per cent of the children we interacted with had working mothers). With consumerism catching on and promoting an ethic which says that you must buy, buy, buy, it follows that parents must work, work and work even harder to earn the means to satisfy newly-created needs. This results in children being on their own or under the supervision of an *ayah* during the afternoon and early evening.

They could go out and play but the reality of city life discourages such activities. 'There are no safe parks and very few nice ones accessible or suitable for young children to play in. Every day you read about people being abducted, run over, and girls being teased. Which parent would send their children out to play unsupervised?' asked one concerned mother. While Delhi does offer dance, music, art lessons and coaching in a variety of games/sports, distances are often too great and the fees charged too high for most middle class families. Much better, safer, cheaper—and easier—to let children watch a Hindi film, a cartoon or a serial on TV.

Growing Concerns

As television options and children's dependence upon it for recreation have increased, so has parental concern about the effect on their children of watching television indiscriminately for long hours. Some parents, who earlier regarded television as an innocent and harmless way of keeping children occupied, have subsequently changed their minds. The parents of a three-year old who has grown up on a rich diet of television, say their child knows not only how to operate the TV set and tune in to particular channels or programmes, but also how to have the local cable operator contacted and summoned to sort out satellite and cable-related problems. That apart, the parents are now beginning to look at television critically to see if it might have anything to do with the way their son has begun behaving:

> He's suddenly become very aggressive, somewhat uncontrollable, and physically demonstrative in ways that disturb us. We are wondering whether his intake of adult programming on television and the high degree of violence that satellite and cable incorporate in their programming might in some way be responsible for the way he is right now. He certainly seems to be aping things that he sees, but does not understand, and it makes life difficult and sometimes embarrassing.

Whether or not the behaviour of this child has a direct correlation with watching TV is of course unclear. The role of television and indeed of films in promoting aggressive, violent reactions continues to be a controversial issue. Different studies have suggested either that there is evidence to bolster the claim that it does encourage violence or that such a connection cannot really be proved.

Nevertheless, existing data on children and television suggests that we cannot ignore the possibility that there is a symbiotic link between violence on TV and violent behaviour in real life. For instance, according to the Committee for Children's Television (Metro Detroit, U.S.A.):

- Acts of violence occur in six out of 10 TV programmes (on American TV).
- Cartoons depict four times more violence than other TV programmes.
- Research shows cartoon violence produces anger, irritability and aggressive behaviour.[30]

Recently, a story in an English daily newspaper in India reported how a young boy had severely beaten up his younger sister after an argument over which TV programme should be watched. His tactics and inspiration were from *World Wrestling Federation* (WWF), a popular satellite TV and cable TV programme.[31]

Whatever be the truth of the matter, for many parents the euphoria of enjoying access to so many channels is now being tempered by a growing sense of unease regarding television. Most of this anxiety relates to the hold television has on children of 8 years and above. Television is bringing in new ideas, a culture that many parents are unfamiliar and uncomfortable with, and diverting children's attention away from creative activities, sports and school-related work.

Significantly, we discovered, that in spite of their growing concern, parents are finding it difficult to control their children's TV viewing habits.

PARENTAL INTERVENTION

In a study which examined the relationship between aspects of family life and children's home television usage, J. Holman and V.A. Braithwaite of the Australian National University, stated:

Recognition of television as a potentially influential medium
has highlighted the need to identify intervening variables which,
if appropriately manipulated, would maximise the positive consequences and minimise the negative. In this context, the role of
parents has been regarded as extremely important.[32]

Our study suggests that parental restriction on the young child's
handling of television is not enforced (or is simply not an issue).
As mentioned earlier, many parents tend to believe that an infant
is too young to be influenced by or understand what's happening
on TV and that television viewing is a harmless activity. A number
of parents (and grandparents) we interviewed expressed admiration
for the skill with which young children handle the TV set and
related technology, including VCRs and video games—gadgets of
modern life many adults are still uncomfortable with.

We asked children as well as parents about their relationship
with the TV set in order to understand the family's perception of
television as a part of family life. Is television seen as just another
device, in this case one that serves to entertain people at home?
Do parents feel the need to intervene and guide their children's
TV viewing habits? Do children end up watching more TV just
because the adults/elders at home are themselves interested in TV
programmes?

Two of the questions we asked children and families were: Who
switches on the TV set and who switches it off? Who decides what
should or should not be watched?

Responding to a list of options, almost 70 per cent of the
children said that they sometimes turn on the TV while 60 per cent
also indicated that their parents often turn on the TV. This trend
held for all three age groups, though one would have assumed that
younger children would be less likely to command their TV sets
than the older ones.

Our research revealed that the act of switching on the television
set is regarded as a casual one. In most families the television set is
seen as an entertainer which can be switched on at any time.
Although the newspapers provide a listing of the day's programmes,
few children indicated that the TV was switched on in order to
catch a specific programme.

There is a great deal of flexibility regarding who takes the
decision to watch TV or, indeed, what to watch. Children indicated
in the questionnaire that, by and large, they do not feel restricted

by any parental diktat on their TV time or on the suitability of programme content.

While a marginally higher number of children in the 5 to 8 years category said that their parents *switch off* the TV, in the older age groups over 60 per cent of the children stated that their parents and they play an equal role in determining when the television set should be turned off.

The act of switching off the TV set by adults could represent an act of control being exercised by them in an attempt to intervene in their children's viewing habits. But clearly parents are faced with several problems when it comes to putting their foot down. We found that it is not until the television habit begins to interfere with schoolwork and impacts adversely on the child's reading and writing abilities, or causes other disruptions in the child's life (such as late night TV vigils), that parents begin to react to it.

Most parents admitted that TV becomes an immediate target when academic pressures on the child increase in the senior classes, because it is then that TV seems to be taking up too much of the child's time. However, by that stage, the child is addicted to an evening routine of leisurely TV watching and takes little pleasure in the alternatives—studying, reading or even learning a skill.

This, parents said, often led to fierce conflict within the household. Children in the older age groups confirmed this view: one 15-year old complained that: 'Earlier our parents used to say "Why don't you watch something on TV instead of making such a noise?" Now they yell when we want to watch something.'

PROGRAMME CONTENT

Parents ambivalent attitude towards television is further reflected in the kinds of programmes children are allowed to watch. The children suggested that there is no active intervention on the part of most parents with regard to what children should or should not watch. However, feedback from parents indicates that there is now greater concern over programme content.

WHO CHOOSES?

In their responses to our questionnaire, more girls than boys claimed that their parents decide what they should watch. More boys said that parents were not concerned with what they watched than did girls.

This gender bias might be due to the parental desire to protect girls from exposure to seamy and steamy scenes and images depicted in many Hindi films and foreign and Indian TV serials. Safeguarding the purity of the girl's mind and body is still considered important by Indian parents. Conversely, it is felt that boys should be aware of the facts of life in order to grow up into men.

A class profile of viewing habits also reflects a gender difference. In the slum and *basti* environments, children said they watched 'whatever was coming on TV', adding that when a choice had to be made it was the elder males who took the decision. Most children from these areas said that their mothers rarely watched TV because their 'eyes hurt'; they were embarrassed to watch with the men-folk; because they could not understand what they saw; or because they simply did not have the time. In sharp contrast, children from affluent homes (particularly in the 8 to 15 years age group) indicated that they were much more in control of their TV sets and they often decided what they wanted to view.

Simultaneously, close to 85 per cent of the youngsters in the 8 to 15 years age group, irrespective of class, said that they were regularly advised not to watch too much TV. When asked why they claimed their parents were worried about the effect it could have on their eyesight. Very few recalled their parents objecting to television on the grounds that the programming might be unsuitable for their age group.

These responses seem to indicate that the majority of children do not feel restricted by active parental intervention in their TV viewing habits and that they enjoy almost unlimited access to TV at home. But, in some measure, the children contradicted themselves when in answer to the questionnaire, they wrote that there were several kinds of TV programming that their parents did not want them to watch.

Significantly, more than 30 per cent of the children in the sample said they were under **no** parental guidance whatsoever with regard to programme selection. How many of these children were merely indulging in wishful thinking remains unclear.

Of those who volunteered information regarding their parental objections to certain kinds of TV habits and programmes, 42.26 per cent said these were related to watching late night programmes and films. Parents, with whom we discussed the issue, said that late night TV viewing eats into the children's quota of sleeping hours, leaving them groggy, difficult to rouse in the morning and inattentive at school. They also objected to the 'adult' scenes in such programmes.

Asked to identify programmes which parents restrict them from watching, the children listed the following:

1. Late night programmes/films : 43.49 per cent
2. Others* : 14.20 per cent
3. Violence and Horror : 11.06 per cent
4. Hindi Films/Films : 9.11 per cent

(*This category includes adult programmes, *WWF*, MTV, and programmes with sexually explicit scenes.)

Inspite of this feedback, we remained unclear about how effective parental intervention really is—even when it occurs. For example, a number of children mentioned that their parents had forbidden them from watching several STAR TV serials including *World Wrestling Federation* and *The Bold and the Beautiful* as well as chat shows on DD which discuss marital, sexual or women's problems. However, a few children, went to the trouble of letting us know in the questionnaire that despite the prohibition they watched *WWF* and the other programmes whenever they could. Parental sanction, it would seem, does not always work.

TV DOES NOT DISCRIMINATE

Several parents, especially those of younger children, told us that they did not want their children watching 'dirty scenes, condom and sanitary napkin ads' or even campaigns for family planning. They felt uncomfortable about exposing their children to such issues: However, given that television does not discriminate between adult and child viewers, they find it difficult to prevent this from happening: Parents cannot always police their television sets or their children. However, some mothers said that although they were embarrassed to discuss these issues especially in front of other family members (especially the men), they were pleased that television was taking on the responsibility of educating their children about them.

We also found that sometimes, despite the good intentions underlying a TV presentation, TV can be harmful especially when children are too young to understand the full meaning of the message delivered. For instance, a Bombay ad film maker found himself disturbed by a satellite TV ad on parental neglect of the child. While he had no quarrel with the sentiments and concerns of the advertisement, he felt a child viewer might end up harbouring unfounded resentment against his/her parents merely because the context of the ad had not been understood. In this particular case, the ad was framed in a western nation where child neglect was legally defined and punishable.

Clearly, television does not take upon itself the full responsibility of showing the right stuff to the right viewer at the right time, and where children are concerned, the onus of discrimination lies essentially with the adults in the household. If parental vigilance is lax or simply non-existent, children tend to watch whatever comes their way. This is particularly important in the context of parental viewing habits. In a chance encounter on the Rajdhani Express from Bombay to Delhi, we overheard a mother recalling a recent episode from a popular TV soap opera. Her 8-year old corrected her as she went along. Surprised and not a little annoyed, she asked: 'How do you know so much about it?' 'Well,' replied the child, 'I was sitting right there while you were watching it.' Visibly upset, the mother exclaimed: 'But I told you not to watch!'

As pointed out in the introduction, there are positive contributions that television can make to children's awareness and learning. Not everything shown on it is harmful; selecting the right programmes for children to watch and discovering relevance or meaning in programme content is a conscious and demanding activity.

To find out just how active a role parents are playing in influencing their children's programme choices and helping them to get the best of TV, we asked the following questions: Do parents look out for good, informative-cum-entertaining programmes on television for their kids to watch? What do they encourage them to tune into?

About 60 per cent of the 8 to 15 year olds said they were encouraged to 'watch TV'. Asked to specify what they were urged to watch, 37 per cent mentioned informative programmes on science and international affairs, quizzes and the news bulletins. Less than 15 per cent of the children, particularly those in the 8 to 12 years age group, said their parents encouraged them to watch entertainment programmes.

However, from the tone of their responses and from the list of programmes they claimed to watch most frequently, it is evident that children resent parental guidance and generally consider parental recommendations to be boring. This attitude may well be a response to the lack of quality programming on TV in areas other than entertainment.

Not a single child drew a link between learning a subject in school and related programming on television which might make it more interesting. Using television to enhance regular learning is not usually attempted either by schools or at home. In any case, very few programmes bear any relevance to topics in science, history, economics, etc., which could awaken children's interest. Since this research was conducted, some TV channels are working to satisfy/target the child audience and more child-specific programming is beginning to appear.

BBC World Service Television has a number of documentary, science and nature-related programmes ideally suited for children. STAR TV's scientific and environmental series are greatly appreciated by some parents and they do encourage their children to watch them. These programmes/series are well made, fascinating and hold the child's attention. They are not viewed by children as an imposition.

Finally, and in the Indian context, the most important TV service is of course the national broadcasting network, Doordarshan. Conceived of as a public service broadcasting system whose primary aim was to educate an illiterate population, Doordarshan has a history of educational programming. The University Grants Commission (UGC) runs a one-hour educational programme on weekdays, and there are regular class curriculum broadcasts on weekday mornings. However, the quality of such programming is largely poor and, as we will see in the next chapter, Doordarshan's emphasis has now changed and education is no longer a priority.

5

THE WORLD OF TELEVISION

WHAT CHILDREN WATCH

Our main focus is on television advertising and its impact on children. However, children's exposure to TV commercials also has to do with *how much* television they watch and *what* they watch.

Three facts became abundantly clear from children's viewing preferences for Doordarshan programmes: children watch a limited number of programme categories; these categories fall overwhelmingly within the 'entertainment' slot; and these programmes have been Doordarshan's biggest money-spinners.

MOVIE MANIA

If there is any one unifying force in India, it is the mania for watching movies. Irrespective of age, class, language, sex or background, children in our survey confirmed—if indeed, confirmation were necessary—that for the vast majority, Hindi films and Hindi film songs are the first choice.

Over 80 per cent of the children between the ages of 8 and 15 years said they watched *Chitrahaar* (a programme of Hindi film songs) regularly, and an almost equal number put the Hindi film next on the agenda (79.67 per cent). Many children named *Rangoli*— the Sunday morning programme of old film songs—as another favourite.

The popularity of the Hindi film and its derivatives will also be noted in relation to satellite and cable viewing habits, reconfirming the involvement of children with the world of the Hindi film and its music.

It was not surprising that cartoons were almost as popular with them (76.53 per cent). Other programmes favoured by the children were as follows (in order of preference): the news—67.56 per cent; sports—67.56 per cent; 9 p.m. serials—64.57 per cent. All other programmes recorded consistently low responses, indicating a big gap between the popular and unpopular.

FIGURE 5.1

Family Preferences for Doordarshan, Local Cable and Satellite TV

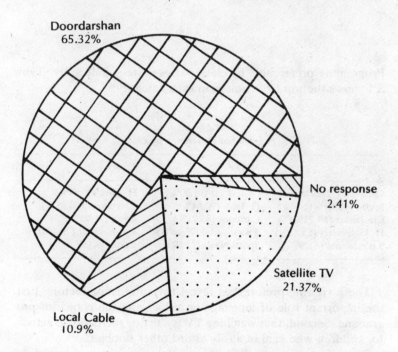

Doordarshan
65.32%

No response
2.41%

Satellite TV
21.37%

Local Cable
10.9%

Roughly 50 per cent of our respondents claim to watch Doordarshan's afternoon fare (which might come as something of surprise to both Doordarshan and advertisers!). Music and dance programmes and the regional film received low percentage ratings.

A closer look at the children's responses throw up some obvious and other, interesting, contrasts when analysed exclusively in terms of age, class or gender.

AGE

Predictably, younger children (5 to 12 years age group) prefer cartoons to Bollywood movies. Only older children watch 'The News' or its Hindi equivalent, 'Samachar' in any significant number—despite the fact that most children (from all age groups) admitted that their parents encouraged them to watch it.

CLASS

Programme preference, by class, varies quite significantly. Table 5.1 shows the top five choices in each category:

Table 5.1
Programme Preference by Class

Upper	*Middle*	*Lower*
Cartoons (71.29%)	Chitrahaar (91.90%)	H. Film (90.64%)
Sports (62.03%)	H. Film (90.84%)	Chitrahaar (80.88%)
Chitrahaar (59.25%)	Cartoons (85.21%)	News (71.95%)
H. Film/News (55.55%)	9 p.m. serial (78.16%)	9 p.m. serial (70.1%)
9 p.m. serial (41.66%)	Sports/News (73.59%)	Cartoons (67.83%)

These viewing preferences reveal two interesting factors: first, the important role of language in influencing the choice of programme. Second, that watching TV is a major recreational activity for children who cannot easily afford other hobbies.

These factors might help explain the discrepancy between the viewing percentages for upper and lower class children, which are much higher for the latter category.

LINGUISTIC PATTERNS

Upper class children seem to indicate a preference for English language programmes (as we will discover a little later, these children and their families are also the highest satellite TV subscribers who, by and large, favour the foreign, English language channels). The significant drop in viewership figures for Hindi films and *Chitrahaar* in this social grouping confirms this trend.

Middle class viewership figures are very high for all programmes, indicating that these children are comfortable with both Hindi and English programming.

If children from the least affluent backgrounds rank cartoons fifth in their listing, it is only because most cartoons on Doordarshan are in English. If they were in Hindi like *Jungle Ki Kahaniyan (Jungle Book)*—the popularity rating would immediately shoot up. In fact, according to the Indian Market Research Bureau, (IMRB), *Jungle Ki Kahaniyan* was the most popular programme on Doordarshan during the summer and autumn of 1993. We can confirm this from our experience in lower class areas of Delhi where, during our interaction with children, we repeatedly heard them singing the theme song from the cartoon. The relatively important position given to the news in Hindi (*Samachar*) reconfirms this language preference.

The language factor also seems to operate for programmes like *The World This Week, Turning Point* and *Hercule Poirot*, which evoked little response from lower class children but have been mentioned again and again by children with greater exposure to English. (Recently serials like *Junoon* and *Dekh Bhai Dekh*, dubbed in Tamil, are reported to have evoked great response. Zee TV, Jain TV and Doordarshan are also running successful regional language programmes.)

TV HOURS

The amount of time spent watching television also seems to be influenced by class profile. For instance, when asked how many hours they spend watching television during the week, children (of the 8 to 15 years age group) from the upper class recorded consistently lower figures than the other two groups. The figures for watching more than two hours of television every day were: upper class—47.68 per

Figure 5.2
Programme Preferences of 5 to 8-Year Olds

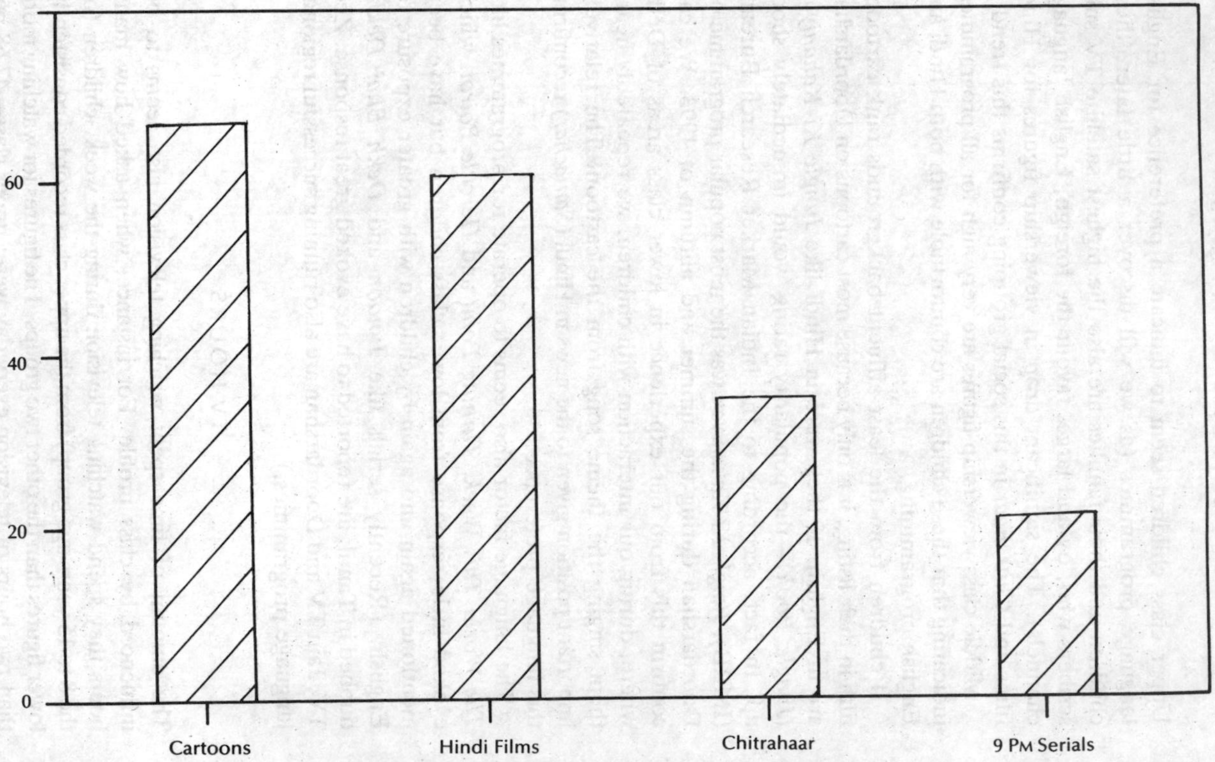

FIGURE 5.3
Favourite DD Programmes: Age Group 8 to 15 Years

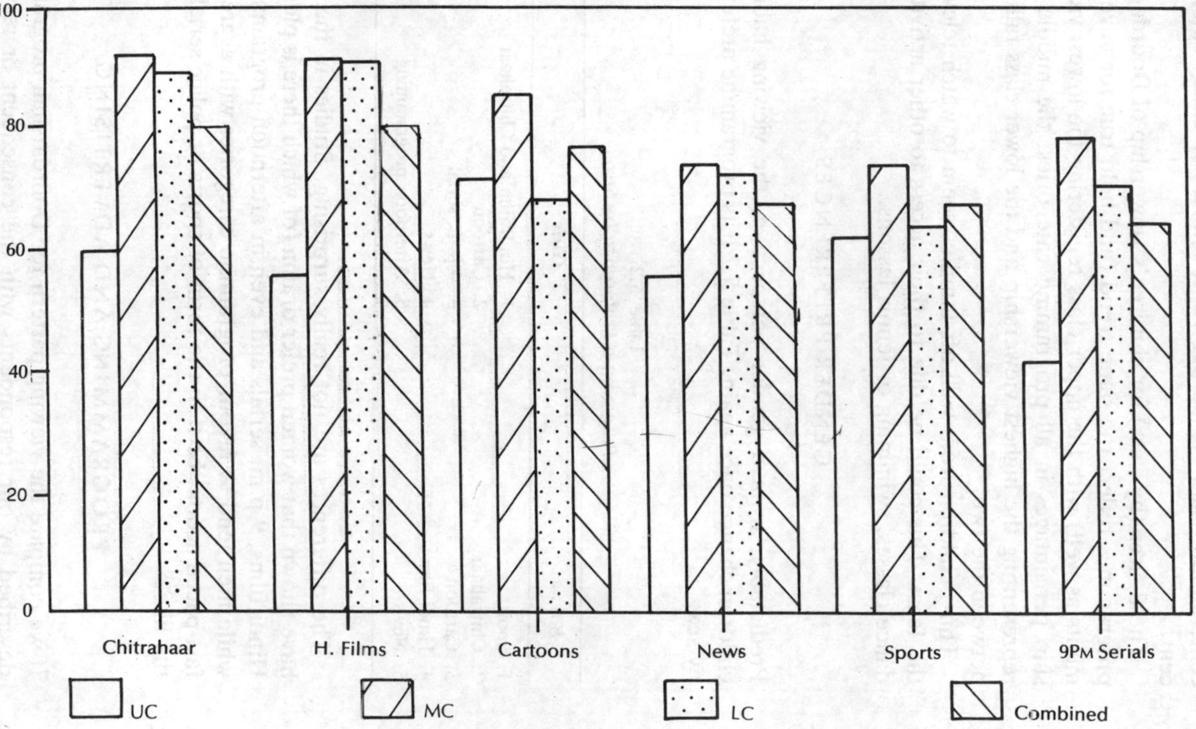

cent; middle class—62.32 per cent; and lower class—55.55 per cent.

The figures (by class) for children's viewership of Doordarshan programmes reflect the same trend (and hold true for advertisements as well) with the upper class registering the lowest viewership percentages in all programme categories, the middle class representing the highest viewership and the lower class falling in between the two.

Thus, children from well off families seem to watch television the least. This could be due to their access to other activities—dance classes, swimming or tennis lessons.

GENDER PREFERENCES

Predictably, from a gender perspective, the viewing habits of children change once again. Table 5.2 lists programme preference by sex:

Table 5.2
Programme Preference by Sex

Boys	Girls
1. Sports	1. Hindi film and Chitrahaar
2. Chitrahaar	2. Cartoon
3. Cartoon	3. 9 p.m. serial
4. Hindi film	4. News
5. News	5. Afternoon programming

The differences are not really surprising. Studies in the West have shown that women prefer drama (of which there is plenty in Hindi films, 9 p.m. serials and even in afternoon programming), while men tend to favour programme categories with aggressive, fast-paced action, be it in the form of sports or police serials and the like.[33]

PROGRAMMING AND ADVERTISING

If we compare the viewing pattern for Doordarshan programmes described by our respondents with the consequent or resultant exposure they receive to advertising, the correlation between ratings and commercial support is reinforced: the Hindi film and *Chitrahaar*, most avidly watched by children, attract the heaviest advertising and Doordarshan's rates for spots or sponsorships of these two programmes are well ahead of others.

Cartoons receive the largest number of child-specific advertisements such as those for sweets and chocolates (Gems, Parry's, etc.) and toys (Barbie, G.I. Joe, video games). Sports events (read cricket) also attract a lot of advertising support and the sponsored serial, depending on its popularity, can attract up to 15 spots. Thus, if we compare Doordarshan's programming package with children's viewing preferences, we can safely conclude that children are exposed to a high quantum of television advertising.

DOORDARSHAN: A PERSPECTIVE

Children's exposure to television, and consequently to TV advertising has everything to do with the manner in which broadcasting in India has developed and is rapidly changing.

If you were watching Doordarshan a decade ago and were suddenly catapulted into the present, you would discover that though much appears the same, much more has changed rather dramatically.

What has remained stubbornly constant is government control of the electronic media. Despite the fact that satellite television has taught us the impossibility—and foolhardiness—of stifling the electronic media, Doordarshan and All India Radio are still wholly state-owned and controlled institutions. Even as CNN, BBC (and now Zee TV too) routinely provide viewers with news about India, Doordarshan and AIR are still subject to government censorship.

Thus radio and television continue to be treated as arms of the government rather than as independent, professional broadcasting units. It should be recalled that when television was first introduced in India (1959), it was with the express intention of using it to educate rather than entertain the public. This public service function of television has often been cited as one of the main reasons for maintaining government control over the media. The other is, of course, the fact that the establishment of a national television network requires huge financial outlays and, in a poor country, the government alone is in a position to generate such funds.

Since the 1960s, numerous government-appointed committees have recommended autonomy for the electronic media, realising that freedom is essential to running a professional media institution. However, the courage to free the media from the shackles of bureaucratic inexpertise and political interference has been suppressed by the much stronger fear that autonomy, or freedom of expression would adversely affect the fortunes of the political elite.

(In February 1995, the Supreme Court of India held that government monopoly of the airwaves was unconstitutional. It further advised the government to set up an autonomous regulatory council to oversee broadcasting in the country. The government is believed to be contemplating a media policy which will offer private companies the right to run local TV stations as well as grant autonomy to Doordarshan and AIR.)

Another justification for state control has been an underlying concern amongst politicians and intellectuals, that if the media were to be owned and operated by private enterprise, it could be exploited by 'anti-national' elements or those peddling a particular point of view. Recent events in the country have lent a semblance of credibility to this fear.

In the western state of Maharashtra, the extremist right wing Shiva Sena Party (which now rules the state having won the assembly elections in early 1995), used local cable operations to broadcast its views when communal tensions had been aroused by the demolition of the Babri masjid mosque at Ayodhya in U.P. in December 1992. The state assembly elections of 1993, saw many political parties using cable TV and video vans to conduct their campaigns, while JAIN TV, a satellite channel launched in early 1994 is prepared to broadcast all kinds of religious and other programmes—the only criterion being the clients' ability to pay.

For these and other reasons, Doordarshan has been denied the opportunity to function as a professional broadcasting service. This must be regarded as something of a tragedy since everyone is agreed that television (and radio) has the potential to play a pivotal role—as a channel of information—in a developing society which has still to resolve large scale problems of poverty and illiteracy.

DOORDARSHAN: EXPANSION OF SERVICES

On 15th September 1959, a small television centre was established in Delhi to see how best the medium could be used for purposes of social education. From this modest, experimental beginning, Doordarshan has now grown into a countrywide—and via satellite communication—an international broadcasting network.[34]

Doordarshan signals were available in 1994 (March) up to 84.5 per cent of India population. This figure must be viewed in relation to the number of people who actually receive the service or own TV sets. The MRAS-Burke National Television Survey IV (conducted in December 1991) put TV households at 22,419 lakhs. Latest figures estimate that there are over 45 million TV households in the country with almost 250 million primary viewers.[35]

Doordarshan's services have been stratified. There is a national network available throughout the country, network programming available as an option, with regional and local broadcasts as well as satellite alternatives. By March 1995, Doordarshan had even launched an international satellite channel.

ETV

As mentioned at the end of Chapter IV, Doordarshan does broadcast educational (ETV) programmes weekday mornings. These consist of classroom instruction and short features (indigenously produced and imparted) as part of the UGC (University Grants Commission) package covering a range of subjects from history to astrophysics. However, there is little consistency in the quality of the programming.

The latest experiment in ETV has introduced interactive learning through TV whereby people in different cities around India are linked by satellite connections to a nodal centre. A viewer in Bangalore can then watch a lecture from Jaipur and also participate and have questions answered.

PROGRAMME BREAK UP

Unlike most foreign satellite TV channels, Doordarshan is not a 24-hour service although transmission time has been steadily increasing. Broadcasting normally begins at 7 a.m. and ends by 11 or 12 p.m.

Before Doordarshan's new satellite/regional channels went on the air, the Audience Research Unit (DART) of Doordarshan estimated that 36.2 per cent of Doordarshan's programming was devoted to entertainment, 34.1 per cent to education and 29.7 per cent to information. Significantly, very little programme time was allocated to rural, health or adult education programming—and certainly none during prime time.[36]

A breakdown of programming by genres is even more revealing:

- Film-based programmes accounted for 24.6 per cent of all broadcasts. Since the DART survey (1993), Doordarshan has increased its number of films and film-based programmes to the extent that it now telecasts 6 films in a week.
- Serials and plays accounted for 21.2 per cent of transmission time; news bulletins for 16.3 per cent.
- By comparison, only 3.3 per cent of total transmission time was devoted to programmes for children and 2.1 per cent to women.

THE COMMERCIALISATION OF DOORDARSHAN

Ten years ago, a child's exposure to TV commercials was limited to advertisements shown with *Chitrahaar*, the Hindi feature film and the occasional cricket event. There were several reasons for this limited exposure: since television in India was conceived of as a public service, commercialism was frowned upon by the authorities and treated as a necessary evil which was not to be encouraged. The expansion of Doordarshan services—the establishment of a national network available throughout the country—and the introduction of colour transmission began only in the 1980s.

TV sets were mainly imported and cost the earth. All of this meant that until the mid-eighties, television did not enjoy a large viewership in the country and was unattractive to business houses who preferred to advertise in the print media.

Faced by an overwhelmingly poor, feudal and illiterate society, successive Indian governments claimed to be using television as a channel of information and ideas aimed at social change.

In this respect, Doordarshan was no different from broadcasting systems around the world, especially in Europe and Africa. Most European countries began their experiments with broadcasting in roughly the same manner as Doordarshan did, treating the airwaves as a scarce national resource to be used for the public good: to inform, to educate and only then entertain.[37]

Over the last three decades the picture has changed dramatically. Most national broadcasting corporations have been compelled to seek commercial assistance in order to remain economically viable as well as to keep apace of the phenomenal technological innovations which are constantly transforming communications. While the BBC continues to support itself solely through revenue from a license fee, it is becoming increasingly clear that it will have to discover new sources of revenue if it is to remain competitive in the new information order. Already its international satellite channel, BBC World, available in India on STAR TV, is a commercial venture.

Almost simultaneously, technology through satellite transmission and better quality cable wiring increased the broadcasting spectrum and governments had to open up television to private broadcasters, the scarcity-of-the-airwaves argument no longer being valid.

The Indian experience has been fairly similar. In the words of the Mahalik Committee Report (1992) on Doordarshan's commercial services: '. . . as the economy of a developing nation reaches a take-off stage, economic considerations cannot be totally ignored. It is in view of the strong dictates of economic self-reliance that most countries of the world have accepted commercial broadcasting as an integral part of their broadcasting services.'[38]

This remark is significant in the light of the new economic policies initiated by the Indian government in 1991. Economic liberalisation has become the watchword and the Indian bazaar has been thrown open to international free market forces. The old socialist philosophy of a planned, government-controlled economic system, dominated by the 'license raj' which moulded government thinking since 1947, now lies in tatters, discredited and discarded.

The new thrust towards liberalisation has, as we shall see, considerably affected the services sector including the electronic media. In fact during the 1993 GATT (General Agreement on Tariff and Trade) negotiations, one of the major differences of opinion between the USA and its European allies was the American desire to enjoy greater access to culture—cinema, television etc.—on an international scale. The Europeans succeeded in keeping culture outside the purview of the final document and even now some governments, particularly the French, are seeking restrictions on American cultural exports and quotas/subsidies for European films or television programmes.

A key component and consequence of the economic reforms in India has been the growth and spread of a consumer culture with the arrival of many more multinational companies. The advertising industry has flourished with growth rates of over 30 per cent per annum as business corporations fight it out in the marketplace.

The Big Leap Forward

In keeping with such changes over the last three years, Doordarshan has steadily and surely commercialised its operations. Apart from the government's economic policies, the impetus for this has come from transnational satellite television broadcasts to India.

The process of commercialisation had begun well before but in a much more controlled environment. The first advertisement appeared on Doordarshan in 1976 but it was the introduction of the prime time sponsored serial in 1984 which highlights the beginning of the commercial era on Indian television. Although the aim was to attract commercial revenue, Doordarshan also sought to provide socially meaningful entertainment of a high standard.

Incapable of producing good in-house programmes, the government went calling on private producers and directors from Bollywood who eagerly responded. Some of the best known names in

Hindi cinema—B.R. Chopra, Ramanand Sagar, Basu Chatterjee, Shyam Bengal, Sai Paranjape, Kundan Shah, Govind Nihalani, Saeed Mirza (and even Satyajit Ray) flocked to the small screen. In their wake came a whole new generation of talented young people keen to exploit the potential of television.

Serials such as *Hum Log, Yeh Jo Hai Zindagi, Buniyaad, Tamas, Rajani, Nukkad, Ramayana, Mahabharat, Mr. Yogi, Malgudi Days, The World This Week, Janvaani*, etc, gave Indian viewers something to watch other than the Hindi film or *Chitrahaar*.

As ratings for such series soared (*Mahabharat* had viewership figures of 80 per cent), advertising responded.[39]

Competition from transnational and Indian satellite TV channels, coupled with the central government's reluctance to continue subsidising the electronic media has culminated in a situation where today commercial interests dominate Doordarshan's policies and actions. The *mantra* now is—entertain, entertain, entertain.

SATELLITE TV: DOORDARSHAN'S RESPONSE

The arrival of STAR TV (Satellite Television Asia Region), a Hong Kong-based company which broadcasts five 24-hour satellite channels to 53 Asian countries, including India) virtually coincided with the return to power of the Congress Party in June 1991. The government, caught unawares responded at first by simply ignoring STAR. Next it pooh-poohed any possible threat STAR might pose; and, finally, it acknowledged STAR's existence but dismissed reports of its growing popularity by saying that only an elite minority in the big cities were hooked on to it, turning a blind eye to the fact that almost everyone in the government was watching STAR TV.

It was the launch of Zee TV in October 1992 which finally galvanised the government into a flurry of precipitate action. As per the recommendations of the Mahalik Committee, afternoon entertainment slots were increased on Channel 1, prime time slots for sponsored programmes were increased from one to two, and more films were included in the schedule. Channel 2 was launched in January 1993.

Superhit Muqabala best exemplifies Channel 2's new commercial culture. One of the first programmes to be introduced on Doordarshan's metro entertainment channel in early 1992, it is, as the name suggests, a film song hit parade. But that's not all: there are star presenters, zany computer graphics, street smart talk of the MTV kind—and of course the film songs. The series was an instant success.

The success of *Superhit* is the success of Doordarshan's Channel 2 (metro entertainment). A satellite channel, it is steadily being converted into an all-India terrestrial channel. Unlike the national channel, Channel 2 has worked on the principle of selling time slots to private producers. This allowed for greater freedom and innovation. The Channel offers film-based series, soap serials like *Junoon, Ajnabi, Kismet, Sri Krishna*, talk shows, quiz programmes, and even current affairs and teleshopping. According to the Doordarshan Audience Research Television Ratings (12–18 March 1995) the channel recorded ratings over 55 per cent.

After, Channel 2, Doordarshan embarked on a massive expansion effort. By June 1993 there were plans to launch five more satellite channels offering time slots to private producers on a first-cum-first-served basis—a policy which, upon being challenged in the Delhi High Court by several private companies, was found invalid. Regardless, Doordarshan went ahead with the channels on its own and doubled its transmission time. However, conceived in haste and executed in a hurry, the channels failed to draw audiences and the whole scheme was abandoned by the end of 1993. In March 1994,10 regional (language) satellite channels with limited broadcasting hours were introduced and seem to be enjoying a greater measure of success.

CHILD-SPECIFIC PROGRAMMING

Currently Indian television channels offer very little by way of child-specific programming. To the Indian child therefore, entertainment has become almost exclusively synonymous with commercial films, film-based programmes or Bombay TV serials. So far little or no imagination is being invested in offering children viable, wholesome viewing alternatives.

If this is so, it is because Doordarshan's priorities have changed. The almost indecent haste with which channels are being launched, planned, or abandoned is an indication of the panic which has set in as Doordarshan faces the first challenge to its 30-year monopoly on broadcasting—a monopoly which had bred a certain smugness and obdurate reluctance to change. The complete absence of a comprehensive blueprint for the expansion of television services has resulted in knee jerk responses to what other TV players are doing.

The trend towards commercialisation of Doordarshan can only continue as more private channels are launched and competition for limited advertising revenue increases exponentially. Already Doordarshan is planning a Hindi film pay channel. Conversely, public service television is likely to be marginalised even further as the government reduces subsidies and Doordarshan is forced to use every available ruse to stay ahead of the competition—not so difficult when it has the advantage of being a national terrestrial channel whose incomparable reach will always be in its favour.

For the child viewer this suggests that programme options on Doordarshan will remain limited until some very conscious efforts are made to step up child-specific programming and strengthen educational TV. While Doordarshan may continue to offer cartoons and a few children's serials, it will rely on its emphasis on films, film-based programmes, live sports and adult serials to retain its child audience.

Thus the child-viewer will continue to be exposed to the values, attitudes and aspirations of the adult world—whether through Doordarshan's programming or TV advertising.

6

CABLE AND SATELLITE TV

Speaking at a school debate, a 16-year-old girl in Delhi had this to say on the influence of cable and satellite television: 'The cable network (which covers satellite) is probably one of the best things introduced into our lives after the video set. I feel strongly about this new development because of the immense exposure it gives us'.

She argued that claims regarding the 'addictiveness' of television were 'misconceived' and that an individual's relationship with the medium was a personal affair. She said:

Watching cable is like looking at the world through a window. The travel shows take us to places where the purse would never allow us to go.

. . . Each individual has dreams and aspirations about their careers and future education. Most of these dreams are set in foreign countries where opportunities are greater. Satellite TV provides an incentive by revealing information about life abroad, for making those dreams a reality.

In her view, since satellite TV does not stop at 'dramas and soap operas' but has programmes on science and technology, cookery, lifestyles and cultures, its daily offerings make adolescents and young people more aware and creative. Watching satellite 'opens up a whole new world for young children . . . and instead of "consuming" precious time it gives children a good way to occupy their time'.

To her, satellite TV is the ideal antidote to the burdens and anxieties of a heavy workload at school. 'These channels provide children the benefit of looking beyond notebooks,' she said, describing her generation as being 'overworked'. Both she and her friends feel that 'teenagers on satellite TV are a great source of inspiration', role models they can look up to.

The fierce defence of satellite TV by children in Delhi will not surprise those who have had the chance to observe them watching and discussing it. Our fieldwork in Delhi provided many opportunities to judge the impact that English-language programming, produced in Western nations and now available on satellite television, was having on children with access to it. At one of Delhi's most exclusive private schools, a group of 12-year olds looked at the questionnaire we had handed them with some perplexity. 'These questions are mostly about Doordarshan. But ma'am, *we* only watch STAR.'

Satellite TV invaded our lives in 1991 and began very quickly transforming the thinking and lifestyles of those it reached—particularly those of the children. For example, when asked what she wanted to be when she grew up, one young girl replied: 'A V.J. like Sophiya.' She is just one of the many youngsters like Rishi Prasad, a young man who, short of plastic surgery, has done everything to look like MTV's 'most wanted' V.J. Danny McGill. It certainly has not taken long for new look role models on STAR TV to steal young Indian hearts.

At the start of the nineties nobody knew what a V.J. was. Today, there are several young aspiring Dannys and Sophiyas around and in all likelihood we will soon have a whole new generation of children who want to be 'just like them', what with Michael Jackson look-alike contests to encourage them further.

Many children whose horizons have expanded beyond their 'narrow domestic walls' (to borrow a phrase from Rabindranath Tagore) have turned away from Doordarshan's narrowcasting and are glued to programmes like *WWF, Santa Barbara* and *The Crystal Maze*. Satellite TV has provided them new programme alternatives—and also their first real taste of children's programming, created to hook them to their sets. Along with the bait comes a new agenda for life, which our children are quick to pick up.

On the one hand, children in urban India (where satellite TV has made significant inroads) are being exposed to a world without frontiers. They are learning about new realms of experience, stretching from one end of the globe to the other. Issues, events, interests, people and places, so far unfamiliar to most children, are now bombarding their consciousness. Satellite TV is opening the windows of the mind and many adults in this country are grateful for its fantastic role in bridging continents and peoples.

Certainly TV teaches. There is much to be learnt from it and children are learning, consciously or unconsciously, as they watch. But what exactly are they learning? Does this exposure to trans-national satellite television contribute significantly to their development? In what way? Does their viewing require guidance and monitoring?

SATELLITE TV AND CHILDREN

Our interaction with children gave us some indications on the role satellite and cable television plays, and will continue to play, in their lives. Among other things, our study reveals:

- That satellite and cable TV have carved out an important market niche amongst children by filling the lacunae left by Doordarshan which provides little child-specific programming.
- That the number of cable/satellite TV subscribers is increasing to include the poorer sections of society.
- That as in the case of Doordarshan, language is playing a decisive role in channel and programme preference.
- That satellite TV is offering children a viewing experience that is qualitatively different from what they have so far been exposed to on Doordarshan. Along with more child-specific programming, there is more crime, violence and adult programming, creating an entirely new dimension in the lives of growing up children.
- That this exposure to foreign satellite TV is forging a whole new cultural identity for many children.
- And, lastly, that local cable TV is very popular as a separate entity from satellite TV, offering independent programming, largely, Hindi films.

THE GROWTH OF SATELLITE TV

In 1991, the Gulf War introduced us to the charms of satellite television—courtesy the American Cable News Network (CNN)—and few people suspected then that cable and satellite TV would spread through India like a forest fire. But spread it has, specially through the easily inflamed urban, affluent India.[40]

More than 80 per cent of our respondents told us that satellite/ cable connections were available in their areas of residence. Almost 45 per cent of our sample said they subscribe to cable TV. According to Doordarshan's Audience Research Cell, by January 1993 Delhi had 94,000 cabled households. The figure has gone up substantially since then.

These figures reflect the phenomenal growth of satellite TV in India since that day in January 1990 when CNN's Peter Arnott stood outside his hotel and described the bombing of the Iraqi capital, Baghdad, by Western allies.

At the time, even as the Indian public sought to understand how it was possible to catch CNN or, for that matter, any of the transnational satellite networks through a contraption which resembled an upside-down open umbrella, Indian air space was under threat from an entirely different source:

Twinkle, twinkle little STAR,
How I wonder what you are,
Up above the world so high,
Like a diamond in the sky.

The nursery rhyme aptly describes our initial response to STAR TV. In April 1991, STAR took its first timid steps along a foot-print (the path of the satellite signal) that would offer five 24-hour channels to 52 Asian countries: STAR Plus, Prime Sports, MTV, BBC World and the Chinese Mandarin language channel. The Hindi channel, Zee TV, became the sixth channel in September 1992.

Along with it, satellite television brought an unanticipated bonus: the local cable channel. Whereas cable TV had made its Indian debut in the early 1980s, until the advent of transnational TV it was restricted to hotels and high-rise apartments in the more affluent parts of cities like Bombay, Bangalore and Madras. The arrival of satellite TV laid, quite literally, the foundation for cable TV. Cable channels proved more popular than the ones satellite offered, especially to children, since cable TV provided an almost uninter-rupted flow of films, *Chitrahaar*-type programmes and cartoons. This popularity can be gauged both by viewer ratings (including this study) and the increase in advertising both on video film cassettes and on the channels.

PATTERN OF GROWTH

From the responses to a question on *when* cable/satellite TV connections were first acquired, we detected a pattern of growth fairly representative of the pattern in many cities in India: under 10 per cent of our sample began receiving cable three years ago (beginning of 1991); over 30 per cent were cabled two years ago (end of 1991) and 60 per cent subscribed a few months before the survey was conducted (autumn 1992).

To keep apace with this continually changing media scenario, market research organisations like IMRB, Mode and Frank Small Associates have been regularly investigating viewership patterns across the country. Meanwhile, advertising agencies and their clients are trying to successfully weave their way through this media maze. The only problem with market research data is that the change is so rapid that today's figures become outdated a month later.

The most recent figures (1994–95) for satellite and cable TV indicate that the viewership is as high as 80 million (all India) and not lower than 50 million. The latest estimates suggest that there are between 10 and 14 million cabled households in the country. Surveys conducted at the beginning of 1993, revealed that whereas cable connections were continuing to increase, there was a decline in the pace of this increase. For instance, between February and July 1992, there was a 210 per cent increase which dropped to 157 per cent in the next quarter. This can at best be explained as a process of levelling off after the initial enthusiasm. In all probability the growth pattern will continue to follow this trend as small town India acquires the cable habit. In 1993 there were an estimated 12.28 million satellite TV households representing an over 30 per cent penetration.[41]

CLASS AND LANGUAGE

The data generated by our study reflects that the growth of cable TV is an inescapable urban reality: 58.79 per cent of upper class children said they have cable connections, 28.52 per cent of the

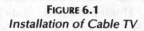

FIGURE 6.1
Installation of Cable TV

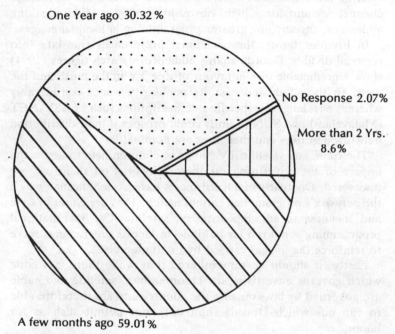

One Year ago 30.32 %

No Response 2.07%

More than 2 Yrs.
8.6%

A few months ago 59.01 %

middle class children have access to satellite TV and 21.05 per cent of lower class children enjoy cable TV at home—a figure higher than what might have been expected.

Two factors may be responsible for this pattern of demand for cable TV: first, cable connections can be expensive (the average cost of a connection is between Rs. 300 and Rs. 1,200 for installation and monthly charges vary from Rs. 30 to Rs. 175 or even higher). Significantly, the price of a dish antenna has been steadily declining. From a high of Rs. 40,000 to Rs. 50,000, the tag on a 9-inch dish today reads only Rs. 10,000 and may come down even further encouraging the spread of cable TV.

Second, available satellite TV channels are predominantly English language services and attract largely the affluent, English-speaking population. Since the study was conducted, the accent has been on developing/improving Hindi broadcasts and channels as well as on offering more channels. Conversely, Zee TV and the local cable channel account for a high viewership amongst Hindi-speaking audiences, encouraging greater programming in local languages.

In broader terms, these channel preferences translate into regional divides: Doordarshan's audience research figures (1994) show a predictable bias in favour of Zee TV in the north and the west. In the south and east its popularity wanes considerably whereas new language-specific satellite options such as ASIANET (Malayalam) and SUN (Tamil) could prosper if their distribution network improves and their fees are nominal.[42]

The cable and satellite TV habits of children help to assess the impact of the advertising on these networks on them. As we discovered, Doordarshan advertisments have a sophistication which the network's programming cannot match. They are closer in style and slickness to ads appearing on satellite TV. Transnational programming is not too far behind—in fact its programmes serve to reinforce the images carried by its commercials.

Lastly, it should be remembered that while there is a code which governs advertising on Doordarshan, satellite and cable are governed by laws outside the country and are therefore able to run ads which Doordarshan does not permit such as for liquor.

What do children watch on satellite channels? As we look at the channels they favour and the programmes they enjoy, we shall also see the level of international advertising they are exposed to. Furthermore, with Indian advertising now prominently claiming time on these channels, children are also witnessing the globalisation of the Indian economy and a transformation of the image we had of our country.

WHAT CHILDREN WATCH ON SATELLITE TV

'I love STAR. I never bother with Doordarshan now.'
— *10-year-old boy*

'We don't have cable or satellite because my mother says it will affect my studies.'

— *11-year-old girl*

'MTV—Most Wanted!

— *15-year-old girl*

Children who have a loyalty to satellite TV are delighted with it. Some of their parents are however dismayed or disconcerted, while others are relieved and feel they can 'leave it to satellite TV to teach and prepare' their children for the outside world. Parents may praise satellite TV for 'the knowledge it imparts and breadth of its vision', or defensively ask, 'What's wrong with it?' A few condemn it outright: it affects the child's scholastic abilities, it has too many 'bad' English movies, too many intimate sexual scenes, is 'alien', and it's making them behave oddly (such as dressing up and talking like Sophiya or Danny!).

In 1993, the *A & M* magazine conducted a survey which revealed that because of cable/satellite TV, children were doing less homework, paying less attention to their studies and sleeping later—and less. So were their parents.

Many parents have become perturbed by this satellite TV mania. They are not the only ones. Fearing a cultural invasion, the likes of which we have not witnessed since British rule, several government agencies, politicians, social scientists, media analysts, psychologists and others concerned with the psyche of the nation, have voiced serious misgivings about the impact of satellite TV. Those who favour satellite television and think that the influence it will exert on Indian society could liberate us from our retrograde ways, are apt to dismiss such fears as xenophobic. They consider these reactions as alarmist and narrow-minded, springing from a desire to remain cloistered in an outmoded and outdated, culturally backward context, one that is at variance with the modern, market-oriented, hi-tech world.

While there is some argument over the influence these space invaders might have on grown-ups (who are supposedly mature enough to absorb the impact without detriment and old enough to make the right choices) there is more concern about the impact it might have on children.

CHANNEL CHOICES

Our experience with children in Delhi has shown that concerns notwithstanding, children are having a wonderful time enjoying their new 'toy'. Some of them are enjoying it even more than they do Doordarshan: 21.37 per cent of the children in our sample said that they prefer satellite TV, as compared to 65.32 per cent who are Doordarshan die hards. Just over 10 per cent are partial to the local cable channel. Given below are the children's ratings for satellite channels:

Zee TV:	75.00 per cent
STAR Plus:	68.85 per cent
Prime Sports:	66.57 per cent
MTV:	55.27 per cent

BBC comes in a poor fifth while CNN and ATN hardly enter the child's world at all (primarily because at the time hardly any cable operators regularly provided either channel. Both services run on satellites whose footprint axis is different from STAR TV's and therefore require a separate dish antenna for reception).

Upon closer examination, these figures reveal gender, class and language distinctions.

GENDER

Girls like Doordarshan more than boys (73.78 per cent: 59.70 per cent) while on the whole, boys favour satellite more (25.87 per cent: 14.60 per cent). The viewership figures for Prime Sports and MTV make it clear that these two channels are especially dear to the boys, who therefore prefer satellite TV fare.

Prime Sports is watched by an overwhelming majority of boys (who also rated sports telecasts on Doordarshan as a top favourite); MTV is also watched by more boys, who lead the girls by a two-thirds margin.

CLASS VARIATIONS

Satellite channels rank highest with children from more affluent backgrounds (44.44 per cent of those who receive cable). Only 10

FIGURE 6.2

Channel Preference in Families of 8 to 15-Years Olds -

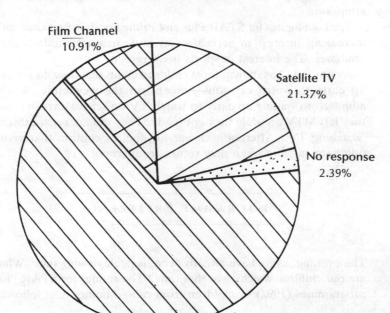

Film Channel
10.91%

Satellite TV
21.37%

No response
2.39%

Doordarshan 65.32%

per cent of the children from middle class and less affluent families like to watch satellite TV though over 20 per cent have cable connections. These two categories overwhelmingly (over 75 per cent) prefer Doordarshan. The local cable channel is equally popular with all three social categories.

The following Zee TV has won is largely due to it being a Hindi-language channel while all the other satellite channels are in English. Zee TV's staple diet consists of Hindi films and Hindi film-based programmes/serials and prize game shows.

The local film channel also devotes most of its output to Hindi films, averaging two to three if not four Hindi films a day. Together with Doordarshan's generous doses of Bollywood, this adds up to a figure of approximately 40 to 50 Hindi or regional films transmitted every week to the TV viewer. (Likely to have gone up considerably since this study was conducted.) All TV networks are furiously introducing special movie channels as they compete for viewer attention.

The high figures for STAR Plus and Prime Sports reflect children's increasing interest in serials/series and cartoons/children programmes. The interest in sports is evergreen.

As our data has shown, most children claim that they do not get up early to watch cartoons—except on the weekends. A few admitted to waking up early to watch TV on school days but said they left MTV on while they got ready. They did not regard this as 'watching TV'. Afternoon viewership figures confirm that many tune into satellite when they return from school.

PROGRAMME PREFERENCE

The evening, as we have already seen, is peak viewing time. What are our children watching at that time? The ratings for STAR Plus programmes (1992) by children from cabled homes is as follows:

Films:	41.28 per cent
Santa Barbara:	35.98 per cent
Robin Hood:	35.22 per cent
Remington Steele:	33.33 per cent
Hollywood Stars:	33.33 per cent

Tour of Duty, *The Bold and the Beautiful*, *Crime Story*, *Treasure Island* and *Lifestyles of the Rich and the Famous* received approximately 30 per cent viewership support.

Of the top 10 programmes/serials selected only two are specifically for children. More significantly, the other three children's programmes listed received negligible responses, confirming that the Indian child tends to watch a lot of adult programming (a habit deriving from the heavy diet of films and other programmes, not specifically for children, watched on Doordarshan).

As mentioned earlier, more boys than girls watch STAR TV. A gender analysis for serials like *Tour of Duty*, and *Crime Story*

FIGURE 6.3
Favourite Satellite Channels by Cable Viewers

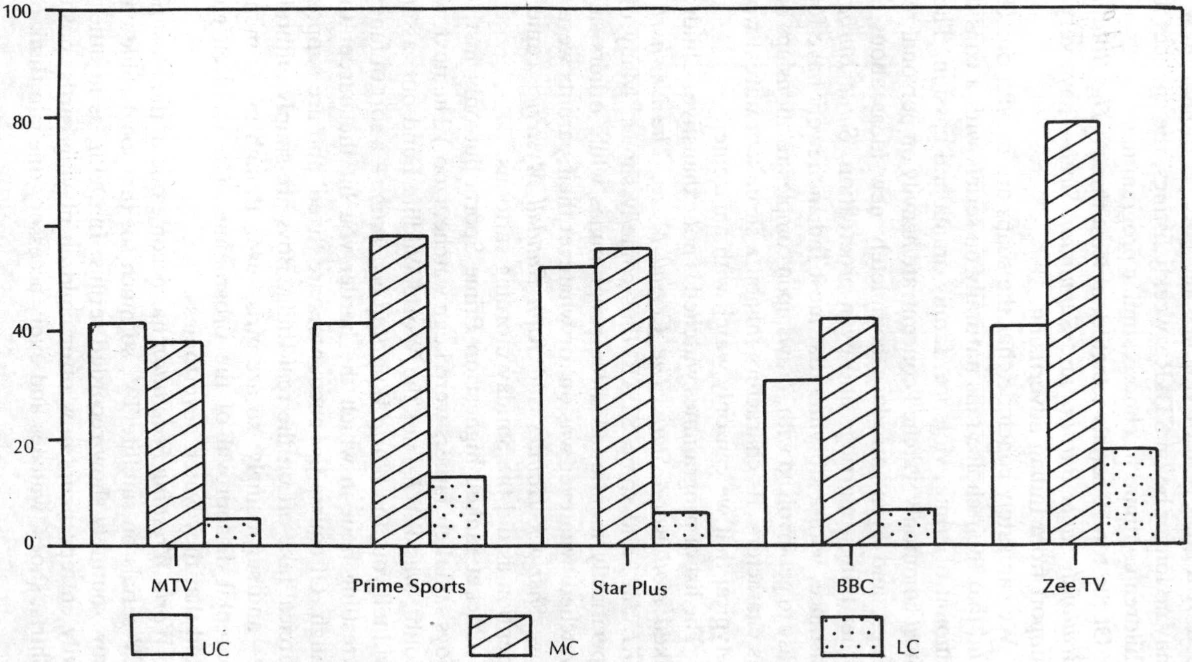

reveals that boys heavily outweigh girls. These serials are characterised by a great deal of violence and gore. Although these serials may no longer be on STAR's weekly listings, the chances are that children continue to choose similar programmes.

Of the top 10 serials selected, at least three—*The Bold and the Beautiful*, *Santa Barbara* and *Remington Steele*—have very strong support from Indian advertising.

We can safely conclude that the soaps are in with our children and that their choice falls naturally on serials with a considerable amount of crime, violence, family drama and passion. The soaps most commonly watched concentrate heavily on personal relationships, and even introduce completely new ideas about, among other things, marriage and even procreation. *Santa Barbara*, for instance, with a storyline that most Indian viewers have found so easy to get involved with, draws upon complex relationships between its characters. Its characters inhabit a shrunken, unreal world, so a-typical that we can only watch with amazement.

The list of programmes watched is not exhaustive. Children also liked *Hollywood Stars*, *The Crystal Maze*, *The Newhart Show*, *G.I. Joe*, and some STAR Plus comedy shows. Many of them specifically mentioned these programmes while others said they watched 'whatever was on' or whatever their parents were watching. *Sherlock Holmes* and *Ruth Randall Mysteries* came in for mention as did the Sunday morning cartoons.

Cricket ranked highest on Prime Sports but only just. (Many boys said their fathers were keen watchers too.) The next, without doubt, was *WWF*—not the World Wildlife Fund but, as any boy will tell you, the *World Wrestling Federation*—a sort of fancy dress wrestling bout in which the harder you hit the harder the kids laugh. Of course the encounters are 'fixed' and are supposedly a farcical take-off on the real thing. Boys are simply enthralled by it—and surprisingly, so are girls—even though many mentioned parental disapproval of the programme. The children gleefully said that they watch nevertheless.

World Wrestling Federation has become one of the most popular TV serials on satellite TV, so much so, that local cable channels now routinely show recorded reruns. In Delhi, as in other cities, wily entrepreneurs now offer children playing cards, posters, T-Shirts, shoes, watches and every accessory one can think of, with the *WWF* insignia prominently emblazoned. Visits to major Indian cities by WWF hulks have added to the obsession.

The influence and impact of *WWF* is, however, beginning to disturb parents and teachers alike who have found that children are becoming increasingly aggressive in their behaviour. As noted earlier, there have been newspaper reports describing how children use *WWF* fighting techniques to settle arguments with siblings at home.

And so to MTV: MTV went off STAR in 1994 (but was quickly claimed by Doordarshan). It has been replaced by STAR TV's own music channel—Channel [V]. [V] has made an extra effort to attract the Indian viewers by putting on a series of India-specific programmes including *BPL Oye*, *Mangta-Hai* and *Videocon Flashback*. MTV's popularity was obviously based on its musical appeal, though its sophisticated visual imagery (referred to by many as 'complete or ultimate television') was also a crowd-puller. Another side to MTV's popularity is that MTV type channels appear to represent more than just music. Music channels are benefitting the music cassette industry which is reaping huge profits from the increased interest in TV promoted music.

A study released by the U.S. National Coalition on Television Violence in 1992, reported that for the major music video networks (of which MTV is well known in India), there were

few time periods which were free from harmful effects: Over sixty per cent of the music videos contained at least one of the following elements: explicit violence, suggestions of violence, degrading sexual portrayals, sexually suggestive themes, profanity, smoking and/or alcohol consumption.

The report identifies MTV as the most violent music video network, averaging over 29 instances of violent or hostile imagery per hour.

In response to these findings, child psychiatrists in the U.S. caution that while the violence and aggression, sexual or otherwise, depicted in music videos may not be as overt or intense as in several Hollywood films, it must be remembered that the target audience of MTV-type networks is children, teenagers and young adults.

In a speech on the US Senate floor, Sentor Robert Byrd said in September 1991:

> The central message of most of these music videos is clear: human happiness and fulfillment are experienced by becoming a sociopath and rejecting all responsibility . . . . (Music videos are) a particularly reprehensible television influence on children . . . . If we, in this nation, continue to sow the images of murder, violence, drug abuse, sadism, arrogance, irreverence, blasphemy, perversion, pornography and abberration before the eyes of millions of children, year after year, day after day, we should not be surprised if the foundations of our society rot away as if from leprosy.[43]

Without getting into the rights and wrongs of where Senator Byrd's attack on the music video industry leads up to (is he suggesting a ban, which might be seen as an interference with the freedom of expression by those who feel that viewers should, in the ultimate analysis, be the decision-makers of what they do or do not want to see?), we quote him here to make the point that many of our children who watch MTV (or other music channels) are being exposed, as the Americans themselves are sensing, to retrograde and destructive visuals whose impact could be dangerous in the long run.

The subjects of many heavy-metal songs are sex, violence, death, Satan and alienation. The images don't always hang together—they flash on and off, staying only momentarily on the screen, bewildering you, confusing the mind until you ease off, and stop trying to make sense of the whole. The question that is being raised in this context is: Does the music video industry bear no responsibility for providing good role models or does it use negative messages because they sell?

7

THE FUTURE

In 1988, *Newsweek* published an article entitled 'The Future of Television' by Harry F. Waters. He wrote:

. . . Enough of memories and visions. As television prepares to mark the 50th anniversary of its coming-out party at the fair, it is time to face up to a startling (some would say chilling) reality: watching TV has become What We Do. On a typical day, the average American family spends no less than seven hours and five minutes in front of the screen. Has any society been held in thrall by a single passive activity for nearly one half of its waking life? Has any technological instrument ever exerted such immense influence over how we think and act?

As we pass from what might be called the era of TV I to the era of TV II, from decades of network dominion to the dawn of viewer liberation, an explosion in communications technology has rearranged the entire video landscape.

Let us count the ways:

- The growth of cable TV has outstripped the most grandiose projections. Cable's copper strand now reaches more than half of all U.S. households; its subscribers devote as much time to watching its programmes as to network shows.
- The video-cassette recorder has emerged as the fastest-selling domestic appliance in history. VCRs currently hold sway in six out of every 10 homes. Last year alone, Americans purchased 65 million prerecorded cassettes and rented over 2 billion.
- The number of independent TV stations has nearly quadrupled over the last decade. And as the independents proliferate, they are spawning a vast surge of syndicated programming. Once largely confined to airing network reruns, the in-die-syndie system now reaps enormous ratings with its own

productions and own stars—the sort of people who wouldn't get past a network's security guards . . . .

The proliferation of remote-control devices and the profusion of cable channels have already radically altered how we watch television. A recent study by Channels magazine suggests that the American viewer's fear of commitment is approaching pathological dimensions. More than half of the study's respondents in the key 18–34 age group reported that they regularly use their remote controls to watch more than one programme at a time, while 20 per cent watch three or more shows at once. There's even a new term for this behavior: 'grazing'. Permanently jittery, instantly bored, loyal to no network or station, grazers incessantly roam the dial in search of . . . . Something Better. Imagine the grazers of the future confronted with the hundreds of channels envisioned by most televisionaries. There will be, you might say, no holding them.[44]

The *Newsweek* article gives us a sense of things to come. India and, to a lesser extent perhaps, Asia are on the threshold of a communications explosion which will alter the entire fabric of our lives. It seems safe to predict that with the continuing decline in prices of dish antennas and cable connections and the dizzying proliferation of channel choices—foreign, Hindi or regional language—satellite and cable TV will spread to the smaller cities and towns of India.

Present indications suggest, for instance, that in the next few years, the Indian viewer will be able to have access to as many as 40 to 60 channels. The figure has already reached more than 30. Some enterprising cable operators are even offering Burmese, Kuwaiti, Bangladeshi, Thai, Dubai and Iranian TV.[45]

STAR was slated to launch ASIASAT II in 1995 (which will offer another possible 12 transponders with double digit channel possibilities). With Rupert Murdoch now in control of the company, the services will include specialised fare: films, drama, music, and interactive services (like banking, shopping etc.), many of which could well be 'pay channels, pay-per-view' available only to subscribers unlike the present five STAR TV channels which are free

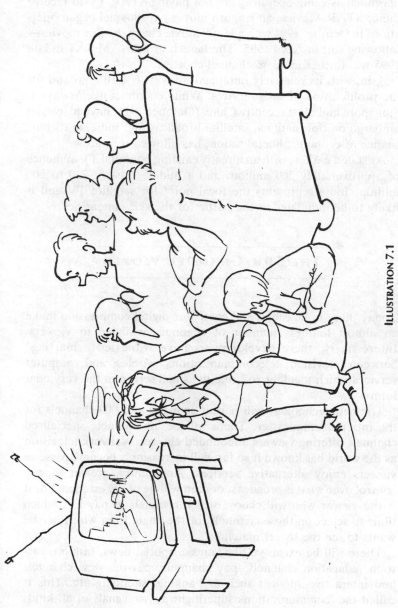

ILLUSTRATION 7.1
All the Time, TV Time

inasmuch as cable operators are not paying STAR TV to receive them. STAR Movies, an English movie pay channel began operations in October 1994 with a Hindi movie channel—Zee movies—following suit in April 1995. The launch of PANAM SAT in late 1995 will further increase channel choices.

Asia, with its relatively untapped market, is fertile ground for the proliferation of such services. While countries like Malaysia, Singapore and most recently China (October 1993) have placed an embargo on transnational satellite broadcasting, India, in its pursuance of economic liberalisation, has allowed it to grow.

As stated earlier, with an already existing potential TV audience of approximately 200 million, and a middle class of 250 to 300 million, India represents the focal point for satellite TV and is likely to be inundated as the battle for the skies intensifies.

THE 500-CHANNEL WORLD

Today, fibre optic cables and computer-digital compression make an almost limitless number of channels available to viewers. Interestingly, these developments have witnessed a marriage between television, telecommunications, wireless and computer services which together will rule the small screen in the very near future.

The new technology will permit as many as 1,000 channels for the intrepid broadcaster. There will be innumerable specialised channels offering viewers unbounded choices. Network television as the world has known it so far, will increasingly become passé as viewers enjoy alternative services. Apparently, greater viewer control over what is broadcast or seen will be of the essence. For it is the viewer who will choose which channels to pay for, which films to select on those channels, or the angle from which he/she wants to see the soccer match.

There will be exclusive film, music, sports, news, fashion, cartoon, education channels, pay channels, pay-per-view channels and interactive services such as banking, shopping etc. This is called the 'communications superhighway' as signals of all kinds controlled by digital computerised technology zoom up and down the telecom lines. All of this will make it possible for us to sit at home in front of a console and do just about everything we need or want to without ever stirring out. Fantastic or frightening?

There are, of course, many positive aspects to this information explosion. One, as we have mentioned, is the viewer's increased control over what is seen and therefore, shown. Individuals will watch what they want to, when they want to in accordance with their own inclinations and tastes. The whole idea of television supplying the world with a shared experience will be reduced to the fact of watching TV (as opposed to performing some other activity). Beyond that, nothing will be the same. Thus individualism will flourish within a homogenous context.

Cable television offers exciting possibilities that are immediate. It contributes to loosening the control of TV magnates and monopolies by offering the opportunity to develop community television. The quality of what we watch could also improve or at least we would have the ability to choose better programming instead of being at the mercy of network, satellite or cable schedules. For example, in the era of pay-per-view and pay TV, you could, on the music channel select an endless stream of classical Indian instrumental or vocal music. Or watch only art films or visit an exhibition. Competition will also enhance the quality and nature of programming and cater to specialised interests—something unimaginable on network programming.

There will be so much information on almost every conceivable subject that the frontiers of the mind will expand beyond present expectations. From the education point of view, the possibilities of satellite and interactive TV are breathtaking if, of course, they are pursued.

However breathtaking the possibilities, this new information order will initially be expensive and almost invariably require changes in dish antennas, decoding machines and television monitors. This would mean additional expense for everyone—from the satellite owners to the cable operators and the viewers.

What will hopefully, from the viewer's point of view, offset these expenses is the competition: all major American—and some European—entertainment/information organisations and telecommunications giants are merging with one another to prepare for the viewership battle ahead. The greater the competition, the greater the likelihood that prices will be held down in order to make the services competitive. However, the vast outlays of money required in the satellite and fibre optic revolution will mean that only the biggest companies or conglomerates will survive.

Furthermore, we have seen in our own study that despite the high costs involved in home entertainment services—Rs. 18,000 for a colour TV, Rs. 20,000 for a VCR—most urban homes own one and 50 per cent own both. The huge success of cable and satellite television also suggests that families are willing to pay a high, sometimes unaffordable, price for TV and related services.

Thus the factors governing the continuing success and spread of satellite TV will be: financial viability, technological advances and viewer fatigue. Till 1994, none of the satellite channels available in India were charging operators or viewers a fee. This was deliberate, the idea being to capture the Indian market, get it hooked and then slap on a price tag. While STAR TV does not propose any surcharge on the current batch of five channels, all future channels will be encoded so that only those who sign up will receive the transmission. The introduction of pay channels is an indication of things to come.

The Indian government has enacted legislation for controlling/ standardising cable networks (which earlier fell under the antiquated 1933 Wireless Act). Some state governments like Bihar, Maharashtra and Tamil Nadu have also imposed taxes on operators up to 35 per cent.

The second aspect of the financial package relates to commercial support. Is advertising revenue going to be able to keep up with the growth and commercial needs of satellite TV? Given that Indian advertising must also feed Doordarshan and its channels, it seems unlikely. There were reports that Zee TV was facing a financial crunch forcing it to raise money in the share market. Other TV companies including BITV, and Jain TV are following suit.

But while Rupert Murdoch's acquisition of a 50 per cent stake in Zee TV might improve its financial standing, it is unclear how long the media moghul can continue to sustain losses. For instance, STAR TV was losing a million dollars every week in 1994. Most satellite TV experts claim that it takes at least five years for the losses to stop.

Finally, one must take into account the viewer's ability to absorb the visual blitzkrieg. TV manufacturers are already experimenting with the marketing of large screen TV sets, three-dimensional TV sets and split screen sets which offer at least eight screens simultaneously. But just how much TV can a person watch? Even 24 hours would not cover all the choices that will become available. Saturation or viewer fatigue will be a major factor in determining which channels and services survive and which fall by the wayside.

The wider impact of this revolution will have to be assessed, as things change. Who controls the technology represented by television and how this influences the content of programming remains to be seen.

For our children, life on earth will be an experience very much like something out of their favourite science fiction serial. For them, the majority of whom have already leapfrogged from a one-channel TV experience to a 20-channel one, and for those who are largely illiterate in terms of their ability to read and write but are becoming sophisticated visual literates, the world will effectively be reduced to the size of the TV monitor they choose. What will this do to their hearts and minds? What kind of human beings will be fashioned out of the new world of television?

NOTES TO PART I

1. Television, its spread and accessibility have been the subject of research and debate for many years now. Many varying perspectives have emerged on 'the television experience'—how it should be seen and defined. Winick and Winick refer to television as a 'member of the family', suggesting that TV constitutes a very significant experiential component of a child's development. Jan-Uwe Rogge in *The Media in Everyday Family Life*, says: 'The media form part of the family system, a part many can no longer imagine living without.'

   Another aspect of the debate is the extent to which the audience/the television determine the use and impact of the technology. The audience is perceived not as a monolithic unit (Ien Ang and James Lull) but as a disparate group of individuals who constantly exercise their freedom to choose what they will view and how they will use television. This is disputed by experts who claim that television has the potential to unify audiences, however disparate they might be to start with. This unificiation is distrusted on the grounds that it alienates people from reality and hypnotises them into living in a milieu defined by a handful of TV characters and programmes (Mander 1978).

2. While TV may appear to be a 'window to the world', Jerry Mander, author of *Four Arguments for the Elimination of Television*, argued that:

   > Television is no open window through which all perceptions may pass. Quite the opposite. There are many technological factors that conspire to limit what the medium can transmit. Some information can pass through, but only after being reshaped, redefined, packaged, and made duller and coarser than before. Some ways of mind can be conveyed and some cannot.
   >
   > The wrinkle in the story is that what can be conveyed through television are the ways of thinking and the kind of information that suit the people who are in control.

3. For a profile of respondents see Figure 2.1 entitled Sample.
4. Indian Market Research Bureau (IMRB). Survey conducted in June 1993.
5. *Basti*: slum; *gali*: small lane.
6. Jan-Uwe Rogge, 'The Media in Everyday Family Life' in *Remote Control TV, Audiences and Cultural Power* edited by E. Seiter, H. Borchers, G. Kreutzner and E.M. Worth. 1989. Routledge, London.
7. According to latest Government of India statistics (see *Development of Education in India 1993–94*, Department of Education, Ministry of Human Resource Development) there were 320.41 million illiterate Indians in the age group of 7 years and above (1991). The literacy rate for men was estimated at 64.20 per

cent while for women it stood at 39.19 per cent. Regional disparities are indicated in the state-wise break up of literacy levels, with only the states of Kerala, Goa and Mizoram claiming that more than 68.01 per cent of their population is literate while the populous states of U.P., Bihar, Rajasthan, Madhya Pradesh and Andhra Pradesh and Orissa fall into the group of states where levels of literacy are below the national average.

8. Krishna Kumar, *Social Character of Learning*. 1989. Sage Publications, New Delhi.

9. James Lull, *Inside Family Viewing—Ethnographic Research on Television's Audiences*. 1990. Routledge, London.

10. M.P. Winick and C. Winick, *The Television Experience—What Children See*. 1979. Sage Publications, Beverly Hills.

11. This view, that television is distinctive from other experiences, is expressed by many researchers and media critics including Jerry Mander, whom we have repeatedly quoted in our study. In Mander's view, television affects the human being negatively, interfering with basic human instincts and curbing the desire to know one's world. It creates this effect by replacing direct experience with indirect experience and providing an artificial information field which the viewer feeds off. Sari Thomas in Downing et al. *Questioning the Media* reiterates this point: 'Television especially provides a window on many matters which most of us have relatively little or no real life experience of.' In *Television and Children*, while emphasising the special qualities of television when compared with other media, Aimee Dorr says:

> '. . . it is clear why television can be singled out. It presents lifelike experiences for viewers to enjoy and it presents them much more effectively and often than do such other communication media as radio, newspapers, books, magazines, computers, films and comics . . . . Television stands out from other media . . . because it can present more lifelike content than most other media and is generally used more than any other of them. These characteristics make the medium important for everyone but especially for children . . .'

Reflecting on a wide range of research over several decades, Dorr, assesses various perspectives on children and television. One of the aspects that this research has drawn attention to in the past quarter century is a number of age-related differences in the way children understand TV: 'A major shift in their transactions with television seems to occur sometime between the ages of 6 and 9, and a smaller shift probably occurs around adolescence.' According to Dorr:

> . . . preschoolers tend to think of it (TV), as completely real because everything looks so lifelike . . . By about the age of 7 or 8 most know that even programmes featuring real people are not necessarily glimpses of real life. They recognise news, commercials, cartoons, entertainment programmes as different forms whose content has different ostensible reality values.

12. See Ellen Wartella's 'Cognitive and Affective Factors of TV Advertising's Influence on Children'. *Western Journal of Speech Communication*, Spring 1984.

13. Joli Jensen, *Remote Control TV, Audiences and Cultural Power* edited by E. Seiter, H. Borchers, G. Kreutzner and E.M. Worth. 1989. Routledge, London.
14. Jerry Mander. *Four Arguments for The Elimination of Television*. 1978. Quill, New York.
15. Patricia Marks Greenfield, *Mind and Media—The Effects of Television, Computers and Video Games*. 1984. William Collins Sons and Co Ltd., Glasgow.
16. Joli Jensen, op. cit.
17. Eric Barnouw, *The Sponsor: Notes on a Modern Potentate*. 1978. OUP, New York.
18. David Littlejohn, 'Communicating Ideas by Television'. In *Television as a Social Force—New Approaches to TV Criticism* edited by Richard Adler. 1975. Praeger Publishers, New York.
19. Aimee Dorr, op. cit.
20. Patricia Marks Greenfield, op. cit.
21. The negative affects of watching a split screen, over a quarter of which is taken by a band of continuous advertising, was brought to our attention by doctors at the National Institute of Mental Health and Neurological Sciences (NIMHANS), Bangalore. Reacting to current media trends, they also told us that in Bangalore, video parlours had on offer cassettes of taped TV ads which were largely borrowed and watched by children. The doctors felt that a dependence on watching such short and unrelated audio-visual materials could be detrimental to a child's ability to concentrate.
22. Marie Winn, *The Plug-in Drug*. 1977. Viking, New York.
23. Daniel R. Anderson. 'The Influence of Television on Children's Attentional Abilities'. Paper commissioned by the Children's Television Workshop, University of Massachusetts, Amherst MA., U.S.A.
24. Vance Packard. *The Hidden Persuaders*. 1981. Penguin, Great Britain.
25. Jerry Mander. op. cit.
26. Ibid.
27. See Figure 3.1 on frequency of TV viewing.
28. See Figure 4.1 entitled 'TV Viewing Patterns of 8 to 15-Year Olds'.
29. See Figure 2.1 (families owning TVs and VCRs) and Figure 6.2 (favoured channels in families of 8 to 15-year olds).
30. *Strategies for Change*—a booklet produced by the Committee for Children's Television, Metro Detroit, U.S.A.
31. *The Pioneer*, April 1993.
32. J. Holman and V.A. Braithwaite, 'Parental Lifestyles and Children's Television Viewing'. *Australian Journal of Psychology*, Volume 34, No. 3, 1982.
33. John Fiske, *Television Culture*. 1989. Routledge, New York. See Chapters 10 and 11. Fiske discusses how different kinds of programmes appeal to different viewers on the basis of sex, colour, class etc.
34. For Reports on Doordarshan, please see Bibliography.
35. MRAS-BURKE National Television Survey IV (1991); Doordarshan-1994-An Update. Audience Research Unit. Directorate General: Doordarshan; Doordarshan 1995. Audience Research Unit: Doordarshan.
36. Doordarshan's Audience Research Unit brings out a handbook of statistics every year. The figures mentioned here are from its 1992–93 handbook.

37. In the USA, there was never any pretense that broadcasting was anything other than a commercial proposition that could only expand and survive if it was economically self-sufficient. Interestingly, American broadcasters argued that government control or interference in the electronic media was, in essence, a contravention of the fundamental right to freedom of speech.

38. The Mahalik Committee Report on Doordarshan's Commercial Services. Ministry of Information and Broadcasting, January 1992.

39. See IMRB: TRP Ratings (Television Rating Points), for public response to Mahabharat; See Annexures for a detailed break-down of Doordarshan's commercial receipts. Between 1984–92, Doordarshan enjoyed a growth rate of roughly 15 per cent each year. However, in 1993–94 this fell to just over 5 per cent.

40. In India, satellite and cable TV are virtually synonymous since cable TV is the major public distribution system for satellite TV in most parts of India. The number of families which own their own dish antennas is still small enough to be irrelevant. According to Doordarshan 1995 (Audience Research Unit: Doordarshan) in 1985 there were 450 cable networks in the country. By 1993 the number had risen to 40,000.

41. See Lintas, *Media Guide* (India): January 1995; *Doordarshan 1994*; IMRB-Zee Survey & FSF Study 1993.

42. ASIANET's Malayalam satellite channel began in September 1992. Indications so far suggest that cable operators in Kerala are not keen on transmitting the service because ASIANET's fees are too high and in order to receive the service, cable operators would have to acquire another dish antenna since the orientation of the channel's footprint is different from ASIASAT I (STAR TV). If ASIANET can improve its marketing, provide free or subsidised dish antennas and equipment, the chances are that it will be much more successful.

43. See National Coalition on Television Violence (NCTV) News. Volume 13, Nos. 1–4, Jan–April 1992. Champaign, Illinois, USA.

44. Excerpts from the Newsweek article, October 17 1988.

45. Soon after CNN and STAR arrived on our horizons, Asian Television Network (ATN) entered the market. ATN has a tie-up with the American Network ABC, the English company Thames TV and CNN. Its popularity ratings are much lower than STAR Plus or Zee, primarily because it uses a Russian satellite and cable operators require another dish antenna to receive its signal.

    Pakistan TV had the foresight to hire a transponder on ASIASAT—something the Indian government balked at, considering the price too high—and began broadcasting in December 1991. Most cable operators in India shy away from the channel except when the immensely popular and well-made Pakistani plays are on the air.

II

ADVERTISING

INTRODUCTION

Find some consumer desire, some widespread unconscious anxiety, think out some way to relate this wish or fear to the product you have to sell; then build a bridge of verbal or pictorial symbols over which your consumer can pass from fact to compensatory dream, and from the dream to the illusion that your product, when purchased, will make the dream come true.

— *Aldous Huxley*

The Hollywood film *The Godfather* was immensely popular with English-speaking urban India. Marlon Brando as the Godfather lived by the code—'make him an offer he cannot refuse'—a code which advertisers understand only too well. Colossal sums of money are spent by the advertising industry all over the world on creating, packaging and presenting the most fantastic images to propel people into the buying game.

India had a Rs. 2,800 crore advertising industry in 1993, (an estimated 25 per cent increase over the previous year) which was growing by leaps and bounds, thanks not only to the changing economic environment but also to rapidly expanding media options. Today, more than ever before, people are being bombarded by advertising signals exhorting them to become defiantly consumption-oriented. On their part, manufacturers are looking to the enormous domestic markets—both urban and rural—still waiting to be tapped. Millions of Indians have money to spend and every producer of goods and services would like them to spend their money on his/her products. Even by conservative estimates, the market segment targeted by the consumer industry today would be several times the population of a country like France.

This section considers some of the major views on the role advertising plays in society. The opinions expressed by the critics and defenders of advertising will, we hope, help to initiate a much-needed dialogue on the function and relevance of current-day TV advertising and its implications for our children.

Since our study set out to examine the impact of TV advertising on children in Delhi, the chapters that follow deal with children's general reactions to advertising on television. Their responses to product-specific TV commercials are analysed in Part III.

Advertising is, of course, the best and the most convenient route to reach the consumer's mind. To make their venture successful, advertisers sink money, resources and time into carefully studying the intricacies of the human mind in order to understand where the individual's vulnerabilities lie. It is on these vulnerabilities that they play to make the consumer feel that redemption lies in the possession or use of a particular product or service. This role ascribed to advertisers—of a snoop whose aim is to find out where and how you are most likely to hurt—has led to their being labelled 'the mind manipulators' or 'the hidden persuaders'. Indeed, many publications and research studies on advertising and its impact have focused on the behind-the-scenes operations the advertising world conducts. Needless to say, many of them have concluded that the methods employed by advertisers to trap consumers are 'unethical'.

In India campaigns, such as the one for Maggi Noodles, are believed to have played on the 'guilt syndrome' experienced by mothers. When children return from school hungry and tired, most mothers would like to give them something 'hot, steaming and fresh' to eat, but they do not always have the time, energy or imagination to come up with an attractive dish. Advertisers, selling '2-minute noodles' (the nutritional value of which is highly debatable), targeted women by exploiting their feelings of maternal guilt. They also enticed children by presenting the snack as a 'fun' food—easy to make and great to eat. The advertisement, as we know, has worked wonders. However, the Ahmedabad-based Consumer Education and Research Centre (CERD) has argued that the ad (from Nestle) is unethical from a medical standpoint. Maggi, they say, uses monosodium glutamate which, research has shown, can result in brain damage and obesity.[1]

Vance Packard, the celebrated author of *The Hidden Persuaders*, has attempted in his book to

> explore a strange and rather exotic new era of modern life. It is about the way many of us are being influenced and manipulated—far more than we realise—in the patterns of our everyday lives . . . . Large-scale efforts are being made, often with impressive success, to channel our unthinking habits, our purchasing decisions and our thought processes by the use of insights gleaned

from psychiatry and the social sciences . . . . The use of mass psychoanalysis to guide campaigns of persuasion has become the basis of a multi-million dollar industry.[2]

Packard describes a number of psychoanalytical techniques used by the advertising world to probe and manipulate consumers' minds. Among these is what he terms the 'life-style approach to selling or psychographics', developed by psychologists to investigate the lifestyle variable of consumers. Describing this technique, the British advertising trade journal, *Campaign* quoted:

Psychographics tries to classify consumers and segment markets in terms of psychological dimensions. Instead of looking at demographic attributes like age, sex and social class, it looks at the motivations, needs and attitudes of consumers.

Psychographics are often developed on a product-specific basis—for example, to explain the different consumer attitudes to buying toothpaste. The best known exception to this rule is Young and Rubicam's 4 Cs (Cross Cultural Consumer Characterisation), which attempts to provide a universal system for understanding people's values and lifestyles. (It even aroused the interest of Margaret Thatcher at one point.)

The first is that of conformity; all teenagers, they argue, fit into one of three categories—those who follow the mainstream fashion and social trends (conformists), those who opt for cult or minority trends (anti-conformists), and those who shun all such trends (independents).

A second dimension is that of control—one group believing they control their own destiny (internals), the remainder believing events are controlled by external forces (externals).[3]

This is but one technique used by advertising to understand and exploit the human psyche. Newer techniques are constantly being developed to study human frailties and these evoke some impassioned, angry feelings and even distrust.

Advertising has also been criticised for being a vehicle of social propaganda. Eric Barnouw says of television advertisements:

Often produced and exhibited at staggering cost, the network commercial is likely to promote not only a product but a way of life, a view of the world, a philosophy. Commercials are the main instrument of corporate image-glossing . . . . Often under the guise of merchandising, commercials are deeply involved in ideological conflict.[4]

But not everyone concurs with Barnouw. Advertising has many votaries who consider it an ideal media for modern-day communication. They respect and admire the high professionalism of the advertising industry: advertisers, they say, are among the best and the brightest—a breed apart; they are the high priests of communication and their expertise in the technologies of the audio-visual medium is unparalleled.

Supporters of advertising feel that advertising alone cannot be blamed for trends such as the level and nature of consumption in society. To bolster this argument, they claim that advertisers do not have the knowledge or the tools to manipulate people. This, they argue, is evident from the fact that the advertising world does not succeed in selling everything it sets out to sell. Nor, they insist, can it *create need*. It merely offers information about available choices to help consumers satisfy their own perceived needs. In a nutshell, they believe that the consumer exercises a rational choice and advertisers are not powerful enough to intervene in that process.[5]

Mainstream writers as well as proponents of industry point out that advertising and consumerism are natural allies and go hand in hand. In this scheme of things, it is advertising's role to take consumers from an ill-informed wilderness into the real world of commodities. As it does this, it also provides the necessary impetus to keep the market buoyant, helping to maintain a high level of production and affluence.

For a nation like India, the question remains: what sort of role does TV advertising play in an economy where consumerism is now emerging as a major force and where economic inequalities imply wide disparities—both in terms of need and the purchasing power of the population?

In this book we discuss some major issues related to TV advertising and specific to India—the development model it chooses to adopt, the impact of aggressive consumerism on the majority of Indians who still have to taste the first fruits of progress, the need for more education, housing and better health care as well as the question of just how valid the concept of unlimited consumption is.

Some writers like Jerry Mander believe that consumption cannot be unlimited. People cannot go on buying nor can the earth's resources support such high levels of production. Where consumerism has been a way of life, sooner or later markets must become saturated. Logically, therefore, as markets of the rich North 'burn up', large corporations and existing multinational giants are forced to move further afield to look for fresh pastures:

> With operations geared to nations that are just emerging as markets, the multinational corporations are taking television into places in Asia, Africa and South America where there are often no telephones or paved roads. Satellite television systems have been installed in many countries ahead of modern transportation or sanitation systems. TV provides pre-training for the commodity life that is coming up fast. People in villages where electricity has just arrived are watching ads filled with ecstatically happy people using artificial milk, Coca-Cola and electric shavers.[6]

Mander's distrust of television leads him to eventually recommend its elimination—a suggestion that many people find unpalatable and unrealistic. But the logic of his arguments cannot be dismissed altogether. The current situation in India matches Mander's/description of TV advertising's role as a harbinger of 'commodity life'. For us to avoid a discussion on the relevance of advertising would be an evasion of reality.

That we, in India, are perturbed by the fast-paced changes we observe in the economy, in the market-place and in the lives of people around us is evident. Almost without exception, individuals writing on the media, appearing on television and participating in discussions find themselves embroiled in discussions on the subject of television, advertising and consumerism. Their views represent, essentially, two approaches: first, that India will benefit greatly by trying to 'catch up' with the Western model of development and that the media is the best barometer of the transformation taking place in our society; second, that India is heading for disaster by allowing this kind of consumerism to shroud and obscure developmental priorities. Commentators in the latter category feel that attention is being diverted from very real problems which in turn are being trivialised.

A colleague who edits an advertising industry journal argued in favour of advertising saying that it has a vital role to play in India. From a marketing perspective, he said, mass media advertising is the only viable and economic way of providing marketing information to India's enormous population, spread as it is over a vast geographical terrain. Television, he explained, is the most cost-effective medium and the high price that industry pays for putting ads on TV evens out in terms of the number of consumers each ad manages to reach.

We found this proposition somewhat confusing. Firstly, only a handful of big companies—dominated by multinational firms like Hindustan Lever, Colgate–Palmolive, Nestle and Proctor and Gamble—advertise on TV. The medium is beyond the reach of most producers because of the astronomically high commercial rates charged by TV networks.

Secondly, some large companies including multinational firms such as those selling new brands of cigarettes (the advertising for which is prohibited on Indian TV) or even VCRs, have made a successful breakthrough into the market, without ever having used TV to sell their products! This seems to suggest that success does not rest exclusively on the use of television for mass advertising.

Thirdly, while the argument that consumers need information is a familiar one, the fact remains that little advertising is purely 'informative'. Advertisements that provide pure information are usually placed in the classified sections of Indian newspapers. TV commercials, on the other hand, do not always highlight product benefits and seldom reveal prices. They do however sell us (and our children) a handful of dreams invested in material products and communicate the ultimate consumer code: buy, consume, own.

Television commercials are thus created with the aim to impart information but instead use persuasive techniques that have very little to do with either the product or with the consumer's need for it. Many ads make the viewer believe that the products they peddle could magically release them from day-to-day problems and anxieties. The Colgate gel advertisement on TV draws a futuristic 'zing' around its user, a college-going youngster who is 'electrified' into popularity thanks to the spiky toothpaste used in the morning.

If we look critically at the business of advertising, it would seem to involve spending huge sums of money to orient consumers towards a growing dependence on material goods. The investment is not in the production or quality improvement of products but in their sales. This raises the question: where does this money come from, where does it go, and who picks up the tab?

Douglas Kellner, commenting on the U.S. advertising industry in *Questioning the Media*, says:

> In 1986 more than $102 billion, or roughly 2% of the U.S. gross national product was spent on advertising. When one considers that an equal amount of money is also spent on design, packaging, marketing and product display, one see's just what is squandered on advertising and marketing. Only eight cents of the cosmetic sales dollar goes to pay for ingredients, the rest goes to packaging, promotion and marketing. Advertising commands tremendous resources and talent and is a crucial component of the capitalist economic system.[7]

Kellner's reading of the whole business of advertising and marketing products indicates, rather disturbingly and ironically, that it is the consumer who ends up paying for being persuaded. After all, if only eight cents of the cosmetic dollar goes on the product itself, the consumer is handing out an additional 92 cents per dollar merely to receive information and market accessibility to attractively packaged goods! The most common counter-argument to this is, of course, that the ultimate price of the commodity reflects the value that consumers attach to it.

Following the logic of these arguments, the consumer might well arrive at the central question raised by them: is advertising beneficial to society or is it unfair and exploitative? This dilemma has never been satisfactorily resolved and perhaps never will be, since there seem to be irreconcilable differences between the supporters and detractors of advertising as well as between different interest groups.

As consumers and social players, it is imperative for us to debate the manner in which we in India are being, willy-nilly goaded into lifestyles determined by market forces. It might be worth our while to re-examine the relevance of this path of 'progress'. (Of course, it follows that in questioning the relevance of advertising we would be, in effect, questioning the very economic model that creates, supports and furthers the goals of advertising.)

Such a debate may ultimately conclude that advertising is an essential and harmless economic activity which society stands to gain from; that advertising and the forces it represents will steer us down the desired path of development. Conversely, the debate could conclude that we are being gradually programmed into accepting an ideology of consumption that will stereotype us as consumers and deflect us from more pressing economic and social concerns.

What follows is a brief description of the arguments commonly used in the worldwide debate on advertising. These could form the basis of a debate on the subject in this country. We feel that these views should be considered bearing in mind that the Indian child is learning how to respond to the outside world as much from television and TV advertising, as from other influences.

CRITICISMS

- Advertising is wasteful. Expenditure on it raises the price of commodities—a price that is ultimately paid by the consumer.
- Advertising permits a few large companies monopoly status. Smaller concerns cannot afford to advertise. Thus, it not only reduces competitiveness but also helps create a situation where power is concentrated in a handful of companies.
- It therefore restricts rather than expands choices and is to that extent undemocratic. It allows a few large companies to control demand, supply and prices.
- Advertising creates false needs, encourages an ethos of conspicuous consumption and manipulates the human psyche to make the consumer buy products. Products that are really needed require no advertising and therefore advertising promotes products that are not needed.

- Advertising encourages people to overvalue the material world. It sells the belief that happiness lies in possessing and consuming material goods.
- It thus distorts values, increases individualism and conversely, decreases social commitment.
- Advertising eventually generates dissatisfaction, frustration and unhappiness because the products/services it promotes cannot create or substitute happiness. Since advertising has to constantly push new products, it eventually sells the notion that consumption is unlimited and that in order to 'stay happy' the consumer must keep buying, replacing one product or brand with a newer, stronger, better one to attain even greater satisfaction.
- Advertising advocates the idea that consumption rather than production is the purpose of life.
- It provides little product information and can even be misleading.

DEFENCES

- Advertising is just one aspect of a market economy. It provides information about products/services thereby promoting economic growth by educating the public about goods available in the marketplace.
- Through the mass media, it performs the vital function of sharing this knowledge about commodities and developments in the marketplace with a larger section of the public than might otherwise have had access to such information.
- It provides economies of scale by helping to increase overall sales through this widespread dissemination of information.
- Advertising presumes that the consumer is a 'rational' being who cannot be manipulated into buying whatever advertising sells him or her.
- Advertising, therefore, only helps the consumer make market choices.
- Advertising is not powerful enough to create need where none exists. It might increase consumption but does not

create the basis for it. Consumers will buy available products according to their personal and individual perceptions of what they want or need. Advertising does not force them to buy unwanted goods but merely encourages shifts in brand loyalties.

■ Advertising uses persuasion much in the same manner and with the same sort of licence associated with the arts and literature. It seeks to present a vision, partly derived from existing human fantasies, to influence and change perceptions by breaking down, for instance, the ethic that saving is good and spending futile. By assigning itself this creative spirit, it is not required to tell the whole truth.

■ There is nothing special or unique about advertising. It is just one of many social forces at work in modern society.[8]

It would appear from these arguments that, essentially, advertising is charged with the following missions:

■ It has to get you to buy.
■ It has to provide a justification for spending on commodities which you may not need.
■ It has to, therefore, break down social resistance to new products and to consumption patterns, thereby changing the social ethic—from the need to work hard, save and live frugally to the need to work hard, spend and forget about the future!

Advertising achieves this by promoting the belief that gratifying individual, material desires is morally acceptable. In India, where 40 per cent of the population lives below the poverty line and where, for decades, we have been taught to believe in the essential rightness of a frugal, unostentatious way of life, it is clear that in order for the new consumer culture to succeed, advertising must replace the old value system with a new one. We can see that it has already succeeded in this endeavour, insofar as frugality is increasingly giving way to uncontrolled spending and lavish life-styles.[9]

It is, of course, not advertising but the advertiser—that is, the manufacturer of goods and services—who dictates this consumer ethic and stands to benefit from its success. It would be futile to attack advertising agencies for any misgivings consumers may have about the nature and content of TV advertising because these agencies are merely doing the best job they can to promote their clients' interests.

The most effective means of communication available to both manufacturers and advertising agencies is the television—which has consequently become the pulpit from which they preach their new religion. As Eric Barnouw says:

> To manufacture a product without at the same time manufacturing a demand has become unthinkable. Today, the manufacture of demand means, for most large companies, television—its commercials as well as other programme elements. The growing scale of mass production has inevitably made advertising more crucial, but this understates the situation. As society becomes more product-glutted, the pressure on the consumer to consume—to live up to higher and higher norms of consumption has become unrelenting.[10]

Barnouw and others suggest that in fact, advertising infiltrates a whole system of consciousness, guiding individuals towards a 'culture' created to sustain the high levels of consumption that it argues are imperative. This is seen as a 'mass culture' which, because it is supported by a unified message conveyed to millions of viewers simultaneously, becomes embedded in the national psyche.

Critics of this 'mass-produced contemporary culture' say that advertising is aimed at creating substitutes for feelings, for love, for curiosity of the mind. It seeks to manipulate anxieties about ourselves and, by appealing to a fraction of our intelligence, ends up shortchanging us. Fred Inglis in *The Imagery of Power: A Critique of Advertising* asserts that consumption based on the arbitrary characteristics assigned to material objects (by which these products acquire meanings other than those related to their utility) is socially harmful. Put in simpler terms, the promise held out by advertising of personal enhancement through the utilisation, say, of a particular brand of toothpaste, creates what he considers the wrong reasons for product consumption.[11]

Referring to the 'magic' that advertising creates in the market-place, whereby material products assume such importance, Leiss, Kline and Jhally acknowledge that:

> Consumers are also manipulated by an advertisement's promise that the product will do something special for them, something magical that will transform their lives. Commercials promise all kinds of things: goods can make us stunningly attractive in an instant, give us power over other people's affections; cure us of all illness, capture and package nature for our use, lift our emotions, act as a passport into a fantastic future.[12]

Bob Dylan, the (famous singer and lyricist), sees it like this:

> Advertising signs that con you
> Into thinking you're the one
> That can do what's never been done,
> That can win what's never been won,
> Meantime life outside goes on
> All around you.
> (From *It's Alright Ma [I'm Only Bleeding]*)

Despite the many warnings and danger signals, the average consumer, blissfully unaware of the power that advertising is exerting upon his decisions or choices, may well turn around and ask: 'What's all the fuss about?'

After all, television and TV advertising are now a way of life. For millions of people, television represents a 'reality' which is an integral part of the modern world. Children, like everyone else—and perhaps more so than adults—must be socialised to handle this reality. Any attempt to direct, change or control the content of television might be considered tantamount to interference in normal processes, an infringement of the right of free access to the media. It is a move which could have dangerous repercussions. Any discussion on advertising and television and the need to regulate either, must take into account such arguments in order to avoid accusations of seeking to 'control' the media.

We have found that in India proponents of the media and of the technology that television represents are very uncomfortable with this kind of questioning. This is largely because they feel that in the relationship between a viewer and television (or TV advertising), the responsibility rests with the viewer who, they say, exercises the right to choose what to watch, when to watch, how to watch and what to internalise from the messages that come across the screen.

Is this reading of the relationship between a viewer and television accurate? Or does it stem from an acceptance of television as an inescapable reality—one that has its own logic and will develop irrespective of how people may see it? A report, published recently in *The Times of India* (2 March 1994) about villagers in Bihar watching the televised broadcast of the Finance Minister's speech on Budget Day, is a case in point. According to the report, since the broadcast was in English and the general awareness level of the audience about the significance of the budget was limited, the programme was more or less irrelevant to them. As viewers they, (and this applies to all those who do not understand English), had no choice or role to play in determining how such information (of importance to them) is being or should be conveyed. Under such circumstances, television appears undemocratic and far from fulfills its social commitment to the mass of the TV audience. One might well ask, television by whom and for whom?

We think this is an issue for serious introspection and debate—especially in the context of children. Viewers undoubtedly have the right to choose between different kinds of TV programming, and may accept some and reject others. However, they do not belong to any decision-making framework and cannot therefore intervene in what appears on TV or in its presentation. They have to take the content and perspective of TV fare as a given. Is the viewer's opinion really reflected in what appears on TV or is it so much a one-way traffic in ideas that the only choice before the viewer is to 'take it or leave it'?

Can children who do not have easy access to other forms of learning and information, children who have little real-life experience of what they see on television, children whose dreams have been magnified by the mystique of advertising until they extend way beyond their means of fulfilling them, critically judge what they see on television?

Is it possible that children could acquire false notions about the world and even about their own society from images created to spread the cult of consumerism? Conversely, is it right to question the content and context of TV advertising when so much else on television, including the Hindi films, present equally harmful if not retrograde ideas. Is the technology of television value-free or is it bound by the rules imposed upon it by those who control its purse-strings?

We believe that answers to such questions are imperative and will contribute to our understanding of the role of television and TV advertising and indeed, to our relationship with both.

8

ADVERTISING AND TELEVISION

While we, in India, are swiftly on our way to becoming a nation wired to TV sets, people in the advertising world are losing their sleep navigating the many channels that will give them access to the TV viewer. Welcome to the new battlefield in advertising: television. It is here that marketers have declared war for supremacy over the consumer's mind.

Television and advertising together present a lethal combination. TV offers the advertiser the most effective way of reaching the consumer's mind. Advertising, on the other hand, exerts an influence on TV which is no less significant—it plays a vital role in shaping the priorities and the quality of television programming.

Advertising has affected the fortunes of the media the world over. It has especially courted television and, in most countries, become the major source of revenue of television networks. Today, television *without* advertising appears an unrealistic proposition. But there are few exceptions to this rule: BBC is still one of them; Doordarshan once was.

This commercialisation of the media, notes Jerry Mander, comes eventually to be dominated by just a handful of advertisers. In the case of the U.S.:

> Since virtually all media in this country depend upon advertising for survival, it ought to be obvious that these one hundred corporations, themselves dominated by a handful of wealthy people, can largely determine which magazines, newspapers, radio stations and television stations can continue to exist and which cannot.[13]

It is not hard for a regular TV watcher in India to identify the major competitors for Doordarshan's commercial time. The list would include companies producing brands such as Ariel, Pepsi,

Rin, Nirma, Nescafe, Titan, Colgate and a handful of others. In most product categories, only two or three brands can and do advertise on the national network, with the rest confined to their regional strongholds. According to *The Best of Brand Equity* in 1992, out of 34 hair oils, only three made it to the national network; of 37 brands of edible oils only four advertised on the national network; and in the washing powder segment, five out of 34 made it to the big time. The really successful brands included Nirma detergent, Rasna and Colgate tooth paste. TV advertising came to be dominated by the war between detergent ads. As Rin, Nirma, Surf, Wheel (later joined by Ariel) competed furiously, detergents emerged as the highest ad spending category on television.

Television companies clearly stand to gain from advertising given the huge revenues they earn off it. Sadly, however, the history of broadcasting suggests that advertising support to TV, while benefiting the advertising industry, does not necessarily encourage an improvement in the content or quality of programming.

David Halberstam, describing the growth of commercial TV in America, says:

> . . . by 1954 there were 32 million TV sets throughout the country, CBS television's gross billings doubled in that single year, and CBS became the single biggest advertising medium in the world. The real money, money and revenues beyond anyone's wildest dreams, was in television and above all in entertainment.

The result was that afternoon papers and magazines that had a mass circulation were suddenly in serious trouble. Starved of ad revenue, many were doomed to die. Television profits were, according to Halberstam, staggering:

> More, the profits seemed to escalate every year, gradually corrupting and changing the nature of broadcasting. Greater profits did not mean, as some altruists had hoped, greater experimentation, more money invested in higher quality programming. On the contrary, profits brought merely the expectation of more profits, and policies designed to create them. The impulse to take risks in quality programming, to serve national

interest in public affairs, became weaker all the time . . . . Now broadcasting was obsessed with the ratings, and the ratings had a morality of their own, they dictated their own reality and their own truth . . . . What was rated high was good, and what was rated low was bad . . . the ratings system seemed to destroy all that was in its way. The lowest common denominator of taste prevailed . . . . It was no longer a matter of the right audience, it was a matter of total audience.[14]

Likewise, for commercial TV and TV producers, the new code became (as it has in India): create programmes for television guaranteed to win support from big-spending advertisers.

Some people may object to the use of the phrase 'lowest common denominator' as being unfairly elitist. But the argument relates to why, when TV begins to earn such enormous revenue, does this not lead to better, more relevant and useful or experimental programming? Also, is the attempt really to justify the kind of programming that gets precedence on television (sex, violence and even horror) by claiming that it conforms to the taste of this 'lowest common denominator'? Does this sort of programming have anything to do with the sponsor's view of what will sell? Do they have a role to play in deciding the nature of the programming they will financially support? Commenting on Doordarshan's attempts to win back the audience it has been losing to satellite TV and on the network's commercialisation, a former secretary of the Information and Broadcasting Ministry, S.S. Gill, wrote in *The Times of India* (7 March 1994): 'It is a sad commentary on our times that instead of establishing benchmarks of good taste and excellence, Doordarshan is aping those who should be emulating its high standards.' He argues that good films like *Padosi, Devdas* and others did exceedingly well at the box office while retaining high aesthetic standards. 'Then we corrupted the people's taste by exposing them to excessive violence, crime and sex. And now we argue that that is what the viewers want.'

According to some researchers and media experts, the communication of 'serious thought' or the replacement of mediocre programming by quality programming is prevented by several factors. David Littlejohn feels that TV has 'an in-built obsession with the largest possible audience' who 'expect skillfully packaged entertainment on network prime time. And those who provide them with these entertainments expect them, in return, to keep watching, and can risk little or no diminution in the number of prospective customers for their sponsors' products.'[15]

Recent developments on Doordarshan in India seem to reflect a similar trend. Rather than pay to have quality serials and programmes produced, or to promote sponsorship for 'good' ones, Doordarshan has been taking the easy way out and using more and more film-based footage with less and less discrimination. What might have been considered lewd and offensive and to be kept off the small screen until a few years ago, is now part of regular TV fare.

Commercialisation paves the way for longer hours of broadcasting. Advertising costs sky rocket and commercials, expensive to make, strive to be technologically superior to regular TV programming. There is a reason for this: in order to stand out from all other forms of programming, television advertising must be qualitatively different so as to catch viewer attention and to make a lasting impact. This is the axe that hangs over advertisers' heads. With so much else available on television, an advertisement has to successfully squeeze its way through the jumble of audio-visual fare. If it failed to do so, advertising would negate the very reason for its existence and have little justification for the vast amounts of money that it pours into television in order to claim a small percentage of transmission time. Advertisers would then have to withdraw support to television and the very survival of television would be at stake.

In the case of a network like Doordarshan where, as we shall see, advertising is cluttered and unrelated ads have to compete for viewer attention in high density clusters, advertisers have to work even harder to ensure that their advertisement stands out in a crowd.

This brings us to the fact that the huge corporations which sponsor and provide the financial backing for programmes by lending advertising support to them (in 1992–93 these included the weekly Hindi film, *Chitrahaar, The World This Week*, etc.) are clearly not concerned with an appropriate definition of entertainment or with the commitment to use television to spread information. They see programming merely as a bait to attract viewer attention for a few seconds during which they implant their message in people's minds. A TV network's lofty aims of educating,

ILLUSTRATION 8.1
Children: Hooked Up and Easy Prey

informing and generating social awareness are easily pushed aside as aggressive players in the selling game take over. We have, in recent years, seen the Doordarshan charter make way for an overkill of the ultimate entertainment carrot—the Hindi film—the easiest and most painless method by which to deliver the audience to the advertiser.

The Joshi Working Group on Software for Doordarshan noted in 1984 that

> the most attractive programmes for the sponsor, because of their high audience-rating, are those of sheer entertainment, film-based or otherwise, and sports. There is no harm in this so long as the entertainment is not vulgar or lewd or likely to degrade public taste. But harm will certainly be done if Doordarshan is tempted to increase the time devoted to entertainment . . . at the expense of . . . assisting in the process of social and economic development in the country.[16]

Since then, as we have pointed out, these fears have indeed been realised.

Douglas Kellner takes the argument a step further:

> One of the gigantic swindles perpetrated on the public today, is that commercial television is free, that advertising pays for network television. In fact, consumers pay for the programming through higher prices for the goods they purchase. Many television series like *Dallas, Dynasty* and other prime time soaps, are themselves advertisements for wealth, luxury, fashion and a high-consumption life-style.[17]

Today in India, not only are the programmes that Kellner refers to being avidly watched by those who receive satellite TV in their homes, but indigenous programming too seems to be dominated by similar fare. Even if we accept that the advertiser functions within the limited framework of acting as a conduit between the individual consumer and the marketplace—and believes that this role enables people to exercise their right to information so as to widen their area of 'choice'—many questions that relate to Indian conditions remain unanswered.

Subrata Banerjee writing in 1989 on the relevance of advertising in developing nations, raises some of them:

The social relevance of advertising in some developing countries is confined to a very narrow elite, comprising the political leadership, the civil and military bureaucracy, top corporate managers, professionals and rich farmers. It is they who use advertised products. In India such an elite would number about 10 crores, while there are 20 crore destitutes and crores living below the poverty line. They are outside the market for advertised goods. Thus advertising has no social relevance for the majority of the Indian people . . . . In such conditions advertising does not play an integrating role except in relation to 10 per cent of the population. The democratic choice that it offers cannot be realised by the vast majority of the population. It cannot create conditions to earn rewards to create social mobility as jobs are not available.[18]

India's market is more complex than we might wish to believe. In an article published in *Brand Equity*, Raghu Roy of Operations Research Group refers to the PACRIM study on 'India—Asia's Next Consumer Challenge'. 'Going beyond the "haves" and the "have-nots", PACRIM approaches the entire complex structure in continuum and attempts to create segments of super-haves, have-somes, near-haves and have-nots where the have-somes are defined as Asia's genuine middle class in terms of values, aspirations and lifestyles.' The results of the PACRIM analysis, he says, are as follows:

▪ The country's present urban-based have-somes number around four million households, perhaps 25 million individuals.

▪ India's traditional urban elite and band of super-haves number less than 400,000 households, under two million individuals.

'Outside of perhaps toilet soaps, fabric wash and a few personal care products, it is the above set of 4.4 million households where the battle for consumer products and conspicuous consumption would take place.'[19]

In other words, the trend in the marketplace is for advertisers, bringing in a whole new range of products, to woo this relatively tiny segment. Advertisers seem aware that once this segment has been saturated and sales drop, acceptance of these products will come up against a series of barriers—attitudinal, cultural and cost.

In this context, television advertising comes to represent future investment, a process aimed at changing attitudes and altering mass perceptions.

The British scholar, Stuart Hall, has argued that this notion of 'the freedom of choice' (commonly put forward by American mass media research) as supposedly being made available to mass audiences through the media, has little democratic value. The concept of such freedom is, he feels, ideologically positioned to support capitalist requirements. Consequently the so-called choices offered by the media are truncated and constrained.[20]

Indeed, one might ask, is the choice between drinking Pepsi and Campa Cola really fundamental and is that the freedom to which we must aspire? Likewise, is TV advertising democratic when it presents a set of options to all Indians although only a small segment can afford them? What about alternative options which never get advertised?

Children, we feel, are learning to accept the ideals imposed on them by television and advertising and are not equipped to protect themselves from these influences. They unconsciously learn advertising codes and are not trained to evaluate the real worth of products against what might otherwise have been considered the priorities in their lives.

One example of this can be had from the nutritional learning acquired through TV ads by children—an issue that has vexed parents and researchers concerned with what children learn from TV advertising. Charles K. Atkin reports that

> Not only does food advertising influence food preferences, but it also can shape the basic nutritional beliefs and attitudes of the child . . . . Since nutritional aspects of foods are not emphasised, youngsters may make food choices, based on non-nutritional criteria and/or nutrition may not even be a salient dimension for evaluating products.[21]

In India, a large number of TV viewers are becoming visually literate although being illiterate they cannot have access to vast amounts of important information that could be vital to their personal and social development. Advertising, in our view, cannot really provide them with 'choices' when they are excluded from other sources of information which might have put them in a better position to judge advertising messages.

It becomes important to examine what advertising says to those who have internalised the dreams and desires conveyed through advertising, but may never be in an economic position to realise them. In the next section we will examine the responses of the children interviewed by us to TV advertising, its messages and its magic.

9

TV COMMERCIALS
AND CHILDREN

Children are fascinated by TV commercials, and as our fieldwork in Delhi confirmed, so are most adults. Few of us fail to react to these glamourous, fast-paced visuals on TV with their heady, exciting music and their determined sales pitch. Before we present the results of our research on the way children react to TV commercials, a word about the advertising scene in the capital city of India.

According to reports, more and more of the action in the world of advertising is taking place in Delhi. This suggests that whereas Bombay may be, as the ad world calls it, 'the Madison Avenue of India', the advertising business in Delhi is now growing at a rate faster than in Bombay, giving it the reputation of being the fastest growing ad centre in the country. Delhi-based multinationals such as Pepsi, Nestle and HMM spent a total of Rs. 30 crore on advertising in 1992, while the Delhi chapters of agencies like Hindustan Thomson, Contract, Mudra and Lintas have been recording stupendous growth rates. Smaller agencies are also making their mark rapidly. The increase in advertising is in part related to the fact that the industrial belt around the city is growing into a major industrial region and that government spending on advertising is huge. With the changing economic environment, producers in a hurry to make a mark are looking to become visible. Not surprisingly, large corporations have moved to the capital (Reckitt & Coleman) and others plan to follow suit. This means that there will be a lot more advertising to be seen, absorbed and taken into account on a daily basis. One advertiser in Bombay assessed that the average viewer might get to see around 5,000 commercials on TV every year, but that was before the multi-channel options came our way. The figure could actually be several times higher as it does not include the advertising that appears on film videos.

In our study we went from a preliminary assessment of the child's relationship with the TV set to a more detailed analysis of children's responses to TV advertising. While interacting with children from different parts of Delhi, we observed that TV advertising has indeed seeped into the daily life of children—young and old. It colours their conversations and even the games they play. We watched 14-year olds from an English medium school play *Antakshari*, a popular Indian game. Two teams alternately sing verses from songs, nearly always from Hindi films, starting with the last letter of the previous verse. These days the game is played using ad jingles and product slogans.

Several school-teachers talked of the popularity of TV commercials. The impact, they felt was greatest on childrens' language. They said that children now speak to one another in a 'lingo' dotted with words, phrases, and expressions from TV ads. According to them the common favourites included the slogan for Pepsi, the Amul chocolate line 'I think you're just right for Amul chocolate', Eveready's 'Give me Red', and 'Go G.I. Joe'. Almost every ad that appeared on TV seemed to have something to contribute to their vocabulary. Jingles like the Nirma washing powder and the Vicks' *'Khitch-khitch door karo'* and Maggi ketchup's, 'It's different!' are it seemed, not only embedded in the psyche of children but part of their modern-day vocabulary.

Although we could have safely presumed that a majority of children 'like' TV commercials very much, we asked them nonetheless. *Do you like TV advertisements? Do you appreciate them better than programmes?*

Responding to these questions, 75 per cent of our respondents said they *loved* watching ads on TV (see Figure 6.3). When asked whether they liked them *better* than programmes, their reactions were less favourable. Those answering a clear 'yes' were as follows: 5 to 8 years: 63.90 per cent; 8 to 12 years: 43.54 per cent; and 13 to 15 years: 36.60 per cent.

There is, as we can see, a sharp drop in the number of children who actually prefer ads to other forms of programming as you move from the youngest age group to the oldest age group. Is there, then, a process of 'growing out' of advertising? Do children, as they become more skilled, better informed and more

FIGURE 9.1

Response to the Question 'Do You Like TV Ads' by Age, Sex and Class

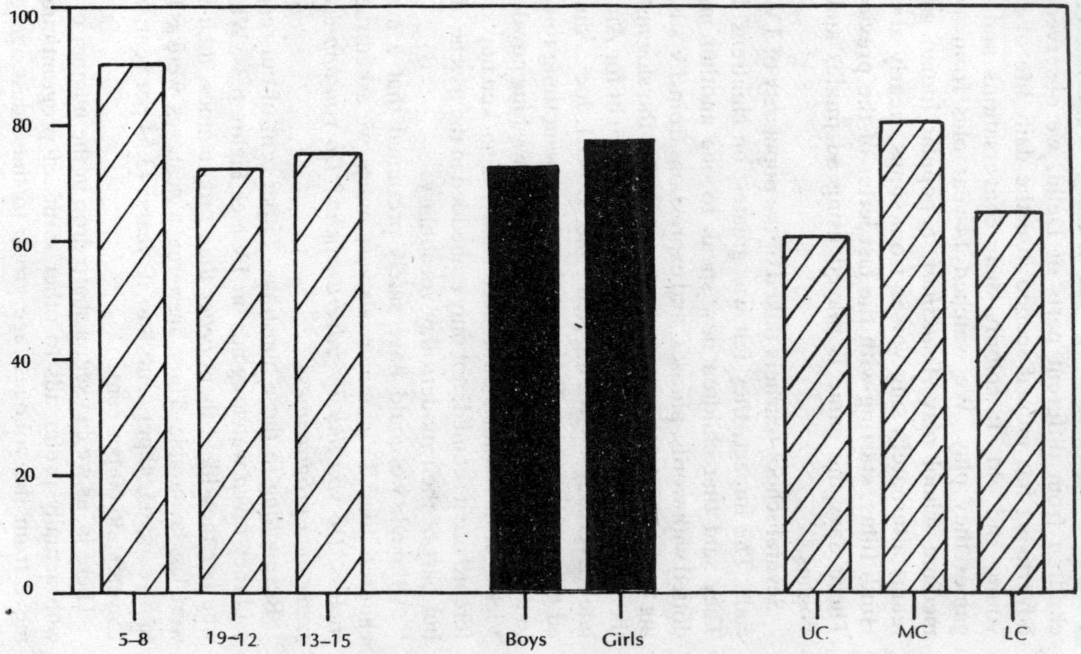
100
80
60
40
20
0
5–8
19–12
13–15
Boys
Girls
UC
MC
LC

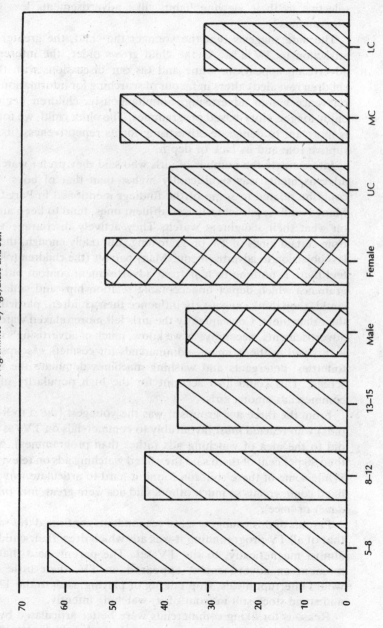

FIGURE 9.2

Response to the Proposition 'Ads are Better than Programmes' by Age, Class and Sex

(Bar chart; x-axis categories left to right: 5-8, 8-12, 13-15, Male, Female, UC, MC, LC; y-axis scale: 0, 10, 20, 30, 40, 50, 60, 70)

selective in their viewing habits, like advertisements less than programmes?

The data suggests that the younger the child, the greater the attraction to TV ads. As the child grows older, the interest in advertising appears to wane and (as our discussions with these children revealed) alters in favour of searching for information and relevance within advertising. Simultaneously, children begin to enjoy longer, story-based programmes. The older child, we found, is more apt to denigrate advertising for its repetitiveness, its disruptive role and its lack of depth.

Interestingly the number of girls who said they prefer watching advertisements was significantly higher than that of boys. This could be related to some of the findings mentioned in Part One. Many families, particularly less affluent ones, tend to keep an eye on what their daughters watch. They actively discourage them from certain kinds of TV programming. But oddly enough, there is less objection to advertisements. Many parents (the children told us) feel there is nothing to fear from advertisement content but programmes which depict unacceptable relationships and situations could, they think, negatively influence their children, particularly their daughters. Consequently the girls felt more relaxed watching advertisements. Secondly, as we know, much of advertising's focus is directed at the woman—commercials for cosmetics, soaps and toiletries, detergents and washing machines dominate the small screen. This could also account for the high popularity of TV commercials among girls.

From the three age groups it was the youngest (the 5 to 8-year olds) who reacted *most* favourably to commercials on TV (as they did to the idea of watching ads rather than programmes). More than 90 per cent of them said they liked watching ads on television. While some of these children found it hard to articulate *why* they liked commercials so much others said ads were great 'fun' (*mazedaar*) or 'nice'.

Parents of this youngest set of respondents confirmed this saying that of all TV programming it was ads which drew their children, almost magnetically, to the TV set. The parents said that the moment an advertisement appeared on TV, their little ones would interrupt meals, stop talking or playing, rush to the TV set and stand stock-still in front of it, watching intently.

Reasons for liking commercials were better articulated by respondents in the 8-plus age group. 'I think ads are thrilling,' said one child while another proclaimed, 'Ads are full of excitement.' Often, children attempted to justify their attraction to commercials: ads were informative, showed them how to live the good life and were important because they helped them decide what to buy. Some of the children told us that they liked watching ads more than programmes because they were more entertaining and 'better' than programmes (which bears testimony to the huge investment advertisers make to create spots that are technically superb). But there were also many children who responded with a 'I like ads because I like them', offering no further explanation to this simple, but definite statement. Those who thought programmes were better, argued that these were more informative and enjoyable; followed a story-line and were longer.

Talking about TV commercials, many older children (13 to 15-year olds), acted as though they were 'nothing-to-write-home-about': advertising exists and you can't get away from it. These children came across as 'old hands at the game of "buy and sell."' Greater discrimination and stronger likes and dislikes were reflected in their reactions to different kinds of advertising, indicating that children's appreciation of, and attitude to, TV advertising *do* change as they grow up.

Responses to the two questions—'Do you like watching ads on TV?' and 'Do you like them better than programmes?'—were compared. We found that while 75 per cent of the combined sample said they liked ads, only 42.05 per cent said they were better than programmes. The response in the youngest and most enthusiastic age group, the 5 to 8-year olds, also dropped sharply from 90 per cent to 60 per cent. This fall is significant but does not undermine the fact that over 40 per cent of all children consider commercials the best entertainment available to them on television.

That so many children are enamoured of TV ads will come as no surprise to the reader, but the number who said that they *do not* like ads, might. Significantly, 25 per cent of the children told us they did *not* enjoy TV ads—most of them from the older age groups, confirming that as children become more discerning, they look for a different kind of entertainment from television. Many of the children who shared this view displayed some degree of contemptuousness and complained that TV ads were 'boring', 'repetitive', 'irritating', 'interfered with programmes' or that they 'did not tell a story'. Only a few resisted elaborating and said they simply 'did not like them'.

But age or 'growing up' is not the only factor that prompted this response from the children. The second major reason was the grave resentment that TV advertisements appear to be causing, especially amongst children who feel they cannot satisfy and fulfil the desires that commercials inspire in them.

As they got deeper into a discussion on the subject of advertising, some children expressed anger and frustration saying they would rather not watch TV advertisements than feel they could not have the products it made them want to acquire. Others took the position that they did not 'need' the goods promoted by advertising. 'Need' became a matter of debate with several groups of children we met. Eventually we realised that the 'need' argument by and large mirrored the children's resentment at being tempted by so many goods that their parents could not or would not, buy for them. One child said that the ads made them yearn for a better life and, it seemed, the sadness and sense of deprivation that followed got translated into a negative attitude towards the business of advertising. 'No one likes to say that their family is too poor to buy this thing or that,' said a child. Other children, reluctant to admit their low purchasing power also used the 'need argument' as an escape route. But 'want' was another issue.

While one boy said he thought ads should not be watched because everything in them was 'imaginary', a girl told us how in her school, keeping abreast of TV advertising was imperative as discussions on advertising were routine. However, there were some children in her school from less affluent families who, she said, refused to be drawn into these 'chats'. At birthday parties, she remarked, one of the games played was to get children to guess at advertisements from clippings taken from the print media.

These discussions highlighted the important and worrying fact that many children were beginning to see themselves as 'deprived'. At the same time, the consumer instinct that was awakening in them and their peers, together with the fear of social ostracism and isolation, prevented them from being able to reject 'the high consumption model' promoted by advertising. Many conceded that not everyone could, or should, possess every new product advertised.

Some middle and upper class children also said they did not like ads. Many of them did not want to explain their reasons. A few said they thought ads were boring. However, their conversations revealed that parental discouragement of consumerism was a major reason for their attitude.

It is important to mention here that children's responses are often complex and cannot be taken at face value. For instance, when we collected questionnaires from a group of students, we noticed that a few of them had stated that they did not like watching TV ads. However, minutes later, the same children were leading a spirited defence of TV advertising during the group discussions. It became plain that not only were they keen watchers of TV ads, they were also better at analysing and recalling them than many others.

We found that children have a tendency to conform to what they think is required of them and therefore provide what might be a 'suitable' answer. Although we repeatedly told them that there were no right or wrong answers and what we wanted were their opinions, some children tried to draw us into conversations in order to ascertain how we felt. The group discussions left us in no doubt that whether or not they like advertising, children know they cannot get away from it.

Having established that children not only enjoy advertising but are being deliberately targeted by advertisers, the next obvious question is: What makes children so important to the industry?

THE CHILD AS CONSUMER

The foundations of a market economy rest firmly on a consumer ethic. From the history of the rich North, where consumerism has flourished we know that the advertising industry, in order to instil and sustain that ethic, gradually extended its focus to include children. It realised how beneficial it could be if they were groomed into becoming good, future consumers.

While writing on contemporary American culture in 1960, Jules Henry pointed out that advertising on TV was deliberately working on young children to prepare them for their future role as buyers in a replete marketplace. Since then, virtually every study which has critically examined the relationship between advertising and children has drawn attention to the effects of TV commercials on the minds of children. Henry wrote:

> The brand image created on TV and embedded in the minds of children assures good volume for these items . . . . In America, children must be trained to insatiable consumption of impulsive choice and infinite variety. These attributes, once instilled are converted into cash by advertising directed at children![22]

Unsympathetic to advertising in the United States, Henry described it as:

> an expression of an irrational economy that has depended for survival on a fantastically high standard of living incorporated into the American mind as a moral imperative. Yet the moral imperative cannot of itself give direction . . . this function is served . . . by advertising which day and night, with increasing pressure reminds us what there is to buy.

In marketing textbooks, 'positioning' is described in a rather passive way as a platform for a brand or a product. But true positioning is an active process of getting through to the ultimate target, the consumer. Positioning is not something you do to a product, it is what you do to the consumer's mind.

Of course, viewpoints differ and researchers also argue that 'just because children like and enjoy advertisements, there is no strong evidence to suggest that their attractiveness automatically translates into children wanting or buying things they wouldn't otherwise have wanted'. Fair enough; but this argument is obviously limited as it refers only to the link between seeing an advertisement for a product and going out to buy it. It does not deny or reject the impact that commercials may have in shaping a child's values, attitudes and aspirations.

A senior advertising executive in Bombay (who has led serious ad-related research), said that children had become an important audience segment for Indian advertisers and that television had been instrumental in targeting them. He pointed out that before television became a major social force, Indian children were less exposed to aggressive advertising and became aware and sensitive to its claims only as young adults. Today, children graduate into becoming consumers much earlier. They begin watching TV almost at birth and, since no skills are required to absorb ideas from television, they become part of the advertising audience fairly soon. The fallout of early exposure to TV commercials could be greater cynicism and higher expectations, especially by the time they reach their mid-teens and are part of an active consumer audience. 'These children will not be satisfied with the nature of information that ads provide. They will also look beyond executional gimmicks and as advertisers, our job of persuasion will get much harder,' the ad executive explained.

The indisputable fact is that TV has played a significant role in extending the frontiers of consumption. Jerry Mander, himself a former ad executive, says of television: 'I learnt that it is possible to speak through the media directly into people's heads and then, like some other-worldly magician, leave images inside that can cause people to do what they might otherwise never have thought to do.'[23]

What makes children such an attractive target for the advertising industry? Market research organisations in India have studied the 'dynamics of child behaviour as a consumer' and defined it both in terms of the child and the environment.

A preliminary study by Search India notes that the child is now receiving a huge amount of market-related information. According to the study:

Information is the key to availing wider choices and, perhaps more rational decision-making . . . given the spate of information flow, the child has opportunities to receive a wide range of information on products or brands, in some of which, as it appears in the advertisements, the child is seemingly playing a key role in decision-making.

Pathfinders—a subsidiary of Lintas: India, conducted a survey that covered over 4,000 children in 1988. (Pathfinders' clients, understandably included some of India's best known consumer goods manufacturers.) Presenting highlights of the survey (better known as P: Childsnap), *A & M* (an advertising trade journal) explained:

> Attention is being focussed on these little men and women for three basic reasons: one, most of them have more money at their disposal than ever before. Two—and this is more import-ant—they are seen as major influencing factors in family's brand choice in a number of product categories. And three, it's a question of catching them young and instilling brand loyalty.[24]

In order to instil loyalty, advertisers have to outdo one another in the game of establishing control over the consumer's mind. This brings us to the questions of ethics, the rights and the wrongs of tactics used by advertising agencies in seeking supremacy for their products.

A MATTER OF ETHICS

If we agree that children are particularly vulnerable to the influ-ences of advertising and to what they see in commercials, then the forms of manipulation in many advertisements might well have us worried.

Before commenting on some of these, we feel it is prudent to state that our repeated references to advertising, research and writing on this subject in the developed West is not without reason. Advertising in India is an off-shoot of international advertising and reflects the same values, attitudes and issues that have characterised advertising in the West. We are, of course, a couple of generations behind—a gap swiftly being covered. In the West, advertising certain product categories to children has raised serious concern. For instance, pitching advertising for various kinds of drugs at children. Many writers argue that the practice of appealing to children to buy pills (even if they are harmless, such as vitamins) is dangerous as it promotes a dependence on drugs per se and establishes in their minds that pills can do quicker what, for example, a balanced diet will do over time: so pop a pill.

At a workshop organised by the Media Advocacy Group in Delhi in 1993, an advertiser discussing new images of women appearing on TV (to justify the ad industry's use of certain personalities), showed us an ad made for TV but not yet on the airwaves. The ad for anti-depressants was targeted exclusively at women. It suggested that a large number of them suffer from depression during various phases of their lives. It reassured them with the promise of an over-the-counter remedy, soon to become available with every Indian chemist. The ad film featured a lonely and lost girl, isolated from everyone and everything.

The ad made us sit up and think. Watching it many girls might believe that they indeed suffer from a drug-solvable problem. Nowhere did the ad advise human comfort and understanding or even interaction as the first option. It also chose to ignore the fact that girls (and boys) often suffer from huge emotional swings during puberty. The question is: can such ads put ideas into the heads of people just to ensure sales of a new drug being introduced into the market? The fact that the ad has still to appear on television is reassuring.

Already several advertisements have evoked the ire of Indian consumer groups. These include the Maggi Noodles ad (mentioned earlier), the advertising for toothpastes containing flouride (which, with prolonged use, can lead to a crippling disease), the sale of gripe water as a 'tonic' to keep babies healthy (when gripe water is merely aniseed water, good perhaps for relieving colic and gas but in no way a health tonic), the Complan ad which consumer groups have argued exploits the anxiety of parents and the ad for Action shoes which has a man stopping a car with his foot indicating the power of his shoes. These ads have been attacked for their potential to mislead the public or (in the case of gripe water) for imparting misinformation (it has been pointed out that many illiterate parents might be greatly influenced by these ads to the detriment of their children's development). In the case of children, commercials which depict acts like hanging on a fridge door, stopping a car with a foot, traipsing off to a movie hall unaccompanied or a young girl taking charge of the kitchen and producing a meal unaided and unsupervised, could encourage children to imitate such behaviour.

In 'Conclusion and Recommendations' we deal with those TV advertisements which we feel contravene Doordarshan's Code for Commercials Advertising and some which for other reasons we suggest should be looked at critically.

10

UNDERSTANDING
ADVERTISEMENTS

'Ads are made well to attract us to them.'
'No yaar, ads are made so that kids do zid.'[25]

Children's understanding of TV advertisements begins with their ability to differentiate commercials from programmes. A majority of our respondents in the 8 to 15 years age group were able to make this distinction insofar as they identified commercials as *information capsules*. Confusion over the difference between a TV advertisement and a TV programme was expressed largely by either very young children or children with very limited exposure to the media and/or education.

Despite these observations, we found, while interacting with children from varying backgrounds in Delhi, that, by and large, telling commercials from programming was problematic for very many children. They viewed TV commercials in much the same way as they would a TV serial or film. This was particularly true for several children from poor homes, out-of-school children, and children with a limited exposure to the media. Many of them merely shrugged their shoulders when asked how advertising stands apart from the rest of TV fare.

In some cases there was a problem articulating and explaining the difference. With others whose experience of television was relatively limited (such as children of migrant workers), the problem seemed to be that their visual literacy skills were still developing and they were not very familiar with television as a medium. We also noticed that for children with little or no learning environment to interact with, the distinction was very blurred.

Almost without exception children believe that the purpose of television is to provide entertainment. The informative role that TV can play is secondary in their thinking and this colours their

reactions to all TV programming, be it advertising or other telecasts. Many who appeared puzzled by the question 'how do ads
differ from programmes?' told us that TV *picture dikhata hai*' (TV
puts on pictures/films) and claimed that the advertisements shown
by us to them were also just 'pictures'.

Studies on the cognitive development of children suggest that
while a younger child may 'like and believe' commercials because
they are short and exciting, from the age of 8 years onwards, a
child begins to recognise the actual intention of advertisements
which is to sell—a product, a lifestyle, an image—anything. However, not until children are well into their teens are they able to
analyse advertisements and develop a more realistic/adult approach
towards them. Research on cognitive factors affecting TV advertising's influence on children has suggested that 'such advertising was
deceptive . . . young children do not understand the persuasive
intent of commercials and are more likely to perceive them as
truthful messages.'[26] If children, as research on their behaviour
indicates, expect all TV presentations, including ads, to be essentially honest, then they are likely to absorb misinformation or
deceptive messages especially if they take 'hyperbole' and 'magic'
quite literally. Some people think that such a danger does exist.

> Parents in the United States (where TV is a purely commercial
> venture and TV advertising an important part of the child's
> exposure to the medium), tend to fear the teaching potential of
> commercials. Because advertisers have perfected their teaching
> techniques, this fear is justified. Children do attend to and learn
> from commercials. They remember slogans, jingles, and brand
> names. They often try to influence their parents to buy advertised
> goods. Children below the age of seven or so, are particularly
> vulnerable to such effects, probably because they do not discri-
> minate between the programme and the commercial and do not
> realise that the purpose of commercials is to sell goods. They
> simply accept commercials as presenting information like any
> other television format.[27]

Understanding commercials also implies recognition of the persuasive intent of commercials. This too develops gradually, starting
around the age of eight. However, the nature of persuasion and its
aims are not, we are told, always easy for a child to comprehend.

This persuasive agenda poses problems for child viewers, since they tend to process other persons' behaviours at face value, assuming that people tell the truth . . . . Therefore, it is difficult for young children to comprehend that an unseen agent is creating a commercial message with a purpose other than to entertain or inform them.[28]

Younger children are often unable to distinguish between make-believe and reality, which applies to and can interfere with their comprehension of ideas presented by television. The well-known U.S. paediatrician, Dr. Benjamin Spock, refers to this problem in his book *Baby and Child Care*. He focuses special attention on childrens' reactions to their all-time favourites—animated cartoons. He warns that these may promote violence among children because children understand from them that cartoon characters never get seriously hurt and always recover—even from the most violent assaults—rather miraculously. Children may interpret this to mean that even in real life, people who are injured do not really suffer and will be all right in a jiffy. By the same logic, children watching advertisements that use fantasy and magical transformations are apt to believe that a product will touch them with the same magic. The mother of a 7-year old girl told us how her daughter cried her heart out for a pair of Power sneakers which she wanted to buy and wear to school on sports day. The child insisted that the commercial promised greater running speed to anyone wearing the sneakers and said she was afraid that her peers would outrun her if they and not she, had the shoes.[29]

Before the group discussions, children answered a questionnaire and watched some taped advertisements. They were then asked: 'What is an advertisement and what is its function?' Most children were quick to identify the informative role of advertising: 'Advertisements tell you about new products and new things that you should have.' During discussions and in the questionnaire, children said that advertising shows the way to a better life, provides product data and creates a set of tempting images for the individual to copy.

Some children, mainly the older ones, seemed to recognise the persuasive intent of advertising: 'Companies make ads to convince you to buy their products.' They do this, the children said, by revealing how superior *their* product is compared to other, similar ones. Such statements always brought us back to the debate on 'truth'. Do commercials on TV really tell the truth? Do they clearly establish why their product is better than any other? Are these claims justified?

Children, are essentially believers. They believe what they see and are told unless experience teaches them otherwise. Instinctively they trust the adult world, unquestioningly accepting its authority and the veracity of its claims. Consequently television, which is mainly peopled by grown-ups, inspires them with the faith that whatever appears on television is real and not to be doubted. Few children are aware that TV content is 'an illusion created by clever production techniques'. As Aimee Dorr points out: 'Children who do not know about television production processes do not have so ready a reason to reject the apparent reality of what they see and are more inclined to feel it must be real.'[30]

In any case, TV viewers rarely associate programming with the minds behind the screen. They tend (and children in this respect are more vulnerable) to believe that TV is almost sacrosanct and that the visions it provides are immaculately conceived and are, therefore, an honest representation of reality. If adults appearing on TV are sanctioning and encouraging the use of a product, then it follows that the product must be good.

It was interesting to observe that the common spontaneous response was 'Yes, of course advertisements tell the truth!' 'Why in the world should they not?' That's when the inevitable group cynic came up with a counter-offensive on advertising: it lies, it makes a fool of the customer, it's a load of rubbish!

We let the children argue over these statements and also urged them to critique familiar TV commercials such as for Glucon D. Most children would have loved to believe that a glass of Glucon D would turn them into 'Superheroes' but ended up admitting that the advertisement was far-fetched. Of course, childhood and innocence are a time when the imagination can run free, unhampered by reality and unfettered by experience. Such advertisements are accepted and loved; placed in that special niche reserved for fairy tales and romantic figures. But precisely for this reason the role of ads (as persuaders) becomes even more pronounced.

Children, particularly those in the 10-plus age group, said they had at one point or another questioned the honesty of TV commercials. Most often this seems to have resulted from a conflict with their parents over a demand made by them for an advertised product, or out of a sense of betrayal when a product failed to match up to expectations. Such disappointments are particularly hard on younger children.

One boy was particularly upset by a Thums Up advertisement. In this commercial, two little children are feeling dejected by the 'House-full' notice outside a movie hall showing a film starring the actor Salman Khan. Suddenly the actor himself comes to their rescue and makes their day by giving them tickets to the show (and shares their Thums Up).

Visibly annoyed the boy told his class mates that the ad was 'bogus'. He was angered by the fraudulent hope generated by the commercial: 'These things don't happen in real life' he said. 'Salman Khan would never walk up just like that and give *us* tickets to a show!' While the advertisement had brought Salman Khan down from his pedestal and into the lives of the two little children on the TV screen, this child on the other side of the idiot box felt cheated. To him the commercial had been 'real' enough to make him a little jealous of the two children in it—even though he seemed to realise that it was just an advertisement! Tragically the child felt that he was not good enough for such a windfall.

Another child, an 11-year old (who from the sound of it had driven his parents to distraction demanding Le Sancy soap), felt he had been conned by the ad. 'The ad is not true,' he said, his annoyance and regret showing in the way he shouted during the discussion. 'I bought the soap and it dissolved and got soft in the water though the ad said it would not.'

Yet, why should the advertiser care? A 15-year-old Bengali boy working as a household help, told us he was going to buy Le Sancy with his next salary. He was prepared to spend Rs. 15 on just a soap and was as influenced by the ad as the son and daughter of well-to-do businessmen. If children in the U.S. have been known to jump from 10th storey windows believing that if Superman can fly so can they, then by the same criterion our children are gulping down glasses of Glucon-D, hoping to be transformed into Super-heroes. As far as the advertisers are concerned, they have accomplished what they set out to.

So how persuasive *are* TV advertisements? According to several studies, there is

> growing evidence of the persuasiveness—and the factors which enhance persuasiveness—of advertisements to children. Children

do positively evaluate products they see advertised; they do request commercial products; and lastly, their eating behaviour is influenced by the type of food commercials they watch. Moreover . . . a major factor which may enhance the persuasive influence of television advertisements is the affective or emotional appeal of commercials . . . .[31]

While several studies suggest that children who do understand the purpose and intent of the TV commercial, could learn to defend themselves against advertising appeals, Ellen Wartella remains unconvinced: 'The evidence regarding advertising's influence of purchase requests for the products, however, finds that there is little reason to believe that children do employ their cognitive understanding of advertising in defending themselves from advertising messages.'[32]

Our experience with children strongly indicates that their innocence and lack of defenses against the influences of advertising makes them particularly easy prey. Part of the problem lies with the fact that children learn cognitive and social skills by watching other people (in real life and on TV). Their values and behavioural patterns are established through a process of observation. Television is the most powerful 'image-creator' and children who absorb ideas from TV cannot help but translate some of them into acts of daily life. Nowhere is this more evident than in the impact that TV advertising has on them. As it often promotes a product linked to a whole lifestyle or attaches special attributes to products which create hopes beyond the utility value of the goods that are purchased or desired, children tend to believe that by buying, using and owning such products their own lifestyles will undergo a change.

The attitudes that children develop towards a business such as advertising are to some extent rooted in their social backgrounds— that is the value and belief systems operating in their immediate worlds. Our discussions with children enabled us to look into this attitudinal structure and we discovered that while there may be some commonality in the way children think, there are also several variations.

In India there are worlds within worlds and advertisers are themselves aware that the Indian consumer belongs to one of two categories—those who have had a high degree of exposure to the Western world and way of life and those who have not. This, advertisers are aware, is one major factor influencing consumption patterns. By and large, as our analysis of advertising on Doordarshan shows, advertisements on Indian TV cater to the first group and present a picture of life in India that has little to do with the way it is really lived.

Many children in our sample talked of the hardship of their lives. They had noticed that advertisements never portray their sort of families and people. 'Perhaps,' said one child, 'we are really not worth showing. Who would buy something that people like us use?' For them TV advertisements hold a deeper and more special meaning. These ads, offer them a social agenda. They lay down the kind of life people should live, the way they should dress and behave and even have 'fun'.

An 11-year-old boy from the Bapu Dham *basti* told us that TV had changed his life. Our encounter with him was remarkable. Full of zest, he came across like a walking-talking advertisement. Every ad we mentioned, he knew. He was full of eagerness to talk about the TV commercials that had captivated his imagination. 'Ads work magic on us . . . they show us a dream world,' he confided, adding determinedly, 'I'm going to live that way, one day!' His current obsession was to possess '*Hava mein udhane wale joote*' (shoes that will make you fly!).

If we consider what these children from the least affluent strata had to say, we find that while most of them love advertisements, some are uncomfortable with the glorious visions the dream-merchants sell, primarily because they know them to be brilliant illusions, far removed from the realities of their lives. However, they hungrily soak in the messages communicated, hoping to imbibe enough knowledge to be able to fit into that world one day.

In an article on children and advertising, Dr. J.S. Yadava, Director, Indian Institute of Mass Communication (IIMC), describes how advertising influences children's behavioural patterns. '. . . Television advertising familiarises the young ones with the world outside and helps them to pick up its mode of expression, its mannerisms and ways of facing it when they grow up.' He feels that given the situation in which most Indian children live, 'stimulated feelings of needs or desires tend to acquire the form of powerful imperatives. The intensity with which children experience

desire and their inability to assign priorities and accept delays in
satisfying them, is the common experience of most parents.' He
also fears that when these urges remain unfulfilled, such children
may 'grow up with lots of resentment against their parents and the
existing social set-up.'[33]

We learnt that the impact of TV advertising is greatest among
children from middle strata families. Not only do these children
like TV commercials more than children of any other social group,
they are also more deeply influenced by the promises advertisers
make: that the products promoted will greatly enhance the quality
of their lives; that seeking comfort through gadgets and conveniences is a meaningful endeavour; that to keep up with others you
must not only own all the products that the ads are peddling, but
must also model yourself upon the image of the modern-day
individual created, projected and sustained by advertising (and TV
programming). Most of these children faced no active barriers to
consumption. As a value, consumption was acceptable, and secured
by the purchasing power their families enjoyed.

For children from the upper crust of society the story is, qualitatively speaking, a little different. For many such children advertising is just another aspect of life—sometimes exciting, definitely
fun to watch but also something they can afford to ignore. Television
advertising gave them a sense of social superiority. They felt that
they already belong to the 'chosen' class of TV ads and were
aiming to be even 'better'. Some of them seemed eager to distinguish
themselves from run-of-the-mill Doordarshan viewer and be identified with a special kind of satellite TV audience. They said that
advertisements on STAR TV were far better than those shown on
Doordarshan (notwithstanding the fact, that many commercials
are common to both services).

Asked to name the TV commercials they liked best, many of
them mentioned multinational brands such as Coke, Reebok and
Nike and even international hotel ads. They felt that Indian ads
and products were not on a par with Western ones. Some children
also expressed a disinterest in the commodities TV suggests they
ought to be buying. Clearly, having everything they needed and
more, these children could set standards for themselves that are
different from the common ones laid down by TV for the rest of
society.

This suggests that, by and large, children from very affluent, elite homes can and do disregard the social propaganda contained in Indian TV advertisements, although they are far from immune to it.

Second, it appears that the social agenda of many such children is set outside their own country. Their lifestyles are influenced by international role models and their desires centre around the latest products available on the international market. They occasionally travel abroad and shop in South-East Asian or West Asian countries. If not, then they know and have enough indirect access to such goods to make them feel part of a larger mass of consumers. They can therefore ignore the charms of, say, a Barbie doll—something other, less privileged children pine for; instead they plague their parents for the latest Nintendo computer games or some new gismo that children abroad are lining up to buy.

This attitude was best illustrated by a group of sixth standard children who informed us that they *never* watch advertisements on Indian TV and know nothing about Indian advertising. While this suggests, as it is intended to, that they watch only satellite TV (confirmed by their questionnaires), it also indicates a somewhat contemptuous attitude towards Indian advertising which they presumed was way below international norms (though Indian advertising is today considered to be of global standard).

Children's attitudes to TV advertising were most poignantly reflected in their conversations about the models and characters they see in advertisements—i.e. the world of glamour, glitter and gold. For example, in the advertisements for suiting materials like Vimal, Raymonds, JCT, Siyaram etc., the lifestyle of the male models that children see and admire, is defined by expensive cars, posh apartments and beautiful women which become, in a sense, synonymous with the man himself. His counterpart would surely be the Ivana (perfume) woman.

Upper class children in our sample were the only ones who could comfortably identify with such role models. The rest looked with some wonder at this world. Even in commercials wherein models appear to represent a middle class environment, their homes, their clothes and their appearance, are still beyond and away from the everyday experience of most families. Saritaji, while being in some senses 'a typical Indian woman', is nonetheless unlike the mothers of most Indian children. She represents a modern personality but one who is not commonly sighted. Children are enthralled by her aura of competence, particularly when it is combined with the loving qualities they associate with the mother figure.

As mentioned earlier, children from all class groups shared the opinion that TV advertisements provide a formula for the 'good life'. However, hidden behind these statements was the rather tragic anxiety of many children who felt their current lifestyles are simply not good enough.

11

ELEMENTS OF ADVERTISING

One of the conclusions easily drawn from our data is that children love television advertising. What is it about commercials on TV that so attracts their young minds?

Some studies point out that TV's use of

> auditory features other than dialogue, such as lively music, sound effects, peculiar voices, non-speech vocalisations, and frequent changes of speaker attract and hold children's attention . . . . High levels of physical activity or action elicit and maintain children's attention. Thirdly, changes in scene, characters, themes, or auditory events are especially useful for eliciting attention, though they are less important for maintaining it once the child is looking.[34]

Studies also indicate that once children. 'gain age-related conceptual abilities or as they become more familiar with a particular stimulus situation, they shift to the search mode'. It is then that children begin to look for, and assimilate information and relevance within the visual presentation.[35]

Advertising's use of these features is designed to attract a child's attention. Through repetition, advertising ensures that its messages are internalised (whether or not these translate into buying decisions is another matter). Advertising messages could, in fact, lead to generic consumption rather than brand specific consumption. The advertising for a product such as non-stick cookware may serve to increase sales of all non-stick brands rather than a single one. Similarly, ads for a fizzy drink encourage consumption of more than one brand of aerated beverages.

Our research shows that the main characteristics of advertising that draw children to commercials are:

1. *Brevity and repetitiveness*: Advertisements, being short, are ideally suited to the concentration abilities of very young children. Television ads get repeated with such regularity that children 'learn them'. They are, in this respect, perfectly tied to early learning processes based on the rote. Nursery rhymes, children's stories and songs are learnt by repetition, comprehension not being the issue. (Think of 'Mary, Mary quite contrary, how does your garden grow?' Many children from English-speaking homes in India may remember this nursery rhyme but almost none of them really understand it and nor, possibly, do their parents.) Similarly, a 5-year old may sing 'Go, GI Joe' or 'Aaj Bhi, Kal Bhi . . .' without understanding much of the ad jingle.

2. *Complete capsules*: Ads put together a series of rapidly changing, exciting visuals to highlight a product, a service, a message. Although children may not be able to grasp the full meaning of individual shots, they do not require skills linked to memory or continuity to respond to advertisements: The focus on the product leaves enough impact.

3. *Music*: Music is universally loved by children of all ages; They react instinctively to it. Recall of advertisements is often inspired by musical scores. The use of music in advertising helps children, we found, to distinguish between ads and programmes. As one child pointed out 'music plays all through an ad' whereas in a programme like *Jungle ki kahani*, the theme song plays only at the beginning and the end. So, ads are sometimes more lively than verbose programmes.

4. *Colour*: Colour is a visual ingredient guaranteed to attract and hold a child's interest. In the last few years Indian advertising has taken a leap into 'rainbow land' with brilliant colours filling the TV screen. Think of ads like Frooti, Cinthol, Dollops, etc.

5. *Technical superiority*: The sophistication and technical excellence of advertising make TV commercials a visual experience par excellence. Irresistible. Breathtaking.

6. *Emotional manipulation*: In several ads the advertising intent is not overtly stated. Instead the ads play on emotions like 'excitement', 'fun', 'humour', and 'sentimentality' as well as a sense of 'mischief', which appeals to children. Many ads touch upon very real problems and personal anxieties (as

in the Clearasil, Ariel and Close Up ads) which are easily understood and appreciated by children. Whether it is pimples on a young man's face, conflict between mother and daughter-in-law or bad breath, the ads provide commodity-linked solutions to all of them.

7. *Role models*: Stunning models and the clothes they wear are an important influencing factor in advertising. These role models extend from the Saritaji kind of competent super-woman created by advertising (Surf), and the sexy Kamasutra star, Pooja Bedi, to Sunil Gavaskar with his confidence and aura of success, draped in Dinesh suitings. Of course, the images of the modern individual vary considerably. Teenagers are apt to take their cue from the macho men in TV advertisements like Thums Up, Hero Puch, LML Vespa and Bombay Dyeing. Younger children look to G.I. Joe, Barbie, He-Man and Superhero (Glucon D).

AN ANALYSIS OF TV ADVERTISING ON DOORDARSHAN

During the first phase of research for this project, we taped and classified one month of advertising on Doordarshan: 1,166 advertisements. We looked at them from the child's viewpoint. We, studied them for the product categories they represented, the language and music they used and the social class of the models and situations presented by them. We also looked at the manner in which children are used in advertising, and at the nature of advertising's appeal to them. We believe that children are attracted to *all* advertising. However while some ads appeal *indirectly* to children (such as Ariel which neither uses a child model nor promotes a product of interest to children), others appeal *directly* to the child (Hajmola candy and other ads for sweets, chocolates and toys). Some even *use* children in order to appeal to the adult consumer (such as the Videocon washing machine and refrigerator commercials). Lastly, we analysed *patterns of advertising* and the concentration of ads with specific programmes to see if there was a weekly trend. This helped to ascertain the degree of children's exposure to TV advertising. We deal with some of our findings in the following sections; the rest are presented in Part Three. These findings form a backdrop to childrens' reactions to the elements of TV advertising that leave an impact on them.

Advertising on television incorporates many different elements. Most of us as viewers do not consciously evaluate them because they are integrated with the whole (just as the technical tricks used by advertisers pass us by as we concentrate on the end product rather than on a sequence of cleverly put together shots).

What is it about a television advertisement that appeals to the child viewer? Do children react to individual characteristics of advertisements? Without getting into the more technical aspects of advertising, we sought a reaction from children to a few of the more easily identifiable elements of TV commercials, such as music, idea, visuals, models and lifestyles.

MUSIC

When children were asked what aspect of advertising appealed to them, the all-time winner was, as we had expected, music. Over 75 per cent of them said they loved the music in ads. They described the music as 'very good', 'exciting', 'fun' and 'stylish'.

Marianna Pezzella Winick and Charles Winick, the celebrated authors of *The Television Experience: What Children See*, say that: 'Music is almost a universal language for children because it elicits spontaneous bodily movements. Its rhythms encourage clapping, whistling and humming. Music stimulates individual association and its enjoyment is not necessarily dependent on any knowledge of words and language.'[36]

What sort of music does Indian advertising employ? Our study of advertising on Doordarshan provided us an opportunity to look into this more carefully (see Table 11.1).

A few examples would be in order to explain how we categorised the music. The jingles/music for the Titan, Maaza, Atlas, Street Cat, Ivana and Frooti commercials fell into the Western group while Santoor, VIP suitcase, Tata Chai, BSA SLR, Nycil Prickly Heat Powder and Wheel soap were placed in the Indian category. An example of 'East–West fusion' is, of course, Pepsi but there was also JCT Suitings and Percy Sip. It was mainly public service ads (e.g. safety warnings against bomb attacks) that used no music,

Table 11.1
Type of Music Used in Indian Advertising

Week	Western	Indian	Ind/West	None
One	187	72	8	–
Two	180	83	18	7
Three	202	82	30	4
Four	189	73	20	11
Total	758	310	76	22

and the rare product commercial (Colgate toothpaste) which depended on verbal commentary, and perhaps, a sound (Ting!).

The analysis revealed that 65 per cent of the advertisements on Doordarshan in 1992 used Western music, 26.58 per cent Indian music, and 6.51 per cent, a combination of Western and Indian scores. Under 2 per cent used no music at all. Children's responses to music identifiable as Western, suggest that this form of music enjoys a popularity on a par with Hindi film music.

Indian advertisers clearly favour pop, rap and other similar forms of music which rely heavily on rhythm. Although, in essence, this music evokes an association with the U2s and Madonnas, it is being 'Indianised'. Instead of the English lyrics one would expect, many ads are in Hindi. This, of course, is a tactic long used by the Hindi film industry, which has traditionally picked up popular tunes from Hollywood. The Close-up advertisement is a good example of adapting Hindi lyrics to Western beats.

By this ploy, advertisers have found a way to reach out to a larger audience. Non-English speaking viewers can appreciate such ads better when they can understand their lyrics, although the commercials may continue to be somewhat culturally irrelevant. (The Maaza cold drink advertisement is a good example.) When seen in combination with other influencing elements such as the lifestyles promoted by advertising, music turns into a socialising factor. It is not just one of many forms—rap, jazz, rock and pop—but establishes mental associations related to a whole way of life. Think of MTV.

The music video industry has, as we all know, transformed the listeners' relationship with music. There was a time when music was appreciated as music: it had no accompanying dimensions to colour the imagination—the listener reacted to lyrics, rhythms and composition and liked or disliked what was heard. Today's music (which is predominantly modern American) has a strong visual element to it and consequently, it is not just the music that matters. The listener becomes a viewer who learns to negotiate a series of somewhat unrelated images which flit across the screen.

ILLUSTRATION 11.1

Mein Bhi Madonna: *Aping the Michael Jacksons and the Madonnas*

The commonality shared by music videos and TV commercials is very striking. The visuals accompanying the Eveready advertisement, immensely popular with Delhi's children, could be straight out of MTV. In the ad (to the accompaniment of a soul-stirring beat) we see a rough rider take his motorcycle right into a bar; a pony-tailed, barrel-chested bartender's fist comes crashing down on the bar counter to tip over a can placed high up on the shelving as, in the background, a woman in red swirls on and on. The advertisement purports to sell a battery but other than a fleeting glimpse of the product right at the end of the ad, it offers no information about it. The Evita soap commercial goes one step further: it blithely plagiarises Roy Orbison's song 'Pretty Woman' from the film of the same name, drawing the thread between Hollywood and Indian TV commercials even tighter. Ads such as 'Jumpin', with its Michael Jackson-style dancing, and others like 'Thums Up' and 'LML VESPA' use music with the same sort of emotive appeal.

The strong flavour of modern Western music in Indian advertising can hardly be denied. It might be seen as part of a process which began years ago. 'The influence of American television on international popular culture is a concentration of a process begun by the movies, and is complemented by American domination of other popular arts such as music.'[37]

What impact does this predominance of Western music have on Indian children? One obvious fallout of listening to this sort of music is the feeling that many children, especially those from middle to upper class schools, expressed to us: that music of this kind has become a 'status symbol'. Not only do these children keep abreast of the latest developments in this world of music, but even 10-year olds are looking to acquire the latest and most popular music cassettes and videos. These have consequently become sought-after birthday gifts. The children's interest does not appear to stop at this: responding to our questionnaire, 53.51 per cent of the children in the 8-plus age group made it clear that owning a music system was very high on their personal shopping list. Over 48 per cent said they would also like to own a two-in-one (a radio-cum-cassette recorder).

Since our fieldwork, much has happened to reinforce the growing obsession that children have with pop music. More and more big business is attracting attention by inviting superstars like Michael Jackson, Bryan Adams, Apache Indian and even Madonna to hold live performances in India. The fervour and excitement built up over Michael Jackson's aborted Delhi concert in November 1993, is an indication of how deeply this music culture has taken root. A sixth standard child from a very up-market school explained his desire to purchase and own a music system: 'I think Michael

Jackson is the "greatest" and I want to be like him—I need a music system to practice dancing at home.'

Indeed, India has been well co-opted into the MTV universe, what with Apache Indian, Baba Seghal, Rock Machine, Indus Creed and Alisha Chinai appearing regularly on MTV—and now on Channel [V]. This, we must mention, is viewed as a cause for celebration by those who feel that it signals a recognition of Indian talent.

While modern music may dominate the advertising scene (paving the way for an emphasis on youth culture), other kinds of music can also be heard in ads. To an older generation of Indians exposed to Western culture, Western music was once synonymous with classical music. The fondness continues and the Indian advertising world uses some of the best known compositions and symphonies. Cars waltz to the 'Blue Danube', Beethoven orchestrates the sale of watches and the 'Four Seasons' comes in handy to create the right mood.

One child was suitably impressed. 'I'd like a music system to hear Vivaldi's "Four Seasons",' he said. But reactions like this are far from the norm. Classical music is the advertiser's bait for a very small segment of the TV audience. It's the hard, rock'n roll beats that really sell. No wonder then that Surf has emerged with an overnight hit 'Bol baby bol, Rock-n-roll', which really says it all.

INDIAN MUSIC, FILMI STYLE

Popular and successful as Western music has been in TV commercials, our analysis of advertisements on Indian TV revealed that the Indian advertiser, though dangling the Western music bait, cannot resist exploiting the decades-old Indian passion for Hindi film songs. Over 25 per cent of the TV commercials in our sample had music based on popular *filmi geet.*

Children interviewed by us reacted spontaneously to these familiar tunes. Even those from comparatively elite/Westernised backgrounds, who are less enamoured of Indian *filmi* culture and derisively laughed at the 'Ilu-Ilu, BSA SLR' ad when we showed it to them, could not help but respond with tapping feet to its bouncy, rhythmic score. Other jingles like *'Tata Ki Chai De De'* (a copy of the hit song *'Chumma, chumma de-de chumma'* from the film *Hum*) are straight lifts and extremely successful with children.

Indian classical music, we found, is still considered 'high brow' by the average television viewer, including most children. The reach of such music and people's exposure to it is so limited, that the advertisers who have made the National Integration advertisements using some of the finest Indian classical musicians and dancers to promote Indian cultural diversity, can claim credit for attempting to popularise India's rich heritage. They have at least had the imagination to go beyond the standard music format of the Western ad upon which most Indian TV commercials are modelled. Children responding to these ads were not, however, as interested in the music as they were in the children who appear in the commercials.

While analysing TV commercials for their use of music, we found that though only a few use Indian folk music, those that do are surprisingly successful. This music evoked a response in most children and there was singing or humming from the children as they watched the ads. Interestingly, commercials which have chosen folk beats and rhythms include the JCT, Siyaram variety of upper class, Western-oriented commercials.

The Nycil Powder commercial, targeted at children, has used the popular children's song, '*Chhumak, chhumak chalta ghoda*' and children's enjoyment of this simple melody bears testimony to the lasting appeal of childhood favourites.

One last observation on the use of music. It is an extremely interesting and telling exercise to look at the choice of music for different kinds of products. It appears that advertisers tend to choose modern American music when selling items such as chips, cold drinks, ice creams and even toothpaste. This music also seems to be the favourite for creating a certain ambience for gadgetry which alters the traditional way of life (i.e. washing machines to replace the local *dhoban* or washerwoman). The market segment appealed to includes young working people and couples—men and women in their twenties and thirties and children who know the value of being 'a chips-and-Pepsi' kind of person.

Conversely, when it comes to selling music systems, the range of music goes from classical concertos to wild, hard rock but Hindi film music does not get a chance to prove the audio sensitivity of the systems.

Sometimes, the use of Indian film or popular music is noticed for products that are 'low-market' such as toothpowders and the lower priced varieties of detergent soaps.

Children are not unaware of the status awarded to products by this selection of music. While watching advertisements they tended to denigrate commercials which used Indian music especially when the product was targeted at the lower income bracket consumer. This was true for the *Ilu-Ilu* advertisement which sells a cycle, and commercials for toothpowders.

CONCEPTS AND IDEAS

A senior Doordarshan official said to us: 'TV ads are made along the lines of radio advertisements in India. They accentuate the verbal message. If the visual message is clear enough, what is the need for a verbal qualification? The viewer is treated like a fool who cannot understand the simplest things.'

Our reading of current-day commercials on TV is, however, quite different. Advertising in India is no longer simplistic or naive: it uses the best known techniques for seduction, including hyperbole. Advertisers in their attempt to catch children young and mould them into consumer-conscious brand loyalists, use any and all tools including 'magic' and 'fantasy' to attract a child's attention. Television, as we have mentioned earlier, is an ideal medium for fantasy and make-believe—a potential advertisers exploit to the hilt.

The hyperbole used by ads is as hypnotic as the use of magic in fairy-tales. On an irrational, purely emotive and spontaneous plane, children love the concepts that go into making the advertisements a journey into fantasy land.

We observed children's reactions to this aspect of advertising by drawing them into an exercise in which three commercials had to be analysed and understood by them. The ads chosen were: Glucon D (health product), Godrej Puf (refrigerator) and Cinkara (tonic). All three ads suggest that the product on sale can instantly enhance an individual's capabilities to almost superhuman levels or that a product is linked somehow with magical external forces, such as the mysterious spaceman 'Puf' in the Godrej Puf ad.

Most children, we found, were at first reluctant to examine these ads from the point of view of realism, veracity and clarity of message. They felt that the TV commercials stood by themselves and should not be measured against such mundane concepts. It was like asking a child if fairies and ghosts really exist or destroying a fantasy they enjoyed.

The commercial for Godrej Puf was an interesting case study. The ad uses (but does not explain) the term Puf—an odd-sounding name designed to intrigue most children, perhaps because of its association in some of their minds with the story of the *Three Little Pigs* (remember the wicked wolf says 'I'll huff and I'll puff . . .'). The ad also targets the child by introducing a Superman-like character, dressed in a cloak with an insignia on his chest. 'New Godrej with Puf', declares the slogan urging the consumer to acquire something quite unique—though what exactly that is, remains unclear.

Puf is represented by a character from outer space who flies by night, walks through walls, is invisible to most people—and makes magic wherever he goes. Only the little girl in the ad has the purity and innocence to see him and to thank him too—but what exactly is she thanking him for? Presumably, advertisers fondly hope that little children, enthralled by this performance, will pester their parents to choose Godrej Puf when the time comes to buy a refrigerator.

In our conversations we discovered just how perplexed children were by the ad. They had paid little attention to its product-related information. At a subliminal level, they had enjoyed the visuals, the suggestion of fantasy and the wonder of the magical man. They longed to share in the little girl's experience, and did not bother to evaluate the advertisement. They had, of course, identified the product being peddled.

In the same way, Surf Ultra (with Ultrons) professed to have miraculous dirt busters that thrill the schoolboy in the ad with their amazing power. This piece of scientific jargon—'ultrons'—is used to lend a special credibility to the product. More and more TV advertisements are riding piggyback on so-called scientifically endorsed claims. Spaceships herald the arrival of a toothpaste, the man-on-the-move is graphically transformed into a computer-animated character for whom all the doors to success lie wide open and the simplest everyday products from soaps to shampoos and cosmetics are unquestionably effective because 'they are products of the latest scientific research'.

Magical transformations are employed as an effective gimmick to make the viewer and potential consumer believe that a particular brand or product could instantaneously give them a new image, make a dream come true, provide superhuman strength, or transform their appearance, just as the fairy godmother transformed Cinderella with a swish of her wand.

In most group situations children generally concluded that while such ads provided 'some information', they did not tell them anything about a 'real' product in a 'real' world.

> Television advertising is especially suitable for portraying magical transformation and metamorphosis, building on fantasy imagery borrowed from myths, fairy-tales, or contemporary media. Television is our primary storytelling medium, and ads provide brief narrative dramas that vividly present the agonies and ecstasies of life in the consumer culture.[38]

Many children we met said they 'loved the idea that Superhero could jump over a wall and hit one six after another to help the losing team win' (in the Glucon D commercial). Not surprisingly, it was mainly the boys who were in awe of Superhero. Many advertisements, as we all know, exploit sex stereotypes, use traditional role models, and also develop product-related personalities in order to inspire potential consumers to become like these TV models. For example, many boys said their ambition in life was to become a 'sports star', 'a cricketer'—ambitions reinforced by advertisers through the use of sports and sports personalities in ad campaigns. Cricket stars Sunil Gavaskar, Kapil Dev, Sachin Tendulkar and more recently Vinod Kambli, regularly appear in TV commercials.

Commercials for cosmetics, with their promise of instant beauty, had the deepest impact on girls. Irrespective of economic or social background, the concept of beauty, we realised, had been successfully commodified and could be bought and sold for a price. Moreover, it had come to represent an essential of life. On Indian television, advertising for cosmetics and other personal care products accounts for the bulk of commercials in the consumer nondurable category. Consequently, the concepts underlying the sales of these products are bound to target and influence young and fertile minds.

A girl from a run-down slum prattled on and on naming all the creams, powders, lotions, shampoos and beauty soaps she wanted to try. She said she longed to be as lovely as the models in the advertisements. Her mother, who had three daughters, was exasperated and said she was constantly pestered by them to purchase beauty products. Not only were these way beyond their means, they were also non-essential and wasteful items of expenditure. She said, she had found a fairly effective but brutal way of handling her children's demands. 'I let them try at least one product they like and then I hold a mirror up to them the next morning and ask: "Has it helped? Has it made you any prettier?" These ads are full of lies to make you buy things that will not change you.'

Despite parental attempts to keep their daughters away from the cosmetics bazaar, almost everywhere we went, girls of all ages— some shyly, some aggressively and some matter-of-factly—told us that they believe in the bottled and packaged hope provided by TV commercials.

Occasionally, however, bold advertising ideas and concepts miss their mark and are not understood (although the commercial may still be popular and arouse interest in the product it presents). For example, the Atlas Rebel cycle advertisement. Though it targets teenage children, we were surprised to learn that the ad had made little sense to the majority of children we interacted with. In every group discussion with the children in the 8 to 15 years age bracket, we asked two questions related to the ad: what exactly happens in it? What was the ad trying to say?

The advertisement has no dialogue but zooms in on a teenage boy sitting with his legs resting on his desk. In front of him is a poster which reads, 'Rebel without a cause'. Frenetic music creates an atmosphere of tension as the boy's father walks in and reprimands him, presumably for wasting his time. The boy throws his papers (he's supposed to be studying) into his father's face and 'escapes' from the house on his Atlas cycle. The song 'Let the rebel in you break loose' is then played, urging the teenager to defy social pressures and parental authority (though it does not offer a constructive alternative). Riding over rough terrain, the boy meets up with his girlfriend and dreamily watches the sunset with her.

Trying to recall the advertisements, children were quick to describe the product being advertised: almost all of them said: 'It tells you how tough an Atlas cycle is' or that 'Atlas is the fastest bike'. So far so good, at least from the advertisers point of view.

It was only when the children had to relate what had gone on in the advertisement that they ran into trouble. Children who did not belong to an English-speaking background did not comprehend the verbal text of the ad or the words of the song. They also found it hard to identify with the older character in the ad. Some thought he was a friend who had come to tell the boy that his girlfriend was waiting outside for him! They were astounded when we suggested that he might be the boy's father. Which father, they demanded, looks or behaves like that? Boyish, jean-clad and with it, the man simply did not match their mental description of a typical father-figure.

Children who did not face a language barrier were also confused. Most of them had to think hard to recall the events in the ad and even then, describing them proved very difficult. Apart from a small number, the others offered inaccurate descriptions.

It became clear that a large number of children had not under-stood the ad and, more significantly, seemed to have paid little attention to its details or storyline. The exercise of trying to piece the ad together was an eye-opener even to the children and many said: 'Please could you show it to us again. We did not watch it properly.' Interestingly, Atlas figured very high on the list of favourite cycle ads (dealt with in Part Three) and our analysis revealed that boys liked the ad better than girls; children from affluent backgrounds liked it least of all (though they were the ones who understood it best) and lower class children ranked it as the best cycle ad but understood it the least.

The subliminal absorption of ideas, messages and concepts used in advertising is demonstrated by these reactions. Comprehension has little to do with appreciation. Therefore a child who senses excitement and defiance as central emotions in an ad could well be influenced, affected and incited without understanding the context within which such feelings are exhibited. How, then, are the ideas in commercials to be judged from the child's point of view (especi-ally when the child represents not a monolithic social segment but belongs to such varied backgrounds, levels of education and ex-posure)?

A creative director based in Bombay said that talk about pro-duction values tends to overshadow discussion on the relevance and credibility of ideas for the consumer. Attempting to define what an idea is, he said: 'Rosser Reeves called it a unique selling proposition. The redoubtable Bill Bernbach described an idea as a dramatic moment in a commercial. And David Ogilvy categorically states that unless your campaign contains a Big Idea, it will pass like a ship in the night.' He admits that real ideas behind Indian commercials are still too rare.[39]

We might add that as far as television advertising goes, ideas in advertising belong to a largely fictional world familiar perhaps to a tiny segment of Indians.

MODELS, ROLE MODELS
AND PERSONAL IMAGE

A young girl from a middle class family said with a dreamy expression on her face: 'I want to be a VJ like Sophiya'. This was more than wishful thinking. It was, at least for the moment, a serious career ambition.

A few children said that their desire to imitate what they see on television, creates conflicts within the family, perplexing and irritating parents who cannot understand or appreciate their 'get-ups'. Older children (especially teenagers) have an even worse time as they want to develop and test their newly-acquired identities but come up against parental disapproval of their dress code, their mannerisms and their activities. Many children from fairly Westernised homes said: 'Our parents don't like the way we want to be and they always tell us that MTV is responsible.' This growing unease at MTV's influence (and of music channels in general) seems fairly widespread: in a middle class home in Old Delhi, the parents of a 14-year-old girl told one of our researchers: '. . . (Our daughter) looks, walks and talks like a stranger. We don't recognise her as the daughter we had just a few years ago. What happened? Could this be a result of her addiction to MTV? She watches 3 to 4 hours of MTV a day and will not take 'no' for an answer.'

Conversely, in a number of other middle to upper class homes that we visited, children watched a great deal of MTV and their parents did not feel threatened by their exposure to it. A teenage girl and her 8-year-old brother said they 'call MTV' occasionally, and enjoy aping the dress styles and movements of the pop stars and dancers they see on the channel.

MTV is, of course but one of the factors influencing the appearance and behaviour of children; as we shall see, new fashion codes are also being dictated by TV advertising.

In a *basti* in outer Delhi, we heard some women and children talking about the 'white soap' many of them had recently bought. Why did you buy it?, we asked. 'Because we want *chikna* faces (smooth complexions) like the woman in the ad,' they replied. Their daughters giggled and touched their skin, re-enacting scenes from their favourite soap commercials.

A group of 13-year-old girls from middle class backgrounds told us that they want 'all the creams and beauty products advertised' because they believe, 'these will make us more beautiful'; a 12-year-old boy claimed that the Pepsi ad was his favourite: 'I like it because it has *style*.' Style, we asked him? 'Yes,' he said. 'This is the style of the new generation—our generation.'

The interest that girls displayed in cosmetics overshadowed their desire for good clothes although a few said they wanted to be 'fashionable' and wear fancy shoes like Puma pumps. The majority, however, insisted they would prefer to invest in accessories and trinkets like hair bands, hair pins, nail polish, etc.

Talking of role models: advertisers in Bombay told us that the Ariel ad is based upon a carefully conceived global format, guaranteed to touch the hearts of a huge segment of consumers. The format was delicately altered for India but continued to be played upon the traditional mother-in-law–daughter-in-law conflict common to all cultures. 'In India this conflict is very real. Consequently, creating the ad was a tricky task. The tone and expression of its main character had to be just right and not sound aggressive or bossy. You could hurt the sentiments of older women by crass insensitivity.' It worked beautifully. The mother-in-law, though naturally bossy, is funny enough to take the edge off the conflict and ends up admitting that the younger woman is right without quite relinquishing her position of authority.

The element of humour, the comical expression on the older woman's face and the resolution of domestic tension thanks to Ariel have made the ad an instant hit. The Ariel *dadi* (grandmother) is typical of her ilk and the 'mother' an ideal role model.

A 14-year-old boy from a middle class family said he was very much taken with the 'modern yet traditional' women featured in ads such as Ariel and Rin. He said he loved 'their style'. One can only

PLATE 11.1
Images to Live Up to

wonder whether he will carry this image in his mind when it comes to bride hunting!

Most children have favourite 'ad stars'. These stars fall into different categories, ranging from the human to the supernatural. In between there are cartoon characters and, of course, famous people. Together, these models present children with someone (or something) to admire and emulate. They are, therefore, crucial components of successful TV advertisement campaigns.

Take the young girl in the advertisement for Barbie dolls. She does not do or say very much but looks the part. The message of the ad is that 'every doll deserves a Barbie'. Talking to a class of teenage girls (from families badly hit by inflation and poverty), we realised how great an impact the little girl in the commercial had had on them. For these girls an early marriage was already around the corner, and with it adulthood, motherhood and a life of responsibility, but they were wistful at the sight of the little model in the Barbie advertisement. Having watched a number of advertisements they said that of all the things they see advertised on TV it's the *'sunehri baal wali gudiya'* (the golden haired doll) they want most of all. As one girl said: 'We have been working at home since we were very little. It must be nice to be pampered.' For them, owning a Barbie would represent the fulfillment of one of their dearest dreams.

As we screened a selection of advertisements for children, we observed that the older male children were watching the LML Vespa ad with hawk-like expressions—studying the rider's gestures, admiring the clothes worn by the models, aping their behaviour.

When it comes to commercials they know well, children can hardly contain themselves. They roar and impatiently call for their favourite stars to appear. During the screenings, when the Pepsi ad came on, the children behaved as though they were at a rock concert and could not wait for the end of the ad when they could chorus along with ace all-rounder Kapil Dev, *Yehi hai right choice, beb-be!* They chattered loudly and giggled delightedly when Sunil Gavaskar hit a baseball into an innocent bystander's ice-cream cone (Dinesh Suitings).

Cartoon characters like Fido Dido (Lehar 7 Up) and 'Gems Bond' (Gems candy chocolates) are also a great hit with children of all ages. A little boy from Bapu Dham said his elder brother was a Fido fanatic and spent all his free time sketching Fido. This, despite the fact that the rather adult language used by Fido and his arrogance (he describes himself in the Lehar 7 Up ad as 'intelligent, witty, handsome and smart') is lost on many children who do not understand English and cannot grasp the humour.

Models are models. They look good and seem completely at home in glamourous surroundings. Television commercials are essentially fashion oriented and assiduously promote a new look through their products. TV commercials promote tight leggings and T-Shirts (Jumpin'), flouncy skirts (Sunny), jeans (Hero Puch), designer dresses (Ivana), and even ball-gowns (CEAT tyres). The various suiting ads like Vimal and Siyaram, often recalled by children, also offer a dress code. In all these advertisements, the overwhelming importance of clothes is emphasised without being stated. The impact is evident. The more discerning children can now give you a low-down on what kind of dress is suitable for different occasions, clearly associating garments with behavioural patterns and situations.

If, in the past, boys seemed to have no particular fascination with clothes and were not really concerned about the texture of their skins or the cut of their hair, today many in the 11-plus age group are obsessed with the way they look. A beauty parlour owner in Delhi told us that most parlours were opening 'exclusively male' sections to cope with the rush (older men too are sprucing up). These men and boys not only want to have their hair trimmed: they want everything—from perms and facials to bleaching, manicures and pedicures. Never before has the Indian male been so openly and joyously courted: from designer boutiques to accessory outlets, from body building salons to health clubs—everyone is after him!

A 14-year-old boy from a 16-member joint family in old Delhi (which has six TV sets) was particularly concerned with his attire but absolutely clear that he wanted his wardrobe to consist of clothes from exclusive 'collections' such as Harry's. Not surprisingly, he is a 'star gazer', and takes his fashion cues from the Indian rock star, Remo.

'I want to wear S. Kumar suitings and own an HMT watch,' quipped a little boy, while his friend said he'd like a Zap watch and a bow-tie. They broke away from the large group of middle class children seated on a rug in the room where their teacher had placed a TV set for our meeting, just to tell us how they wanted to look. They were barely 10 years old.

Certainly there's nothing wrong with wanting to dress well. But when that ambition translates into contempt for the way other members of their families are turned out, it becomes somewhat reprehensible. Several children told us they did not want to be like their parents and uncomfortably added that they thought their elders had 'no taste', and did not conform to the 'right image'. Some children tried to distance themselves from their backgrounds, denigrating their parents' professions (most of them were drivers, electricians, small-time businessmen or shopkeepers). These children said they wanted to be white-collar workers or professionals.

Parents are not immune to their children's feelings and desires. Most children and parents living in the poorer parts of the city said they wanted a set of 'good' clothes—especially for outings. As one father said: 'Everyone is dressing so well these days. If I take my family out, I'd like to feel proud of the way they all look.' Simply being neat and clean is no longer enough.

VISUALS

Only 25 per cent of the children in our study said they liked the visuals in commercials. Several recalled the Nescafe advertisement claiming they enjoyed it very much because it showed them 'all the places in the world where Nescafe is drunk'.

The lack of enthusiasm for visuals arose perhaps out of an element of confusion in most children's minds. While there was little doubt that children love the images they see on television, the visual element is so integral to 'the ad' that children take it for granted and are seldom able to focus upon it as a distinct component. This emphasises three points: that the images, the graphics and visual gimmickry employed by advertisers are (a) very effective; (b) accepted as a given; and (c) absorbed unconsciously by most children.

> The growing preponderance of visuals in ads has increased the ambiguity of meaning embedded in message structures. Earlier advertising usually states its message quite explicitly through the medium of (the) written text (even if the most outrageous claims were made in the process), but starting in the mid-1920s visual representation became more common, and the relationship between text and visual image became complementary— that is, the text explained the visual. In the postwar period, and especially since the early 1960s, the functions of text moved away from explaining the visual and towards a more cryptic form, where text appeared as a kind of 'key' to the visual.

In all, the effect was to make the commercial message more ambiguous; a 'reading' of it depended on relating elements in the ad's internal structure to each other, as well as drawing in references from the external world. 'Decoding' what is happening in these more complicated message structures requires the use of a method, such as semiology, sensitive to these nuances.[40]

12

THE CHILD IN ADVERTISING

As mentioned earlier, the classification and analysis of TV advertising undertaken during the first phase of our research investigated the nature of the appeal that television commercials hold for the child viewer. Starting with the assumption that children are attracted by, and watch *all and any* advertisement, we attempted to assess how many commercials appeal *indirectly* to children, how many appeal *directly* to them; and lastly, how many advertisements feature a child.

To clarify the point: the first group, i.e., advertisements which do not specifically target children, includes the majority of advertisements. These commercials promote products which children are either not ready to use or to consume, and are directed essentially at the adult consumer. For example, advertisements for tyres, credit cards and investment opportunities are geared towards the adult consumer but are watched (and appreciated) by children as well.

Those classified as directly appealing to the child include ads for toys, sweets, chocolates, ice creams, cold drinks, some soaps, accessories like shoes and cycles, and even certain health products.

Finally, using the *child-as-salesman technique*, advertising for products such as motorcycles, and even refrigerators sometimes cashes in on the emotive and endearing appeal children can lend to an ad by featuring them.

The classification revealed that more than 35 per cent of the commercials taped from Doordarshan during April and May 1992 featured children. Just over 30 per cent of the ads reviewed held a direct appeal for the child audience. In other words, roughly 5 per cent used children although the advertisements *did not in any way target the child*. The remaining commercials appeal indirectly to children.

Children seem to be a particularly good medium for selling products, for justifying the expense on them and for evoking

Table 12.1
Type of Appeal Used in Indian Advertising

Week	Direct Appeal	Indirect Appeal	Child Used
One	92	175	95
Two	92	196	99
Three	97	221	109
Four	75	218	109
Total	356	810	412

certain responses from the audience. The context is the home, where families watch TV together, and where children are so important.

The practise of using children in advertising is a cornerstone of international advertising; advertising agencies tell us that children are routinely employed because of the emotional appeal they lend and their potential for attracting adult attention. Shown together with their parents and siblings, they reinforce the concept of the happy, well-knit nuclear family which is improving its status with the purchase of yet another satisfying product.

On screen, infants, toddlers and young children appear bouncy, at ease, full of verve and joy. But how many takes are required before that look of complete joy—the perfect shot—is achieved? How many rehearsals and hours of simply waiting for the shoot before the ad is canned? What sort of conditions and pressures are children who act in advertisements, subjected to?

Film-makers in India say that while it's not easy to work with children (some of the simplest shots take a whole day), it can be a lot of fun. But, they admit, the most difficult aspect of using children is to get them to rigidly follow a script. Said an old hand at ad films from Bombay:

There's certainly a high degree of sensitivity required in dealing with children. Some children simply will not parrot the words you want them to and may even come up with a spontaneous variation which, because it is natural, sounds good. But most ad agencies are hell bent on sticking to an approved script.

Other film-makers point out that when using children it is better to let them be natural, comfortable in their environment (even if it

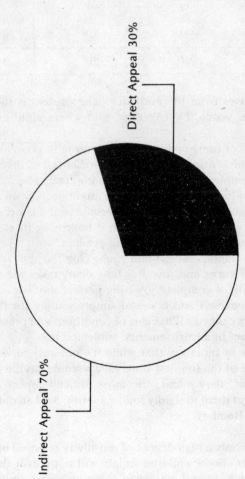

Figure 12.1
Advertising Appeal

Direct Appeal 30%

Indirect Appeal 70%

Note: See Classification of TV Ads by CTA Study.
412 ads used children.

means creating a set in their homes), and not to let them feel as though they are being subjected to adult tyranny.

Regarding the ethics of using children, people in the ad world see nothing amiss and are apt to throw their hands in the air and say: 'Well, if their parents don't mind, why should we?' In a country where child labour is still rampant, this use of children for commercial purposes, may appear almost harmless. However, there is a need for caution, as this could become another form of undue pressure on children turning them into a source of income.

This brings us to the sordid studios with their dismally painted walls and ill-kempt interiors where many ad films are shot. A mother whose little daughter was invited to model in a commercial, told us that there was no time for subtleties, niceties or sensitivity in the making of the advertisement.

Ad film-makers confirm that they have a job at hand which must be done with the minimum of fuss and delay: a deadline hangs over the producer/director's head. Children line up to play the part, one replacing the other . . . until one child does it right and the others shamefacedly walk away with failure written all over them. A handful of parents gloat over their young performing seals—well-trained and obedient. Indeed, as an ad film-maker told us:

> . . . there is a breed of what we call 'professional parents' who
> ⋅ ensure that their children are prepared almost from birth for
> some sort of *Stardom*. And there is money in too: they could be
> earning up to Rs. 10,000 for a film which takes only a few days
> to complete.

However, a mother whose three-year old was requisitioned for an ad said that hers had been a comparatively enjoyable experience. The film-maker who approached them was gentle, kind and understanding and took pains to interact with the child long enough to win the little one's confidence before unobtrusively sneaking some footage. No script. No tutoring. It worked out fine.

Some children come away from shoots wide-eyed at what goes on behind the scenes. Better than anyone else, they know that a commercial is 'created' and the mystique of the 'world-on-holiday' presented by ad films is in some measure destroyed.

PLATE 12.1
A Good Bait for Young Customers

Having established the importance of children to advertisers, we now move on to examine how successful commercials using children are in attracting and influencing the child viewer. How do children watching TV react to children in advertising?

Most of our respondents seemed particularly influenced by ads which had children in them. They identified closely with the child stars in the commercial. Take the Complan ad with its model—a boy—who proclaims: 'I'm a Complan boy.' This was remembered by many children who said they liked the commercial because of the boy in it.

The Le Sancy soap commercial (as well as the Vaseline ad) is another excellent example of how children are successfully being used in advertising campaigns. The Le Sancy ad shows two children in a bath tub playing with a cake of soap, while their fond parents look on. The ad was unusually popular. The Amul Chocolate commercial, the humourous Hajmola candy ad, the Bubble Gum toy depiction and of course the Rasna advertisement make clear the power of persuasion that children in advertising lend to the business of attracting customers.

13

TV ADVERTISING IN INDIA

CLUSTERS, CLUTTER AND CHAOS

Studying the advertisements that were appearing on Doordarshan in the summer of 1992, we found an enormous discrepancy in the quantum of advertising between one day and another. Over the course of one month, this variation remained more or less unchanged, resulting in a weekly pattern (see Figure 12.1).

According to this pattern, the viewer saw very few ads on some days of the week but was subject to an overdose of them on the remaining days, particularly as the weekend approached and over Saturday and Sunday. The swing in the number of advertisements aired from one day to the next indicated a lack of organisation and balance and may be explained by:

(a) the general, amorphous nature of programming on Doordarshan;

(b) the concentration of advertising with a few popular programmes;

(c) the general lack of programme-specific or audience-specific advertising on Doordarshan.

As a result, the advertiser is confronted with a number of serious hurdles in his business of effectively persuading potential customers. To reach them, the advertiser must, first, know that the potential customers will be watching television, and second, that the time slot alloted will suit the commercial. Unfortunately for the ad world, although TV depends heavily on advertisers' use of its commercial time, Doordarshan has not been able to streamline its programming (by which it can ensure a steady delivery of the audience to the advertiser). Nor has it figured out a neat packaging and marketing strategy by which similar ads can appear and compete in identifiable clusters.

Until very recently, Doordarshan's advertising policy dictated that advertisements could appear on Doordarshan only before or after a programme. In 1993 this was reversed by new policies introduced for the Metro Entertainment (DD2) and satellite channels which permit regular commercial breaks in the middle of a telecast. This has had a direct impact on the national network too, with all sponsored programmes now breaking for commercials.

Given the limited number of programmes that were popular with viewers, and the policy structure, advertisers have enjoyed little freedom in positioning their advertisements. Most advertisers have had to opt for the same few programmes resulting in overcrowded, untidy cluttering. As we will see, children's programming and children's advertising form the one notable exception to this amorphous clutter.

This 'clutter' culture on Doordarshan has implied, both for the advertiser and the viewer, that commercials are placed together, haphazardly and very often, without any commonality. Obviously, this is disadvantageous to those seeking publicity for their products since one commercial can hardly stand out in a cluster of 30 to 50 other ads. The best example can be had from the kind of advertising that accompanied the film song programme, *Chitrahaar*. As the most popular programme on Indian television, *Chitrahaar* received as many as 50 ads and at least 25–30 ads for a single telecast. The commercials ranged at the time of this study from the one for the Tata Sierra car, Ravalgaon sweets, Breeze beauty soap to public share issues. The viewer, presented with such a barrage of unrelated commercials, was left bewildered.[41]

Since we conducted our study of TV advertising, the picture has somewhat altered with the introduction of DD2; more sponsored serials on Doordarshan's national network; an increase in the number of films aired every week; and the siphoning off of a sizable chunk of commercial revenue by alternative satellite and cable TV.

However, until 1992, the pattern of advertising on Doordarshan was something like this: a low starting point on Mondays and

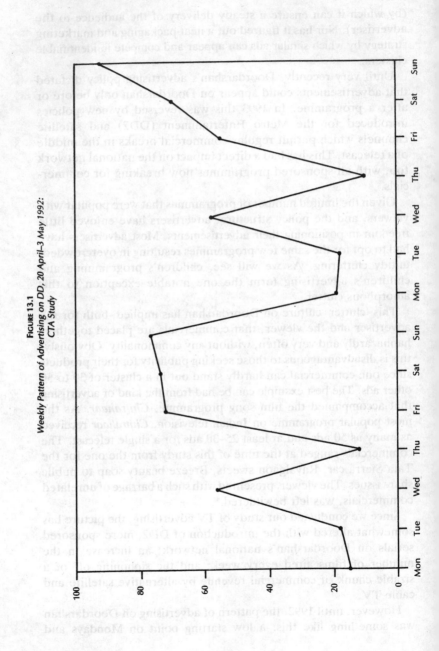

FIGURE 13.1
Weekly Pattern of Advertising on DD, 20 April–3 May 1992: CTA Study

Tuesdays with the national programme recording under 20 ads on both days. A quantum leap on Wednesdays with close to 60 ads appearing over just a few hours during the evening. Commercials slumped again on Thursdays to a figure even lower than Mondays but this represented the quiet before the storm which broke loose on Fridays and continued to build up over the weekend. The only difference was that whereas the bulk of Fridays' advertising was concentrated in the evening slot, the week-end fare was spread over the day, especially on Sundays (see Figure 13.1). Thus, as the figure illustrates, advertising is markedly high on Wednesdays, Fridays, Saturdays, and Sundays and pathetically low on Mondays, Tuesdays and Thursdays.

Having established this as a trend over four continuous weeks, we turned our attention to the pattern of advertising on each high density day. The results were quite astounding. On a Wednesday, for instance, of the 56 advertisements aired during the evening transmission (during the telecast of *Chitrahaar* and the national programme, which at the time of our classification had two sponsored serials on its schedule) as many as 36 commercials were concentrated in a *single* hour of television time (between 8 p.m. and 9 p.m.). These commercials appeared along with *Chitrahaar* and the sponsored serial *Talaash*. This unequal spread characterised the advertising pattern on the other days as well: on a Friday, between 7.45 p.m. and 9 p.m., a viewer could be subjected to 53 commercials appearing with just three programmes—the weekly programme preview, *Saptahiki* (13), *Chitrahaar* (26), and the sponsored serial *Sangharsh* (14).

The World This Week, a late night programme for which in 1992, there was considerable advertising support, emerged with an ad concentration of between 15 and 20 ads. Significantly, it was the only Indian-produced English language programme on the air during the period of our study. From an advertising standpoint, *The World This Week* competed favourably in terms of ad support for third place (after *Chitrahaar* and the Hindi film) with the more popular Hindi serials. (That position has since been undermined as support for the newsmagazine has fallen ever since BBC and CNN became available to the Indian viewer.) By February 1995, it had only one sponsor.

Saturdays were important and provided the first glimpse of a cluster of related advertisements appearing together, aimed specifically at a child audience. These commercials, aired just before the children's cartoon serial *Panchatantra*, were predominantly for toys: Barbie doll, Leo toys, Leo guns and some video games. Saturdays also saw the first prime time telecast of a Hindi film in the week. The film collected as many as 50 ads while the 9 p.m. serial (in this case *Sangharsh*) had, on an average, 12 commercials.

On Sunday mornings, cartoons and other programmes for children enjoyed a concentration of advertisements for sweets, which otherwise appeared sporadically through the week. The historical drama serial *Chanakya* drew as many as 24 advertisements and the next highest concentration of commercials during the day was predictably with the Sunday evening Hindi feature film. *Tom and Jerry* and, later in the day, *Superman* brought together more child-oriented advertisements—the range extending from chocolates and Media TV games to G.I. Joe and cold drinks like Frooti and Jumpin'.

These patterns indicate that as audiences go, children were in 1992, already being successfully targeted by advertisements for products of interest to them. For, as we have seen, there was no steady pattern on a day-to-day or programme-to-programme basis for advertising in other categories. The only programme which seemed to attract advertisements with some commonality was the Friday night *The World This Week*. A disturbingly unrelated clutter of advertisements went with all other programming. Commercials appealing to a mixed viewership in terms of age, class and sex battled for attention destroying advertisers' hopes of maximizing impact by target-specific advertising.

This pattern obviously mirrors the strengths and weaknesses of programming on Doordarshan. It indicates clearly that popular films and film-related programmes attract the greatest number of ads. Thus *Chitrahaar* (Wednesdays and Fridays) and the Hindi feature film (Saturdays and Sundays) attracted high commercial interest. (The same held true for *Chitrageet*—a programme of regional film songs—and the Sunday morning *Rangoli*—a programme of old Hindi film songs.)

The pattern also confirmed that sponsored programmes with high viewership ratings and high advertisement support tend to be concentrated over the weekend (starting Friday evening), contributing to the high density of ads over the weekend. By comparison, week-day sponsored programmes were fewer and received far less advertising support.

In 1992, the 9 p.m. sponsored serials on Mondays through Thursdays enjoyed minimal commercial support. Thursdays consistently recorded the lowest number of ads over all four weeks—a curious phenomenon which could be explained by the fact that the least popular serials tended to be broadcast that day (this unhappy coincidence occurred during the entire summer, despite changes in serial telecast).

Fridays saw the beginning of the week-end bonanza with *Saptahiki, Chitrahaar*, the science magazine *Turning Point* and *The World This Week*, heralding the increase in popular programmes and advertising. Saturdays went from a popular afternoon slot, occupied by a re-run of the serial *Hum Log* (and then a re-run of *Tipu Sultan*) to *Panchatantra*, followed by a Hindi Film in the early evening and a sponsored serial at night (*Mashaal*). Saturdays had the advantage of a large number of niches/special programmes with which to lure the advertiser. For example, Saturday nights came in handy for special late night programmes like the *Oscar Awards* and the Miss Universe competition that were likely to attract public attention and therefore viable in terms of advertising support.

Sundays represented the only day replete with sponsored programmes/slots and films, from the morning. The slots/programmes which attracted ad support included:

1. *Rangoli*.
2. *Laurel and Hardy*.
3. *Chanakya*.
4. *Children's Film Society Cartoons*.
5. *Cricket with Mohinder Amarnath*.
6. *Tom and Jerry*.
7. *National Geographic*.
8. *World of Sport*.
9. *Superman*.
10. *Hindi feature film*.

We were left wondering whether advertising perspectives and priorities were influenced not only by programme appeal but also by social bias: on Sundays, the regional feature film and the 9 p.m. serial on Dr. Ambedkar drew a complete blank, having failed to attract any commercial support at all.

CHILDREN'S TV, CHILDREN'S ADS

Advertising in a more and more competitive marketplace becomes more focused and targets very specific market segments to maximise its impact. Children represent one such segment and during the limited time that Doordarshan offers programming meant exclusively for them, they are receiving their first dose of persuasion for products they can use or consume.

'Children's advertising' and 'children's television' are terms that will increasingly be heard on the battleground of TV. Both these terms (already long in use by advertisers and researchers in the West) have a distinct context and meaning and refer to one specific aspect of TV programming. Commercials especially aimed at the younger generation—mainly those for toys, breakfast cereals, candies and snack foods—constitute the bulk of children's advertising. Programmes with 30 per cent or higher child audiences are commonly accepted in Western countries as representing 'children's television' and mainly comprise comedies, cartoons, children's films and serials.

Given that children's TV is so limited in India, Doordarshan has high child audiences for essentially adult programmes including Hindi films and serials.

How much television programming is child-oriented, i.e., made with the child in mind? Doordarshan's Audience Research Unit estimated for 1992–93 that only 3 per cent of programming time on television was devoted to programmes for children. A glance at television programming over a week suggests that in 1992–93, apart from Doordarshan's morning educational TV, afternoon programme transmission and very limited early evening fare (which, being of poor quality, attracts no advertising support), there was almost nothing directed towards children. This results in children regularly watching programmes like *Chitrahaar* or *Phillips Top*

Ten on Zee TV which, by default, now have to be considered within the realm of child programming.

As an example: in the summer of 1992 here is what Doordarshan (DDI) offered children by way of viewing options, during the week:

- Monday: Nil
- Tuesday: Nil
- Wednesday: *Chitrahaar*
- Thursday: Nil
- Friday: *Chitrahaar*
- Saturday morning: Nil
  Saturday afternoon: *Panchatantra*
- Sunday (all day): *Laurel and Hardy*
                     CFSI Cartoon
                     Tom and Jerry
                     Cricket with Amarnath
                     National Geographic
                     World of Sports
                     Superman
- Weekdays: Afternoon TV and early evening
                     programmes.

Afternoons should logically be a good time for Indian television to rope in child audiences and, indeed, in 1992 Doordarshan's afternoon transmission was intended primarily for 'women, children and senior citizens'. But the one-hour entertainment slot, in trying to cater to three different audience segments ended up with no focus and its package was extremely anomalous. Stories, craft demonstrations and other child-oriented programmes seem oddly at variance with burning social issues and adult enactments of real-life drama. (Since we conducted this study, Doordarshan has changed its focus, devoting the afternoons primarily to women. It telecasts two soap operas almost daily—*Shanti* and *Swabhimaan* and repeats of popular serials like *Junoon*.

Our study revealed that TV viewership in the afternoons largely comprised women and girls and that too, mainly from middle class families. Given the minimal advertising support this slot received, it appears that advertisers did not consider the viewership sufficient to justify investment.

If TV time spells money, then this would explain why, by 1995 the afternoon slot had been taken over by serials which big investors were willing to sponsor. *Shanti*, received advertising support from Proctor and Gamble and *Junoon* and *Swabhimaan* have been sponsored by Hindustan Lever. Moreover, STAR TV has undoubtedly stolen a large segment of the afternoon audience, offering as it does many child-oriented serials and cartoons.

Since this analysis was undertaken, television programming has undergone fairly dramatic changes. Children, as programmers and advertising agencies have begun to realise, represent (both in terms of size and decision-making potential), an audience segment which no one can afford to ignore. Consequently, transnational satellite and cable TV as well as advertisers are paying more attention to catching them young. We now find more TV programming geared towards children's interests, although quality programming for children is still a distant dream.

Doordarshan has introduced a few more cartoons and serials during the week on its National and Metro channels. Imported programmes like *The Wizard of Oz, The Wonderful World of Disney, Jungle Book* and *Alice in Wonderland* are just some of the cartoons broadcast (often, dubbed in Hindi). It is significant that though there have been some attempts to produce indigenous serials or cartoons, i.e., *Tur Am Tu* (inspired by the successful American serial *Sesame Street*), Indian television is still heavily dependent upon foreign sources for the limited child-specific programming it offers.

STAR Plus offers more popular cartoon serials like *G.I. Joe, Batman, Ninja Turtles* and *Small Wonder*, while the Hindi satellite channel Zee TV has introduced original material such as *Tyre Puncture Junglee Toofaan* and even a parent/child talk show, *Teer Kaman*. This is a noteworthy attempt, though the quality of such programmes is unfortunately still quite poor. (More recently, Turner Broadcasting's TNT satellite channel has become available. TNT offers cartoons and films. 'Yes', a privately owned satellite channel aimed exclusively at the youth is also on the airwaves and Disney Productions is set to come on soon.)

However, even as viewing options have increased, it must be emphasised that children are essentially still watching more of the same thing. The new channel choices and increased transmission on Doordarshan have resulted in:

- An increase in the number of films, Hindi or English, on Doordarshan's national network, Metro and satellite channels, on Zee TV, STAR Plus, STAR Movies and the local cable network. (In April 1995 two movie channels—Zee Films and Doordarshan's Movie Club were added to the list.
- A large number of cartoons and children's serials, particularly on STAR Plus and the local cable channel.
- More adult programming. This is especially true of Metro Entertainment, STAR Plus, EL'TV and Zee TV.

The increase and changes in programming have wreaked havoc with advertising patterns. But it is difficult to provide a clear picture since these patterns have not so far settled into any long-lasting determinable trend. What is clear, however, is that children are being exposed to more and more advertising as television services expand.

DOORDARSHAN: EARNING A LIVING

In 1992–1993 (the year we conducted this study) Doordarshan earned Rs. 360 crores in commercial revenue. In 1993–94, the figure went up to Rs. 373 crores and in 1994–1995 it touched Rs. 398 crores. While these figures represent an increased earning capacity in absolute terms, they nevertheless, indicate a drop in the rate of growth.[42]

During the same period, Zee TV's commercial earnings read as follows:

1992–1993 = Rs 7 crores
1993–1994 = Rs. 49 crores
1994–1995 = Rs. 100 crores

Zee TV's advertising revenue has been growing at a faster rate than Doordarshan's, though the state-owned, broadcaster is still far ahead in overall earnings. Undoubtedly, Zee TV has made inroads into Doordarshan's potential earning capacity, notwith-standing a rise in advertising budgets. According to a Hindustan Thomson Associates survey of advertising (April–May 1995), total ad spend on the electronic media in 1993 was Rs. 540 crores;[43] in 1994 it had gone up to Rs. 745 crores—a 38 per cent increase.

However, even as Zee TV has established itself as a competitor, Doordarshan's inability to maintain previous growth levels or match Zee's performance, is of its own doing. In 1993–1994, the state-owned television service had expected to earn up to Rs. 400 crores and in 1994–1995 its revised estimates suggested a target of Rs. 450 crores. That neither of these expectations was realised is primarily the consequence of several problems internal to Doordarshan. Firstly, there was a fall in audience ratings for Doordarshan's national network which led to a dip in advertising on DD1. Even programmes such as *Chitrahaar* and the Hindi feature film—tradi-tionally Doordarshan's biggest money spinners—experienced a significant loss in audience loyalty and commercial support. According to estimates, viewership of *Chitrahaar* in the four metros cities of Delhi, Bombay, Madras and Calcutta, dropped from 68 per cent (of adults who watched the programme) to 44 per cent within the space of one year (September 1993–September 1994).[44]

The cause of this desertion is not difficult to identify: Doordar-shan's sponsored programme scheme had run aground in 1992 with charges of corruption and favouritism in allotments; conse-quently, a moratorium of sorts was placed on new serials being aired while the entire scheme was re-examined by the Central Bureau of Investigation (CBI). This meant that Doordarshan's national network was reduced to telecasting commissioned serials not always very good or popular.

The introduction of Zee TV in October 1992 and the revamped Doordarshan Channel 2 on 26 January 1993 were the other two reasons for depleted viewership. The latter was originally created to provide more audience-specific programming for the large and amorphous audiences in the metros. It was essentially conceived as a local channel. However, the increasing popularity of Zee TV by the end of 1992, compelled Doordarshan to deploy DD2 as part of its counter-offensive.

With total entertainment as its motto, DD2 offered films, film-based programmes, serials, quizzes, talk shows and even current affairs. Many of these appealed to viewers.

However, the popularity of DD2 did not translate into increased commercial revenues for Doordarshan because DD2 worked on the principle of offering private producers the opportunity to buy time slots at certain prices (around Rs. 2.7 lakhs per half hour at prime time). Once this fee was paid, the slot belonged to the producer who could do what he/she liked with the slot. Such commercial revenue as accrued from advertising during that time slot went to the producer who sold the allotted Free Commercial Time (FCT) at rates agreed upon between him/her and the advertiser. Thus, funds being generated by advertising were being diverted from Doordarshan to private producers/marketers who were capitalising on opportunities offered by DD2. Commercial revenue once generated by the national channel, DD1, was re-routed to producers on DD2.

Advertisers found DD2 ideally suited to the needs of clients targeting the urban middle class. A series like *Superhit Muqabala* is estimated to have earned anything between Rs. 17–25 lakhs per episode for its producer, Nimbus. The total estimated advertising revenue generated by DD2 at the end of its first year 1993–94 stood at Rs. 150 crores—most of which went to private producers. At the end of 1993 this scheme was abandoned after the Delhi High Court ruled it as invalid. Doordarshan then reverted to the sponsored programme scheme which had worked so well on DD1. The switch paid dividends: in 1994–1995 DD2 earned between Rs. 75 and Rs. 80 crores for Doordarshan. Out of a total ad spend of Rs. 560 crores on Doordarshan, the network actually took home only Rs. 398 crores, the remaining Rs. 142 crores going to private producers.

Even as DD2 undoubtedly succeeded in its primary aim of countering Zee TV and winning back audience loyalty for Doordarshan, its success created a rather piquant situation: the more DD2 prospered, the more it did so at the expense of DD1. In the middle of 1995, Doordarshan's management had become sufficiently concerned by this anomaly to implement steps which they hoped would rationalise its services and make the two channels complementary rather than adversarial.

A SEASON OF PLENTY

The first TV commercial appeared on Doordarshan in 1976. However, the floodgates did not immediately open and advertising brought in less than a crore in the first year (Rs. 0.77 crore). It took a combination of three developments during the early 1980s to boost TV advertising. These were:

— The introduction of colour transmission and the National Network in 1982.
— The rapid installation of TV transmitters throughout the country soon after, which established an all-India signal reach for Doordarshan.
— The impetus given to Doordarshan's sponsored programme scheme from 1984 onwards.[45]

The figures reflect the quantitative (and qualitative) change that ensued: in 1985–86 Doordarshan's commercial revenue stood at Rs. 60.20 crores, in 1988–1989 it reached Rs. 136.00 crores and by 1989–90 it had advanced to Rs. 210.13 crores. Two years later the figure had grown to Rs. 300.61 crores. The reasons for this rapid and increased earning were: Doordarshan's ability to reach out to a nationwide audience; the potentially high viewership it thus offered, and the improved quality of serials under the sponsored programme scheme.[46]

Doordarshan's earnings till 1993 were essentially garnered from spot advertisements and programme sponsorship. Since then a variety óf new schemes have been introduced to augment its revenues: sole marketing rights of popular programmes or time slots is one, the selling of air time was another. For example, the ever green *Chitrahaar* was auctioned to the highest bidder (in this case a joint bid by Drishti and UTV) for the guaranteed sum of Rs. 54 lakhs per week. *Rangoli* and the Friday feature film have similarly been sold out. Doordarshan has also sold air time to MTV on DD2 and will be considering renting transponders on its upcoming satellite INSAT 2C. CNN already leases a transponder on INSAT 2B for $ 1.5 million.

If we take a holistic view of Doordarshan's commercial progress certain interesting factors stand out:

— At no time did advertising on Doordarshan meet or exceed the 10 per cent of broadcasting time allotted by the government to advertising. In fact the figure had not, until 1993 crossed 5 per cent. So whereas Doordarshan's transmission time has increased noticeably, its commercial time has, if anything, fallen.

— Advertising on Doordarshan has so far been concentrated in the hands of the very few: in 1991, 10 advertisers contributed 25 per cent of the total commercial revenue and the top 25 advertisers accounted for 37 per cent of the revenue. Only 45 brands spent more than Rs. 1 crore on advertising. More recently, the Hindustan Thomson Associates (HTA) survey of TV advertising (April–May 1995) found that the top 10 advertisers on TV account for 33.7 per cent of ads on Doordarshan.[47]

These figures reflect worldwide trends. In 1965, 50 of the largest business units in the USA controlled 35.2 per cent of the total manufacturing assets in the country and completely dominated advertising expenditures.[48]

— Advertising on Doordarshan was divided into separate tariff groupings such as Super A Special, Super A, A Special, A, B, C. Ninety-three per cent of the total commercial revenue came from the first three categories. A look at the programmes which fall into these different categories, explains this: all popular programmes belonged to these categories. For example *Chitrahaar* and the Saturday Hindi Feature Film were in the Super A Special category, sponsored serials on all days (at 9 p.m.) in the Super A category and so on.

— This commercial profile confirms that a few kinds of programmes have contributed almost the entire amount earned by Doordarshan. One estimate suggested that 12 per cent of programming time had an overdose of advertising while the remaining 88 per cent had no advertising at all. Viewers complain that *Sri Krishna* on DD2 spends up to 15 minutes on advertising time and only 15 minutes on the serial episode!

This information is partly available in both the Mahalik Committee Report on Doordarshan's Commercial Services (1992) and the Public Accounts Committee report of the same year. As we have stated above, the Government of India has been keen that both All India Radio and Doordarshan be less dependent on it for financial support. The Eighth Five Year Plan had emphasised the need for Doordarshan to become financially self-reliant and led to the setting up of the Mahalik Committee which, amongst other things, recommended an increase in afternoon transmission, more film and entertainment slots on the national network and more live sports events. The PAC's report resulted in a demand for restructuring Doordarshan's advertising policy and for an explanation on why the broadcasting network was unable to utilise the 10 per cent broadcast time allocated for commercials. The PAC also suggested that Doordarshan's advertising policy must be broader-based in order to attract more clients rather than simply consist of increasing rates at regular intervals.[49]

Doordarshan responded to these demands and to the challenge from transnational satellite TV services by increasing transmission hours, the entertainment content of its schedules and introducing several new schemes on its Metro and satellite channels. At this stage it is unclear whether or not these steps will suffice. A great deal depends upon Doordarshan's ability to chalk out a comprehensive programme and commercial policy (i.e. audience-specific programming rather than a generalised menu card) instead of the ad hoc changes it has resorted to so far. As we know, in the summer of 1993, Doordarshan introduced five new satellite channels. Six months later, these channels were abandoned. Plans to introduce a high quality channel for discriminating urban, educated viewers—DD3—were postponed shortly before its proposed launch in October 1994. The channel finally went on the air in September 1995. Such ad hoc moves are not likely to encourage advertisers who are looking for stable platforms with identifiable audience segments.

Second, as mentioned earlier, the Metro channel, rather than increasing Doordarshan's earnings, in fact, depleted or more accurately diverted them. While commercial revenue for television will increase, it will go to private producers also rather than to an organisation like Doordarshan alone. With the introduction of regional language channels, advertising could be spread even more widely and thinly.

Thus, Doordarshan is exploring other avenues to increase its earnings—i.e. it has increased the time slot fees and sponsorship rates, augmented the number of its entertainment slots on all channels, created new regional, local and language-specific programmes to increase its advertising base, introduced new marketing schemes, etc. Such steps have become inevitable with the thrust of government policy moving towards greater privatisation of the media and liberalisation of the economy, a lowering of subsidies for state-owned institutions and an emphasis on encouraging such institutions to become financially self-reliant.

In addition to Doordarshan's expansion plans, there is the possibility of many more private channels opening up. Already the Indian government is considering allowing private broadcasters to own their own transmission facilities. Other entrepreneurs are exploring satellite TV options. Transnational television services are in the process of offering more, specialised channels to the Indian viewer.

STAR TV

STAR TV earned 10 per cent of the total commercial revenue in 1992–93 from advertising on television in India, a figure that is quite remarkable considering that it has been in business for just over three years.

Ever since the summer of 1993, when Australian media magnate Rupert Murdoch bought a controlling share in the company and a 50 per cent equity stake in Zee TV's controlling company ATL (Asia Today Ltd.), Murdoch has repeatedly said that he views India as one of the most important potential markets for satellite TV and he is backing his conviction with tie-ups involving Indian companies. Murdoch brings with him 'better' programming through his ownership of 20th Century Fox, BSkyB (the premier satellite TV company in Britain) and other TV programming companies.

STAR TV is running at a loss and Murdoch has revealed that the losses were as high as $1 million per week in 1993. The *Far Eastern Economic Review* estimates that STAR TV lost $20 million last year. Satellite TV experts predict that losses will continue for at least another two to three years.

Indian advertisers, notwithstanding the government's restraining policies, do advertise fairly extensively on STAR TV, especially on STAR Plus and Channel [V]. Indeed, serials like *The Bold and the Beautiful, Santa Barbara, WWF* and *Remington Steele* have been sponsored by Indian companies. So are many sports events on Prime Sports and Indian music shows on Channel [V].

Increasingly, STAR TV and Channel [V] are orienting programming content and schedules to Indian interests. There are special India-specific programmes—*India Show, India Business Report*—and one-time telecasts of events like Republic Day and the Miss India contest. Rupert Murdoch is already talking in terms of a Hindi music channel, a sports channel with Hindi commentary and regional language services.

All this is aimed at winning high viewership in India and increasing STAR TV's commercial prospects in the country.

ZEE TV

Until Murdoch bought 50 per cent equity stake in it, Zee TV was an independent operation with its own advertising rates. Zee pays STAR a rental fee, and shares its commercial revenue with STAR in a ratio of 50:50. Information on the financial status of the companies behind the Hindi satellite channel is hard to come by, but unlike STAR, Zee claims to have made profits in its second year. The fact that its commercial revenue touched Rs. 100 crore (1994–95) bears testimony to its popularity.

Major Indian companies ranging from MRF and CEAT to Lehar Pepsi, Hindustan Lever and UB, have lined up at STAR and Zee TV's doorstep ever since MRF began the trend by co-sponsoring the World Cup Cricket telecast in February 1992. To begin with, STAR accepted rupee payments but soon changed over to the dollar.

STAR TV is governed by advertising codes laid down by Hong Kong. Jewellery manufacturers who were not permitted to advertise on Doordarshan until 1994, found an outlet on STAR. However, commercials for tobacco, financial issues, gambling and faith healing are prohibited even on STAR and interestingly, liquor advertisements were disallowed on MTV on the grounds that the channel is extremely popular with children.

With the burgeoning of so many channels, the competition to win commercial support can only become stiffer. The effect this will have on network schedules and programme content will be tremendous and television services will vie with each other to maximise their appeal for potential advertisers. Inevitably some will succeed and others fail. The Indian viewer who had lived in splendid isolation will be inundated with choices, gimmicks and populist culture as TV services fight for audience ratings. The dizzying proliferation of channels is already creating a segmentation and a fragmentation of audiences—audiences segregated according to their different programme choices which can logically only enhance a trend (that has already begun) towards more programme-specific, audience-specific and language-specific advertising.

For the child audience the future can thus mean only one thing: an even greater exposure to TV advertising and the consumer ethic it promotes.

The commercialisation of television networks implies more and more advertising. In the next part of this book we shall deal with the nature of television advertising and its impact on children's consumption choices. Before that, we need to mention one other category of advertising which seldom receives the attention it deserves.

SOCIALLY RELEVANT ADVERTISING

Apart from commercial advertising, television services throughout the world also carry what are popularly known as 'socially relevant' or 'public service' advertisements. These are intended to educate and inform people and raise social awareness.

Pursuing its stated objective of using the media as an agent of social change, Doordarshan broadcasts a number of advertisements on issues such as national integration, dowry, family planning, the environment, the girl child, the disabled, health and sanitation, etc. Many people are apt to overlook such advertisements when they appear on Doordarshan, responding with indifference partly because many of them fail to live up to the standards of commercial advertising. Some viewers also feel that these ads are intended for the 'masses' and can therefore be safely ignored.

PLATE 13.1
Raga Desh: *Socially Relevant Advertising — Rejoicing in the Maestros to Promote National Integration*

Compared to commercial advertising, the time devoted to socially relevant advertising on Doordarshan would startle its most vociferous supporters. *Brand Equity* (July 1992) revealed that it was the National Literacy Mission ads and not Nirma or Ariel that held the coveted position of being 'the most advertised' spots! According to the write-up, nearly 800 spots were aired over Doordarshan's national network and regional kendras (at a cost of Rs. 8.18 crore) in 1991. The article suggested that advertising agencies have begun to realise that if a consumer's brand selection can be influenced, they could just as well change attitudes to education, health, sanitation or even sex. The government, as well as some international agencies, have opted to let private professional agencies handle these campaigns.

Advertising agencies and their clients have also identified the need to develop a corporate image which can be associated with socially acceptable values such as being environmentally friendly or concerned with the physical and mental welfare of employees. On STAR TV, for instance, international banks sell themselves not merely as efficient financial outfits but as 'people who care' for the well-being of the public.

Although such advertisements on STAR TV are much like commercial advertisements, those on Doordarshan bear little resemblance to regular advertising. In fact, Doordarshan's public service advertisements usually fail to use the most basic elements that make commercial advertising as mesmeric and successful as it is. While commercial advertising consists of brief, visually sophisticated 10 to 30 second capsules which appeal to viewers' emotions, fears, hopes and desires, public service advertisements are of poor technical quality, and sometimes too long to hold viewer's interest. Sometimes it is hard to differentiate between them and traditional forms of programming. The lack of focus in these commercials pushes their messages to the periphery and often one needs to watch almost to the end before the purpose of the advertisement becomes clear.

What is of even greater concern is the fact that these ads frequently perform the function of a filler. They generally appear between programmes and in the event of insufficient programming—which further reduces their credibility.

Most public service ads on Doordarshan are low-cost and therefore lack the finesse and sophistication of their commercial counterparts. In addition, they lack imagination: the messages are dealt with in a rather heavy-handed manner and the scenes enacted are sometimes too prosaic or dull to be interesting. The exceptions to this in creative terms are the national integration advertisements and some of those for literacy.

By comparison, similar advertisements made for STAR TV are far more successful. To the average viewer, they resemble other commercials: they are slick, interesting and absorbing. Even when they adopt an indirect approach, they use images that might have been selected by any other commercial to ensure that the viewer's attention is held: A man is writing postcards during a flight; the focus shifts to the hospital where he lies, dying. 'It takes only one sexual encounter to contract AIDS' is enough to warn and inform the viewer of the dangers of the disease.

The relative failure of Doordarshan's public service advertising is clear from the poor response to it from children in our sample. Just over 20 per cent of the children in the 8 to 15 years age group identified public service advertisements as commercials. The others were completely confused by what they thought were information capsules or programmes. Even when prompted or reminded of

PLATE 13.2
Children Hold up the Light of Freedom

socially relevant ads that appeared regularly on TV, they failed to recall very many.

These are the only ads directed at the lower classes—unfortunately this in itself is questionable. Social change, after all is a shared responsibility and there is certainly a need to awaken awareness across class.

NOTES TO PART II

* The opening quote is from 'Discrimination and Popular Culture', ed. by Denys Tompson.
1. 'Moralising in the marketplace.' Brand Equity, *The Economic Times*, 17 March 1993. In 1995 Kentucky Fried Chicken was asked to close its operations for a similar reason.
2. Vance Packard. 1981. *The Hidden Persuaders*. Penguin Books. Great Britain.
3. We feel the need to clarify why we have quoted from so many studies and materials emanating from the West—and particularly the U.S.A. In these countries advertising has been a major industry this century and TV's growth unparalleled. Advertisers have spent enormous sums of money developing techniques to successfully win over the consumer's mind. Equally significant is the fact that advertising has been widely and critically studied in these countries for its impact on the public, particularly children. We feel that the lessons learnt from this area of research are valuable for a nation like India which has not had as long an experience of either TV advertising or of consumerism. The relevance of the research is greater now than ever before, given that so much multinational advertising is, and will be, coming our way. In other words, we will be exposed to the same set of advertising messages that our counterparts in the West have been. Almost every major Indian advertising agency has a tie-up with a multinational one (e.g. India's largest advertising agency, Hindustan Thomson Associates, is linked to Walter J. Thomson).

   As more and more foreign-produced goods enter the Indian market, the advertising campaigns for these products will be closely monitored by the parent agencies to ensure that they conform to the product's global image and advertising formats. If Indian advertising had earlier sought guidance and cues from international advertising, the industry has now become part of giant transnational concerns which are using the same techniques, selling the same values, and defining the same culture for the Indian consumer as they have for their domestic markets, albeit with minor modifications which allow for local shifts in emphasis.
4. Eric Barnouw. 1978. *The Sponsor: Notes on a Modern Potentate*. Oxford University Press, New York.
5. For more information on the debate on advertising see *Social Communication in Advertising* by W. Leiss, S. Kline and S. Jhally. 1986. Methuen, New York.
6. Jerry Mander. *Four Arguments for the Elimination of Television*. 1978. Harvester, New York.
7. Douglas Kellner, 'Advertising and Consumer Culture' in *Questioning the Media*. 1990. Sage Publications Inc. USA.
8. A great deal of literature exists on the controversy over the role of advertising in society. For a concise and comprehensive picture see W. Leiss, S. Kline and S. Jhally, *Social Communication in Advertising*; Vance Packard, *The Hidden*

Persuaders; Edward Barnouw, *The Sponsor*; S. Ewens, *Captains of Consciousness*; C. Lasch, *The Culture of Narcissism*; and M. Schudson, *Advertising, the Uneasy Persuasion*.

9. See Douglas Kellner in *Questioning the Media*; Raymond Williams in an essay entitled 'The Magic System' (1980), Vance Packard, *The Hidden Persuaders* (1981) and Stuart Ewens, *Captains of Consciousness* (1976).

10. Eric Barnouw, op. cit.

11. Fred Inglis, *The Imagery of Power: A Critique of Advertising*. 1972. Heinemann, London.

12. See Leiss, Kline and Jhally, op. cit.

13. Jerry Mander, op. cit.

14. David Halberstam. *The Powers That Be*. 1979. Dell Publishing, New York.

15. David Littlejohn, 'Communicating Ideas by Television' in *Television as a Social Force: New Approaches to TV Criticism*, edited by Richard Adler. 1975. Praeger Publishers, New York.

16. P.C. Joshi Committee on Software for Doordarshan, 1984.

17. Douglas Kellner, 'Advertising and Consumer Culture' in *Questioning the Media*. Edited by John Dowming, Ali Mohammadi, Annabelle Sreberny-Mohammadi. 1990. Sage Publications, California, U.S.A.

18. Subrata Banerjee. 'Socially Relevant Advertising and the Developing World.' *Communicator*, September 1989.

19. Raghu Roy. 'Consumerism in the 90s.' *Brand Equity, The Economic Times*, 5 January 1994.

20. Joli Jensen on Stuart Hall, 1982, in *Redeeming Modernity*. 1990. Sage Publications.

21. Charles K. Atkin. 1981. 'Effects of Television Advertising on Children' in *Children and the Faces of Television: Teaching Violence, Selling*, edited by E. Palmer and A. Dorr. Academic Press Inc.

22. Jules Henry. 1966. *Culture against Man: On Contemporary American Culture*. Random House, Great Britain.

23. Jerry Mander, op. cit.

24. 'Inside The Child's Mind', *Advertising and Marketing*, July 1989.

25. *Zid* is an Urdu word which means 'to be obstinate'.

26. Ellen Wartella. 1984. 'Cognitive and Affective Factors of TV Advertising's Influence on Children'. *The Western Journal of Speech Communication*.

27. Patricia Marks Greenfield. 1984. *Mind and Media*. Fontana Paperbacks, William Collins Sons & Co. Ltd., Glasgow.

28. By K. Frome Paget, D. Kritt and L. Bergemann. 1984. 'Understanding Strategic Interactions in Television Commercials: A Developmental Study'. *Journal of Applied Developmental Psychology*, 5, pp. 145–61.

29. Spock, Benjamin. *Baby and Child Care* 1976. Pocket Books, Simon & Schuster, N.Y.

30. Aimee Dorr. 1986. *Television and Children*. Sage Publications, Beverley Hills.

31. Ellen Wartella, op. cit.

32. ibid.

33. J.S. Yadava. December 1989. 'Does Television Advertising Harm Children?' *Communicator*.

34. Aletha Huston-Stein and John C. Wright. 1979. 'Children and Television: Effects of the Medium, its Content and its Form'. *Journal of Research and Development in Education*, Volume 13, Number 1.
35. ibid.
36. Mariann Pezzella Winick and Charles Winick. 1979. *The Television Experience: What Children See.* Sage Publications, Beverley Hills.
37. Lawrence L. Murray. 1979. 'Universality and Uniformity in the Popular Arts: The Impact of Television on Popular Culture' in *Screen and Society: The Impact of Television upon Aspects of Contemporary Civilization*, edited by Frank J. Coppa. Nelson-Hall Publishers, Chicago.
38. Douglas Kellner, op. cit.
39. Suresh Mallik, Creative Director, Ogilvy and Mather Advertising Agency. 1993. 'A Review of Indian Television Commercials: Production Values or Ideas.'
40. Leiss, Kline and Jhally, op. cit.
41. *Chitrahaar* has consistently led viewership ratings over the last five years. This is confirmed, for instance, by IMRB's TRP system, which offers weekly programme ratings.
42. Doordarshan 1995. March 1995. Audience Research Unit. Directorate General: Doordarshan. See also 1993 and 1994.
43. HTA Survey of Advertising. April–May 1995. Hindustan Thomson Associates.
44. Television Rating Point System, *IMRB*
45. Doordarshan–1995
46. Doordarshan–1995
47. Doordarshan Audience Research Unit: Facts and Figures. 1991; Doordarshan 1995; HTA Survey of Television Advertising April–May 1995.
48. Jerry Mander. Ibid.
49. Mahalik Committee Report on Doordarshan's Commercial Services (1992); Report of the Public Accounts Committee (1992).

III

CONSUMERISM

INTRODUCTION

India's consumer population was approximately 200 million strong at the end of 1993. By any standards, this is an incredibly high figure. However, according to one demographic analysis, with a 25 per cent urban population, the country remains one of the *least* urbanised in the world. India's 'urban population at 215 million is the second largest (after China) in the world. At the current rate, it would take another 20 years for the urban population to double, by which time it may be very well the least urbanised country in the world.'[1]

Such predictions are oddly at variance with the increase in consumerism now visible in India's larger cities. The Indian market-place is teeming with choices that had earlier been unavailable. Instead of just one Colgate toothpaste, there is now Colgate Red, Blue, Gel, Paste and Colgate Total, which have collectively all but wiped out the once popular Colgate toothpowder. Similarly, the potato chip is no longer merely a salted potato wafer: it's *pudina*, ketchup, vinegar, *chaat*, or masala flavoured.

Or take a look at the increasing number of choices available for washing machines. There are now at least six different brand names in the market where five years ago there were only two and before that none at all.

The growth in the number and variety of products available to the Indian consumer in the nineties implies a complete transform-ation of the urban Indian shopping experience. Until the late seventies and even mid-eighties, many affluent Indians had looked to foreign markets for electronic goods, designer T-shirts and jeans, cosmetics, etc. Today, with almost every conceivable con-sumer product being manufactured in the country and with popular multinational brand names becoming increasingly available, Indians who earlier shopped abroad can now shop at home.

This boom coincides and, in effect, mirrors the entirely new way of thinking now popular with educated Indians belonging to the upper and middle classes, as well as with the political leadership of the country. In 1991, the Congress government at the centre embarked on a policy of economic liberalisation, which has opened up the market and allowed multinational companies entry into areas that would once have been termed irrelevant to the nation's developmental priorities: Kentucky fried chicken cannot be described as a panacea for poverty; nor can the proliferation of cold drinks and fast foods contribute to the well-being of millions of malnourished Indians.

However, according to current philosophy, a mixed economy and the socialist ideals which inform it (central to the Nehruvian model adopted at the time of Independence) have only weighed India down, impeding development. Consequently, the new thinking is aimed at shedding this ideology and espousing in its stead a market-oriented economy. The promise is of quick prosperity (which will eventually trickle down to the least privileged or so it is hoped).

It is both interesting and surprising that the desirability of this course of action as well as the government's present policies have been so easily and unquestioningly accepted, particularly since they represent a complete reversal of earlier policy. There is no real debate within the country about the wisdom of abandoning a government-controlled and planned economy in such haste or, conversely, the dangers of laissez faire consumerism which, in the space of a few short years, has been allowed to rock the very foundations of our political commitment.

Television advertising is, of course, one of the most visible protagonists of this consumer culture or 'delectable materialism' as the American newspaper *The New York Times* once called it. More effectively than any other medium, it demonstrates and sells to millions of viewers the virtues of consumerism.

Since advertising creates and sustains an ideology of consumption, it is a social force which we, in India, will now have to analyse for both impact and influence. It is said that consumerism encourages a cult of individualism by focusing on the needs—real or artificial—of the consumer and, in doing so, diverts attention from larger societal and economic concerns. By persuading the consumer to concentrate on the goal of attaining personal satisfaction through material purchases, consumerism may focus attention more and more on the products themselves—so much so that the consumer takes for granted the system that designs and delivers them.

Commenting on the relevance of advertising, Subrata Bannerjee has argued that

> The promotion of a psychology of more and more consumption sustains also a value system which is based on ruthless competition for individual achievement, which alone enables ever expanding consumption of an ever increasing range and variety of goods and services. It is such a way of life that alone can sustain an economic system of the primacy of profits. In this entire environment the relevance of advertising is not only economic, but also social and cultural and in the final analysis, even political. After all, a particular economic structure can be sustained by a relevant political structure.[2]

In other words:

> . . . advertising is not just a business expenditure undertaken in the hope of moving some merchandise off the store shelves, but is rather an integral part of modern culture. Its creations appropriate and transform a vast range of symbols and ideas, its unsurpassed communicative powers recycle cultural models and references back through the networks of social interactions. This venture is unified by the discourse through and about objects, which bonds together images of persons, products and well-being.[3]

It is this transformation in people's thinking patterns and particularly those of children, that we are concerned with. Are children in India absorbing this 'discourse through and about products'? If they are, how is it shaping or reshaping them as human beings?

Unlike other influences, consumerism and its effects on children has not been strenuously critiqued even in nations where consumerism is a major force. As long ago as 1955, Joseph Seldin noted in the American newspaper *The Nation* that the 'manipulation of children's minds in the fields of religion or politics would touch off a parent's storm of protest and a rash of Congressional investigations. But in the world of commerce, children are fair game and legitimate prey'.[4]

In an effort to focus attention on the deep and lasting impact consumerism can have on children, in this part of our study we will look at children's responses to specific categories of TV commercials; how these are influencing and changing their aspirations and priorities for both the present as well as the future; and the impact that consumerism can have on children in terms of their identities, language and cultural confidence.

CHILDREN, ADVERTISING AND CONSUMERISM

As mentioned in Part Two, by the early fifties it had become clear to advertisers in the United States that in order to ensure the long-term success of consumerism, they would have to target children. Clearly, the fact that very young children were singing commercial jingles (and unlike the television set, they could not be switched off) indicated to advertisers that infants 'at no extra cost' could be used to prompt and remind adults about available products. One example which delighted American advertising agencies was the singing of beer commercial jingles by four-year old children who, although they had no personal interest in the product, persistently sang the jingles in the hearing of adults![5]

The process by which TV advertising exposes children to a consumer ideology (which they unconsciously imbibe) thus includes the ritual incantation of popular jingles, a phenomenon to which we in India can easily relate today. Children in Delhi routinely parrot advertising slogans, including 'I love you, Rasna', 'Thank you Puff', '*Yehi hai right choice baby*' and even '*Kya karen duty par jana hai*'.

Moreover, we can see that as television viewers, children are easily influenced by the happy, carefree and sumptuous world of TV advertisements. Starting at a very early age, children learn to desire things they see on TV, and eventually become active persuaders in the marketplace and at home.

During our study, we observed that many children in the 8-plus age group seemed more interested in discovering new products than their parents were—and they were particularly attuned to new brands of products they had seen on television—soaps, crisps and hi-tech equipment. In some senses, therefore, they seem to act as the family's antenna, picking up new ideas, noticing new products and keeping a watchful eye on premiums and discounts, free gifts and sales offers. They are far from immune to the lure of attractive goods, clothes and food in sophisticated shops, to the glamour of opulent homes and the sleekness of imported cars. Day after day, they are seduced by media hardsell and peer group pressures into a hypnotic state where the dictates of desire begin to override everything else—even reality. Slowly, we believe, they are learning to redefine themselves and to judge their ability to succeed—or even to be happy—on the basis of the level of their material possessions.

In Delhi, the difference between the haves and the have-nots stares you in the face. More wealth is now on display than ever before: in the marketplace, in people's homes, in corporate offices. Here, in the capital of India, the consumer ethic has overrun the tenet that in a poor nation, self-indulgence is unwarranted. Everybody now seems to be in a hurry—to get ahead, to possess more things, to take the lead. This has resulted in a visible change in attitudes. Poverty is no longer seen as insurmountable (without education, social access and requisite professional skills). A new set of values based on the ability to make money any way has begun to dominate our thinking. The social concern and 'guilt' at other peoples' poverty is also being overcome in the race for personal material advancement.

Success is reflected in the clothes people wear and their material affluence is expressed through the goods displayed in their homes. In other words, consumerism does, at least to this extent, possess an egalitarian face, for there are no apparent barriers of class, religion etc. that prevent the accumulation of wealth and the consequent rise in an individual's status. The local *paan-wallah* could, within a year, rake in more profit by diversifying his business and running a video parlour alongside his shop than he ever imagined possible.

Today's urban Indian child wants and demands more and more. Parents in Delhi are hard put to explain to their offspring why other children of the same age receive cars on their fourteenth birthday and constantly eat out at five-star hotels. Those struggling to meet the basic needs of food, clothing and shelter may feel that it is wasteful to spend their limited finances on superfluous items of consumption like cold drinks, trinkets or candy. But, they find themselves giving in to such demands for fear of causing resentment and a sense of frustration in their children.

Unlike in the West, where consumerism has been a way of life for many decades, in India the cult of individualism engendered by consumerism is still to reach its high point. Consequently, in deference to existing social norms, advertising is forced to recognise the family as a consumption unit even as it peddles the virtues of individualism. Many ads featured on Indian television still appeal to this 'family unit' rather than to individual consumers.

The changes in consumer behaviour that must be wrought in order to promote the interests of consumerism are placing a huge burden on producers, marketers and advertisers. Crawl into and behind the picture tube, the hoardings and the neon signs and you will discover industrious people frantically at work, scrambling about wildly for ideas and concepts which will keep old customers loyal and tap new, potential ones. For instance, it has been estimated that the teenage market size in India could be at least Rs. 2,000 crore a year. Advertisers are therefore, constantly preoccupied with devising, altering and redesigning strategies to claim the largest slice of this cake.[6]

Advertising has to be on the lookout and prepared to change track. Advertisers admit, that with teenagers for instance, 'whether you trust them, distrust them, mistrust them, love them or hate them, the last thing you can do is ignore them'. Similarly advertisers have to look to every new market segment, including the one children make up for they are tomorrow's teenagers.[7] As Clyde Miller says in his book, *The Process of Persuasion*:

> It takes time, yes, but if you expect to be in business for any length of time, think of what it can mean to your firm in profits, if you can condition a million or ten million children who will grow up into adults trained to buy your product as soldiers are trained to advance when they hear the trigger words, 'forward march'.[8]

Seen from this perspective, every child represents an opportunity for advertisers, since one day that child will become a consumer. The child must, therefore, be groomed, tutored and 'programmed' into wanting to own and use material products that advertisers make it their business to promote.

Logically, if this approach proves successful, then by the time children reach an age when they can make market decisions for themselves and have the means and financial independence to purchase what they want, there will be a ready-made army of consumers that will respond automatically—by training and force of habit—to an advertisement every time a new product invades the market or an old one comes back with a facelift.

This is not a very charming account of what growing up in a consumerist society could mean for our children. The fact is, however, that teaching children to become consumers is a task which (a) consumerism as a social ethic makes imperative; (b) TV carries forward with tremendous success; and (c) advertising designs a curriculum for, working both on the content and form of a lifelong consumer orientation course which begins during infancy and is an enjoyable learning experience.

ROLES CHILDREN PLAY

Market research agencies tell us that as the child grows up he/she moves through several phases before eventually becoming an independent consumer. Each of these developmental stages is seen as critical for, as any school-teacher will tell us, early learning lays the foundations for lifelong education. The advertiser, like the parent and the school-teacher, can influence the entire process by which a child learns to establish consumption-related values, sets priorities and develops aspirations. Like an unseen presence, advertising is always there, invisibly guiding the child in these critical, formative years. During infancy the child is principally an information receiver. Advertising selects the information and ideas which will promote a certain kind of consciousness in the child.

As children move up the age and cognitive development ladder, they advance to the persuasion phase. Not yet decision-makers, and still without the means to buy most products advertised on television, children resort to requesting or demanding that their parents buy these things for them.[9]

Children of different ages, socio-economic and educational backgrounds relate differently to the world of material things. Some may focus only on their actual needs and desires—demanding toys, foods, clothes and accessories that they can directly consume;

others may be pushed by advertising and by their level of affluence into demanding bigger things—television sets, telephones, air conditioners and even cars.

The television is a new and powerful entrant into the field of influences; it has muscled in on family life and from that vantage point, plays one of the most powerful roles in a child's life. It is muscling in on other primary influences such as the family and school. Television offers an opportunity to extend this influence, and sets visual standards which the child unconsciously imbibes and consciously imitates. Advertising on television creates a special kind of classroom where the teacher lurks behind a sales counter.

However, advertisers cannot be held solely responsible for tutoring children in the ways of the materialistic world. They are the 'agents' hired to promote almost single-mindedly the interests of the major economic and business forces in a market economy. In fact, one of the main objections to commercialising television was eloquently argued by the Beveridge Committee on BBC. According to its report:

> We reject any suggestion that broadcasting in Britain should become financially dependent on sponsoring as it is wholly in the U.S. and largely in Canada and Australia. Sponsoring carried to that point puts the control of broadcasting ultimately in the hands of people whose interest is not broadcasting but the selling of some other goods or services and the propaganda of particular ideas.[10]

IMPACT OF CONSUMERISM

The sovereign nations shall cross the great mountain range
With offerings of tooth cleaners and coloured water
And of all the native merchants peddling their 200 decade secrets
Of clove oil and coloured water
None but a few shining stars will last.[11]

Advertising is commonly regarded as a business of persuasion which sets about to alter our most basic patterns of consumption.

Socially, it encourages the development of a new and different culture to uphold the changing needs of producers who must sell their wares. Often these contradict existing views on social behaviour, alter societal interaction and overturn guiding principles. In other words, the value system required by consumerism may need to push aside those values that do not fit the cut of its cloth. If, for example, we once considered the stem of the neem tree (many by-products of the neem are today being widely marketed in the West) the best toothbrush, then advertisers had to alter that perception and devalue the traditional stick in order to sell their array of toothbrushes and toothpastes.

For millions of Indians the neem was just another a commonplace tree: no one needed to pay to keep their teeth clean. Moreover, until a few years ago, it was axiomatic that Indians had very good teeth and maintained them well. Similarly, Indians habitually rinsed their mouths after eating a meal or even a snack. Now, television advertising has begun promoting the charms of mouth washes for bad breath; and soon, no doubt we will be gargling with antiseptics rather than water after each meal!

In much the same way, the advertisers' ideal of a consumption unit varies from what might be socially the norm. For instance, the concept of sharing is definitely out. A few years ago, a businessman in Delhi who was speaking to a group of wide-eyed students training for a challenging career, veered off into a discourse on advertising. He felt that advertising was the most important, creative and vital vehicle of change in India (as indeed it has proved to be). Advertising, he said, had the power to alter the course of the nation (India) and completely transform the way people thought. He then rationally and logically explained how advertising could achieve what seemed the impossible:

1. The most ideal consumption unit, as advertisers and manu-facturers, saw it, was the individual.
2. If the advertiser/manufacturer could sell to every individual a long list of household items and personal products, the size of the Indian market would be even more staggering than currently estimated.
3. Given this view, the joint family is not something that ena-mours or interests the advertiser. In such families, there is too much sharing of commodities between too many people.

4. Therefore, the advertiser's first job is to promote the concept of nuclear families, though this has to be done gently and by projecting this unit through visuals which have layers of meaning and ostensibly leave viewers free to interpret the ultimate message as they choose. Eventually, the process would lead up to focusing on individuals, be they single parents or even unmarried persons.

As our study has found, children acquire knowledge about many things from advertising. Today, the most dramatic changes in their way of thinking are reflected in their approach to clothes, to concepts of beauty, to their commitment to a certain lifestyle images of which are being constantly superimposed upon their minds through television. The point we wish to emphasise is that TV advertising reinforces certain patterns of consumption by presenting a visual, modelling perspective.

For instance, if in 1990 there were 42 popular soaps, 93 premium soaps, 116 brands of edible oils, and 81 brands of tea in the Indian market, only a handful of these could afford to advertise on television. Those that did, however, communicated one basic message to the young child: that soaps, oils and tea were important consumption items. As Charles Atkin notes, 'TV commercials may stimulate greater consumption of other brands within the generic product class' since there are very few unique aspects to individual products.[12]

THE SPREAD OF CONSUMERISM: DELHI

Commenting on the spread of consumerism, a leading Indian publication wrote that Napolean once allegedly called the English a nation of shopkeepers. Now this is certainly becoming true about the 'jewel in the crown'. During the last decade, consumerism has invaded the country like 'an untamed virus, to the point where there seem to be only three kinds of people: those who own shops, those who shop and those who do both. Delhi is at the forefront, in the sheer number of devotees at the altar of consumerism.'

In 1993, Delhi's population stood at 9.5 million and it is considered to be one of the most swiftly growing cities in India. Alongside, or perhaps leading this consumer boom, is the growth of Delhi's advertising industry (estimated at Rs. 350 crores last year). According to print media assessments, the advertising business in the Capital is growing at a much faster rate than Bombay, which continues to be India's Madison Avenue.[13]

Delhi, with its strong tradition of being the largest market for loans, has responded to the flooding of its shops with consumer durables by creating widespread instalment schemes that encourage even the 'have-nots' to succumb to temptation. As a city, it leads in car sales and the penetration of washing machines is apparently recording amazing figures. Women and children are prime targets: the women of Delhi are believed to be highest users of cosmetics such as lipsticks, in the entire country. Following a major survey, completed a few years ago by the Bombay-based Pathfinders, on children's media habits, attitudes and their role in decision-making, marketers began to openly acknowledge that in their business 'you can't but take children seriously'.

How successful is the advertisement in its role as the 'hidden persuader', as Vance Packard once called it? If our survey is anything to go by, extremely successful. Children are being groomed into becoming future consumers—they are already in the demand-and-supply framework and advertisements are doing all they can to influence their choices.

14

WHAT TV ADVERTISING SELLS

The merchant of dreams will arrive too
With his 'ten commandments' and his merry tunes
And his allies shall supply him all his needs
For his credo to be embraced by all around.[14]

If we accept that consumerism is being presented (especially by TV ads) as a 'way of life' that should ideally become the norm for every individual, then it is useful to investigate the main characteristics of this presentation. Moreover, children's reactions to television advertising are best understood within the context of *what* television commercials are selling; the kind of orientation they provide to the young and the priorities they set by repeatedly drawing attention to certain categories of products.

In examining the role that television advertising plays in promoting consumerism, one inescapable conclusion we arrived at was that television advertising is a highly selective process, and directs consumer attention to a very limited number of product categories. These account for the overwhelming majority of commercials.

While classifying Doordarshan advertising during the summer of 1992, we were able to identify the main areas of its focus. Not surprisingly, we found that advertisements for less expensive, daily use commodities dominate the TV screen. They fall into product categories which appeal to a larger market segment than do, for example, up-market durables. In other words, many consumers could be persuaded to buy items from the main shopping list prepared by television advertising *because* they are the most affordable, e.g., soaps and toiletries, personal care products and food/beverage items.

Most TV commercials, as our classification shows, were—and continue to be—for non-durable products. There is also a fair amount of advertising for commodities which are described as durables, but hardly any for services or for investment schemes; and there are even fewer corporate ads. Apart from these, there are public service advertisements (PSAs) which are designed to raise social awareness. PSAs are on the advertising agenda of most TV networks across the globe.

We taped a total of 1,166 advertisements appearing on Doordarshan over four weeks. The week-wise break-down of this figure was:

(6 April to 3 May 1992)

No. of Advertisements

Week one	=	267
Week two	=	288
Week three	=	318
Week four	=	293
Total	=	1,166

The kind of commercials and the product categories advertised are listed in Table 14.1.

Table 14.1

Kinds of Commercials and Product Categories Advertised

Week	Durable	Non-Durable	Public Service	Corporate Sector	Service Sector	Invest-ment
One	45	204	18	–	–	–
Two	56	209	21	–	2	–
Three	56	242	12	5	1	2
Four	47	220	21	3	–	2
Total	204	875	72	8	3	4

The break-down suggests that the world of material goods presented by TV commercials consists largely of an array of consumer non-durables, including major product groups such as soaps, toiletries, cosmetics and foodstuffs. As the figures show, commercials for these categories overshadow all other categories. Our findings revealed that the role of such advertising is not limited to creating awareness only about the goods promoted by it. Instead, its function extends to encouraging a generic interest in consumption which augurs well for *all* products—and *especially* the more expensive durables. If we look carefully at each advertisement for non-durable commodities, we find that incorporated in it is a holistic vision of life—one which embraces and is sanctioned by the possession of many other products and the promises they hold out. For example, the advertisement for the cold drink Mirinda serves the interests of a wide range of manufacturers: it deliberately or inadvertently spawns an interest in cars, jeans and other accoutrements; it familiarises us with modern pop music and it suggests of course, that fun is waiting to bubble out of every fizzy drink on offer.

The fact that there is almost no variation in the pattern and emphasis of advertising from week to week implies that the consumption pattern this could be promoting is heavily loaded in favour of items of 'inconspicuous consumption'—products that satisfy an urge here and now.

NON-DURABLES

Commodities that are not meant to last but to be immediately consumed are the most difficult to resist. They do not call for any major investment but represent instead a short-lived but immediate gratification.

Many of them fall within the realm of things we use everyday, such as soaps and detergents. Soap is a category important to all stratas of society: the size and scope of the market is therefore huge. The wide range of choices (in each price bracket) presented by TV commercials makes this an area of advertising that appeals to most viewers. Although it can be argued that no one needs expensive or scented beauty soaps to be clean and that a cheap, ordinary brand or natural soap will do the job equally well, the soap industry does everything in its power to tell you differently so that it can ensure the sales of the latest brands.

At the same time, in order to increase the popularity of the brands they promote, advertisers pitch their sales at different kinds of consumers: there is a soap for the man who has to oversee work at a construction site (Nirma Bath), the woman who wants to look forever young (Santoor), the man whose body odour deters the pursuit of an office romance (Lifebuoy), and soaps for those who believe they can look as enchanting as Dimple Kapadia (Lux).

Of the advertisements we taped, 75 per cent were for non-durable commodities. The classification reveals that the overwhelming majority of them represent five major groups of commodities: toiletries, detergents, cold drinks and foodstuffs, cosmetics, and health products. The Audience Research Unit of Doordarshan confirms this analysis: according to it, in 1993 advertisements for toiletries alone accounted for 30.1 per cent of the ad share followed by food/beverage ads which had a 21.1 per cent share. Of course, soap-based products rule the TV commercials empire.

The monopoly of this small range of product categories is matched by the monopoly over TV advertising of a few companies: in 1992–93, the two major advertisers on television were Hindustan Lever and Proctor and Gamble. Between them, these companies produce almost all the soaps and detergents purchased by the Indian consumer.

CONSUMER DURABLES

Deriving satisfaction from non-durable items is just a first, small step for the consumer. The big buys still lie ahead. Television commercials for consumer durables come in a very poor second and many stories appearing in the Indian press suggest that this is largely because these items are still beyond the reach of millions of Indians whereas soaps, detergents and fizzy drinks can be and are bought by almost all segments of society.

Whether the market size justifies the cost of putting out these commercials or not, the fact remains that everyone (even those who cannot yet buy such household durables) is being educated about their existence. As our data will show, people are learning to view these goods as tomorrow's essential purchases. The products in this category contribute to household comfort and convenience and range from kitchenware, mixer-blenders, TV sets, music systems, washing machines and air conditioners to cars, motor-cycles and cycles. Television ads constantly tell viewers that these products can make a world of difference to their lives. There is not much competition on Doordarshan in the consumer durable ad category although different television brands do vie with one another for viewer attention. Many of the commercials for these products inspire the ultimate consumer dream of belonging to the rich man's world, and carefully place the gadgets they are selling in very luxurious surroundings—the Tata Estate car or a brand new Maruti accompanied by either a tuxedoed male or a woman in a ballgown.

Quick to notice the impact of their commercials on the minds and hearts of the middle income consumers, advertisers are always in search of the right images to use. In TV advertising this amorphous social group includes the daughter-in-law who pleases her husband's family by investing in the 'right' pressure cooker, the one who correctly chooses Parachute Oil for her hair, as well as the one who uses a Videocon washing machine. Among other products that target a large part of the middle class are Bajaj scooters and VIP suitcases.

CORPORATE, SERVICE AND INVESTMENT ADVERTISING

A tiny number of the ads we reviewed were made to promote a corporation (Tata Steel, for instance) or a service (Mastercard or other credit cards). Some encouraged public investment (Gold Bonds and IPCL Issue). However, given current trends and the fact that Doordarshan's competitors—satellite TV—are busy putting out ads for banks, business houses (Mitsubishi, Matsushita) and an array of services including airlines and telecom services, it seems likely that the percentage of similar ads on Doordarshan will increase.

15

RESPONSES TO ADVERTISING

In the first and second parts of this book we have argued that children learn (almost subconsciously) from television. If 75 per cent of all television advertisements are for products such as soaps, foods and beverages, toiletries and cosmetics, then logically these are the products that children learn to desire although not all of them are of direct or special interest to them.

Before we go into children's responses to TV advertising, we would like to state that our study leaves us in no doubt about the success of TV ads with children, a fact that emerges from their high level of desire to own commodities they see in commercials. The following data confirms this. Asked if they would like to *own* some of the products they saw advertised on television, the percentage of children from the three age groups who replied in the affirmative was as follows:

Age Group 1 (5 to 8 years):   63.93 per cent
Age Group 2 (8 to 12 years):   73.69 per cent
Age Group 3 (13 to 15 years):   75.00 per cent

Evidently, the ambition to own advertised products increases with age. This is partly explained by the fact that as children approach an age of active consumerism, they already have more money of their own to spend (be it pocket money or monetary gifts received on various occasions). They also develop, as our data shows, a greater interest in products that represent the adult world—cars, scooters, motorcycles, credit cards, clothes—and more importantly, they begin to see themselves as miniature versions of the consuming adult who invariably has a list of 'I want' and 'I will have'.

The figures presented above seem to indicate that advertising strategies created with the child and the teenager in mind are meeting their objectives. Not only are they successfully breeding a generation of consumers ready to respond to the call of consumerism, they are also creating an avid interest in material goods that hardly relate to the needs of a child—credit cards, airlines and designer wear. As mentioned earlier, unlike in the West, in India there is no demarcation between children's TV and children's advertising as opposed to the same for adults. Children watch a lot of TV with their parents and consequently see and absorb the same kinds of advertising messages as do the adults. (This is not to suggest that child-specific advertising in any way promotes a healthy attitude to consumerism.)

The break-down of responses by social class present some interesting findings. In the 8 to 15 years age group, nearly 80 per cent of children from the middle class said they wanted advertised products while children from the upper and lower classes reacted less enthusiastically—58.79 per cent upper class: 60.23 per cent lower class.

However, in the youngest of our respondents (those in the 5 to 8 years age group) and their families, it was lower class children who were most keen to have the goodies in television's window display. Parents and elders of almost 40 per cent of them said that their children pestered them to purchase products advertised on television. Interestingly, these little ones showed a high degree of interest in soaps, toiletries and cosmetics—a clear indication that the quantum of advertising for these commodities spurs an interest in them. Upper class children in the 5 to 8 years age group were, according to their parents, not as demanding, recording a figure of only 16.66 per cent as opposed to 25.59 per cent of middle class parents who said that their children often urged them to buy advertised products. Of the total sample in this age group, 80 per cent (a figure that matches the responses from the older age group) said they were influenced by TV commercials and wanted to own advertised commodities.

A school principal was eager to discuss the reactions of his students to our questions. He was convinced that children today were possessed by the 'I want' philosophy and did not realise that they were 'being conned.' Parents pointed out that people of their generation (the generation of Indians born in the thirties) were always taught to say 'No, thank you' but that this attitude is now a thing of the past. Other parents said: 'When there is so much available and everyone is interested in acquiring new things, how can children be immune to desire?' A few were anxious and said: 'Of course our children want things that get advertised. We do our best.' Others said their children were still unaffected by an obsession with the marketplace.

As mentioned in Part Two, our classification looks at three types of appeal that TV advertising holds for the child viewer: Ads that appeal *directly* to the child; ads that appeal *indirectly* to the child; ads which *use* children to appeal to a larger consumer audience. These assign the following roles to the child as consumer:

1. The first group corresponds to the role of children as consumers to whom a certain set of *commodities of direct relevance* (toys, sweets, etc.), appeal.
2. The second group corresponds to the role of the child as a future consumer. This group includes ads for all products that are *not of immediate relevance* to the child including as cars, refrigerators, tyres, cooking oils, etc.
3. The last group corresponds to the role of the child as actor, participant and salesperson. In this group are all the ads that feature children.

BEST ADS

Having established that a very large proportion of children who watch TV end up aspiring to become active consumers, we now turn to the advertisements children said they liked best of all. From this list it is possible to assess the kind of advertising and advertising messages that have the greatest impact on children. The list of the top 12 favourite advertisements chosen by the children in our sample comprised the following products:

1. Ariel—Detergent
2. Citra—Soft drink
3. Lehar Pepsi—Soft drink
4. British Airways—Airline
5. Apollo Tyres—Tyre
6. Eveready—Battery

7. Blue Seal
8. Bajaj—Scooter
9. BSA SLR—Cycle
10. Le Sancy—Soap
11. Thai Airways—Airline
12. 7 Up—Soft drink

The list drawn up by the children represents no fairy-tale world. Their modern-day dreams are not filled with sweets, toys and exciting games. Indeed, while children will be children and will enjoy, want, and even pester their parents to acquire many fun things, they are at the same time looking way beyond and longing to play the adult consumer.

As the list reveals, five out of the 12 products named fall into the non-durable category. For the rest, the choice is rather eclectic. Children's obsession with cold drinks helps this product category break past the whole range of consumer choices to emerge as a winner.

However, with Ariel topping the list, the brand certainly deserves special mention. This advertisement has succeeded so well with children that it stays on top of the list under any and every category. The popularity of the Le Sancy ad has already been dealt with in Part Two.

The most important fact that can be gleaned from the list is that children are most definitely being oriented towards the big buys and towards material goods and services that they believe will become essential to them in adulthood. As we can see, two airlines figure on the list of the most admired commercials. Our discussions with children confirmed that flying out and away is believed to be a one-way ticket to success. The interest in airlines reflects this thinking and there is nothing the children would like better than to be executive class customers. A recent Marg–Eyewitness survey conducted at the end of 1993 in the metropolitan cities found that 90 per cent of their respondents, including children, wanted to study or work abroad—a sentiment which seems in keeping with their appreciation of airline ads.

The choice of tyre, battery and scooter ads seems to indicate that the high tension, excitement and aggression played on by most of these commercials to attracts children, particularly teenagers. Challenging and tempestuous, such emotions guarantee a heightened response from the young and appear to ensure better recall.

Our discussions with children about their favourite ads can be summed up thus: While the affluent child in the 8 to 15 years age bracket is very impressed by ads for Mastercard, airlines, hotels and banks, the lower class child is dreaming of washing machines, TVs and refrigerators. The middle class child wants practically the entire gamut of available goods and desire is apt to be dictated by mood, peer group obsession and environment.

DOMINANT ADVERTISING

To get back to the thrust of advertising on television and its resultant impact on the child viewer: Focusing specifically on dominant categories in TV commercials, we asked children about their reactions to soap and toiletry ads. Though such ads are not primarily aimed at children, they are avidly watched by them, resulting, as we found, in a high degree of interest and participation by the children in the products their parents purchase.

A majority of children in the combined age groups (65 per cent) said that they wanted to 'try' or 'use' many soaps, detergents and personal care products advertised on television. New brands enticed younger children more than others and over 80 per cent said they asked for brands they had seen on TV.

Noticeably, too, the girls evinced more interest in these items than boys (68.91 per cent: 59.95 per cent), responding perhaps to the orientation of the advertisements which target the woman who, in her many roles as mother, wife, daughter-in-law and daughter, manages the well-being and cleanliness of the home and simultaneously tries to always look beautiful. (A superwoman, no doubt!)

The impact of these ads—which sell, along with cleanliness, concepts of beauty and status as part of the purchase—was greatest amongst children of the lower classes. There was also, we found, a direct relationship between the advertising on television and the purchase of the products concerned. Almost every single toiletry/cosmetic item listed by our respondents as 'a recent household purchase' was one that had been recently advertised on TV. Look at the ad campaigns for new products—Le Sancy, Evita and Ganga soaps—all three brands were launched and prominently advertised on TV in the autumn/early winter of 1992—just a few months before we conducted our fieldwork. All three figured repeatedly in the children's lists of recent purchases—Evita and Le Sancy getting mention from the upper and middle classes and Ganga from less advantaged children.

Judging from the variety of responses we received (some children listed as many as four brands of soap as having been recently bought), the promise of soft, perfumed skins, everlasting freshness and beauty (and conversely, the fear of smelling and looking un-attractive), propounded by advertisers responsible for the notice-able flux in brand selection. Every time a new option appears in the market, consumers, especially children, are led to believe that the new product on offer will bring better results. Only a few children stated that their parents were die-hards and that the household had stuck to its old favourites: Lux, Colgate, Hamam, Lifebuoy.

The Big Buys

We are still dealing here with goods and products that are not aimed at the child. Commercials for durable commodities such as televisions, refrigerators and a host of other household goods account for only a small proportion of TV ads. What sort of impact do these have on children?

Children have come to believe that not only must *we* look attractive, but so must our homes. Material comfort is high on their aspirational agenda. This understanding is not accidentally acquired but stems, as we shall see, from the images that speak to children from the TV screen.

Two examples come to mind. One of a 16-year-old girl who claimed to be battling furiously with her parents for a telephone connection in her room. The other is of some 15-year-old girls who wanted to break free and be transported magically into another world. These girls, who belonged to underprivileged homes, told us that they had no conveniences at home—no TV, no cupboards, no gas. Shyly they confided that their greatest dream was to get married to 'escape' from hardship and that above all else, they wanted to live in attractive homes. To every question we asked, they responded by saying they wanted 'things' with which to beautify their homes. These were, they said, a Godrej almirah, a proper bed, a sofa set and, of course, a television set.

Clearly the aspirations and needs of the Indian market are undergoing a change. According to a survey conducted by the Indian Market Research Bureau, in households with a monthly income of over Rs. 1000, '74 per cent own some form of transportation, 82 per cent own some means of entertainment and 86 per cent own at least one household appliance'.[15]

To gain a better understanding of the way their minds were working, we listed 11 items—all durables—and asked which of them the children thought they would like to own or have in their homes, now or later when they grew up. Many children looked at the list and simply exclaimed: 'All!' Others said, 'We already have all of these.'

Putting together the responses of our 8 to 15 years old respondents, we derived the following list by order of preference and priority:

1.	TV	63.97 per cent
2.	Fridge	46.71 per cent
3.	Washing Machine	45.00 per cent
4.	Music System	43.42 per cent
5.	Cooler	40.27 per cent
6.	Two-in-one	40.13 per cent
7.	VCR	40.13 per cent
8.	Mixer	39.39 per cent
9.	Air Conditioner	30.27 per cent
10.	Vacuum Cleaner	27.67 per cent
11.	Syntex	21.23 per cent

If there were any doubts about the importance of the TV set in the lives of our children, the fact that it figures as their number one priority (although almost every child we met had a TV set at home) confirms that they cannot imagine life without it. And, if they had the option and the means, they would prefer to acquire more than one set.

Refrigerators are given a special place on the priority list largely because middle and lower class children are realistic enough to choose basic household conveniences above the more luxurious ones (such as air conditioners and vacuum cleaners) which consequently fall on the overall list to the ninth and tenth positions.

Only upper class children place an air conditioner way ahead of a refrigerator, a mixer and a Syntex water tank.

Washing machines are in a bracket of their own and, as we have mentioned, are especially attractive as a convenience to those children from less advantaged backgrounds who appreciate their usefulness. Significantly, as many young boys as girls said they would like to see their mother's burden of chores relieved by the acquisition of a washing machine.

The music system gets high priority almost by default, as it is largely upper class children for whom it holds such importance. However, as discussed in Part Two, the growing popularity especially of modern music, has extended the interest in this expensive piece of equipment so that children from the middle class also hope, one day, to own such a system.

Coolers, two-in-ones and VCRs are important to different social groups reflecting both need and aspiration. The VCR is, interestingly, given equal priority by all class groups indicating that they share a common desire for increased TV viewing options.

Air conditioners and vacuum cleaners are evidently considered to be the rich man's preserve. The vacuum cleaner continues to be an enigma, its purpose still unclear to most lower and even some middle class children.

Table 15.1
Relevance of Advertised Goods by Class

Upper Class	Middle Class	Lower Class
1. Music system	1. TV	1. TV
2. Air conditioner	2. Refrigerator	2. Refrigerator
3. TV	3. Washing machine	3. Cooler
4. Washing machine	4. Music system	4. Washing machine
5. VCR	5. VCR	5. VCR
6. Two-in-one	6. Mixer	6. Mixer
7. Refrigerator	7. Two-in-one	7. Two-in-one
8. Vacuum cleaner	8. Air conditioner	8. Syntex tank
9. Mixer	9. Vacuum cleaner	9. Music system
10. Cooler	10. Cooler	10. Air conditioner
11. Syntex tank	11. Syntex tank	11. Vacuum cleaner

The poor Syntex tank, for all its essential utility, is too mundane for upper and middle class children to concern themselves with. It is noteworthy that the less fortunate children (for whom, even in Delhi, safe drinking water is a priceless commodity), have placed the tank above owning a music system, air conditioner and vacuum cleaner.

This list of durable commodities, now very visible in the markets of the capital and well known to most children, is easy to assess from the viewpoint of social class and the varying priorities that different households have. The relevance or irrelevance of these goods becomes apparent in Table 15.1.

ATTITUDES TO THE CHILD IN INDIA

In India the child was, and still is, seen as a blessing, especially the male child. A large number of families continue to be 'child oriented' and believe that they must invest in the future generation. Interacting with many families in Delhi, we found that parents across the board were, by and large, prepared to make sacrifices to see their children happy. Many parents said that they would like to give their children things they had not been able to enjoy in their own childhood. 'Dream fulfilment' through children seems to exemplify this attitude.

In a *basti* of south Delhi, parents admitted to having bought a TV set just to please their children. In another case, a family with only one child, a seven-year old girl, had also bought a TV set to make her happy. 'We have only one life. If we can't make our children happy, fulfil their dreams and desires, then what have we achieved?' asked the mother.

In middle class families indulgence is a common phenomenon and a large number of parents told us they hated saying 'no' to their children. Yet, although today some parents are compelled to put their foot down, this does not come easily to them.

Among children of affluent homes, the story is a bit confusing. On one end of the spectrum are parents who put a car and driver at the service of their children and make sure they have enough cash on them to satisfy every desire. A 14-year old who received a car on his birthday had, we were told, acquired an awesome image. His opening line became, 'Hi, I'm . . . . I have a Tata Sierra. Want a ride with me?' The girls swooned as he zipped down the road with a flourish.

FIGURE 15.1

Preferences of 5 to 15 Year Olds for Household Durables

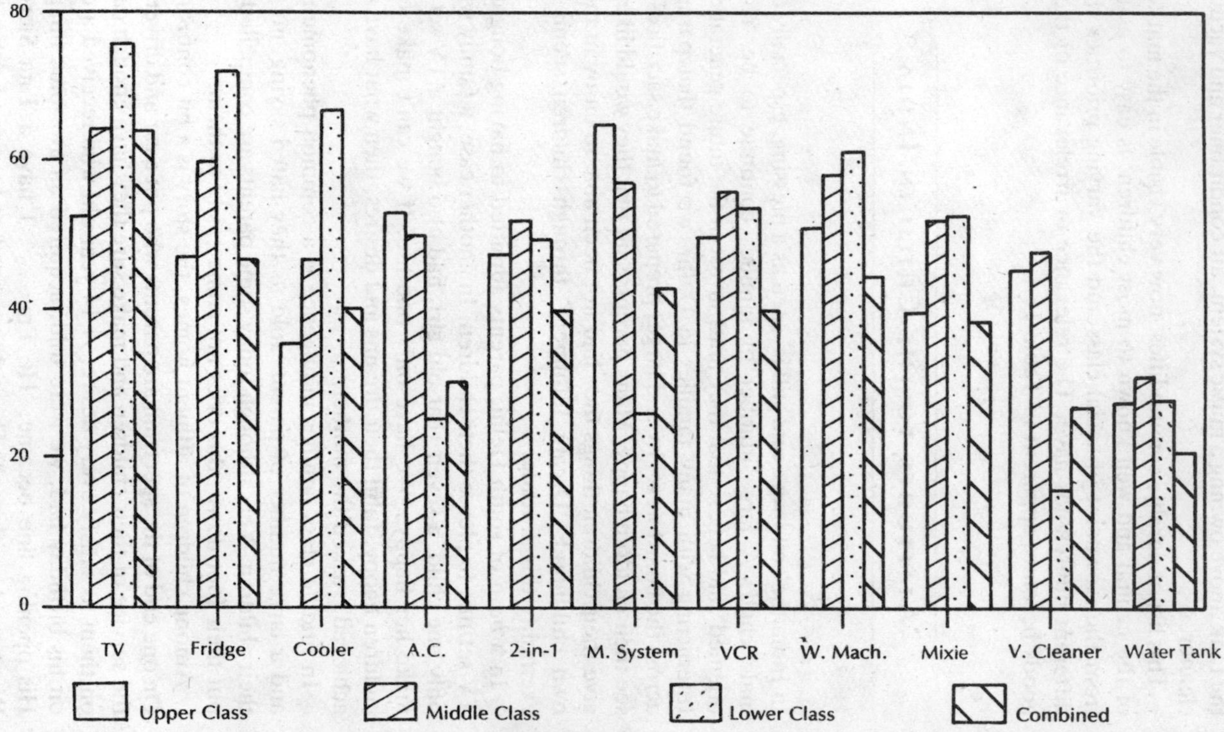

At the other end of the upper class spectrum are children who may be sheltered and cosseted but whose environment remains fairly disciplined and unostentatious. Money is spent on books, on swimming lessons, on acquisition of skills and on travel. Television, mindless shopping and overindulgence are not encouraged.

The point here is that parental attitudes help determine children's relationship with the world: values emanating from influences outside the home are likely to be judged against those nurtured by the home environment. For instance, although children may watch a lot of advertising, their response to it could be tempered or exacerbated, as the case might be, by parental attitudes. However, the pressures on both the parent and child are indeed immense. Not until the excitement of such a sudden spurt in consumerism dies down will parents find it easy to handle their children's desires.

How Parents Respond to Children's Demands

With an environment that is becoming increasingly consumer conscious, it is likely, as our data confirms, that children now want more of everything. And they get it too.

Over 80 per cent of the children in the 8 to 15 years age group told us that their parents gave in to their demands and bought them what they asked for, while 55.73 per cent of the 5 to 8-year olds said their demands were met. Children in the older age groups had indicated that they ask for more products than younger ones. While these responses by and large hold true for children both from the upper and middle class households, the figure drops by about 20 per cent when it comes to lower class responses.

Our experience shows that parents find it harder to handle children's demands as they grow older. The high level of parental accession to children's demands may well be linked to the fact that the older child is more forceful and demanding as a consumer. This also leads to parent–child conflicts.

As for younger children, their parents told us that it was in the marketplace where the goodies were most visible that they found it difficult to curb their offspring's demands. In the 5 to 8 years age group, several mothers indicated that it was the fathers who indulged in the whims and fancies of their children.

With the exception of children from very affluent families who only visit markets when they are on shopping sprees, we found that most children in Delhi have a very active association with the marketplace. By and large, the children know the market quite well. Many contribute to household duties by doing the daily shopping for milk, bread, eggs, biscuits, cold drinks and so on. Some accompany their mothers to the shops fairly regularly.

The demands made by children and the response of parents to them is something that needs to be carefully watched. Not only can this become an area of conflict, it can also lay the ground for dissatisfaction in children who might feel that they have been deprived. On the other hand, without monitoring their children's purchase requests, a parent cannot hope to limit these.

TV commercials, as we have seen, are responsible for putting consumption ideas into the heads of children. According to Charles Atkins, there are

> several ways that commercials may contribute to unhappy feelings among young viewers: (a) when advertising-induced requests are denied or unobtainable, children may become angry and upset; (b) when the child's own social or psychological condition is less satisfactory than life situations portrayed in the commercial, dissatisfaction may result; and (c) when ads create high expectation regarding the performance of products, actual experience with the product that falls short of anticipation may engender disappointment.[16]

These anxieties are reflected by the Code for Commercial Advertising on Doordarshan which warns advertisers against creating such ads as might 'lead children to believe that if they do not own or use the product advertised they will be inferior in some way to other children or that they are liable to be condemned or ridiculed for not owning or using it'. The Code goes on to list all the things that an advertisement appearing on TV should not encourage.[17] Yet, as we are all aware, advertising does in fact promote such feelings, though perhaps indirectly. An obvious example is the ad for Barbie dolls with its slogan: 'Every doll deserves a Barbie'.

Discussing their desire for new products, we asked children if they ever fought with their parents over their acquisition. The responses were interesting in that they were extremely low. While 80 per cent asked for new products, just over 20 per cent admitted that they argued, pestered or even fought with their parents for them. However, the figures for the 5 to 8 years age group were higher, with more than 45 per cent saying that they threw tantrums for the things they wanted, a response that was more often than not prompted by an elder. (Think back to the children's serial on STAR Plus: *Little Wonder*. Harriet, the girl next door tutors Vicky the robot-child on how to throw a tantrum, what to demand and how to ensure parents give in.)

The low figures for the 8 to 15 years age group suggest either that children are still very obedient and are capable of postponing gratification or, that they do not like to admit fighting with their parents, something which is considered disrespectful.

In our assessment, many children have begun to associate happiness with owning or possessing a toy or with simply being indulged. Several children from middle to upper class backgrounds told us that they loved to 'show off' their latest acquisitions in school where there were always some children who outdid them and kept the consumer momentum alive.

When children find that the things they see and want are beyond their economic reach or are not being bought by their parents, they experience a sense of disappointment, rejection, anger, frustration and even anxiety. Whereas the lower class child may want popular sweets to share with other children in school and consequently feel desolated if parents cannot afford them, a middle class child feels mortified when parents do not rush out to buy them the latest sneakers that everyone else is wearing.

16

CHILDREN'S ADVERTISING

Advertisers have known for years that children's television and children's advertising are an important aspect of marketing strategy. As we have stated in Part One, what this suggests is that advertisers use a two-step process to target children. The child is first brought to the advertiser's doorstep by programming which is directed at and meant for children—this could be anything from cartoons to children's films, serials and other entertainment programmes. When the child is safely glued to the TV set, the advertiser steps in with a series of commercials for products that a child is expected to be interested in: toys, sweets and chocolates, cycles and even foodstuffs and beverages, hoping to make enough impact to send the child scurrying off with a new request.

In its survey on children's media habits Pathfinders had concluded that the growing interest that manufacturers and advertisers were expressing in the choices that children made or did not make, stemmed from the fact that children now have more money at their disposal, that they can, and do, influence family choices and, lastly, that they need to be worked upon if the purpose is to instil brand loyalty. 'Catch them young' is the motto of today's ad world and, as we can see, not only is there more and more child specific advertising but also if we take all the channels available into account there is more programming to bring children closer to their TV sets.[18]

By the early nineties advertisers had begun to create and use slots on TV for appealing almost exclusively to children, embedding tiny seeds of desire in the mind of the child viewer. As our classification shows, over 30 per cent of the ads being aired on Doordarshan in the summer of 1992 were, aimed at children and that too for child-specific products. Many other ads appeal to children indirectly, but in this chapter we shall deal with those related to products meant for children and children's responses to them.

Most children, particularly the younger ones, would share the view that the world of sweets, chocolates, ice creams, soft drinks and, of course, toys is *their* world. These products matter to them. They feel uplifted when they hear 'I think you're just right for Amul chocolates' or 'Yes, Vadilal is what it takes to bring the smile back on your face'. Today's child in Delhi is tempted by a whole world of goods that goes beyond the one advertised on TV—shoes, books, accessories such as pencil boxes (the array of these is bewildering), water bottles, attractive tiffin boxes and so on.

Looking over the questionnaires filled up by our respondents, we found that 'fun foods' which TV advertising promotes so assiduously was one of their high-spend areas. Items such as fizzy drinks, biscuits, jams, pickles, condensed milk, ice cream, chocolates, sweets, tomato sauces, instant noodles, etc., are the main food products advertised on Indian television.

The question arises: what does television teach children about nutrition? From a health and nutrition angle, none of these products fit the bill, particularly for children whose normal daily intake is not balanced. In the United States, where nearly every household had a television set by the sixties, and where the advertising for almost exactly the same range of foods has been the norm, efforts have been made to point out that focusing the child viewer's attention on such foods serves to reshape their nutritional beliefs and to influence their food choices to the detriment of their physical development and nutritional requirements.

The Center for Science in the Public Interest (CSPI), a U.S.-based organisation, conducted a survey of advertising on children's TV in February 1992 and found that out of a total of 433 commercials and public service announcements, food ads and PSAs accounted for 61 per cent of ad time in the 8 a.m. to 12 noon programming slot on Saturdays. The study noted that in 1992 (as in 1991) there were no. paid ads for fresh fruit, fresh vegetables, bread and other nutritious food such as fish. 'More than nine out of ten food ads on Saturday morning television are for sugary cereals and candy bars, salty canned foods, fatty fast foods and chips, and other nutritionally flawed foods.' The CSPI report commented: 'How sad that when many adult Americans are trying to change unhealthy eating habits, junk food marketers saturate the Saturday morning airwaves with appeals to youngsters to consume foods that put their health at risk.'[19]

It can be argued that since there are no ads for fresh fruits and vegetables, for real milk, fish, meats and other nutritious foods, nor any warnings that tell viewers that the consumption of only or large quantities of the products advertised on television can be injurious to health, the information that is being communicated by TV advertising about food is misleading and incomplete.

A working mother complained that her children refused to go to school without a box full of potato chips. They brought back the 'food' she packed. 'Its sick', she said, 'and I cannot really afford it'.

Unfortunately, these advertisements have placed a high premium on the foods and beverages they promote by suggesting that consumption of these items is the best way to have 'fun', the most fashionable thing to do and that these foods, like so much else that is sold today, are symbols of modernity. This message has, without doubt, got across and many of the children who said they spend their money on food, added that their idea of having fun and enjoying themselves was to be able to eat or drink with their friends.

Of course, it is also true that the new fast food culture of pizzas and hamburgers has influenced indigenous foods as well, to the extent that the concept now applies in equal measure to foods like dosas. There are many other Indian foods that are now being included in the list of pre-cooked, quick foods to compete with the home delivered pizzas and the TV dinners so famous in the West. Certainly, some of them offer healthier nutritional options.

We know that as advertisers pay more attention to the child as a consumer, the quantum of this kind of advertising is likely to grow. For the present, child-specific advertising is meeting with mixed responses. We found, for instance, that the recall for various brands of sweets, chocolates and ice creams advertised on television is very low indeed. In the three categories the recall level of the TV advertisements never crossed the 15 per cent mark for any one brand. Furthermore, children seem to be quite fickle when it comes to picking and choosing: brand loyalties shift and constantly change. The child consumer seems to make spontaneous decisions based on market-place exposure, peer group pressures and parental choice in their brand selection.

Children were asked to list all their sweet, chocolate and ice cream preferences.

Sweets are sweets and children will consume them. In India the sweets market is generically referred to as 'toffees' and, as we found, a vast majority of children do not seem to worry about which brand they are consuming just as long as it is sweet, small and can be popped into the mouth!

Parry's had the highest recall but *only* at 6.30 per cent, followed by Melody, Nutrine and Hajmola—this, despite fairly regular and heavy advertising for all four. Take the case of Gems: it was mentioned by only *four* children though it is one of the most oft-repeated advertisements on television and was tremendously popular with our respondents when we played the commercial capsule for them. Interestingly, Gems was seen, not as a chocolate, but as a 'sweet'. Chocolates were firmly recalled in their bar or slab form.

Like so much else in a child's world, colour would seem to dominate choices: many children described the sweets they liked by their colour schemes—'the orange one', the 'green-wallah'. As we will see, this proved to be equally true of their ice-cream preferences. The consumption of sweets continues to follow a traditional pattern, and they are bought in ones and twos for immediate consumption. The glass jars containing individually wrapped candies are peered at for the colour and attractiveness of their contents. Sweets also substitute for loose change.

When it came to chocolates, the picture was not vastly different. Asked to name their favourite brands of chocolate, children's responses once again suggested that the recall and impact of TV advertisements was limited: 5-STAR (10.91 per cent) led, with Amul and Nestle next (just over 7 per cent), followed by Dairy-milk and Cadbury's (just over 6 per cent).

There were some variations in class preferences: Nestle is number one with upper class children but almost unknown to less advantaged children. The latter love their 5-STAR which is also the middle class favourite. Children from well off families claimed to eat mostly imported, Swiss chocolates.

These recall patterns suggest that children named chocolates they like to eat while the advertisements took a back seat. Thus advertising seems to have had little impact on their choice of product, except to make the consumption of candy a somewhat regular habit.

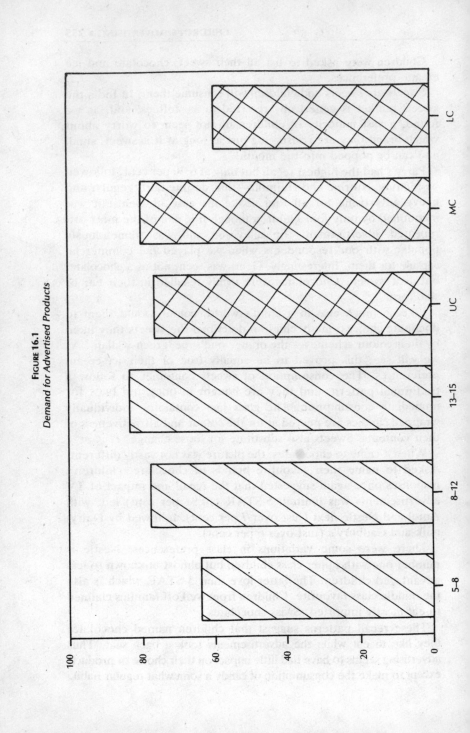

Figure 16.1
Demand for Advertised Products

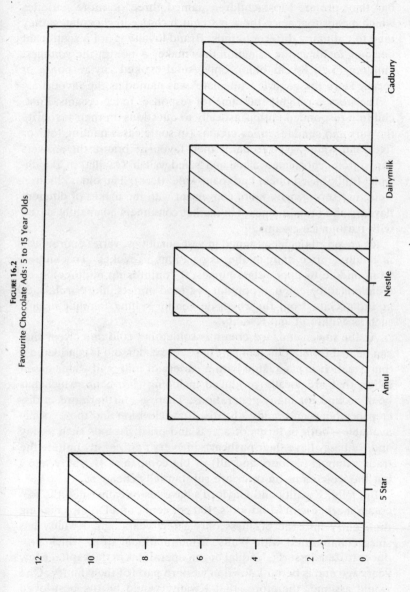

FIGURE 16.2
Favourite Chocolate Ads: 5 to 15 Year Olds

Note: Responses as identified by children.

Although every major chocolate manufacturer offers a range of chocolates children did not discriminate or pin-point which kind of bar they prefer. Most children named three or more varieties which means that since there is so much choice in chocolates, they tend to eat many different kinds. Brand loyalty is not a significant deciding factor in the selection they make. Amongst the youngest children (5 to 8-year olds), only Amul evoked any response or recall. Here the generic 'chocolate' was named as the favourite.

The story is roughly the same for responses to ice-creams. First, children responded enthusiastically to questions on their favourite flavours and sundaes in ice creams (in some cases naming four or five), but when asked to name their favourite brand, the answers varied from 'chocolate wallah' and 'safed wallah' (vanilla) to 'doodh-wale' (milk-based ones) and 'pani-wale' (ices). The older children were, not surprisingly, more conversant with the names of different flavours and brand names. Up-market consumers adamantly stayed with parlour ice-creams.

Ice cream, though consumed in vast quantities, varies enormously in quality, price and, in the associations it evokes. To children from middle to upper class homes, it conjures up multi-coloured creations to be eaten at popular fast food outlets, like Nirula's; or at India Gate from the roadside vendor selling familiar brands such as Milkfood and Kwality.

At the lower end, ice cream is something cold and sweet that can be had from a different sort of street vendor and is considered a 'big' treat! It is associated with a variety of milk and water-based lollies that are locally produced including chus-chus, which has been around for many generations: There is, furthermore, a discrepancy between brands advertised on television and those locally available—both in terms of access and price. Brands such as Jay and Embassy have their pushcarts in every basti. Many imitate the trade symbols (colours and all) of big companies (Kwality, etc.) but the ice-creams on offer are substantially cheaper.

In Delhi, Kwality and Gaylord's have historically ruled the ice-cream market with Milkfood's '100 per cent', and Dollops making their entry into the business only a few years ago. Kwality has since collaborated with Walls, a multinational firm, which produces frozen desserts. Vadilal began operations in the capital a few years ago and is better known in western parts of the country. One would assume, therefore, that Kwality would be the best-loved and best remembered ice-cream brand amongst children in the capital—despite the fact that it does not advertise on television. That, however, is not quite the case.

Responding to the question on ice-cream ads, children from the upper and middle classes preferred Dollops (close to 14 per cent). Next came Milkfood's 100 per cent (just over 6 per cent), while Vadilal scored very high with better-off families (11.94 per cent). Kwality does not figure at all in their ratings.

So whereas the overall response to the questions on ice-cream preferences and advertisements was poor, it is significant that Dollops, 100 per cent and Vadilal, all of whom recently launched media blitzes, scored so well. Vadilal, for instance, is high on children's lists despite its limited availability in Delhi. The advertisement particularly appeals to teenagers whom it targets quite effectively through its ice-cream parlour ambience. New brands of ice-cream, including Mother Dairy ice-cream have also become popular since the study was conducted.

Many children mentioned Nirula's ice cream which, once again, emphasises the confusion in their minds: Nirula's does not advertise on television.

THE COLD DRINKS WAR

In the heat and dust of Delhi summers, children are constantly thirsting for something 'cool and soft' to restore their spirits. The 'cold drink' culture has mopped up the sweat: its cool! The recall patterns for soft drink advertisements fare better than those for sweets, chocolates and ice creams.

In three separate though related questions we asked the children *what* they drank at home, what they would *like* to drink (if they were given the choice), and which cold drink *advertisement* they had enjoyed the most. The answers indicated family consumption patterns and the influence of TV advertising. We present below a list of the ads which children said were their favourites (see Table 16.1).

While Pepsi emerges as the most popular TV ad (it also leads in overall consumption figures—a correlation which seems to suggest

PLATE 16.1
Frooti: Tough Battle Against the Fizzies

that the ad has influenced consumption patterns), it needs to be emphasised that Pepsi is a relatively new entrant into the Indian cold drinks market.

Advertisers in Bombay pointed out that new products coming into a market already served by several other similar brands have a hard time making a breakthrough. The ad must (*a*) instil brand

Table 16.1

Favourite Cold Drink Ads by Class (in Order of Preference)

Upper Class	Middle Class	Lower Class
1. Pepsi	1. Pepsi	1. Rasna
2. 7 Up	2. 7 Up	2. Pepsi
3. Thums Up	3. Citra	3. Maaza
4. Citra	4. Thums Up	4. Rooh Afzah
5. Mirinda/Maaza	5. Maaza	5. Zeera Sip/7 Up

loyalty for a new product by capturing the consumer's imagination; (*b*) compel a shift in loyalties from a known brand; and (*c*) peg consumer interest in their product to an image created exclusively for it. These tasks are part of the brief given to advertisers dealing with the launch of new brands. With its effective advertising and marketing policy, Pepsi has almost effortlessly brushed aside Campa Cola, the long time market leader in Delhi.

It could well be argued that Pepsi is not really a 'new' brand. The giant multinational has etched its name in many countries and its ad campaigns were visible in India even before the product was introduced. The success of the Pepsi campaign exemplifies the influence of international advertising and the power of the multi-national to create an image in markets still outside their area of operation. For instance, middle and upper class families in Delhi told us that they were aware of Pepsi long before they saw it in India. Pepsi, like Coca Cola, was to them *the* American drink. The lifestyle campaign it has conducted over the years seems to have given it an almost unshakeable image in the public psyche. Why else would the Indian market take to Pepsi with such alacrity when, not so long ago, people were quite happy drinking Campa Cola or Thums Up?

Generically, cold drinks belong to a category of products that human beings do not require for their survival and are, therefore, not essential. High visibility of these products and the huge sums of money spent on advertising are imperative in order to create a need for such a product.

Lehar Pepsi uses a global format—a tried, tested and well-researched formula. Based on the belief that consumers all over the world share the same human instincts, such formats are developed

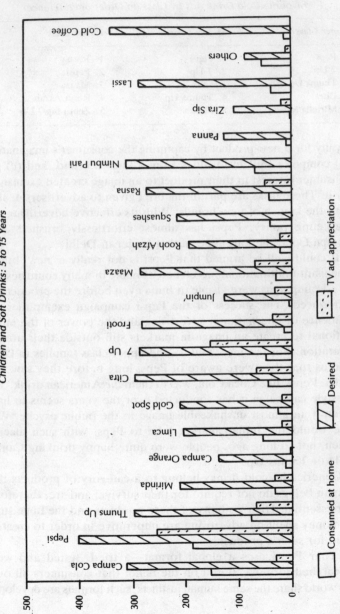

FIGURE 16.3
Children and Soft Drinks: 5 to 15 Years

Cold Coffee
Others
Lassi
Zira Sip
Panna
Nimbu Pani
Rasna
Squashes
Rooh Afzah
Maaza
Jumpin'
Frooti
7 Up
Citra
Gold Spot
Limca
Campa Orange
Mirinda
Thums Up
Pepsi
Campa Cola

500   400   300   200   100   0

TV ad. appreciation.
Desired
Consumed at home

FIGURE 16.4
Responses to Soft Drink Ads of 5 to 15 Year Olds

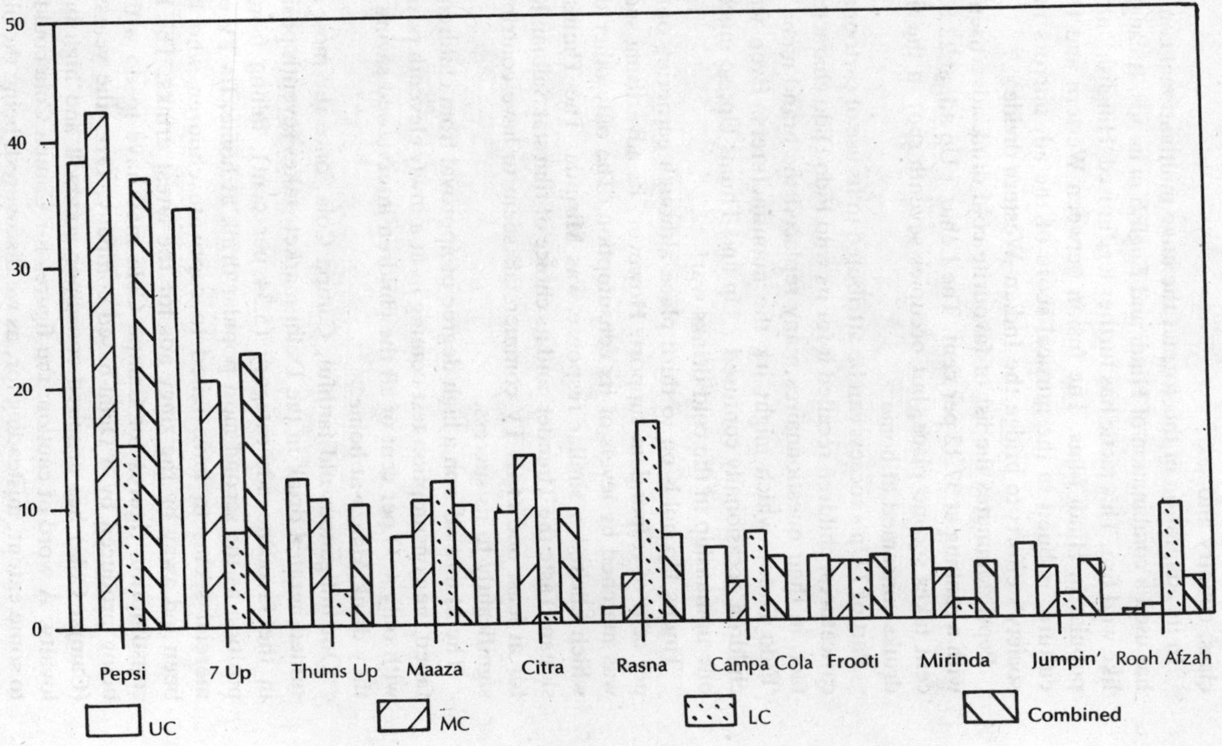

to appeal to the most basic human desires cutting across culture, class, country and sex.

In its adaptation of this format the huge multinational company has used a combination of Hindi and English in its ads. It caught on like wild fire. This tactic has further legitimised 'Hinglish', already popular in Hindi films. The fusion between Western and Indian culture, imbued in the musical score of the ad, mirrors Indian society's efforts to bridge the Indian–Western divide.

Pepsi dominates the list of favourite cold drink advertisements with a ranking at 37.12 per cent. The Lehar 7 Up ad, at 22.87 per cent takes second place, but occupies seventh spot in the list of drinks consumed at home.

Part of 7 Up's success can be attributed to its use of cartoons and caricatures: children recalled it for its wild Fido Dido character. In fact, in their questionnaires many replaced the brand name with 'Fido Dido', which might irk the manufacturers. Even worse, children occasionally confused 7 Up and Thums Up; so much for one-upmanship in the cold drinks war!

Thums Up holds on to third place although garnering only 10 per cent of respondent support. However, its advertising success was matched by levels of its consumption. The only other drink which elicited a similar response was Mirinda. The Thums Up slogan 'Taste the Thunder' and its choice of film star Salman Khan for at least one of its TV commercials seem to have contributed significantly to its success.

The Maaza ad won a high degree of approval from children but failed the consumption test coming in at a lowly eleventh position with only 4.93 per cent of all the children interviewed saying that they drink Maaza at home.

Our indigenous old faithful, Campa Cola, once the most con- sumed aerated drink in the Delhi market, takes seventh position in the favourite ads category (5.34 per cent), falling from its position as the second most popular drink at home. Its TV com- mercial seems to have failed to captivate children who have been led away by the zingy ads for the latest drinks. The high consumption figures for Campa Cola may have to do with its being produced by a Delhi-based company. Over the years CC (Campa Cola) has acquired consumer goodwill and high brand loyalty. A word of caution: the figures for Campa Cola could be, to some extent, misleading for, as we discovered, being the oldest brand known in the Capital, many children refer to *all* colas as

Campa Cola and to the other flavours—orange and lime as Campa—as though Campa were the generic term for all aerated drinks. Alternatively they go by the 'black', 'white' and 'orange' of the drinks, all of which are 'Campas'.

The tetrapack culture seems easily disposable. Only Frooti and Jumpin' receive attention and that too minimal.

Brand images and class choices go hand-in-hand. Up-market commercials such as Pepsi and 7 Up have won favour with children from upper and middle class homes: the media hype that went with the launch of these products was not lost on people with the big bucks! Culturally, the Fido Dido advertisement was best appreciated and understood by these children while the rest responded simply to the animation.

Children from less privileged backgrounds preferred the much advertised TV brands of concentrates such as Rasna and Zeera Sip (also priced considerably lower than the fizzies). The Rooh Afzah advertisement is also fairly high on their list of favourites. A typically Indian drink, Rooh Afzah competes with the aerated ones and, if the responses are indeed an indication of things to come, it appears that the sherbet is rapidly being edged out.

A LOOK AT THE WHOLE PICTURE

A look at the overall consumption figures (see table below), makes it clear that six of the top eight (most consumed) drinks belong to the aerated category, with the top three positions going to Pepsi (26.98 per cent), Campa Cola (24.10 per cent) and Thums Up (11.50 per cent) (see Table 16.2).

These responses reveal that aerated, bottled drinks—like colas—are overwhelmingly the favourites—price being the main deterrent to consumption. As status symbols their value is obvious. In a *basti* near Ambedkarnagar, a family told us that it was the done thing to offer Campa Cola to guests. With the price of each bottle between Rs. 5 and Rs. 6 this is an expensive proposition.

When it comes to appeasing their children's thirst less well-to-do parents stay with home-made drinks—certainly healthier! Lemonade or 'nimbu pani' is still the most popular home-made drink and ranked quite high. Also available in local markets (at Rs. 2 per

Table 16.2
Overall Soft Drink Consumption

Drinks at Home	%	Best Ads	%
1. Pepsi	26.98	1. Pepsi	37.12
2. Campa Cola	24.10	2. 7 Up	22.87
3. Thums Up	11.50	3. Thums Up	10.27
4. Nimbu pani	11.23	4. Maaza	10.00
5. Others	8.76	5. Citra	9.45
6. Limca	8.49	6. Rasna	7.26
7. 7 Up	7.26	7. Campa Cola	5.34
		Frooti	5.34
8. Squash/	6.71	8. Mirinda	4.79
Citra	6.71		
9. Rasna	6.43	9. Rooh Afzah	3.15
10. Lassi	6.16		
11. Maaza	4.93		
12. Mirinda	4.79		

bottle) is a lemon drink sold in bottles with marble stoppers, which continues to be fairly popular.

Putting the two lists together we concluded that advertising definitely plays a role in influencing what children drink. Parents who can ill afford expensive aerated drinks for their children do, however, continue to influence their children's consumption patterns to the extent that 'nimbu pani' and lassi rank highest on the children's lists. The response to nimbu pani was so overwhelming from this class of children that it took its place at number four in the overall listing.

A closer look at the lists revealed that, while a very high overall percentage of families appear to consume aerated drinks at home (26.98 per cent), the majority of these belong to the upper and middle classes. Children of upper class families claimed to drink (in order of favoured consumption):

1. Pepsi
2. Campa Cola
3. Others
4. Thums Up
5. 7 Up
6. Limca

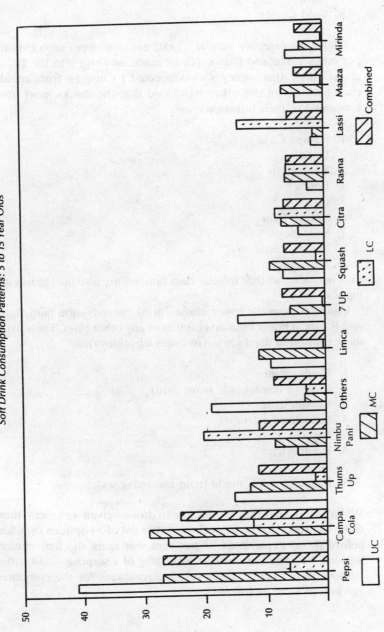

FIGURE 16.5
Soft Drink Consumption Patterns: 5 to 15 Year Olds

7. Citra
8. Cold Coffee

Under the category 'others', 19.02 per cent upper class children put down Coke and Fanta. (Coke made an entry into the Indian market after this survey was conducted.) Children from middle class families on the other hand said that the drinks most often consumed in their homes were:

1. Campa Cola
2. Pepsi
3. Thums Up
4. Limca
5. Citra
6. Nimbu Pani
7. Squashes
8. Maaza/Rasna

This list indicates that middle class families are also into fizzies in a big way.

Children from the lower classes drink more Nimbu pani, Lassi and Rasna at home than do children of any other class. Their list of most consumed drinks was (in order of priority):

1. Nimbu Pani
2. Lassi (a drink made from curd)
3. Campa Cola
4. Squashes (sherbets)
5. Pepsi
6. Rooh Afzah
7. Others
8. Panna (a drink made from raw mangoes)

When asked what they would *like* to drink—given a choice—most children proceeded to tick off the entire list of 34 options they had before them! Pepsi at 54.93 per cent was again the first choice, followed by—and this came as something of a surprise—cold coffee (almost 50 per cent). The overall percentages for the combined age groups were as follows:

Campa Cola	− 47.80 per cent
Pepsi	− 58.00 per cent
Thums Up	− 43.56 per cent
Mirinda	− 30.13 per cent
Campa Orange	− 20.95 per cent
Limca	− 31.23 per cent
Gold spot	− 30.27 per cent
Citra	− 42.46 per cent
7 Up	− 41.50 per cent
Frooti	− 42.19 per cent
Jumpin'	− 18.08 per cent
Maaza	− 41.50 per cent
Rooh Afzah	− 29.17 per cent
Squashes	− 31.64 per cent
Rasna	− 40.27 per cent
Neembu Pani	− 46.16 per cent
Panna	− 18.21 per cent
Zeera Sip	− 15.61 per cent
Lassi	− 42.87 per cent
Others	− 13.15 per cent
Cold Coffee	− 47.53 per cent

Coffee has acquired a remarkably high status value in this essentially tea-drinking part of the country. Commonly considered something that only adults would drink, the interest and desire to become coffee drinkers was so strongly articulated by so many children, that it made us wonder what coffee symbolises for the young.

Shortly after we completed our fieldwork there appeared an article in a leading daily on the launch of a new brand of coffee powder by the multinational, Nestle. The company, which accounted for 39 per cent of the coffee market in India was set to introduce Nescafe Dolca—a chickory-free coffee, priced at 20 per cent less than the already popular Nescafe Select. According to the report, market research had indicated that in the minds of Indian consumers, tea had become an *old fashioned* drink whereas coffee had managed successfully to project itself as a modern drink.

For coffee producers and advertisers, this was the best mind-set they could have hoped to create. The new brand of coffee was aiming at a potential market segment of 30 million 'young, upwardly mobile Indian youth' in the Rs. 2,500 plus income group. It was being presented as an 'all season' drink for jean-clad youngsters with the logic that if you catch them young, you keep them. Our own study suggests some cradle-snatching on the coffee front.

Clearly the Nescafe advertisement had won them over. The children loved the ad and were impressed because in many places in the world people drank the beverage: Coffee drinkers, if advertisements are to be believed, are those who have shed old habits (like tea drinking), have broken through the shackles of tradition and joined hands with the 'moderns'. Not only were children indicating that they wanted to see more of how the 'rich of the world live', but they made it amply clear that if coffee was a symbol of internationalism and Westernisation, they were willing to go for it! There's no mistaking the subtle ideological underpinnings to such ad campaigns.

Not long ago a roadside hoarding peddling a fizzy drink used the line 'Thank God for Thirst!'. Rather insensitive and out-of-place in a country where access to safe drinking water is still problematic and drought a regular trauma. Whatever children might associate with coffee drinking, the fact is that close to 50 per cent of the respondents put the beverage only second to Pepsi. A majority of these responses came from upper and middle class children but even more interestingly, as many as 20 per cent of the children from less affluent families wanted to drink it too.

The grass, they say, is always greener on the other side. We found that in the list of *most* desired drinks, those who had access to all the fizzies and fun drinks wanted to consume the simpler home-made varieties such as nimbu pani or lemonade whereas the others, for whom aerated drinks were still 'special', continued to hanker for them. The highest number of children who wanted to drink lemonade (given the option), were from the best off families. Oddly enough from their list of drinks consumed at home, nimbu pani does not figure as a regular item on the beverage menu (45 per cent).

CYCLES

Commercials for cycles are a distinct part of the TV advertising agenda. These target children of all ages—from the very young to adolescents. There is quite a range of bicycles now available in India and the brands being pushed by TV advertising are developing strong images to go with their products.

Before dealing with children's responses to cycle commercials, we must mention that for many children the cycle is a 'toy'. This became evident when, in response to advertising for toys on television and the children's favourites amongst these, many respondents said the toy advertisements they liked best were those for cycles.

Cycles are important to children and therefore, they keep in touch with the latest developments in the world of cycles. As a result, they find it hard to focus on just the few brands advertised on television.

However, five TV commercials for cycles emerged as favourites, with over 80 per cent of the respondents of the three combined age groups naming one or more of them:

Hero	23.01 per cent
Atlas	21.91 per cent
BSA SLR	18.21 per cent
Street Cat	15.75 per cent
Brute	5.89 per cent

THE ADVERTISEMENTS

For children of poorer families, the cycle is both a form of amusement and an important mode of transport. For them, learning how to cycle is taking one step towards future independence. Children of affluent families see the cycle as a sports accessory and, as they grow older, they want newer and more versatile models to match their ambitions. Whereas the cycle was just a cycle, television advertising has lent the simple two-wheeler a new, dynamic personality. The cycle has been elevated—it is a means of liberation—it is a younger sibling to the motorcycle, but no less daring. The best

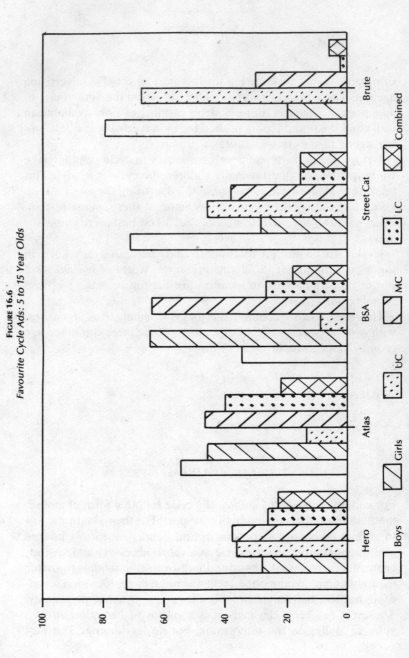

Figure 16.6
Favourite Cycle Ads: 5 to 15 Year Olds

ILLUSTRATION 16.1
Rebels Without a Cause

examples are the up-market brands—Atlas and Street Cat, which
rely heavily on concepts of excitement, challenge and danger.

Both these ads play on high tension scenarios, the cultural
relevance (or irrelevance) of which is discussed further on. The
Atlas commercial with its pushy jingle 'Let the rebel in you break
loose' was one of the commercials shown to children during fieldwork. It invariably evoked tension and excitement in the children.
The Street Cat advertisement highlights danger and presents the cycle

as the saviour, providing escape from all evils. Both advertisements use cultural scenarios which, we discovered, are irrelevant to most Indian children. However, children cannot help but respond to the central message these ads play on—that every child faces a variety of threats, be it on the streets or from the adult world. The ads also link the idea of 'danger' with the 'thrill' of escaping.

Appealing to middle and lower class aspirations, the BSA SLR ad on the other hand is seeped in clean, simple fun. Uncomplicated. Passé?

The responses to these ads and the concepts they peddle, reveal that there is a marked difference between the ways in which boys and girls understand and appreciate them. Over 70 per cent of the

PLATE 16.2
Buy a Ticket to Freedom

children who listed Street Cat as their favourite ad, were boys, despite the fact that in the ad it is a teenage girl who escapes on her Street Cat cycle from a street gang. Conversely, almost 65 per cent of those who named BSA SLR as the best were girls: they identified more positively with both the cultural imagery of the ad and its innocence. In fact, BSA is the only cycle ad that makes any impact on girls. This gender differentiation reconfirms the kind of conditioning that boys and girls undergo: the cycle is still a symbol of male independence and in Delhi very few women/girls use cycles though their numbers are gradually increasing. Similarly, the idea that it is alright for women to drive mopeds, scooters and motorcycles is still not fully acceptable whereas it has become commonplace for women from upper class families to drive cars. The commercials are exploiting this bias.

Children's responses highlighted that the class bias within commercials definitely gets across. The Brute cycle advertisement is clearly an upper class option. Over 67 per cent of the children in the 8 to 15 years age group who named it as their favourite belonged to the upper class. BSA SLR is aimed at the middle class. The responses made this amply evident. Meanwhile Atlas, which for decades has been synonymous with cycles in India, is best liked and remembered by the lower class child.

HEALTH PRODUCTS

Children are also the focus of another category of television commercials—health products. We listed a few of these in our questionnaire (biscuits, beverages, tonics). As energy quick-fixes, nutritional supplements and protein foods, these aim at the growing child—the one who needs Complan, Nesfit and Glucon D, which ostensibly ensure the full requirement of vitamins, minerals and proteins. To push their point, the ads use sports as a theme and the products are promoted by such stars as Kapil Dev, Sachin Tendulkar and Zena Aryton.

The children, however, failed to identify the list of products as health-related and saw Complan and Nesfit, to mention just two, as milk additives worthy of consumption for flavour and taste. They added their own choices such as coffee and cocoa. Some children indicated that they do drink their milk with 'something' in it, perhaps Bournvita, Horlicks or Boost—there are now so many brands to chose from. But it is not the converts advertisers are gunning for.

Clearly the attempt is to change consumption patterns from traditional health foods and natural milk additives (such as ghee, *elaichi* or cardamom and honey) to processed energy-based, ready-to-use ones. But given the low-comprehension of product benefits, it is likely that advertisers will come up with new gimmicks and use every trick in the book to get children to include these products in their list of demands.

An overall look at the children's responses provided the following ranking for the products:

1. Glucose biscuits   43.15 per cent
2. Complan   24.79 per cent
3. Glucon D   19.45 per cent
4. Horlicks biscuits   12.60 per cent
5. Nesfit   11.91 per cent
6. Others   33.01 per cent

Already, despite the hefty price tag on these products, we found that children across class were interested in them. (Any paediatrician in Delhi will tell you that an adequately balanced diet will give a child all the vitamins, minerals and proteins required. An inadequate diet will not be rectified by supplements.)

BEST ADS

Reactions to TV advertising for these health products showed that the recall and popularity enjoyed by these ads amongst children was very low:

1. Glucon D   18.08 per cent
2. Complan   17.67 per cent
3. Nesfit   13.97 per cent
4. Glucose biscuits   5.81 per cent
5. Others   4.93 per cent
6. Horlicks   4.24 per cent

Children (*a*) do not recall advertising for health products easily nor do they, by and large, understand the sales pitch (*b*) they like the ads primarily because they have happy, healthy children and sports stars in them and, (*c*) they would like to become consumers but not because they believe these products will boost their energy or improve their health, but because they wish to emulate the child models and sports stars associated with the ads.

From discussions we gleaned that this product category is still alien to most people. Eating well and drinking milk everyday is what every Indian family would like its children to do. Many cannot even afford that glass of milk. The concept of quick-fix meal supplements is virtually redundant in homes where freshly cooked food is on the table at each meal. Only upper class children seem familiar with the world of additives and proteins out of a box.

Upper class children ranked Nesfit as the number one advertisement and were deeply influenced by its sophistication. Nesfit has broadcast more than one commercial—each introducing a high profile, high class athlete or sports star to sponsor its product, usually someone who has recently achieved success. The ads did not go down quite as well with the other two social groups. The middle class was more comfortable with the Complan ad while lower class children responded best to the humour and excitement of the Glucon D ad with its Indian version of a young superman known as the 'superhero'.

17

TOYLAND

A decade ago, our toy shops were small and insignificant. Empty showcases bore testimony to the paucity of toys and games for children and those that were available were often of poor quality, badly finished and to that extent unattractive. Today, you name it and they've got it. Toy shops have proliferated and their shelves are bursting with colourful, eye-catching goodies. With so much to attract and entice them, taking children to the market has become a dangerous affair.

Yet, as we will see, despite this growth in the toy/game industry, the market is ruled by only a few giants. Monopoly is the name of the game. If television advertising is an indication of what toyland in India is like, then a tiny handful of companies in the business of making children's toys have complete control both of the market and over children's minds.

However, this is not entirely the case. It's more like applying the three-world theory to the world of toys in India. There is the first world of toys which get advertised on television: these are the Barbies, the He Mans and the Leo Mattel variety—rich, expensive, elite. Since they are advertised to the exclusion of all other toys, it might appear that these are the only ones available or at least the ones most desired and most popular.

Then come a vast range of less, or perhaps, never advertised games and toys which nonetheless find a place in all major toy shops—although the buyer has to look beyond the shop displays (which are completely subservient to the big brands) to discover them. The third category comprises local toys, of which there is a large variety. These are hand-made, ingenious and creative, and available at a fraction of the price of branded toys.

Children watching television at the time of our study saw toy ads almost exclusively on the week-ends, when they appeared with child-oriented programmes such as *Laurel and Hardy*, Sunday

morning cartoons (Children's Film Society's Indian offerings like
Jungle Book) and *Mickey Mouse*, or with *Superman, Panchatantra*
and so on, broadcast on Saturday afternoons. Advertisers rightly
assumed that this was the best time to get to children, especially as
the ads piggyback on programmes which children are likely to
watch. Besides they also know, as we all do, that children watch
vast amounts of television over weekends. While classifying television advertisements (in the summer of 1992), we found the list of
advertised toys and games extremely limited. Dominating the
commercials was the Leo collection with toys such as Hot Wheels
and Barbie, TV Video games, G.I. Joe and other Funskool products
mopping up the remaining advertising time.

ADVERTISING CALLS THE SHOTS

Television advertising for toys is more than just an attempt to sell
one attractive toy over another to children with the promise that
they will have a lot of fun with their new purchases.

The story of children's advertising in the United States (which is
the world leader in children's commercial television) tells us something about the relationship between the programming designed
for children and TV advertising for toys. We quote from an article
on the subject, which provides a background on how toy companies
function with respect to finding avenues to sell their goods. As the
reader will find, the same companies have become familiar to us in
India and include those that today account for the largest share of
TV advertising of toys on Doordarshan. The products offered by
these giant toy multinationals are flooding the Indian market,
although thanks to various media, some of these toys are popular
even before they become available—as in the case of Ninja Turtles.

By the late eighties, advertisers in America were already spending 700 million dollars a year to tell children what they should buy.
At the same time, a combination of various factors—including the
low value attached to educational programming for children,
pressures from advertising and long established ties with the toy

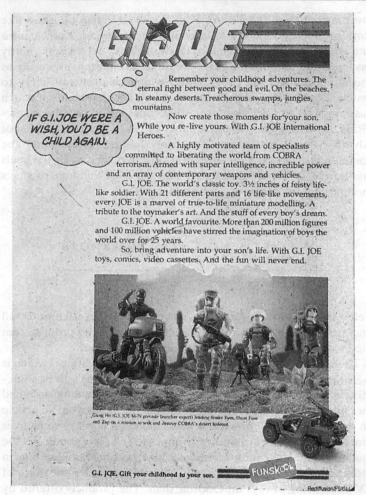

PLATE 17.1
G I Joe: Big Names, Big Claims

industry—were together responsible for programming that was not, as the critics put it, 'good' for children.

In an article entitled 'Public tastes, business demands guide TV programmes for children', published in an American journal in October 1987, the author Bruce De Silva, quotes officials from the children's television industry as saying:

It is true that most children's shows are based on characters drawn from toy lines such as Rambo 'action figures' . . . . Toy companies, which often put up the $ 3 million to $ 20 million in production costs for such programmes, are more interested in promoting toy sales than in producing good shows.

Less than half of today's animated shows try to make children laugh. Most cartoons chronicle wars between 'super heroes' such as G.I. Joe and villains such as G.I. Joe's arch enemy, Cobra. The good guys always win, usually by detonating bombs, shooting laser guns or filling the screen with automatic weapon fire.

The article goes on to say that

. . . thirty-two years ago, there was no children's television industry. Bernie Loomis, a Stanford, Connecticut, toy designer whose career is entwined with the history of children's television, says the young industry was created and then reshaped by two key events: the premiere of 'The Mickey Mouse Club' and the election of Ronald Reagan.

The reason there was no children's television industry, Loomis says, is that there was no children's advertising. Loomis, who has worked as president of three major toy companies, says the thinking at the time was that children had little money so it was pointless to direct commercials at them.

In 1955, an ABC television executive named Vince Francis was looking for an advertiser willing to challenge that belief. He approached Mattel Inc., then a tiny toy company in Hawthorne, Calif, that had only recently moved out of its founder's garage. Francis asked Mattel to spend $500,000 for a year's worth of national advertising on a show called 'The Mickey Mouse Club'. That, Loomis says, was about all the toy company was worth at the time. Mattel took the gamble.

Kids who tuned in the new hit show saw commercials for Mattel's cap-firing 'Burp Gun'. The day after Thanksgiving that year, Christmas shoppers swept Burp Guns from store shelves . . . .

The demonstration that children could influence purchases brought forth a host of children's shows sponsored by the manufacturers of toys, sugared cereal and candy . . . .

In the late 1960s, television and the toy industry abruptly drew even closer when ABC broadcast a Saturday morning programme called 'Hot Wheels' based on a line of racing cars made by Mattel. Loomis, then a Mattel Executive, says this was 'the first show where the inspiration was a toy product'.

Throughout the 1970s, under both Republican and Democratic presidents, the FCC (Federal Commission on Communication) insisted that television had an obligation to serve the public interest. Then Reagan was elected in 1980, and everything changed.

'The public interest determines the public interest,' declared Mark Fowler, Reagan's first FCC chairman. In other words, 'the public interest' would be determined not by such things as educational value but by the ratings.

But it was Mattel, by now one of the nation's largest toy companies, that pushed this approach to its limits. In 1982, the toy company asked Filmation to turn its new He-Man action figures into a television show for broadcast not just once a week, as was customary for children's shows, but five days a week after school.

. . . Filmation syndicated it to independent television stations, in effect creating its own nation-wide network. The result was 'He-Man and the Masters of the Universe', perhaps the most commercially successful programme in the history of children's television.

Success invited imitation. In short order, 'He-Man' begat 'Transformers', 'Centurions', 'G.I. Joe' and about 50 more—all syndicated children's shows based on toy lines from companies including Coleco, Mattel, Kenner Parker, Hasbro Inc., Tonka Corp., LJN Toys Inc., World Wonder Inc. and Ideal Toy Co.

This account of how children's advertising and children's programming evolved out of a set of changing commercial dictates of the toy industry is especially interesting to us in India. Not only is advertising for toys on Indian TV already dominated by the same companies that were responsible for the sea-change in children's programming in America, but for similar reasons advertisers are likely to call for similar programming to be stepped up for Indian children. For the present, we can only watch and observe the changes that are, and will take place.

CHILDREN'S ADVERTISING: HOW DEEP DOES IT GO?

The Delhi child is a strange customer. As mentioned earlier, this child seems overly eager to grow up and do what adults do—hence the deep and abiding interest in hotels, airlines, large companies, and consumer goods such as Ceat tyres, beauty products, ads for suitings and even those for paints. Look as hard as you might you won't find a toy on the list of favourite TV commercials drawn up by the children.

Asked if they could recall having watched ads for toys and games on television? An overwhelming majority (87.39 per cent) said they did remember such advertising. Children from the middle and upper classes seemed to remember the commercials with greater ease and familiarity (over 90 per cent) than children from less advantaged homes (75 per cent).

The reasons for this difference in recall patterns are easily explained. One, the toys that get advertised on TV are mainly targeted at middle to upper class children, both in terms of price and in the nature of their persuasive appeal. Second, these ads are aimed at English-speaking children: the number of toy ads that appear in English far exceeds those in Hindi (the Leo toy gun ad was perhaps the only ad in Hindi at the time of our classification). Nonetheless, as we have said earlier, *all* children watch these ads and many have learnt to parrot them even when they do not fully comprehend the language/message of the ad.

A marginally higher number of boys than girls said they recalled seeing toy advertisements on television. This, as we shall see, is in part related to the kind of toys that are advertised and the fact that the hidden text presents these as designed for the boys.

RECALL

Asked to name the TV advertisements for toys/games they could remember children in the 8 to 15 years age group listed the following:

Leo	(40.35 per cent) 40.95 per cent including 5 to 8 year olds
Barbie	(20.92 per cent) 23.83 per cent including 5 to 8 year olds
Media Video Games	(11.98 per cent) (mainly by boys)
G.I. Joe	(5.30 per cent) (again mostly boys)
He Man	(5 per cent)
Samurai Video Games	(5 per cent)

Leo toy advertisements, as these figures suggest, dominate recall, and Leo is way ahead of the next best remembered toy advertisement, Barbie. As one might expect, the Leo commercial was mentioned by more boys than girls who, by contrast accounted for over 80 per cent of the children (in the total sample) who recalled the Barbie commercial. In overall terms however, the number of girls who recalled the advertisement was just under 50 of the sample of girls. Amongst the youngest children interviewed, 55.73 per cent of those in the 5 to 8 years age group remembered Barbie, the majority of whom were again girls. This figure falls to 24.92 per cent in the 8 to 12 years age group and even further to only 16.96 per cent in the 13 to 15 years age group, owing presumably to the fact that as they grow older, children lose some interest in dolls.

Two factors marred the clarity and accuracy of children's responses to toy-related questions. First, children had trouble linking the brand name of a particular toy or game with the name of the manufacturing company. In other words, if Leo produces a long line of toys, it was the names of the toys that children remembered rather than the fact that Leo produced them all.

Secondly, recall and response were, influenced by strong likes and dislikes for these toys.

Looked at from a class perspective, the recall pattern for Barbie is fairly even. Amongst children of the upper classes, Barbie is marginally less well recalled though they are the most avid collectors of this vinyl-model of the young woman and all her trappings—clothes, accessories of all sorts, a house, a bath and what have you.

The figures also reveal that younger children remember advertisements for toys such as guns and Barbie dolls while TV video games naturally appeal to older children. Of the children who recalled

TV video games, the majority were upper class boys in the 13 to 15 years age group. Just over 10 per cent of lower class children remembered seeing an advertisement for a video game. This was also true for He Man and G.I. Joe, the bulk of recall responses coming from upper class boys.

PARTING COMPANY

Next, we asked children to identify the toy/game company they felt advertised the most on television. Leo, once again came in at number one spot with 41.91 per cent of the children naming the company. Other companies that got a mention included 'Barbie' (not the name of the manufacturer), Funskool and Media Video Games.

A closer look at the responses provides a few interesting pointers. Boys appear to recall company names better than girls: thus 66.99 per cent of those who chose Leo as the most prominent advertiser were boys (as opposed to 33.33 per cent girls); 84.31 per cent of those who thought it was Media TV games were boys. This holds true for almost all the companies that were mentioned, with the notable exception of Barbie. Barbie is produced by Leo Mattel, but that was not clear to the children. Similarly, though children thought that Leo Mattel advertised the most (and it does), they were more clearly able to recall the toys: Barbie, Leo Gun, Hot Wheels and Chook-Chook train rather than the company. Leo was named separately, and in addition to Leo products. Likewise, He Man and Funskool were thought to be mutually exclusive of each other though Funskool manufactures He Man.

In the media games category manufacturing companies—Samurai, Media and Nintendo—were named. (Nintendo, it should be mentioned, is not advertised on Indian TV but ads for the game have appeared on satellite TV.) Children who said that the media game manufacturers advertised most of all on TV seem to have named these manufacturers (to the exclusion of the more visible, Leo) as a result of selective recall. Their interest and desire for such games puts all others in the shadows.

PLATE 17.2
Barbie: The Best Ambassador from the West

When children were asked which toys/games advertised on TV they would like to own, 19.58 per cent of the combined age groups said Barbie (of whom only 8 were boys), 13.15 per cent wanted Leo toys, 15.06 per cent said video games, 8.22 per cent named Media TV games, 3.13 per cent specified Samurai, 2.70 per cent wanted guns, 2.60 per cent G.I. Joe and only 1.75 per cent wanted He Man.

An analysis of the children's answers revealed that there was a distinct and rather sharp fall between their recall of toy advertisements and their desire to own them. The recall of Leo advertisements was much higher than the ambition to possess any of the toys. This pattern cuts across class, age and sex and is partly explained by the fact that many children, especially in the middle and upper classes, already own one or more of the Leo range of toys/games.

The same goes for Barbie dolls where far fewer children (especially from the middle and upper classes) said they wanted to own the doll. However, those who did were not content with what they had. As an 11-year-old girl said, she had several Barbies and plenty of Barbie accessories, but wanted 'everything'. The advertising pitch is to sell not just the doll, but the entire ever expanding 'collection'.

Among lower class children, the figures for ad recall and the desire for the doll were almost on a par. The only other set of toy/games for which recall virtually matched the desire to own was the video games category. Children continue to dream and yearn for TV video games which, because of their exhorbitant prices, remain beyond the reach of most.

Children from less privileged backgrounds naturally want to own toys more than upper class children. From the point of view of age, our analysis revealed that younger children between the ages of 5 and 12 years, are more keen to own toys than the 13 to 15 years old teenagers (23.72: 9.22 per cent). This merely confirms the trend, noted earlier, in children's thinking and behavioural patterns. The teenage child's mind is now geared to more and more adult pursuits. Moreover, most toys and games—with the exception of TV video games—and their advertisements are aimed at younger children.

Lastly, from a gender perspective, boys seem to want to buy toys much more than girls (20.89: 9.73 per cent). This has a lot to do with the fact that most toys and their advertisements are targeted at the male of the species; by comparison, they offer almost nothing to girls.

The variations in responses along gender and class lines mirror the bias of advertising for toys and games on Indian television. A quick glance at what children watching Doordarshan's national network see by way of toys/games, tells us not only that choices are

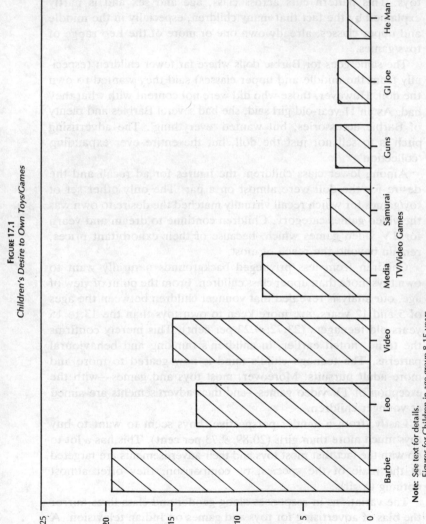

Figure 17.1
Children's Desire to Own Toys/Games

Note: See text for details.
Figures for Children in age group 8-15 years.

very limited but that there is a definite and disturbing orientation to such advertising.

There is only one doll advertised on TV and it is aimed exclusively at girls. Apart from Barbie, the Indian girl enjoys very few options—these include some of the games offered by Leo. The commercials for these depict children of both sexes playing an indoor game together, and sometimes with their parents. A majority of the other TV commercials project toys/games such as Hot Wheels, He Man, G.I. Joe, TV video games and, of course, the Leo Gun as designed for the boys. What these toys share is a combative grounding: epitomised by the likes of He-Man.

This brief analysis indicates two salient points: (*a*) that television commercials for toys constantly reinforce gender stereotypes rather than challenge them (why can't a girl be seen playing with He Man or a video game?); and (*b*) that they encourage (by virtue of the limited nature and focus of games advertised) boys to be violent and aggressive which is, of course, a stereotyping of another kind.

A FLUTE FOR A GUN

In the West, the campaign against war toys is a longstanding one. However, in India, campaigns to consciously steer young, impressionable children away from aggressive games are still to take root and flourish. This, despite the fact that the country has had its share of violence in recent years—there has been an alarming rise in crime, terrorism, communal rioting, caste conflicts and regional disputes.

According to newspaper reports, the Ann-Mary school in Dehra Dun conducted an anti-war toys campaign. The campaign began with posters appearing in the school bearing slogans such as 'Peace begins in the playground: don't buy war toys'.

The Ann-Mary school adopted an interesting method to discourage violent games and aggressive toys. It discussed real violence with the school-children, concentrating on what such toys represented and were teaching them. In response, some children began to consider giving up their guns and swords. The school offered a pleasant barter: any child prepared to bring in a gun could swop it for a book, a ball or a flute.

The experiment was a huge success despite the fact that for many children (and their parents) the decision to give up a gun was not an easy one. In several cases, the economics of the trade-off were discouraging (in which guns were much more expensive than the substitutes that the school could offer). Confusion was also expressed by those who saw the toys as objects of wonder (guns with flashing lights, sonic sound effects and bright colours) which confused and obscured their violent character. In such cases, both children and their parents were unsure about how to respond. But in the end, apparently the campaign worked, and worked well.

What it Costs

A visit to any toy shop in India is an awe-inspiring experience. Children are awe-struck by the number of toys and games that fairly spill off the shelves; their parents, meanwhile, are stunned by the price tags. As every mother and father has discovered, indulging in children's hunger for playthings can be a very expensive business.

Take the Barbie doll. It tops the shopping list of girls of all three age groups and especially of those from poorer families. However, in 1993, Barbie dolls were priced at between Rs. 80 and Rs. 200, with accessories, such as the glamour bath costing as much as Rs. 500 (a figure which represents roughly half the minimum wage in India).

In contrast to the Barbie doll, Leo toys were within the reach of many more children. Leo prices ranged from about Rs. 70 for a Hot Wheels car, Rs. 30 to Rs. 90 for a gun and anything between Rs. 100 and Rs. 200 for the games.

G.I. Joe and He Man, high on the priority list of upper class children, were more affordable (Rs. 65 for an individual piece but almost Rs. 600 for a complete set of He Man and the Masters of the Universe). These toy men cater to predominantly English-speaking, video-watching families who have seen these characters in cartoons on TV and video. More recently, Batman, Jurrasic

Park, WWF and other muscled hulk figures have become available. Imported, these cost Rs. 400 upwards.

Video games are very high on the recall and desirability scale of children from wealthier families. They are also horrifically expensive—indeed, they are the most expensive toys/games in the market: they cost anything between Rs. 1,500 and Rs. 3,500 and some are being sold for Rs. 10,000—almost the same price as a video cassette player!

The manner in which comic strip cartoon heroes and toys complement each other all over the world is one of the great marketing success stories of all time. Each spawns and supports the other so that wherever the child looks, the same toys or characters are on display. For instance, there are the cartoon serials, *He Man and the Masters of the Universe* and *Superman*, both of which ran on Doordarshan. Their trademark has been used to sell a variety of products from chewing gum to shoes and water bottles, pencil cases and T-shirts (mostly by unauthorised manufacturers capitalising on the appeal of these well-known characters). And it works: youngsters, bowing to peer group pressure and exposure, pester their parents to buy them shoes with a Ninja Turtle insignia, or insist on a water bottle with the same—irrespective of price or quality.

The Ninja Turtle phenomenon is something of an enigma. Ninja Turtle cartoons did not appear on television in India until very recently, nor were the toys available in Delhi toy shops. Yet the Ninja Turtle had taken over the marketplace with Leonardos and Michaelangelos embossed on every other child-related product. The Turtles enjoyed such a high degree of popularity (surely the only way children could have become acquainted with them is via the video cassette network?) that even confectioners were turning out squat brown and green turtle-shaped cakes for little boys' birthdays!

The appeal of He Man, Ninja Turtles and every other childhood hero pales when compared with a phenomenon known as *WWF*. As we have mentioned in Parts I and II of this book, *WWF* or the *World Wrestling Federation* is one of the much watched programmes on satellite and cable TV. When we conducted our study at the end of 1992, we found that *WWF* was being watched by many of our respondents, notwithstanding parental objections. Also, in response to a question on their favourite advertisements, quite a few children singled out the *WWF* programme commercial.

Since our fieldwork, the situation has altered quite dramatically: *WWF* is now so popular with children that in a study (quoted in the *Economic Times*, 4 February 1994) school-children in Delhi named wrestlers like Hulk Hogan as their favourite heroes and idols—far outstripping Indian film and sportstars. More than that, *WWF* has spawned a whole new industry: its accessories and spin-offs flood the urban Indian market today. There are not only T-shirts, shoes and shorts available, but also posters, post cards, playing cards, belts, costumes, etc. all bearing the *WWF* insignia or pictures of the wrestlers.

18

MONEY, MONEY, MONEY

The money that children between the ages of 6 and 15 years have access to (either through gifts or pocket money) makes them potential buyers of a special kind since this money is not necessarily earmarked for determined expenditure. It could be saved. However, it does not *have* to go towards paying bills, or satisfying essential needs.

For many children interviewed (only the 8 to 15-year olds were asked), assessing the amount of pocket money they receive every month was not easy. A large number claimed that they were not restricted by fixed amounts. Indeed, they take as much as they want or need, and accept whatever parents are willing to part with on occasion.

Nonetheless, children were asked to give us a figure that best approximated their monthly pocket money. Although we asked for monthly figures, some children gave us weekly amounts.

The figures for pocket money in 1992 were as follows: In the 8 to 15 years age group, 26.90 per cent said they receive Rs. 10 per month. Just 19.43 per cent claimed to receive between Rs. 50 and Rs. 100, while 12.10 per cent said they got up to Rs. 150. To look at these figures a little differently: 43.19 per cent children are given between Rs. 10 and Rs. 40, and another 43.64 per cent receive pocket money within the range of Rs. 50 to Rs. 250. Interestingly, age does not seem to dictate the amount received—roughly, an equal number of younger and older children get the same sum in all these categories. For instance, 4.50 per cent of the 8 to 12-year olds and 4.16 per cent of 13 to 15 years age group said they got up to Rs. 400 in pocket money. In some cases, the sky is apparently the limit. A few children claimed that their parents dished out considerably larger amounts.

We next asked how much pocket money the children would *like* to receive. Here the figures ranged from the very modest—many children saying that the Rs. 10 to Rs. 30 they were getting was ample—to the astronomical: nothing less than one million dollars, with the emphasis being on the currency! Over 43 per cent of the children said they would like to receive between Rs. 50 and Rs. 250 per month while more than 31 per cent said they would be happy with Rs. 100 to Rs. 150. Roughly 26 per cent of the children were willing to settle for Rs. 10: this figure corresponds with the number of children who actually receive Rs. 10 each month, indicating perhaps that the expectations of these children do not exceed their limitations. (Alternatively, the figure does not really reflect a stringent limit on expenditure, since many of the 'treats' and 'fun things' children desire are, in any case, paid for by adults.) Under 10 per cent wanted between Rs. 250 and Rs. 500. Interestingly parents do not appear to differentiate between boys and girls when it comes to pocket money.

What happens to this money? Is it put into the bank by parents? Does it go towards meeting everyday demands for sweets, cold drinks and so on? Is it saved for a big buy? In order to ascertain children's attitude to money and their shopping priorities, we asked children in the 8 to 15 years age group how they would spend Rs. 150 if they had it.

Food: Almost 30 per cent of all children said they would spend their money on sweets, chocolates, ice creams, chips and eating out, particularly at fast food parlours. For instance, some dreamed of 'treating' their friends to a meal at Nirula's (the ultimate in fast food for many children), but with rates going up steadily, the money would certainly not buy very much.

We found that upper class children were most influenced by this 'food culture' and mentioned a variety of foods, drinks and confectionary they would like to indulge in. The figures dipped somewhat when it came to middle class children and fell dramatically in the case of lower class children (upper class: 38.42 per cent; middle class: 30.99 per cent; lower class: 13.45 per cent).

Most food items mentioned by the children were straight from the Western kitchen. It seems that samosas, chaat and other snacks from the Indian kitchen, which might once have excited children are steadily being replaced by chips, cold drinks and pizzas. This could explain why, when middle class children emerge as leaders in consumption on almost all other fronts, they lag behind the upper class in spending on food, now associated with a

Figure 18.1
What Children Want to do with Rs 150

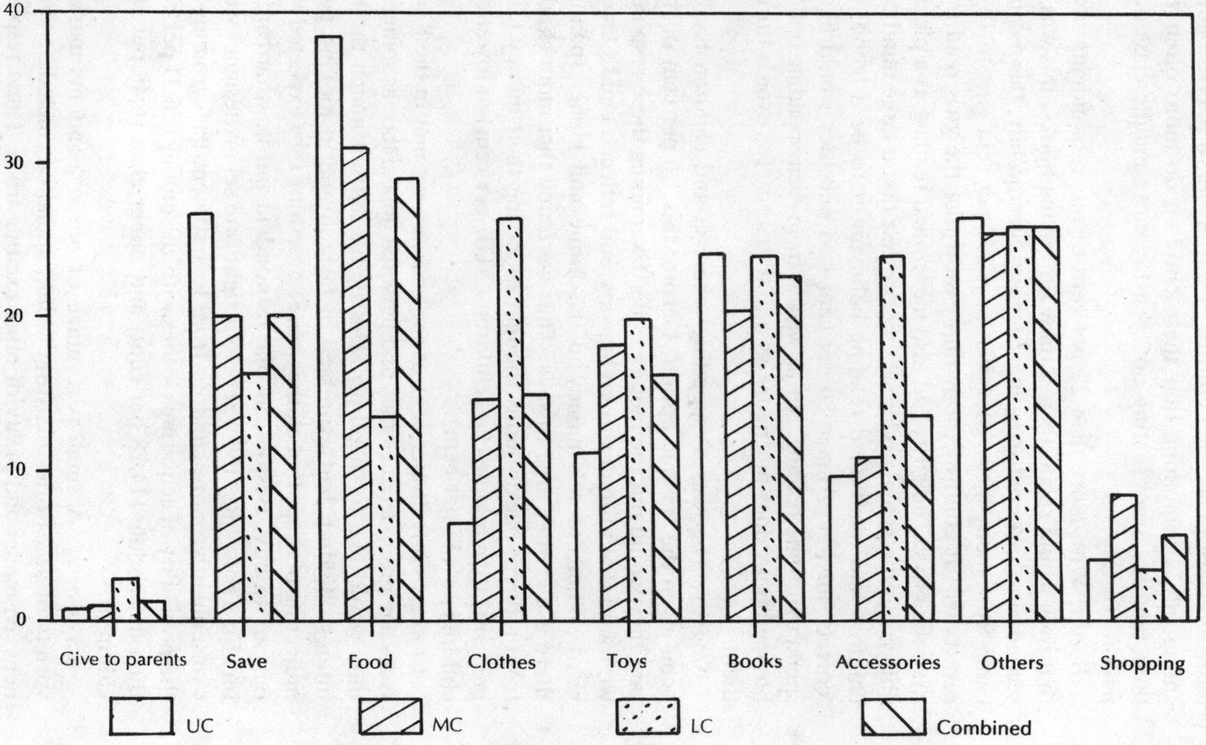

more Western palate and culture. Then, again, it is possible that eating out is something that these children do more often with their families, since 'eating out' is a favourite middle class occupation.

Books: With more than 22 per cent of our respondents saying that they would spend their money on buying books, this was the second most favoured spending category. Significantly, this response came from many more girls than boys (32 per cent girls to 16 per cent boys). It confirmed our impression that the girls read more than the boys. The girls, had also mentioned reading as a pleasurable free time activity. Conversely, we felt that a large number of children had mentioned reading believing it to be a 'good' and 'correct' answer. Almost 80 per cent had said they would like to spend their time reading, but as we see from their spending options, buying books does not figure as a first priority for even a third of them.

Savings: This was a 'spending' exercise and children had not been given the 'saving' option. Despite this, 20 per cent of them said they would put the money aside. Examining these responses, we found that attitudes to saving vary and reflect a child's level of need. Where there's money in the home and higher spending, there is a greater urge to save. Thus we found that more children from affluent backgrounds thought of saving their money (26.61 per cent) than middle class children (20.07 per cent) or lower class children (16.37 per cent).

Clothes: Only 15 per cent of the children we met in the 8 to 15 years age group cited clothes and personal appearance as something they would like to spend on. This figure did not match the high interest children had expressed in fashion and in looking good, indicating perhaps that clothes were something they expected their parents to buy. Besides, as one respondent put it, what can you buy for a paltry Rs. 150 when your sights are set on designer wear? Consequently, more children from less affluent backgrounds saw the possibility of acquiring clothes with the money (26.31 per cent) than did middle (14.78 per cent) and upper class (6.48 per cent) children.

Accessories: A small percentage of our respondents named a variety of accessories that they would spend on, including shoes, pens, cosmetics and plenty of other exciting trivia. These responses followed much the same logic as for spending on clothes, with more lower class children willing to part with their own money to acquire these things than children of other social groups.

Give to parents: A handful of children, most of them from less fortunate backgrounds, said that they would not spend the money, nor save it. They would give the money to their parents, who would find it useful.

Amongst the minority who considered giving away their money, some said they would like to help someone whose need was greater than theirs. But, as we must point out here, this empathetic response came almost exclusively from children (almost without exception by girls) of the least affluent families (not a single respondent from the middle or upper class families suggested this).

The evidence suggests that there is no single monolithic entity as the Indian child. We are a nation in which people with vastly different realities coexist, so much so that the values, aspirations and imperatives highlighted by the mass media mean very different things to different people. Take, for instance, a set of children (8-year olds) who were completely perplexed when asked how they would spend Rs. 150. They said they simply could not answer the question. When asked 'Why?', they answered: 'Because we never shop in India', or 'We always send our shopping lists abroad' and even 'There's not much that is worth buying here'.

In sharp contrast, sitting on a *charpai* (a string bed) in a *basti* talking to a 6-year old and his mother, we raised the same question. Only this time we left the amount unstated and merely asked: 'If you had a little money to spend on yourself what would you like to buy?' The child smiled back shyly and said nothing. When the question was repeated, the answer was devastating. 'Didi,' said the child, 'I have never eaten a real orange. That's what I would buy.'

Despite such conflicting realities, television, that great unifier, is at work influencing both the child whose unfulfilled dream is to eat a piece of fruit and the 8-year old who shops in foreign markets. Consumerism tells these children different things, making the poor child desire so much more than can be had and reassuring the rich ones that as long as they are buying, consuming and wanting material goods, they're doing just fine.

By promoting this ethic, television provides not just a way of thinking but also a series of images to conform to and identify with. It is this vision, this presentation of a value system and the

PLATE 18.1
We are Going to Look Right

negation thereby of other alternative viewpoints that we are concerned with. To the child who is watching and absorbing the messages that emanate from television and advertising, what do these images mean and how do they translate into models for behaviour, lifestyle and individual growth and development?

In this context, some of the fears related to the very technology of television (dealt with in the first part of this book) stand out as particularly disturbing and it would be relevant to return to some of these.

Given current trends, we are likely to find ourselves succumbing to the modern standards that appear to be evolving in a somewhat automatic, natural and impersonal manner around us—guided by forces that we cannot easily identify. These standards become visible in a myriad forms within society, and are replicated and reinforced in many ways. The market has changed face—indigenous products are no longer the showpieces of shop windows; they have been replaced by the better packaged, multinational brands which, we are taught to believe, are superior to anything produced in this country.

The media send out millions of impulses to nudge the individual into focusing on personal benefit and private gain—entertainment programmes produced within and outside the country promote similar values and project lifestyles that support in large measure the acquisitive and consumerist fashions of the day. And so it goes on. Nothing in this scenario is intended to make the television viewer sit up and question the worth of this new thinking. With greater options for the use of television, more and varied programming available, it would seem that genuine competition is being encouraged just as it is in the marketplace. But is this true? Or does all the competition related to programming options in fact concentrate on a few chosen themes, and reflect a growing standardisation of content? Are the new stereotypes so strong as to deny the viability of many other images today?

In *The Power Elite*, C. Wright Mills expressed the view that 'The media not only give us information; they guide our very experiences. Our standards of credulity, our standards of reality, tend to be set by these media rather than by our own fragmentary experience.' He argues that gradually people wait for confirmation and acceptance by the media of even those things that they have learnt from their own experience. They do not, in other words, trust their own experience until it is mirrored by the media.

He goes on to state that:

The media have not only filtered our experience of external realities, they have also entered into our very experience of our own selves. They have provided us with new identities and new aspirations of what we should like to be, and what we should like to appear to be. They have provided in the new models of conduct they hold out to us a new and larger and more flexible set of appraisals of our very selves. In terms of the modern theory of the self, we may say that the media bring the reader, listener, viewer into the sight of larger, higher reference groups . . . which are looking glasses for his self-image.[20]

For the Indian child, caught in the media blitzkrieg which has overnight altered the use and public expectation of the media, what are the strongest images that television and particularly TV advertising are presenting as the ones to emulate? Are these likely to become the only acceptable ones in India?

19

DOMINANT IMAGES

The dominant images being created and sustained by television (and by the advertising that appears on it), acquire special importance in the context of children. Children derive and absorb many of their ideas from television, which has become one of the main and most influential sources of information available to them.

To understand what these images represent in our classification of TV advertisements we included an analysis of the language, music, culture, class and, of course, the relationship of these to the major product categories advertised.

In the following section we shall look at the culture and class images that are most strongly being communicated by TV advertising. The brand of images promoted by this advertising is unique and follows its own persuasive logic. Take soaps. With the recent proliferation of brand names, the soap industry is forced into greater and greater competition. Product benefits (this product/ soap is better than any other because . . .) have been left behind, forgotten as a sales pitch. The soap industry is packaging and selling soap as a beauty product, a cosmetic, a magic recipe. While Le Sancy sells itself by highlighting that its cake of soap has a unique curvaceous shape and firm body, Evita unmistakably replicates the visuals and theme song of the film 'Pretty Woman', appealing to romantic instincts. Beauty soaps sell. Sexual stereotypes too.

None of this misses its mark on children. The obsession with soaps has made the product a high priority item for families and for children of all ages. The main images communicated by advertising in this category are youthfulness, beauty, freshness and sensuality or even a clean, strong masculine odour. All these are set in milieus that convey modernity—presenting the office worker, the woman who cares about herself, or fashionable society and even feelings such as liberation.

To turn then to toothpaste, toothpowder, shampoo and talcum powder ads. The message here is twofold: (a) that natural body odour is undesirable and you must do something about it or else . . . .; (b) that if you want to get ahead of everyone else, you need to use a particular brand, with each brand promising the earth. The underlying threat of failure (if you don't comply with advertising sermons) is that you may lose out on a 'beautiful relationship' or just remain boring, dull and unimpressive. Put a sheen to your hair. Breathe sweet.

Detergent ads use words like 'strong' and 'powerful', and also throw in lots of 'scientific' jargon like 'ultrons' (which no one really understands). They play on prices without actually mentioning them. These ads create the image of the modern, Indian superwoman—efficient, aware that she's both an exemplary housewife and a working woman who is still concerned with her husband's reputation (judged by the whiteness of his shirts) and the effect of the detergent on her hands—and she's great at balancing the budget too!. All this is designed to make you race off to the nearest store, buy one of the detergents advertised and try it out in the hope that it will transform you and your life.

Just how effective this kind of advertising can be is clear from the phenomenal success of Ariel Microsystem. Ariel conducted a massive ad campaign on TV and children's responses to the ad indicate that its impact has been stupendous: it is their number one favourite TV advertisement. Ariel is extremely expensive and would appear to be beyond the means of most salaried families but, if children are to be believed, almost everyone has bought the product at least once.

Advertisements for cold drinks sell images that range from a consumer who is young and modern to that of the devastatingly attractive woman who lives dangerously and finds salvation with a macho rough rider on a motorcycle (Thums Up). Jumpin' is a straight lift from the Western screen, incorporating a strong dance element with an aggressive male leader for the troupe. He points at you through the screen, arrogance and confidence writ large on

ILLUSTRATION 19.1
Image Building: A Unifying Experience

his face as he wants more . . . . Pepsi, as discussed in earlier
chapters, has played on a cultural synthesis and stolen the show.

Music and pop stars, dancers who use their bodies to communicate, youngsters drawn to one another, irresistible men and women,
high frolic and lots of fun are the salient images that all cold drink
advertisements peddle.

Lehar 7 Up, which uses the overtly Western Fido Dido cartoon
character 'Cool, light and easy' is clever, witty and handsome,
while the Mirinda ad draws successfully on the Indian/Western
cultural mix that is Pepsi's strength using, this time, a delivery boy
in a baseball cap in juxtaposition with a traditional Kathakali
dancer who clasps a bottle of Mirinda in each hand as he goes back
to his dancing. Both sell a way of life obtainable to very few but
ostensibly subsumed in the products. The Kathakali dancer lives in
a modern bungalow, lush green all around. Painted a stark
white . . . .

Aerated drinks create images for the fun-loving, the idealists, and the freedom that youth signifies. Most ads feature the older child, the adolescent, and the youth. Of course, there is the Citra ad which homes in on a science practical at school with the students, hot and sweaty, looking for a break (so what if their antics are not likely to find favour with their teacher?). The day is saved by a carry pack of Citra drawn up with a lasso made from an assortment of school belts and hair ribbons.

Collectively, these advertisements are drawing attention to the individual who is a winner, someone who is both daring and of course, extremely trendy—in behaviour, style and taste.

Culturally, advertisements for the more indigenous beverages such as sherbets still stay with the image of the homely, happy family.

Cosmetics have established their own space in television advertising. They have a wide range and appeal as they move from perfumes (Ivana) to hair oils that promise to turn the woman into another Sridevi. The cosmetic commercial is geared to the woman from that super rich, international class of people who recognise no cultural or national boundaries. The Ivana ad is strikingly Western and upper class and has no distinguishable Indian element in it at all. The whiff of money is central to the power these ads exert on the minds of consumers. Every little girl hankers after the look created by these ads.

Of all cosmetic ads, it is the one for fairness creams that are the most worrying. Here the image of the woman is still traditional. The concept and idea that fair is lovely, however objectionable, is very Indian. The commercial does not hesitate to suggest that the cream can put you back into the marriage market and, conversely, that with a dark complexion a woman has no future and can never be considered beautiful or attractive. The advertisement thereby reinforces a colour consciousness which democracy should have been erasing.

Health products like Complan, Eno's fruit salts (for those with indigestion), Glucon C, Glucon D and Cinkara could be straight out of Alice in wonderland—with labels that read 'Eat me' 'Drink me' for instant energy, revitalisation and growth.

What the commercials do is not just promote the product for its possible benefits but deliberately suggest that with them comes a tiny key that will open the secret door to success (Superboy saves the match in the Glucon D ad) and superhuman energy (the Cinkara consumer turns from a wilting man at work into a Superman bursting with energy).

The world of toys as represented on TV is grotesquely shrunken. Dominated by Leo Mattel and Funskool and various kinds of media TV and video games, these toys fly the multinational flag and are looking for undying loyalty from children. The toys themselves are an advertisement for a look epitomised by the blond-haired Barbie.

Advertising thus plays on the obsessions of many Indians—go foreign, buy foreign, be foreign. If TV advertising is pushing a viewpoint then advertisers will do their best to ensure it is understood and appreciated. They employ the tools of language and music to their best advantage, honing these with carefully chosen visuals to create a tiny capsule that will elevate the viewer into a perpetual state of entrancement.

LANGUAGE

Language, we believe, is one of the dominant elements of identity in any culture. In the Indian context language has played a major role in assigning social status and has even influenced the access that people may have to certain kinds of education and jobs. English language education has been held up as being a notch (indeed, several notches) higher than education in any Indian language and speaking English has for long been associated with the elite.

Indian advertising needs to reach a much larger segment than is represented by the English-speaking minority. It has to 'speak' to this broader segment which has money to spend on the goods and services that advertising promotes.

As we can see from the classification of advertisements (in May 1992), there are essentially three 'languages' that are commonly used in Indian advertising. The break-down of languages used in advertising on Doordarshan is given in Table 19.1.

Table 19.1
Languages Used in Advertising on Doordarshan

Week	English	Hindi	English/Hindi	None
One	68	193	6	–
Two	88	191	9	–
Three	108	189	20	1
Four	76	201	13	3
Total	340	774	48	4

As the figures indicate, the majority of ads (in this sample, over 65 per cent) on Indian TV use Hindi to communicate with the audience. A fairly large percentage (almost 30 per cent) use English. On the face of it, this seems to indicate that the advertiser is sensitive to the needs of the vast majority of TV viewers who are not English-speaking. However, the number of ads appearing in English would probably be disproportionate to the size of the English-speaking audience. The use of English, not understood by a majority of viewers, is dictated by several factors: (*a*) that the ideology of consumerism is closely associated with the Western development model. A lot of the goods and services that are now becoming available here have long been part of the lifestyles of people in developed nations. English assumes the role of initiator—a language that will draw the Indian consumer into an international world enabling communication; (*b*) as for the rest of the non-English speaking viewership, the use of the language signals the direction towards similar lifestyle. The elite, whose language is the one that advertisers use so much, is at home with new technologies (be they computer or washing machine related) which are part of India's new consumer priorities. This section of society is thus presented, by using English, as the one to emulate—in every sense—because they are already consumers of these products.

Children have a lasting impression that English is the language which dominates TV advertising. To test their language recall patterns we asked children in the 8 to 15 years age group to identify the language used in three different commercials which appeared frequently on television just before and during the period of our fieldwork.

The advertisements chosen were Close Up toothpaste (Hindi), Lehar Pepsi (English/Hindi) and Siyaram suitings (English). The percentage of children who correctly identified the language was respectively 35.27 per cent, 37.81 per cent and 46.93 per cent for the three ads. Over 50 per cent could not identify the languages used by these ads. Although the figures are not remarkably high, the English language commercial (Siyaram) received the largest number of correct answers and the Hindi language (Close Up) advertisement the least. Many of those who got it wrong thought Close Up was in English and Siyaram in Hindi. Upon closer analysis we discovered that this confusion arose, at least in part, because of the cultural impact of these advertisements.

The Close Up commercial is shot on a beach: a group of teenagers is dancing to pop music being played by a band. The dress code is T-shirts and jeans or dresses. But the lyrics of the song are in Hindi. What stayed with most children was the completely western ambience of the ad: naturally, then, it must have been in English!

The Pepsi ad has Indian rock star Remo singing a duet with a young girl, Penny Vaz, which ends in the famous slogan, 'Yehi hai right choice baby'. The advertisement incorporates the odd Hindi word here and there and has a musical interlude in which the notes of an Indian classical *raga* enhance the bubbly, frothy, rippling visuals of the drink.

The third advertisement, Siyaram, creates a union between traditional aristocracy and the ultimate in fashion. The ad is set in an old Rajasthani *haveli*. Deep Indian colours flutter across the screen: the women are dressed in the finest traditional *ghagra-cholis*. A male, as rugged as the landscape, steps out of his jeep wearing a well-cut suit. Here are two people at home with the best of two worlds. Folk music provides a rigorous beat but the lyrics of the haunting melody are in English: 'Oh Siyaram . . . coming home to Siyaram'.

The visual and the musical elements in an advertisement seem to influence the overall impression it creates far more than its choice of language. While both the Close Up and Pepsi ads are more Western-oriented in their imagery and music, suggesting thereby that they must be in English, the Siyaram ad with its Indian setting and folk music strongly suggests that its lyrics must be in Hindi.

Logical. But there's no apparent logic in the selection of language except from the point of view of *which* class of Indians these ads target. Siyaram is clearly intended for the well-heeled, English-speaking businessman and those who aspire to be like him; whereas both Pepsi and Close Up represent product categories that are accessible to a much larger segment of consumers—both, therefore, play off the Hindi/English tactic—stay with the modern image but let the viewer in just enough to understand what is being said.

The impact of the language used for communication in TV ads is clearly mitigated by dominant and overt cultural images and symbols. Our response data shows that this generates confusion. The inherent contradiction and gap between the two cultures that ads seek to bridge leaves many children befuddled.

The fact is that a very large number of people who watch TV do not know enough English to fully comprehend the verbal messages of ads appearing in English although they are most definitely influenced in other ways by the commercials.

We met many children who, as we have mentioned, responded enthusiastically to ads such as Eveready, Gems and Atlas. It was however, emotive appeal that communicated itself to them. These children did not understand the verbal or even the cultural messages clearly and, in some cases, misunderstood the ads completely, but were wholly 'with' the ads while watching them.

Hindi seems a deliberate choice when advertisers are trying to communicate culturally new concepts or, of course, when the product is targeted at a 'non-English speaking segment' of viewers. This leaves its scars, creating a class bias which, as we can see from children's reactions makes them want to reject and even laugh at such ads. They see these ads and the products they promote as being 'less important', and lower down on the consumption ladder.

Then there is also the attempt to run down regional accents which characterise the way we speak English. Take the advertisement for Ortem fans which has a smart young woman repeating 'Ortem' correctly pronounced, while several male characters attempt to imitate her but fail, their accents being strongly Punjabi or Tamilian, or what have you. Only one young man gets it right and he's the winner. He gets the woman's heart. Franz Fanon, the noted author of *The Wretched of the Earth*, might have said that such an advertisement is a classical example of a colonial hangover: the Indian putting down the rest of his kind in a desperate bid to become a 'white man'.

CULTURE

Culture, defined in anthropological terms, is a 'whole way of life'. In aesthetic terms it implies 'high' culture represented by 'works of art' as opposed to 'popular' culture such as the kind represented by Hindi films or television. We have looked at culture as a part of social interactions reflected and informed by television. We are well aware that in the urban Indian context it is becoming very hard to define modern-day culture and its exclusive elements as distinct from Western culture. In many parts of India, where regional identities are strong, it might be argued that the local culture is so deeply rooted that it would be hard to shake its foundations. A city like Delhi, however, has no identifiable cultural base or homogeneous population and seems more open to new influences.

The new culture we see evolving combines many elements of the Indian and the Western. But it is still restricted to a small proportion of the population even in big cities. In Delhi, we found reason to believe that certain elements of modern culture, as represented by the Evita advertisement, are still unacceptable to many families. On the other hand, it has been pointed out by social commentators and even advertisers that, behind the cloak of conservatism, 'the Indian' is quite another person. He has internalised the new culture and lives by its norms. In other words, Indian society is in a state of flux. Change, we know, is rapidly taking place and is following patterns of Westernisation which are the bedrock for homogenisation of consumers under a single culture exemplified by the MacDonalds and the Benettons. As one advertiser said: 'In India, people derive their ideas of consumerism from the West, and most of their role models belong to that part of the world as well.'

In attempting to classify TV commercials for their cultural expression we looked at elements such as the language, music, dress, lifestyle, behaviour, relationships and cultural symbols that today's ads choose to employ. From Table 19.2 it is clear that Indian advertising was dominated by elements of 'Western culture'.

Increasing Westernisation (reflected in Indian advertising's choice of style, music and visual message) characterises the best of television commercials, while a predominantly upper class bias

ILLUSTRATION 19.2
"India? But Mom I've Been Down this Street Before"

Table 19.2
Elements of Culture in Advertising

Week	Indian	Western	Indian/Western	None
One	80	127	60	–
Two	93	159	36	–
Three	76	179	60	3
Four	86	138	62	7
Total	335	603	218	10

dominates and sets the tone for cultural images swiftly becoming popular and being internalised despite being alien to the majority. One of the problems that advertisers say they face is that since there are so many cultural variations in India, it's hard to choose which one to reflect. The easy way out is to deny all of them. But surely this infinite variety should be a goldmine for the advertiser in search of ideas! How much more exciting than the unification of culture that current advertising promises us. Wait a few years and no matter where you go things will begin to look as though whole cities were factory-made. Already, walking down the Mall in Shimla is a changed experience because one cannot get away from the Intershoppes and the Batas. However, producers may well need to 'go Indian' once they begin courting the rural market. Right now, as a senior Doordarshan official put it, it is easier to sell Western culture and Western music because we really do not have a culture of our own in urban India.

During fieldwork we asked a number of children what they thought of the 'culture' or the way of life depicted in TV advertisements. Their reactions provide some clues to the way in which this culture is making itself understood to children of different social backgrounds and varying life experiences.

While most upper class children felt that the culture in Indian advertisements was 'their' culture, at the other end of the social spectrum children, who could neither comprehend the language of a great many ads nor identify with the lifestyles portrayed, felt that the culture was alien or *'paraya'* (someone else's). They also expressed a degree of confusion, being unable to connect what they saw with *their* vision of the India they know.

Relevance is not the only criterion by which an advertisement may be judged. To ascertain the impact of commercials with different cultural emphases on children, we selected twelve ads and asked children in the 8 to 15 years age group to choose the ones they liked best. While half the commercials listed had a stronger 'Indian' context, the rest were overtly 'Western'. The overall order of preference expressed by the respondents was as follows:

1. Ariel (I)
2. Eveready (W)
3. Atlas (W)
4. Godrej Puf (W)
5. Bajaj (I)
6. BSA SLR (I)
7. Glucon D (W)
8. Vimal (W)
9. Weekender (W)
10. Tata Chai (I)
11. Emami Cream (I)
12. Bandar Chaap Kala Dant Manjan (I)
   (*Note*: I = Indian; W = Western)

Of the five most popular ads, three had strong elements of this Western culture—Eveready, Atlas and Godrej Puf. These commercials are characterised by their use of Western music and cultural symbols that in no way belong to the Indian ethos. They present characters such as a bartender, images of a pub-like joint, a jean-clad father and a spaceman of the Superman variety.

An analysis of the children's responses to these ads by social class provides an insight into the importance they attach to such advertising and to the product it sells. Ariel receives the most favourable overall response from children. However, even in the case of this ad, it is clear that children of the middle class appreciate it best (upper class: 38.42 per cent; middle class: 65.14 per cent; lower class: 44 per cent). Perhaps their overwhelming support for the ad has something to do with the fact that the ad plays on a theme of great relevance in the middle class (mother-in-law and daughter-in-law tensions) and yet retains the sophistication they are learning to associate with the modern household of the ad world. Above all, it gently but surely allows the usually oppressed daughter-in-law a slightly more positive role. Children from the upper class did not share the same level of enthusiasm for the ad. Instead, the upper class selected Eveready as their number one favourite and Weekender as the second best. Lower class children, as we can see from the figures, like the Ariel ad better than do upper class children (owing to much the same reasons that apply to children of the middle class), but do not match the middle class response. Many of their mothers, as our survey also shows, are still denied several of the rights that the middle class working woman enjoys.

From the responses of lower class children we learnt a great deal about how relevant or irrelevant certain kinds of advertising was for them. The ads which rank lowest in the overall readings—Tata Chai and Emami Fairness Cream—obtain the highest responses from children from the least affluent class. Table 19.3 provides the way children ranked the ads (by class):

Table 19.3
Ranking of Ads by Children of Different Classes

Upper Class	Middle Class	Lower Class
1. Eveready	1. Ariel	1. Bajaj Scooter
2. Weekender	2. BSA SLR	2. Atlas
3. Ariel	3. Atlas Cycle	3. Godrej Puf
4. Atlas	4. Eveready	4. Ariel
5. Godrej Puf	5. Godrej Puf	5. Tata Chai
6. Vimal Suitings	6. Bajaj Scooter	6. BSA SLR
7. BSA SLR	7. Glucon D	7. Glucon D
8. Glucon D	8. Vimal	8. Emami Cream
9. Bajaj Scooter	9. Tata Chai	9. Vimal
10. Emami Cream	10. Weekender	10. Eveready
11. Bandar Chaap	11. Emami Cream	11. Bandar Chaap
12. Tata Chai	12. Bandar Chaap	12. Weekender

These lists show that while upper class children are most impressed by ads promoting a battery and a fashion house, the middle class responds best to commercials for products of immediate relevance to their families such as Ariel and BSA SLR. The lower class appreciated the Bajaj scooter and Atlas cycle ads—both consumer

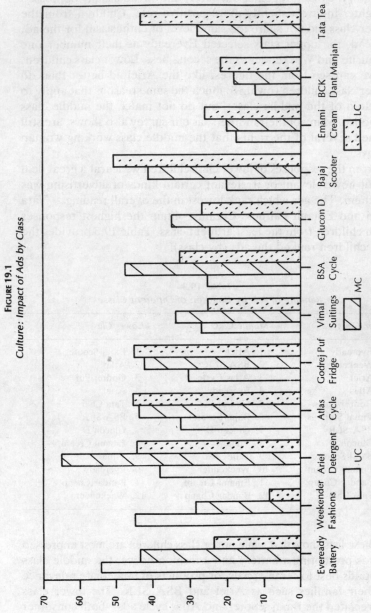

Figure 19.1
Culture: Impact of Ads by Class

Note: See text for details.
Figures for children in age group 8-15 years.

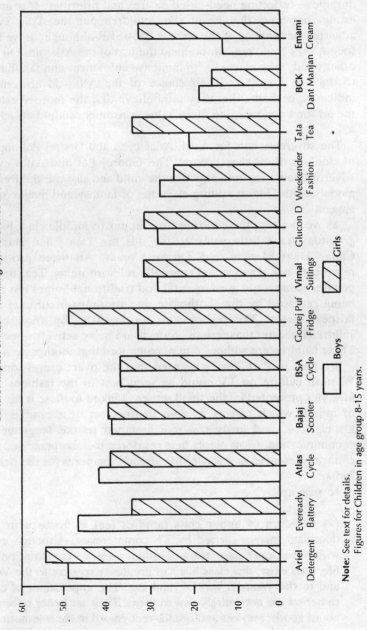

FIGURE 19.2

Culture: Impact of Ads — Ranking by Preference and Sex

Note: See text for details.

Figures for Children in age group 8-15 years.

durables—reflecting need-based desires and priorities. It is interesting, however, that lower class children put the Atlas cycle advertisement ahead of the one for BSA SLR although, as we had found, they could not comprehend the text of the Atlas ad. On the other hand, they reacted with immense enjoyment and familiarity to the one for BSA. Their choice of the Atlas advertisement indicates, perhaps, that they too believe that the more Western the ad for a product, the more value consumers should attach to it.

The advertisements for Ariel, Atlas cycle and Godrej Puf appeal to children of all class groups. The Godrej Puf and Atlas cycle advertisements are both aimed at the child and also use children as models, with Godrej adding elements of fantasy and magic to its appeal.

As we can see, the children from upper to middle class backgrounds attach little value to the ads for Tata Chai, Bandar Chaap Dant Manjan and Emami Cream. All three products represent once popular and culturally relevant items: Tea, toothpowder (commonly used by rural and traditional homes but now being replaced by the toothpaste and toothbrush culture) and fairness cream. The rejection of toothpowder by lower class children indicates that certain products are being actively rejected. These children are without doubt, convinced that toothpaste is in.

We had, in Part Two, suggested that the overt expressions of Western culture on TV could be seen best in the fashions and lifestyles promoted by the small screen. Linked to these is the use of music, which carries its own distinct set of meanings and associations, and lastly the role assigned to the language of communication. Class biases help reinforce the acceptance of this culture, presented as a way of life already the norm for the rich in India.

To sum up:

(a) Children of upper class families feel at home with the dominant images carried by TV commercials. Although even within the upper class strata of Indian society huge variations in lifestyles exist, this class has had greatest exposure to the West and to the Western way of thinking. The imperatives of consumerism are not entirely new to them. They are better informed about goods, services and brands recognised in the international market and, therefore, require little preparation for their entry into the Indian market. The children of this class reflect a keen interest in those aspects of consumerism that promise to help them become more active as members of a larger international community of consumers. They watch more STAR TV and dream of flying international airlines and owning a well-known credit card. They also feel, as one child articulated, that the rest of Indian society (which does not speak English and does not wear the kind of clothes that echo American fashions) should not try to conform to this kind of lifestyle but should instead hold on to the 'rich traditions' of Indian culture. This child, obviously well travelled and well-informed, also pointed out that in European countries such as France, people take great pride in their language and customs and, therefore, 'Indian Indians' should do the same. The argument was interesting, although the child excluded himself and all the others who belonged to his class of Indians from the responsibility of upholding 'Indian culture'.

(b) That the children from middle class families are concentrating on changing their appearances, trying to transform their status by, for instance, listening avidly to modern Western music and are very consumption-oriented. To them the culture of TV ads is exciting and creates high aspirations for change. These children watch a lot of Hindi films and the film world reassures them by reflecting a growing cultural similarity with the world of ads. Much of the lifestyles, fashions, music and dance in Indian films are now straight lifts from the American screen.

(c) For children from lower class backgrounds, the cultural images in TV commercials are alien but fascinating. Some of them react with passivity, responding to the emotive appeal of the ad, ignoring the relevance of its context. In this class of children we sensed a growing unease. Their parents, told us that they felt helpless to handle the changes in society and that they could not guide their children into a world they did not themselves know or understand. 'Let TV teach them since we cannot,' was a common remark. In this social grouping there was also confusion about whether the people they saw in TV commercials were at all Indian, (except where easily identified as such). To many children ads were peopled by foreigners and Indians who were 'different' from the rest.

If one were to go solely by the image of India as created and reflected in TV advertising, one might conclude that it is, by and large, a nation of great affluence and wealth. In the ads on Indian TV there are few 'real' people, everything is beautiful—almost perfect. This vision is developed by projecting the needs, aspirations and lifestyles of mainly one social class and that too, not always realistically. This projection is at the expense of the rest of Indian society which constitutes almost 90 per cent of the population but finds itself excluded from the world of Indian television advertising. Yet the aim of the advertiser seems to be, essentially, to entrap the burgeoning middle class—that large and amorphous section which is so difficult to pin down or define. To them advertising, in recent years, has provided an alternative class image, which it seems, is fast becoming acceptable.

In 1993, a senior Doordarshan official told us that in his assessment, TV advertising was essentially geared towards the middle class. However true this may be, the standards being set even for this class of Indians are fashioned by the norms of the miniscule, Westernised upper class.

Our classification of TV advertisements revealed (Table 19.4) that over 55 per cent of the ads on TV in 1992 were predominantly upper class in that the lifestyles portrayed could only be associated with that class of people in India who are the best

Table 19.4
Classification of Indian Ads by Class

Week	Upper Class	Middle Class	Lower Class	Cut Across	None
One	132	98	5	30	2
Two	184	87	7	10	–
Three	198	91	12	17	–
Four	156	88	14	35	–
Total	670	364	38	92	2

educated, rich, influential elite. They are so exposed to the Western way of thinking that they can respond to it with the same confidence as can similar elites in the North and in other countries as well. This projection stands out in ads such as JCT, Vimal and other suitings, Ivana perfume, Le Sancy, Titan watches, Citra, Mirinda, Vadilal Ice cream, Archies and so on, It should be remembered however, that the products promoted may well appeal to a broader segment of Indian society than simply the so-called upper class. The upper class depiction serves merely to create a mental association between the product and the lifestyle, and to lay the foundation for the rest of society's aspirational development in that direction.

Just over 30 per cent of Indian advertising on TV uses middle class images and lifestyles to sell its goods. The selection of products that are thus promoted include detergents such as Rin, ads for pressure cookers, non-aerated drinks such as Percy Sip and Rasna, condiments and so on. In hardly any of these commercials is the middle class depicted in its real sense. However, the characterisation in the ads and the scenarios chosen are indeed of relevance to what is termed the middle class. While advertisers choose not to focus on crowded family homes, unkempt exteriors in DDA/government colonies or on the continuance of the joint family norm, they nonetheless project the concerns of the typical middle class, seeking out, in particular, the housewife and the working woman.

Only a little over 3 per cent of TV advertising brings into focus the rest of Indian society—the least affluent majority in the country. Since this figure is accounted for in large measure by socially relevant ads on immunisation, drinking water, dowry, the girl child and so on, commercials with a selling intent targeted at this class are extremely limited. Advertising, on Doordarshan's national network, is not particularly concerned with winning over these millions. The few ads that do appear use lower middle class environments to sell products like toothpowders, medicated shampoos, locks and a few brands of soap. The class images imposed upon millions of non-English speaking Indians are creating an enormous gulf while at the same time the demands of consumerism are making it impossible for them to remain at such a distance. They will have to bridge the divide if only to establish that they too are part of India. In other words, the largest section of Indians (40 per cent of all Indians live below the poverty line) see their lifestyles, their realities and their faces mirrored in under 3 per cent of largely non-consumer product advertising while the tiny affluent and elite section sees its lifestyles presented in a majority of ads.

While discussing the India portrayed in the world of TV advertising with children in Delhi, we realised that though children still think of India as a poor nation, they tend to accept the lack of realism in advertising unquestioningly. They become aware of this discrepancy only when asked to analyse TV advertising. Group discussions with children usually concluded that TV commercials do not use real people and real, identifiable situations and that, like the Hindi film, advertising is another form of escapism—it depicts lifestyles that are dream-like. A number of children said that it was nice to see so many beautiful people and homes and exciting situations in TV ads and that these made you want to buy the product. They also felt (and this was true for children across class) that the advertiser could not be successful if the people shown in TV ads were ordinary. No one, they said, would buy a product that was shown being used by an Indian who was not 'modern' or was 'unsophisticated'. This raises the question of where and how we evolve our understanding of what is sophisticated and what is not and in what respect we are willing to show those who do not conform to advertising stereotypes. Tragically, the truth is that we are all deeply influenced by media and other forces that tell us constantly that the acceptable definition of modernity is the one that is handed down to us by the West. The challenge: match the lifestyles and consumption patterns that go with it.

If it is the affluent class whose lifestyles serve to promote consumption best, then do TV commercials portray them accurately? The Indian upper class is still quite feudal in its way of life. Almost every upper class household teems with helpers and has a long list of services it depends on. Self-help is by and large unknown. However, practically no TV advertisement pays any heed to this. The ads never include people who work as household help although servants, cooks, bearers and maids are very much part of upper class lifestyles. Service people such as the milkman (*doodhwallah*), the garderners (*malis*), the washerman (*dhobi*) or even painters, carpenters and others regularly employed by well-to-do households find no place in the commercials. What is more, these ads would have us believe that the affluent are, as is the case in Western nations, completely self-reliant—the lady of the house cleans even the toilet bowls, the children fend for themselves, people tend their own gardens and, in short, believe, as much of the West does, in self-help.

This absence of 'real people' is at variance even with what goes on in Western advertising. In ads produced in Europe and America, for instance, a construction worker wipes the sweat from his brow and takes a break with a packet of really crunchy, irresistible chips . . . . The milkman is a consumer and the people at pubs could hail from just about any walk of life. People from different regions (identifiable from their accents and their dress) feature in commercials and enliven them.

Children, we discovered, felt that the 'rest of India' (which does not have the means, the interest or the sophistication to share in this business of consumption), does not have the right to be seen on the screen. Those belonging to that section of Indian society which is excluded from TV advertising, told us that they feel alienated from the 'other India'. They expressed a feeling of low self-esteem and said that they were not worth emulating. Worse still, they considered it alright for their existence to be completely denied. Yet they also felt discounted and degraded as human beings and felt that salvation lay only in their ability to conform to the image of the modern Indian.

At one school in South Delhi, the children (11-year olds from affluent backgrounds) spent some time considering the aspirations that would grow in people who were being left out, as it were. One child said that the least affluent parents would secretly desire to see their children turn out like the ones in TV ads but added: 'They'll never be quite like us.' She went on to say that the 'traditional Indian' should be protected from all this 'Western culture' because 'it will spoil their culture'.

When we pointed out the contradiction between illusion and reality to one advertising executive, he countered it with the argument that advertising was a ray of sunshine in what would otherwise be a bleak picture. 'Advertising is doing a great job. It's a source of positive, gay and happy emotions and offers people an escape from the depressing realities around us,' he said. Undoubtedly the country has more than its share of problems and for millions life is a gruelling experience. We certainly deserve breaks but is deliberate distancing from social reality the answer? What does it lead to?

As the *Human Development Report* points out, it is not the strength of the country's currency (or the visible affluence in the marketplace) that determines development but the social achievements judged in terms of how far the nation has provided the basics of a decent life (health, nutrition, education) to its people.

In this respect, India figures at the bottom of the list and has little to be proud of.[21]

In the end we must add that while children are getting used to these dominant images of life in their country and are likely to discount as unimportant the other realities they know and experience, they believe that commercials are not made with the intention of helping you to understand the world around you. Yet the same children believe, like and even act on such advertising.

AMBITIONS

The responses of children in the 8 to 15 years age group when asked what they would like to be when they grew up are detailed in Table 19.5. The top ten professions preferred account for over 75 per cent of the response.

Table 19.5
The Top Ten Preferred Professions

1. Doctor	157 (97 girls, 60 boys)
2. Business	73 (68 boys)
3. Teacher	62 (61 girls)
4. Engineer	53 (48 boys)
5. Army	39 (35 boys)
6. Pilot	37 (35 boys)
7. Police	30 (21 girls)
8. Cricketer	25 (All boys)
9. Scientist	21 (10 girls, 11 boys)
10. CA	17 (11 boys, 6 girls)
Total	514 (Total Sample of age group: 669)

From the responses in Table 19.5 we concluded that traditional professions such as medicine and teaching are still attractive and even considered 'noble'. The fact remains that many children, especially those from the less privileged sections do not have the requisite financial resources and educational background to realise their dreams. Yet they are conscious of the need for strong education-related and medical services, both of which are sadly lacking in their own environments. Many children also know that being a local, private doctor is one of the best ways of making a quick buck.

Significantly, once the most sought after job, government service does not figure in the list of top ten professions. This seems to indicate a growing awareness that money is to be made from 'private enterprise'. There is also a degree of cynicism with regard to the administrative services.

The special mention of the police force (21 girls and 9 boys said they would like to join the police) had a direct relationship with the impact of the TV serial, *Udaan*, in which actress Kavita Chaudhary (also remembered for her appearance in the Surf ad as Saritaji) plays a police officer. As the figures tell us, Kavita Chaudhary's performance in both the serial and the ad have created, especially among girls from the lower classes, a very high aspiration to emulate her. Respondents reinforced this during their discussions, leaving us with little doubt about the influential role of television in shaping their aspirations.

We also got some unusual and interesting answers. One 14-year old told us cockily that he wanted to be a smuggler—and even asked us how the word was spelt. Another boldly wrote into his questionnaire (and followed it up with several exclamation marks) that he would be satisfied with nothing less than becoming the President of the United States of America! Three cheers!!

The professional preferences of girls and boys shown in Figure 19.2 indicate clearly that girls would like to become doctors and teachers above all else, whereas the boys are rooting for business, engineering, flying and professional sports.

The study conducted by Pathfinders (quoted by us earlier) had confirmed that these were indeed the most favoured professions in the child's mind.

Children from upper class families (Table 19.6) were the only ones to come up with the following professions:

1. Archaeologist
2. Badminton player
3. Brain surgeon
4. Car manufacturer
5. Cartoonist
6. CBI
7. Film director
8. Film star
9. Flautist
10. Forest officer

Table 19.6
Ambitions of Children by Social Grouping

Upper Class		Middle Class		Lower Class	
Doctor	= 37	Doctor	= 69	Doctor	= 51
Engineer	= 29	Business	= 34	Teacher	= 27
Business	= 20	Teacher	= 29	Police	= 22
Pilot	= 10	Army	= 19	Business	= 19
Scientist	= 10	Engineer	= 18	Army	= 15
Cricketer	= 8	Pilot	= 14	Pilot	= 13
CA	= 7	Cricketer	= 14	Engineer	= 6
Teacher	= 6	Scientist	= 10	Cricketer	= 3
Army	= 5	CA	= 9	Scientist	= 1
Police	= 0	Police	= 8	CA	= 1

11. Geologist
12. MBA—join multinational
13. Millionnaire
14. Missionary
15. Model (this response came from a couple of girls and, more interestingly, from three boys)
16. Mountain climber
17. Neurologist
18. Pathologist
19. Prime Minister
20. Tennis player
21. V.J.
22. World champion
23. Writer

Others are guided by the limited, and real options open to them. Lower class children were the only ones to mention:

1. Carpenter
2. Customs officer
3. Driver
4. Electrician
5. Farmer
6. Labourer
7. Nurse

8. Painter
9. NCC Cadet

Some children of construction workers said they could not aspire to anything beyond the profession their fathers were following and even within that, could not see themselves improving on the status or level of professional competence attained by the older generation. On the other hand, middle and upper class children had a much wider range of options open to them and were certain that they would eventually take up professions that would monetarily and in terms of status match (and even go beyond) what their parents currently enjoy.

Nearly a third (32.88 per cent) of our respondents said that studying abroad was important to their career ambitions. Certainly, at least 6 of the top 10 professions listed by them could enable them to seek positions here or abroad—doctor, businessman/ executive, teacher, scientist and chartered accountant. Hard work and a good education were identified as the major stepping stones to success by 83.25 per cent and 69 per cent of the children, respectively.

It was on the role and significance of money that there were major differences. While 60 per cent of the lower class children attached a high premium to the role that money plays in building the future, just over 25 per cent of upper class and 35 per cent of middle class children pointed out its worth.

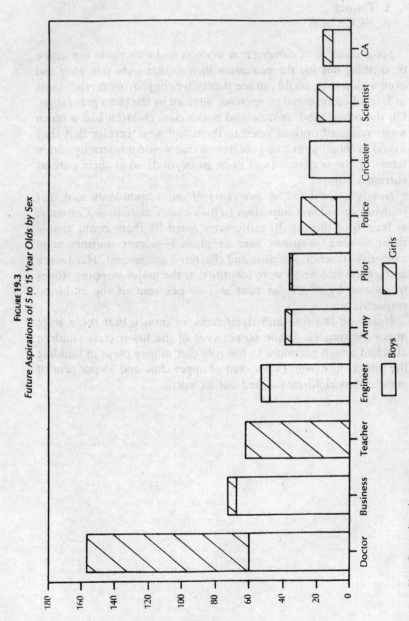

FIGURE 19.3
Future Aspirations of 5 to 15 Year Olds by Sex

Note: By number of responses.

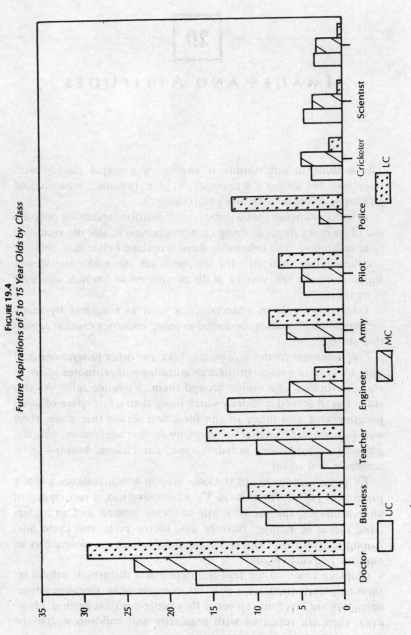

FIGURE 19.4

Future Aspirations of 5 to 15 Year Olds by Class

Note: By percentage of responses.

20

IMAGES AND ATTITUDES

The attitude to entertainment undergoes a **major change** with television. No longer is it necessary to plan, **organise, seek** out and pay for individual or family entertainment.

Television encourages a complete abdication, **requiring** only the use of an index finger to bring on a programme to **suit the** receiver's taste and mood. The belief that there is nothing **better than** relaxing and unwinding in front of a television set **can make the** viewer throw away the last vestige of discrimination **and watch** whatever is on offer.

Television's role as entertainer is seen as **harmless** by many viewers, though studies conducted in many countries **caution** against this attitude.

Entertainment carries a price tag. Like any **other programming,** it upholds certain values, influences attitudes and **promotes** ideas. It chooses themes and builds around them. Violence **sells.** As this study has observed, children watch more than a **fair share** of adult programming and many of the films and serials **that** come their way incorporate violence in its many forms: **aggression,** threats, physical intimidation, murder, rape, car chases, **bomb** blasts, accidents and so on.

TV programming is not the only area in which violence **holds** a prominent place. There is, in TV advertising too, **a recurrence** of violent images, the use of music to create **tension and an** underlying threat of failure. Battery ads, motor cycle **and cycle** ads, commercials for toys and tyres and many **others use** violence as an emotive response plank.

Children react. Some feel frightened and **disturbed;** others let their heightened reactions pass off as excitement. **Because** advertisements are brief, the violence they project is **disregarded.** However, they are repeated with regularity **and children** watch the same scene again and again.

TV VIOLENCE AND CHILDREN

Studies conducted on violence and TV in developed nations suggest that TV influences children in three ways:

(i) It creates characters they can imitate;

(ii) It immunises them to violence by showing them so much of it in so glamourised a manner that after a time it fails to register as something to be avoided; and

(iii) It justifies violence. If the behaviour is, for instance, sanctioned by a film hero (Amitabh Bachchan playing the angry young man and taking the law into his own hands) children may be willing to accept it as appropriate.

Dr. Leonard Eron, psychologist, Chairman of the American Psychological Association's Commission on Violence and Youth, testified before the U.S. Senate on 31 March 1992 that: 'Television violence affects youngsters of all ages of both genders, at all socioeconomic levels and all levels of intelligence, and the effect is not limited to children who are already disposed to being aggressive and is not restricted to this country'.

Explaining how TV/boosts violence in children Dr. Eron suggests that a heightened state of tension, including a strong physiological component, results from frequently seeing high-action (violent) sequences. Another aspect deals with the rehearsal of behaviours observed by the child on television. The more often the child rehearses sequences involving his/her favourite character by continued or repeated viewing, the more likely it is that those very acts will be remembered and re-enacted when the child is in a situation which he thinks is similar. Also, by watching consistently aggressive behaviour, the youngster may come to believe that this is an expected, appropriate way of behaving and that most people solve problems in this manner.[22]

NCTV's research study (1991) of 100 nationally-distributed cartoons showed that 50 per cent glorified violence or used it to entertain. According to the study, cartoons have three times as many acts of violence than prime television. Among those listed as the *most* violent were: *Teenage Mutant Ninja Turtles* (which has

·already created an obsessive following for itself in India) and *G.I. Joe* (also familiar in India largely due to TV commercials for the toy set). Also listed were *Tiny Toons, Peter Pan* and *The Pirates, Dragon Warrior* and *Toxic Crusaders*.

Warner Brothers' cartoons featured the most violence containing 50 acts of violence per hour (almost one act per minute). Even Disney's *Gumni Bears Talespin, Duck Tales, Chip 'N Dale* and *Rescue Rangers* (all of which are available in Delhi's video libraries) exceeded the overall average, recording 29 acts of violence per hour.

The top ten most violent cartoons have *Tom & Jerry Kids* with 88 and *Bugs Bunny and Pals* with 68 acts of violence per hour. According to NCTV data, by the age of 18 years, the typical child in the US would have witnessed more than 200,000 acts of violence on TV, including 25,000 killings.

The National Coalition on Television Violence chair and research director Dr. Thomas Radecki, said

American children continue to be inundated with screen violence for the purpose of attracting children for advertisers. From an early age we teach our children to enjoy unrealistic and glamourised violence. With 33 out of 37 research studies finding a harmful impact on normal children from cartoon programming clearly this must be stopped.[23]

Despite this, many of these cartoons are still popular and are broadcast in several countries of the world including India: *Tom and Jerry, Woody Woodpecker* and *Mighty Mouse*. NCTV identifies three cartoons (which thanks to satellite TV will sooner or later come our way) as the 'worst': *Beetlejuice, Dragon Warrior* and *Dark Water*. According to its newsletter, NCTV planned to launch a campaign for an advertisers boycott of at least one of these cartoons and *G.I. Joe*.

Child psychologists suggest that while cartoons are 'funny' and many people find it hard to see them as being violent, it is a misconception that they do not harm children. Dr Benjamin Spock recalls a nursery school-teacher telling him that her children were crudely bopping into each other much more than usual without provocation. When she remonstrated with them they protested: 'But that's what the Three Stooges do on TV.' The theme of cartoons such as Popeye is that any problem can be solved by 'brute force' which you get by eating spinach. Cartoons in being funny and fast paced reduce a child's perception of danger, pain and suffering. Investigations suggest that where children are addicted cartoon watchers the tomfoolery among children can assume frightening proportions when they become more violent than fun.[24]

It is forcefully argued (at home and abroad) that it is unfair to blame violence and aggression on TV. Television as a medium merely reflects (sometimes in an overt, exaggerated manner) the violence and frustration that already exists in society. The attempt, therefore, must be to rid society of its guns, its drugs, its unemployment and other distortions that nurture human and social antagonisms. The August 1992 issue of TV Guide, a New York publication carried an interesting debate on violence on TV. The experts included Peggy Charren, President, Action for Television, George Gerbner whom we have earlier quoted and John Leonard, a TV critic.

Leonard pointed out that American society/culture has always been more violent than any other culture, and that this tendency has been fed by cult figures like *Superhero*, implying that the violence has little to do with what people watch on TV and more to do with the culture that has developed around them. He compared the U.S. example with that of Japan (the only country in the world that watches more television than the United States). In Japan television programmes are surprisingly violent. However, the emphasis on violence and excessive TV watching does not seem to have the same effect on Japanese culture and life as it does in the United States.

George Gerbner, Dean Emeritus, Annenburg School of Communication, University of Pennsylvania, countered the argument: 'We did a comparative study and found that Japanese violence, unlike our own, is not happy violence. It's painful, it's awful, it teaches a very different lesson.'[25]

These debates and studies have been quoted because many readers will recognise a number of cartoon titles mentioned since the Indian child is now receiving a large helping from the same dish. According to Mander, 'Fear is one of the most desirable emotions for advertisers. Loneliness and self-doubt are good ones. So is competition.'[26] Fear is a common feeling that advertising plays upon. By creating strong images that people want to live up to, it suggests that the failure to meet those ideals will result in social rejection.

SELF IMAGES

One of the loudest messages that comes across the television screen through advertising is that 'becoming rich must be the ultimate goal of every consumer'. All the 'super rich ads' (Titan, S. Kumar, Vimal) are aimed at creating in the ordinary, average Indians the desire to belong to that class of people who have it all—money, education, culture and class. The stress is on fashion, accessories, gadgetry, cosmetics and internationalism.

Television advertisements, also put a premium on being beautiful. Kellner's comments on advertising suggest that this new 'involvement with appearances' mirrors American society where 'corporations, politicians, and individuals are all obsessed with image.' Advertisements for clothes, he states, 'show the proper image, for specific social groups and classes'.[27]

Many television commercials in India pitched at young, and hot-blooded adolescents, still to learn who they really are, attempt to forment their restlessness. The message for them is: 'To be rebellious is right'. The youth who will accept no rules is the favourite role model. Again and again this character appears to sell cycles, cold drinks and even shock absorbers, always enveloped in a strangely solitary and aggressive garb, he is a 'rebel without a cause'. Unlike his counterpart in the Hindi film who has a cause, this youth is given individualism, bordering on self-indulgence, as a motto.

For the Indian who is gradually joining the ranks of committed consumers advertising has developed a code which dictates everything from behaviour and dress to personality.

What about programming? Imagine what the world looks like to a child who watches only Star TV. The images that come across the screen paint an odd version of the world:

(a) English is *the* language people converse in.
(b) The music played on MTV is the only kind of music people throughout the world listen to Nitha the notable exception of the enigmatic Yanni!
(c) All personal relationships outside India resemble those portrayed in soap operas such as *Santa Barbara*.

The child may never have the opportunity to visit other countries or to directly experience different cultures. Gradually the child may become so comfortable with the standardised culture shown on STAR TV that anything else may seem odd or out of place. Will the child *value* other, less visible cultures?

Talking to senior advertising officials in Bombay, we tried to understand where the ad industry thought it was leading us. They assured us that the ad industry merely reflected what the consumer himself desired and that the images that today dominate the screen are part of the young Indian's dream. But surely, we said, that is not true of all Indians? What about the little girl who is baffled and a little unnerved by what she sees on TV because it is so far removed from her reality?

We questioned an ad film maker and an ad executive. Did advertisers in India have to use the symbols and values of the Western world to sell products in this country? How was advertising creative if it merely used and reworked ads made abroad? Why didn't the Indian advertiser reflect the Indian for what he/she is? Why did the advertiser discount the culture and ways of his own country?

'Look, we are merely doing a job. We do what we are expected to. We work with a brief. What you see is what the big firms want you to see in advertisements', came the response. They reluctantly admitted that while India has some of the best advertising talent in the world, this talent could get stymied by the imposition of international commercial formats which reduce the freedom of the advertiser. Instead of having to come up with brilliant and creative ideas, born from the cultural soil of this country, ad people were getting used to merely substituting the characters and situations of commercial made elsewhere with Indian ones. But that is old hat. It is well known that creative people in advertising agencies spend much of their time watching and rewatching foreign commercials, many of which get replicated simply because it's easier than selling a new line.

'Yes, advertising is reinforcing what might be culturally alien values for many Indians but the change had to come some day. And when there is change it is always accompanied by pain,' said one advertiser who has spent much of his time researching the Indian market. This pain is aggravated by the fact that many Indians are still struggling to meet their basic needs, even as the concept of need undergoes transformation.

If we take the word 'need' to mean something basic to human survival—food, shelter, clothing—or basic to human content-ment—peace, love, safety, companionship, intimacy, a sense of fulfillment—these will be sought and found by people whether or not there is advertising. In fact, advertising intervenes between people and their needs, separates them from direct fulfillment and urges them to believe that satisfaction can be obtained only through commodities. It is through this intervention and separation that advertising can create value, thereby justifying its existence.

The goal of all advertising is discontent or, to put it another way, an internal scarcity of contentment. This must be continually created, even at the moment when one has finally bought something. In that event, advertising has the task of creating discontent with what has just been bought, since once that act is completed, the purchase has no further benefit to the market system. The newly purchased commodity must be gotten rid of and replaced by the 'need' for a new commodity as soon as possible. The ideal world for advertisers would be one in which whatever is bought is used only once and then tossed aside. Many new products have been designed to fit such a world.[28]

Children are in some ways a sort of litmus test in this context: no child is born with a need or desire for tomato ketchup for instance. It is something he/she learns to want—from other human beings or from the ads that urge the child to buy it.

More than 65 per cent of the children in the 8 to 15 years age group felt they *needed* the products they saw on TV, with the middle class children way ahead (72.18 per cent) of the upper (43.05 per cent) and lower (57.30 per cent) segments.

Does the upper class boy who claims to watch 14 hours of TV on holidays need yet another TV when there are already five sets at home? Does the middle class child need more of the latest toys in the market? Does the child in the *basti* need even one television set when there isn't enough food to go around?

Why not, some people might ask. After all, there's nothing wrong with a lot of things TV advertising teaches. It makes people aware of the *need* for personal hygiene, encourages them to have fun, helps them focus on themselves. That's fine, except that hygiene is not the plank on which soap-sellers stand. No, it is beauty, erotic perfume and youthfulness that they sell. Nor does cleanliness have anything to do with the brand of soap, toothpaste or shampoo that you acquire.

Mander feels that 'television limits and confines human knowledge. It changes the way humans receive information.'[29] Rather than learn from direct experience or respond to real need, children from every strata of society are walking around with images of beautiful homes, gadgets that make life comfortable—washing machines, fridges, mixies, coolers and air conditioners—fun foods and fancy clothes in their minds. These images come to them repeatedly, day after day. They appear on the picture tube and unobtrusively wedge themselves into the subconscious where they are carried around like germinating seeds. But many of the ideals, dreams and aspirations linked to the sale and advertising of commodities, appear to contradict the social definition of need as we once understood it. When so much of the country is still to be provided with electricity, how important is the microwave oven?

Our deepest concern is directed at less advantaged children who are being urged to conform to the ways of a society and to a value system they can hardly comprehend. They are frightened and frustrated not having the resources to keep up with the demands of the new, emerging order.

21

CHANGING VALUES

Up to the late seventies we were, as a nation, guided by a set of values given to us by the Independence movement. These values are best ascribed to the fierce pride in 'being Indian, buying Indian'. We never failed to remind ourselves that our's was a poor nation and that there were millions of Indians who did not have the basics—*roti, kapada aur makan* (food, clothes and shelter).

This awareness did three things: (*a*) created a belief that citizens had a larger responsibility and that poverty was a collective concern; (*b*) stemming from a sensitivity to other people's poverty, a vulgar show of wealth was discouraged; (*c*) efforts were made to contain consumerism, protect the Indian market from being overrun by multinational companies and to let the flag of self-reliance fly high. The political justification for this was that India's hard-won freedom could not be allowed to be pilfered away by permitting dependence on foreign manufacturers. It has, of course, been argued that this protectionism, be it of industry or even television, served the interests of a small group of people.

However, the fact that we produced a wide range of products and ran our own heavy industry was, at the time, reason enough to be proud of the country. In sharp contrast to us, some developing countries were staggering under the burden of economic debt.

In the mid-eighties, liberalisation became the new philosophy and the swift changes in the commodity market completely altered the priorities in the nation's shopping list. It replaced the old approach, the cult of protectionism and the politics of 'third world unity' which had harped on the 'threat from Western nations' and even warned against attempts at 'cultural imperialism'. This fiercely independent spirit had made India one of the few nations that did not depend, for instance, on imported TV programming to fill in transmission time.

These planks upon which policy was formulated, have long since given way to a new ethic which hungers for a free market economy, and believes that technology is the primary vehicle for attaining quick, sustainable economic growth. The old fear that the transfer of technology would be 'loaded' and that the consequences of joining the queue for technology would have adverse ramifications beyond the economic sphere, seem to have dissipated or have at least been set aside.

Television represents a form of technology with infinite potential for disseminating ideas to huge audiences across huge distances. The 'cultural imperialism' debate, now set at rest (except when industry feels threatened: for example, the consternation of Indian newspaper owners over the question of foreign newspapers being allowed direct access to the Indian reader), is still alive elsewhere in the world and is, if anything, giving rise to even deeper anxieties. In fact, with regard to media technologies including satellite, several West European nations are exercised over the threat to local, regional or national identity from the prospect of a multitude of satellite-transmitted foreign programmes being aired in their countries.

Marit Bakke, in *New Media Politics: Culture at Stake* says:

A concern about national cultural identity has particularly been expressed in Italy, the Netherlands, France, Finland and Denmark, with governments as the most ardent defenders of this aspect. The French government has talked about the 'English language imperialism', while the Italian government is concerned about 'cultural colonization'. Naturally, the launching of a series of satellites can generally be seen as a serious threat to a nationally-oriented cultural policy. And satellite transmissions combined with local and regional cable-television will in a few years time offer impressive communication networks, which will be very difficult to control. The import of foreign video programmes is also seen as quite problematic and, so far a few counter measures have been tried.[30]

In 1982 the French government stated that the general objectives of broadcasting should be to defend the national culture and encourage programmes which present local life. The development and regulation of cable has, in keeping with this perspective, played a central role in the government's media policy. A general rule for programming on cable television was decided upon in April 1984, in which the government stated that at most 30 per cent of total programme time might be of foreign origin. In an attempt to control the amount of foreign video programmes, the government imposed restrictions on the import of video hardware, e.g. a high tax and particular technical specifications. The government also tried to encourage associations and cultural industries to establish a multi-media group which could compete with the huge production from American companies. Very high ranking committees have been set up in several European and other countries with senior statesmen such as a former President of France, heading one such committee to assess, monitor and regulate the transmission of foreign programming.

In this context, it is worth recalling that the French Government has also been at the forefront of the attempt by European nations to stymie the ever-increasing domination of American media in their countries. The Uruguay Round to regulate international trade, popularly known as GATT, became the battleground between the USA and the Western European nations on the subject of 'culture', which included a debate on films and television services. The European countries successfully resisted American attempts to gain unlimited access to their markets, arguing that American 'cultural' exports were killing their own cultural traditions. The fear was not unfounded: in 1993, of the top 100 worldwide box office successes, over 80 were Hollywood productions and the first 'outside' film to break the American monopoly came in at number 27.

In sharp contrast, India has passively watched the spread of satellite TV and abdicated from serious and informed discussion on issues of *who* controls transmission, *how* relevant programming is and *how* it affects the nation's image of itself. What is more, the nature of programming that is beamed to us (and to 53 other countries in Asia and West Asia), is considered the worst example of TV fare that could be had from the developed West. Instead of the better programmes for adults and children, we receive outdated serials and soaps such as *The Bold and the Beautiful*.

However, it is argued that the

image of the media as ideological state apparatus is particularly important in international settings, where American media fare has tended to dominate developing nations. The fear is that people in the Third World are being educated, by this content, to become capitalist consumers. Their own traditional social and cultural mores are being eclipsed by commercial American values embedded in media fare. This is cultural imperialism, an attempt to educate and thus transform Third World nations into passive and dependent outposts of American cultural values. The education metaphor, based in notions of the media as cultivating particular kinds of values, underlies much of national as well as international criticism of media influence.

The MacBride report had warned in 1980 that

In setting up ever more powerful, homogeneous and centralized networks, there is a danger of accentuating the centralisation of the public or institutional sources of information, of strengthening inequalities and imbalances, and of increasing the sense of irresponsibility and powerlessness both in individuals and communities . . . by intensifying competition, it may lead to the standardisation of content and, at the international level, accentuate cultural dependence by increasing the use of imported programmes.[31]

'Existing outside the boundaries of the country, the multinational companies, in concert with banks, are capable of the economic domination of entire nations. Governments slip slowly into a new role subordinate to and supportive of them' is a warning that we ought to consider.[32]

With growing transnationalisation of the media and the tendency of nations to respond by permitting, as India is doing, more and more commercialisation of its own television, the stage is set for a radical change in the way a whole people think and react. When new media technologies put a country such as India into the shadow of a satellite footprint they:

(a) create an opportunity to address a new and enormous audience which also represents a huge market.

(b) they secure a new avenue for multinational giants (who are slowly edging their way into the Indian market) to transmit commercial messages through advertising. Both these factors could more or less force an international tilt to media policy, particularly as satellite networks have a transmission capacity far beyond that of our national capability.

As discussed in Part One, there is a genuine fear that the media depends upon advertising for survival, which in turn does the bidding of big business firms owned by a small number of very wealthy people. Being in powerful positions, these handful of people can decide the fate of print and television media. Logically, these media will promote a content and programming which is acceptable to those who hold the financial reins in their hands. As a powerful influencer, television serves the interests of this tiny community by spreading their messages far and wide and thereby enabling them to consolidate their hold. As Jerry Mander has said:

The spread of television unified a whole people within a system of conceptions and living patterns that made possible the expansion of huge economic enterprise. Because of it, our whole culture and the physical shape of the environment, no more or less than our minds and feelings, have been computerised, linearied, suburbanised, freewayised, and packaged for sale.[33]

Creating and sustaining values in society is a task that is left to the family and education systems. However, many media critics point out that the dangers of learning from the media are associated with its inherent ability to make viewers believe that *no attempt at educating them is underway*. As Joli Jensen puts it:

We are deemed at risk when viewing television or listening to rock music or reading comics or watching movies, because we are not alert. We are not sufficiently charged and wary of these attempts to seduce and persuade us. We become passive, enervated victims, lulled into complacency and then shaped by the forces that take over when we are least aware.[34]

Jensen also tells us that the 'uses and gratifications' approach to research on media audiences took the stance that the individual was motivated by particular needs or desires which could be fulfilled by certain media behaviours. This implied that the individual was eventually free to choose how to interact with the media and what to gain from it. Arguing against this, Jensen points out that this approach has been charged with being blind to the more 'general and ideological influences on society' of the media.

People in India are today being forced to take positions on the changes that are taking place in the media. There is a sharp dividing line between those who welcome the transnationalisation of the media and those who are uneasy about what TV mania, given the nature of its content, implies for the country.

'Satellite TV is a liberator' was the way one newspaper headline put it. The author argued that since other parts of the world were at last, thanks to satellite TV, getting to watch *India's* Republic day parade and the budget day speech of the finance minister, and that Indians were now appearing on MTV, the question of 'cultural invasions and cultural imperialism' could be laid to rest. Whereas we could not have 'spread the message about India's Rennaisance' this was being done for us by satellite TV, the argument went on to state. For Aiyer, the cross-cultural sharing enabled by STAR for Asian countries represents an opening up rather than the imposition of a cultural image. He also points out that Indians have been exposed for long enough to BBC and Pakistan TV and the fact that they have not been 'deculturised' is reason enough to believe that the Indian viewer can protect himself and has enough grounding to know what to reject and what to absorb from foreign programming.

Aiyer wraps up his argument with an attack on 'the self-appointed guardians of Indian culture', saying that satellite TV has proved them quite wrong. This viewpoint is not uncommon in the debate on media that ensues within and outside the country, and has its own merits and demerits. While the author may like to believe that in a democracy everyone—the rich and the poor, the educated and the illiterate—share equally the responsibility of choosing their leadership and that, therefore, they will act with equally sound judgement in relation to the acceptance or rejection of certain kinds of media programming, it remains that

(a) the impact on India of such a sudden but intense change in the world of television is still at a nascent stage and cannot as yet be fully comprehended;

(*b*) that TV appears to give viewers a choice but, as we have already argued in this book, essentially only forces the viewer to choose between a set of similar menus;

(*c*) as mentioned in Part One, the very technology of television, based as it is on a one-way traffic of ideas, does not allow for an interactive and constantly altering picture to emerge from it but tends to provide *a* view of the world, one kind of entertainment and to lull the viewer into believing that what is presented is the whole and unaffected truth;

(*d*) that when it comes to children, the influences of the media are more extreme in that children are more likely to accept what they see as being real. It is equally true that much of what the Indian viewer does get to see is not only unreal but the images misrepresent reality;

(*e*) lastly, it is hard not to agree with Aiyer in his dismissiveness of the 'cultural imperialism' argument in the sense that the threat exists as much from within the country as from outside. While, for instance, the world of advertising chooses to focus on only a handful of Indians and presents them as *the India* to which it appeals, on the other hand chauvinistic forces are likely to use the 'cultural imperialism' slogan to their own advantage. But such fears should not, we feel, make us reject the need for a widespread social debate on the use of television or the increasing commercialisation of the media. After all, there are other people and issues that are affected, perhaps adversely, by the imposition of certain values and attitudes upon them.

As Krishna Kumar, in his book entitled *Social Character of Learning* points out:

A curriculum which does not represent cultural data of all social groups in a proportionate manner can act as a means of aggression on the groups whose data are excluded or poorly represented. The children of such groups are forced to identify with the symbols of dominant groups and therefore have to perceive themselves as 'backward'.[35]

According to Douglas Kellner, 'threats to individuality, democracy and community from consumer culture' have been the focus of the group of critical theorists known as the Frankfurt School. They include Max Horkheimer, Erich Fromm, Theodor Adorno, Leo Lowenthal and Herbert Marcuse who were forced to flee Nazi Germany in the early thirties and emigrate to the United States where, Kellner says, 'they developed one of the first systematic critical perspectives on advertising, fashion, and the consumer society.'[36]

According to Cees Hamelink:

> Information imbalance leads to the cultural integration of the peripheral countries in the culture promoted by the core. Imported cultural programming encourages consumerism and individualism, and diverts attention from any regard for the long-term needs of the country. Internal gaps develop as urban elites become part of the international economy while the rural poor get left behind. A nation needs cultural independence to develop its own language, forms of musical expression, literature, theatre, educational system, suitable technologies, and what it chooses to preserve from its cultural heritage. Information imbalance thus undermines cultural self-determination.[37]

The concern expressed here relates to the access that nations and people have to useful information: information capacities, information hardware and software and the content of information. Core nations which are the rich, industrialised countries—the United States, Canada, Western Europe, Japan and Australia— largely control the flow of information to the rest of the world subjecting what the writer calls 'peripheral' nations (which comprise the poorer, predominantly rural countries of Africa, Asia and Latin America) to a worrying form of dominance.

Television and TV advertising are, as we have argued, a vital component of social communication. They too, reflect the imbalances just discussed. Television, however, has been hailed for its tremendous potential for supplying information to the widest possible audience and this has influenced policy, especially in developing countries which set out to use it as a public service broadcast system. We would like to point out here that that such an imbalance can be seen with regard to information flows even within India. If Indian television, as mentioned in Part Two, uses English to convey to non-English speaking Indians information on some of the most vital events and issues in the country such as the Annual National Budget, then clearly television is excluding these people. Similarly, with regional television still in its nascent stages, non-Hindi speaking viewers who are offered programming in Hindi over the national network feel justifiably angered at this cultural imposition. It therefore stands to reason that if an honest assessment of the use and role of television in India were to be undertaken, we would in all likelihood find that it serves, within the country, the interests of a particular viewership and does not act as a conduit for information important to all segments of Indian society. The choice of programming and its cultural relevance might also be called into question. In any case, as we can see, for all practical purposes, television in India has become an entertainment channel.

NOTES TO PART III

1. Brand Equity, 'Consumerism in the 90s', *The Economic Times*, 5 January 1994.
2. Subrata Bannerjee, 'Socially Relevant Advertising and the Developing World'. *Communicator*, September 1989.
3. William Leiss, Stephen Kline and Sat Jhally, 1986. *Social Communication in Advertising*. Methuen and Co.
4. Quoted by Vance Packard. 1981. *The Hidden Persuaders*. Penguin, Great Britain.
5. Vance Packard, ibid. See also Patricia Marks Greenfield, *Mind and Media*. Fontana. 1984.
6. *Advertising & Marketing*, May 1993.
7. Ibid.
8. Clyde Miller, *The Process of Persuasion*. See Vance Packard, *The Hidden Persuaders*.
9. Child—The Consumer: A Study in Urban India, Research Proposal October 1991, Search India.
10. The Beveridge Committee Report on the BBC.
11. Nostradamus. Quoted by Brand Equity. *The Economic Times*, 5 January 1994.
12. Charles Atkin, 'Effects of Television Advertising on Children' in *Children And The Faces Of Television: Teaching Violence, Selling* edited by E. Palmer and A. Dorr. Academic Press Inc., 1980.
13. *The Best of Brand Equity*, 1991.
14. Nostradamus, op. cit.
15. IMRB. Brand Equity, 8 April 1992. 'Gambling on the rural roulette'.
16. Charles Atkins, op. cit.
17. See Annexures. Code for Commercial Advertising on Doordarshan.
18. Pathfinder's study: 'Inside the Child's Mind'. A and M, July 1989.
19. CSPI (Centre for Science in the Public Interest) News Release, July 1992.
20. C. Wright Mills. *The Power Elite*. 1956. Oxford University Press, NY.
21. *Human Development Index Report* (Annual). UNDP.
22. Leonard D Eron. Testimony on behalf of the American Psychological Association before the United States Senate Committee on Government Affairs, *Violence and the Media*, 31 March 1992.
23. NCTV: Report on a study of cartoons. *NCTV News*, Vol. 12, Nos. 3–5, June–August 1991.
24. Dr Benjamin Spock, *Baby and Child Care*. 1976. Simon & Schuster, NY.
25. Debate carried by *TV Guide*, August 22, 1992, New York. (Other participants were Rosalyn Weinman, Vice President, Broadcast Standards and Practices, NBC; Dick Wolf, Television Producer; Ronald Slaby, Senior Scientist, The Education Development Center; and Deborah Prothrow-Smith, M.D, Harvard School of Public Health.
26. Jerry Mander, op. cit.

27. Douglas Kellner, 'Advertising and Consumer Culture' in *Questioning the Media*, edited by John Downing, Ali Mohammadi and Annabelle Sreberny-Mohammadi, Thousand Oaks, Sage, 1990.
28. Jerry Mander, op. cit.
29. Jerry Mander, op. cit.
30. Marit Bakke, *New Media Politics: Culture at Stake*: Comparative Perspectives. In *Western Europe*. Edited by Denis McQuail. The Euromedia Group.
31. UNESCO. *Many Voices, One World: The MacBride Report*, London Kogan Page, Paris, UNESCO.
32. Jerry Mander, op. cit.
33. Jerry Mander, op. cit.
34. Joli Jensen, *Redeeming Modernity: Three Dominant Metaphors*, Thousand Oaks, Sage Publications, 1990.
35. Krishna Kumar, *Social Character of Learning*, Sage, New Delhi, 1989.
36. Douglas Kellner, op. cit.
37. Cees Hamelink. 'Information Imbalance: Core and Periphery' in *Questioning the Media*, edited by John Downing, Ali Mohammadi and Annabelle Sreberny-Mohammadi, Thousand Oaks, Sage, 1990.

CONCLUSION AND
RECOMMENDATIONS

Children's perceptions of TV and their reactions to TV advertising have led us to conclude that (*a*) television is one of the most important influences in children's lives; and (*b*) that children are watching more television than ever before and this is only likely to increase with time as TV services extend their reach and offer greater viewing options.

The TV viewing habit is already altering the pattern of family life and social interaction in urban centres like Delhi, and the more people watch television, the less attention they pay to alternative other activities at home and outside.

We found that by and large, television is accepted as a given and there is little questioning of either the nature or content of programming or advertising. Most people feel resigned and accept whatever appears on TV as inevitable since there seems to be no way or opportunity for viewers to intervene in the process by which TV content is determined. Television is therefore looked upon by most people almost as a natural phenomenon—beyond people's control.

This study has enabled us to understand how children of different social backgrounds react to television. TV messages have different meanings for children from different social segments. This is particularly true in India. On the one hand, there is undoubtedly a shared sense of an 'opening up', culturally and in terms of information. A far larger number of people and children now have access to images, knowledge and entertainment they might otherwise never have had. On the other hand, TV is, we feel, negating the kind of lives many people actually live.

Within this changing environment we noticed that children are displaying greater curiosity about the outside world. This interest is more clearly focused on countries that enjoy high standards of living.

It is questionable whether TV is truly broadening children's appreciation of the diversity in cultures, lifestyles and role models that exist around the globe. The argument that television (as we know it today) *must* be welcomed because it has the unparalleled potential to offer viewers an experience of people and places and expose them to socio–cultural information of a kind that they cannot hope to obtain *directly*, holds true only in part. Sensitisation to the world's diversity is translated by TV programming to mean greater awareness of a limited range of information and ideas.

Children in India, we feel, are being exposed to what might be termed an *unreal reality*. Television (barring what might appear on regional networks) often depicts a 'reality' which fails to mirror Indian society or life for what it is. Moreover, the very technology of television lends it a sterilised and untouched air: the tube speaks to the viewers. It leads the viewer to feel, perhaps, that television is innocent and can be *trusted*. Television, can confuse people, particularly children, into believing that what they see on TV is the real and complete truth. All children, irrespective of their economic or social status, are influenced by what they see and hear on TV, although the meanings and messages are understood and absorbed differently by children as they bring, into their negotiation of TV information, their own experiences. There is some evidence that this perceived reality can and does influence the real world beliefs of children.

We believe that television has

the potential for regular viewing in the long run to cultivate the values and beliefs represented by the characters, situations, themes and topics emphasised recurrently, and thus give shape to the worldview on which behaviour is based, as well as for the unusually compelling portrayal to affect immediate behaviour among teenagers and adults as well as children, sometimes in non-trivial ways.[1]

As far as TV advertising is concerned, we have seen how it is all too easy to be lulled into believing that it is a harmless and inconsequential activity. Advertising, especially when it targets the child, powerfully promotes a consumer culture and the values

ILLUSTRATION C 1
Drinking in a Vision of the World

associated with it. It is an investment for the future which manufacturers expect will pay off many times over.

Television advertising extends its domain by working hard at creating, for all of society, the right images to carry off the material products that it entices the consumer with. In this respect advertising assumes a larger influential role.

In India, advertising on TV is, today, creating a set of images especially for the Indian child, alongside a host of other dominant images for the rest of its audience. Once internalised, together these become a test of personal success and levels of achievement. This presentation does not sensitise children to their own or other people's realities. The affluent child might feel convinced that only his or her class of Indians really count. On the other hand, the child from a poor family class may be forced to acknowledge that the lifestyles of the affluent class are the *only* legitimate ones (since advertising chooses to ignore his).

Since the ideology of consumption turns the spotlight on the individual, the individual is, in effect, freed from the burden and responsibility of caring about the rights and development of others in society. The primary aim is personal enhancement. As Leiss, Kline and Jhally put it:

because advertising as communication is essentially a form of social interaction, a range of concerns about society at large has been raised. Advertising has been criticised for perpetuating racial and sexual stereotypes, for unduly influencing children and disrupting the normal socialisation process, for perpetuating socially inappropriate roles, and for promoting goals, values, and imagery that oppress or dehumanise people. In other words, controversies about what is occurring in society at large—materialism, sexism, racism, lack of diversity, and inequality—are transferred to the domain of advertising.[2]

Jerry Mander feels that:

If you accept the existence of advertising, you accept a system designed to persuade and to dominate minds by interfering in people's thinking patterns. You also accept that the system will be used by the sorts of people who like to influence people and are good at it. No person who did not wish to dominate others would choose to use advertising, and choosing it, succeed in it. So the basic nature of advertising and all the technologies created to serve it will be consistent with this purpose, will encourage this behaviour in society, and will tend to push social evolution in this direction.[3]

Mander is involved with very fundamental arguments on the purpose and intention with which advertising has become such a major force. We urge readers to critically evaluate what children are learning from advertising, not from the narrow framework of a single ad with its brilliant and fun-seeking dimensions but from a larger, societal point of view and from the angle that sustained viewing can become an avenue for unlearning and learning values which may not benefit children in the long run.

We came across some extreme reactions amongst the children we interviewed in Delhi. A child, whose parents are rarely at home and who therefore looks upon the television as his mentor, told us in all seriousness that he was determined *never* to marry and raise a family as he felt this would prevent him from fulfilling all the desires he had for *himself*. He aspired to a very high level of personal affluence. He argued that education was expensive and bringing up children, he felt, would be too great a drain on his resources.

This is probably a very atypical reaction. However, it does serve as an example of the thinking that could set in and the cynicism that such ideas might inculcate. The fact that a young boy can think so far ahead and conclude that he would not be able to share his life with others because the material pressures on him would be too great was a bitter indication of what individualism can breed.

The purpose of this study is not to paint a completely black picture or to suggest that advertising or even television can be done away with. We are faced with the reality that both these are tied up with a whole process of development and change and that at best the TV audience can become a critical participant rather than a passive recepticle for the ideology that is delicately being handed out.

Television, we recognise, has the ability to spread information and knowledge. It also, therefore, has the power to shape or at least influence our behavioural patterns (more so in the case of children and young people). As television technology rapidly expands and diversifies there will be a constant need to take stock, question and analyse developments as they unfold. This analysis might begin with fundamental questions such as: Is the role of television (as it is evolving), the role we wish it to play? Are the values, the attitudes and the role models being propagated by television the ones we wish our children to emulate? Will television increasingly serve only the purposes of entertainment, filling the airwaves with gory or even vulgar scenes from Hindi films or programming, so poor, that it becomes an assault on the viewer's taste and intellect? Will television help to divide or unite people by providing more regional-specific, language-specific, audience- and interest-specific programming? Do we really wish to see the chasms in our society grow wider because the media does not adequately represent the diversity of culture in India?

Indian television appears at present to be following the path of networks elsewhere in the world where privatisation and commercialisation together act as major forces capable of influencing and shaping the very nature of the medium.

In the United States, the proliferation of cable and network channels created as many as 1,300 options for the TV viewer and efforts to sustain a children's channel *without commercials* and other channels offering high quality programming had to be abandoned because of commercial pressures. TV time is expensive. At the 1993 Grammy Awards ceremony, the famous singer and entertainer Frank Sinatra was receiving a Grammy in the Living Legend category when live TV coverage of the ceremony was interrupted for a commercial break. Subsequently, a rather annoyed Billy Joel (the American pop star) departed from the words of his song to rather mockingly chorus: 'Valuable advertising time is going by, valuable advertising time is going by . . . dollars, dollars, dollars . . .'

That STAR TV is dishing out to Indian audiences some of the worst serials produced by the United States suggests that countries not being charged for such services are likely to be fed the cheapest and oldest fare available on the international market. The question is: should society accept without so much as a debate, anything that is put out on the airwaves because a few people have the money to pay for programming and they place their bets on very mediocre fare?

We reject the notion that Indian audiences will watch only Doordarshan's Channel 2 or some of the Zee TV kind of entertainment. Equally, we believe that though viewers are addicted to films and film-based programmes, they do watch other, better quality programmes—*when* and *if* the option exists. Quality programmes with a difference have succeeded. A case in point is the TV serial *Nukkad* which was immensely popular with Indian viewers, adults and children alike. Not only was it well made, it also provided a fresh perspective and depicted life as it is led in a typical urban, Indian environment. Good cinema and informative serials/programmes have done equally well.

Therefore, the primary recommendation this study makes is that a process of critical viewing be initiated by the viewing public in the interest of their children's development. It is presumed that if we, as television audiences, feel we have the right to question TV where it deserves to be questioned, then eventually TV may respond to public opinion. Such a process could well begin with taking a long, hard look at TV advertising, particularly in the context of existing regulations which attempts to restrict 'unfair' advertising and protect consumers.

This study is in no way comprehensive or complete. While some of our findings will apply to children in other parts of India, particularly the metropolitan cities, it is imperative that more research be conducted and that it focus attention on children as a special and vulnerable segment of the TV audience. In order to make recommendations it is first essential that greater awareness be generated on the rules and regulations that govern TV advertising. A starting point, therefore, could be Doordarshan's Code for Commercial Advertising. Viewers might then have a better understanding of their rights as consumers vis-à-vis television advertising. In the future it may become vital to exercise the right to react, accept or even reject what appears on television.

ETHICS OF TV ADVERTISING

Now take another look at advertising in the context of the code that supposedly seeks to ensure that TV commercials are fair to the viewer.

Until recently, Doordarshan's Code for Commercial Advertising was a fairly stringent one, attentive and sensitive to the unwholesome influence some kinds of advertising can exert on viewers. However, like so much else in this country these days, the Code has been 'liberalised'. In a major departure from earlier policy, Doordarshan permitted advertisements for banks (Indian as well as foreign) and jewellery to appear on its channels (February 1994). The only industries still prohibited from advertising on Doordarshan are cigarette and alcohol manufacturers (an area that STAR TV advertising more than makes up for).

Whereas the Code is exhaustive in its do's and don'ts, being loosely phrased it allows for almost any interpretation or bending of rules. Indeed, many advertising agencies complain that if one were to follow the letter rather than the spirit of the Code, there would be very little advertising on Doordarshan.

The Code emphasises that particular attention must be paid to advertising related to specially vulnerable groups such as women and children and outlines a series of portrayals and images in TV advertising which it deems undesirable and therefore, unacceptable.

Analysing Doordarshan's commercials against the tenets of the Code, we found that advertisements which appear to misinterpret or ignore the recommendations of the Code, still manage to obtain clearance. It is worthwhile studying some of these cases to decide whether or not the Code requires revision and to alert the government, the general public and adults responsible for children's development, about the need for corrective measures. While conducting such an analysis, we must also ask the following questions:

(a) Does the advertisement raise or appeal to unreasonable or unacceptable emotions in the child?

(b) Does it show either an adult or a child doing something that is not safe?

(c) Does the advertisement make false claims or suggest that the product will?

CASE STUDIES

In a Thums Up advertisement taped by us off Doordarshan, two very small children are shown going to the movies alone; subsequent shots show them accepting tickets from a stranger—in this case the actor Salman Khan, whose film *Toofan* is running at the cinema hall. Principle 24 of Doordarshan's Code specifically states: '*any advertisement which endangers the safety of the children or creates in them an interest in unhealthy practices shall not be shown*'. While some people might defend the advertisement, claiming that the children recognised Salman Khan and therefore accepted the tickets from him, there are many child viewers who do not know who Salman Khan is (and will view him as a stranger). In any case, should two little children be frequenting a cinema hall alone? This advertisement, it might be worthwhile to note, is similar to a musical video by pop icon Madonna, which also showed two children cavorting on their own. The video was banned in the USA.

Two other advertisements—the Footfun shoes ad in which a little girl and boy slip quietly out of the house (while the mother reads) and navigate hazardous rocks and streams and the Vicks ad in which a young boy is out late at night in the rain looking for his kitten—should also raise a few eyebrows.

Does an ad really give you accurate information about a product and its performance?

Code No. 16 of Doordarshan's Commercial Code states: '*Slimming, weight reduction or limitation or figure control—No advertisement should offer any medical product for the purpose of slimming . . . .*' Yet take the example of the sweetener, Sugar Free: while it is true that this product is not advertised as a medicine, it is equally true that the claims made by the advertisement—that Sugar Free transforms its users from overweight hulks into curvaceous beauties ('now I'm happy as can be, I've discovered Sugar Free . . . .')— assume properties the product cannot possibly possess. In any case, one might argue, this is not the best way to shed weight.

Are children shown using instruments etc., which are beyond the skill or capability of the child?

The ad for Minute Milk shows a little girl playing mother and using every gadget in the kitchen unsupervised—from the mixie to the gas stove—in order to produce a five course meal. Such a performance could hardly be deemed safe for such a young child.

Does the ad make parents feel that they are less caring because they have not bought their child a particular product? And does the absence of such a product in any way make the child feel less loved or inferior to those children who do possess the product?

According to Doordarshan's Code No. 23: '*No advertisement shall be accepted which leads children to believe that if they do not own or use the product advertised they will be inferior in some way to other children or that they are likely to be ridiculed for not using it.*' The advertisements for Barbie dolls are aimed at not only trying to make every girl want one but invoke the value judgement: 'Every doll deserves a Barbie', suggesting that every girl is entitled to the doll and that not to possess one is a deprivation.

WOMEN

'*Women,*' says the Code, '*must not be portrayed in a manner that emphasises passive, submissive qualities and encourages them to play a subordinate, secondary role in society.*' In any number of advertisements women and girls are portrayed exactly in this manner—indeed advertisements generally reinforce the stereotype of the woman in a 'subordinate, secondary role': whether it is the

Relaxo Shoes commercial which has a little girl playing cheerleader to the boy who is winning the race or all the women who appear in household advertisements—cooking and cleaning for their men and children. The principle that a woman's place is in the home is continually reiterated. There is also the Go-Kool ice-cream advertisement in which the women appear as seductive flavours for the sole delectation and enjoyment of Kabir Bedi. As we have noticed throughout this study, gender stereotyping both in TV programming and advertising is widely prevalent and though there has been some increase in the 'modern, liberated' images of women, advertisers are now plugging into the image of the woman who tirelessly carries the burden of the household and is also the breadwinner.

Code 2 (iii) argues against violence in any form. Its portrayal, incitement or desirability is another area of violation. As we have noted, from advertisements for toys such as G.I. Joe and the Leo Gun to ads for cycles and other commodities, violence and aggression are commonly used to promote products in TV advertisements. The Leo gun advertisement has a man holding a gun to a woman's head until she is rescued by the Leo gun-toting hero—a little boy. Other ads link their products to mental associations with violence—attacks by gangs, chases and personal frustrations that require an aggressive release or response. These are crude examples but there are other lifestyle advertisements which champion aggression or suggest it explicitly e.g., the Roadmaster Cycle advertisement in which a woman is being chased by a gang of men or the Atlas cycle ad which exhorts teenagers to let 'the rebel in you break loose'. In this commercial, flouting parental authority is romanticised as desirable behaviour.

'The picture and the audible matter of the advertisement shall not be excessively loud.' We don't know what decibel count is being employed by Doordarshan but to us the level reaches a crescendo every time the commercials begin! A great many advertisements are very loud and might well shock or startle viewers, particularly little children (which the code strictly prohibits): the music in most ads is almost invariably ear-splitting. People might argue that we are refining the point too much, that one can always turn down the volume. However, we feel that in the case of children, this is not always possible though they are the ones most affected by the sound effects.

Many distortions can be spotted in the advertising for medicines or health products. *'No advertisement should contain a claim to cure any ailment or symptoms of ill health . . . .'* says the Code. Many advertisements do just that: Eno Fruit Salts cure heartburn; Nature Cure, constipation; Zandu balm, headaches. Whereas these products might indeed *Help* alleviate the symptoms of the ailment, contrary to their claims, they seldom actually *cure* it.

Do advertisements tell the truth? Do they mislead children? According to Code No. 28: *'Advertising shall be truthful, avoid distorting facts and misleading the public . . . .'* The truth is, advertisements by their very nature, seldom tell the truth. In their book *Social Communication in Advertising*, William Leiss, Stephen Kline and Sat Jhally emphasise the genetic quality of dishonesty in advertising messages and images which are selling something short of the honest truth, be it equating beauty with a particular soap or social acceptability through the right toothpaste. Advertisers assume a degree of visual sophistication in the audience who take commercial 'white lies' in the spirit they are intended. Our only query would be: are children visually or otherwise literate and mature enough to make such distinctions?

The storyline of the Glucon D advertisement would have us believe that an ordinary boy is transformed into a 'superhero' after a dose of Glucon D. He develops extraordinary powers and saves all the other children. This is misleading, untrue and gives children the wrong notions not only about Glucon D but also fills their heads with the impossible ambition of emulating 'superhero' or Superman (the original model). In the West, serious questions have been raised about the Superman myth and the danger it represents to children who try to imitate his antics.

Should well-known personalities be allowed to promote products?
The use of 'stars' to sell goods is a very well known marketing technique. Indian advertising is increasingly falling into the star trap. A large number of testimonials by well-known personalities—film and sports stars, the rich and the famous who lend their name and status to everything from oils and soaps to cars and cold drinks—have great influence on the public, particularly children. One should always be aware of the fact that the stars are in no way responsible for the quality and safety of the products they promote—they are simply there to make some easy money. Whereas Code

No. 29 does warn against testimonials other than those of government-recognised standardisation agencies, there is nothing in it that questions the advisability or indeed, desirability of people masquerading as doctors selling toothpastes.

Code No. 9 states: *'Scientific or statistical excerpts from technical literature etc. may be used only with a proper sense of responsibility to the ordinary viewer. Irrelevant data and scientific jargon shall not be used to make claims that appear to have a scientific basis they do not possess. Statistics of limited validity should not be presented in a way as to make it appear that they are universally true.'* Ultrons in Surf, the microsystem in Ariel, the Puf in Godrej refrigerators are all being promoted as wonderful new scientific properties possessed by the products which make them better than the rest. But what are ultrons, microsystems and PUF?

Do advertisements promote values that are unhealthy?

Perhaps the most objectionable advertisement on Indian television is the Emami Fair Skin Cream one. It should never have been permitted on Doordarshan. Unashamedly it propagates the virtues of fair skin, suggesting its necessity if, for instance, one is to find a bridegroom. What could be more deeply offensive and contemptuous of the Indian Constitution? By articulating the pathological Indian dislike of dark skin, the advertisement flouts all the most cherished principles of the Code.

We have chosen only a few examples to illustrate the effete and misconceived nature of the Advertising Code and the disregard for some of its stated tenets. It is clear that the norms of advertising as laid down by Doordarshan are being enforced in an arbitrary manner, possibly reflecting the interpretation of individuals entrusted at different times with the task of enforcement. Advertisers might claim that the Code is impossible to adhere to, that to follow it would mean there would be no advertising whatsoever. Similarly, Doordarshan might argue that it would have to reject commercials if officials strictly followed the letter of the Code—and then where would the whole commercial policy be?

These may be valid arguments: they suggest that the Code needs to be drastically revised to reconcile it with reality. Only those principles which can be realistically enforced should be retained and the rest eliminated. A streamlined policy would permit fewer violations and eliminate the corruption that attaches itself to a system where rules have to be constantly flouted in order to get an advertisement passed. Also, for any code to have authority it is necessary that it now be enforced for cable and satellite TV as well as video programmes and films which broadcast many advertisements not permitted on Doordarshan. Advertisers will argue that if people are being allowed to watch ads for beer on satellite TV, why should those who do not own satellite connections not enjoy a similar exposure?

As the competition for commercial support increases in a multichannel world, Doordarshan might feel that it is being unfairly discriminated against by being burdened with a code which though it now applies to satellite and cable TV is not being adhered to. In the process it is being deprived of the ability to earn revenue that other channels are siphoning off.

We believe our analysis shows that the following issues related to TV advertising demand urgent attention and rectification:

1. *The concentration of a very high number of ads within a single hour of programming (up to 60 ads with* Chitrahaar) *is a cause for concern. Serials like* Sri Krishna *and* Chandrakanta *being shown on DD2 in 1994–95 had so much commercial support that viewers complained that these were ad slots. The serials provided small breaks in-between.*

2. *The imbalance in programming whereby a small fraction of the four per cent of TV programming is designed for women, youth and children should be corrected.*

3. *Advertisers and producers should, in the interest of the child audience, make efforts to limit the use of programming which is excessively violent, gory and based on horror.*

4. *Advertisers must bear in mind that all children—those who can and those who cannot afford advertised products—learn from commercials and eventually desire many promoted products. If advertisers insist that nothing should prevent an individual's determination to own a material product and that aggressive or dishonest behaviour are acceptable, the consequences could be disastrous.*

5. *Advertisers and adults must critically view the messages of all advertisements whether they relate to a child's nutritional beliefs or to norms of social interaction. As long as the objective of TV is to act as a major avenue for raising awareness among Indians, whereever advertising's values contradict the development of a better and more healthy understanding of what is important to the health and development of people, questions must be raised to correct misconceptions.*

Things to Watch for in TV Advertising

1. *Is the size or performance of the product made clear?*
2. *If batteries are needed, is the disclosure audio as well as video?*
3. *If assembly is required, does the ad say so clearly?*
4. *Is a child or adult shown doing something unsafe?*
5. *Are children shown using a product in a way that is beyond the skill or dexterity of a child?*
6. *Are children shown using a product not intended for children?*
7. *Does the ad suggest that a child will be superior to friends or more popular if he/she owns a given product?*
8. *Does the ad suggest that an adult who buys a product for a child is better or more caring than one who does not?*
9. *Does the ad employ any demeaning or derogatory social stereotypes?*
10. *If fantasy elements are used, are they clearly 'just pretend'?*
11. *In ads featuring premiums, is the premium offer the main feature or is it clearly secondary?*
12. *Is a child-directed advertising appeal being used for vitamins or medication?*
13. *Is there anything misleading about the product's benefits?*
14. *Does the ad suggest that possession or use of a consumer item endows a child with physical, social, or psychological characteristics superior to those of his or her peers?*
15. *Does the ad falsely lead a child to believe that for the regular price of a consumer item the child will obtain all the items and/or accessories advertised?*
16. *Does the ad use a program personality or character (either live or animated) to promote a consumer item?*

Courtesy: Committee for Children's Television (Metro Detroit, USA)

RECOMMENDATIONS

In Part One of this book we have drawn attention to the relationship evolving between children and their television sets and have indicated that extensive viewing of television can interfere with other learning processes that every child needs to undergo. The television takes children away from their natural environment and places them in the artificial confines of a darkened room. It may affect their natural curiosity to explore and discover the outside world and may also interfere with their socialisation by isolating them from other children and even adults. That it may affect reading and writing skills is a problem that many parents and schoolteachers throughout the country are now beginning to address. In India children tend to watch anything and everything that appears on TV and therefore form part of an active audience for essentially adult programmes.

AT SCHOOL, AT HOME

We know and can help our children to appreciate that television is simply another machine which like the washing machine, mixer, cooler et al., can be controlled by human beings. The choice to switch it on, switch it off, change channels, rests entirely with us and it is imperative that parents and children be made to realise this truism. The fact that people attach little or no importance to the act of watching television is most tellingly illustrated by the following conversation heard in almost every household around the globe: 'What are you doing?' 'Oh, nothing—just watching TV.'

On the basis of our study, we discovered that a child's relationship with the TV set is a casual one: children tend to switch it on and switch channels at will. They treat it almost like a toy which they can play with whenever they so desire.

This casual attitude on the part of both children and their parents must alter so that children understand and appreciate the importance of watching TV. Parents should encourage children to 'switch on' only when there is a programme they want to or should be watching. To simply graze in search of something, anything to nibble at should be discouraged.

Parents can play a vital role in shaping children's attitudes to television. In the United States, various studies have shown that in families where parents watch television with their children and explain what is happening on the screen and draw the distinction between real and fictionalised events, children learn more positive information from TV than those children who are left to negotiate television and its messages alone. Sharing television with their children gives parents the opportunity to make them aware of how TV programming comes into existence and to explain that there are people and real faces behind the screen like puppeteers holding the strings of marionettes.

Another area of concern is the nature of a child's exposure to the media. This study confirms the fact that children watch a great deal of television, particularly (a) Hindi films, and (b) adult programming. In this respect, action must be taken at different levels: first, the entire programme structure of Doordarshan's channels should be overhauled so that schedules include (a) good quality children's TV programmes, and (b) that children's prime time is free of retrograde adult programming. Similar measures for other TV channels should also be adopted.

Second is parental intervention. Parents should be careful not to employ the TV set as a baby-sitter for their children. For a start, parents could discourage 'watching TV' during mealtimes. Above all, *children need to be helped both by their elders and their teachers to critically evaluate what they see on television so that they become discerning viewers better able to protect themselves from negative influences*.

Good software, that is to say programming which is well produced, child-oriented and attempts to use an Indian cultural idiom for expression, must be generated so that our children can appreciate indigenous programming and talent. Otherwise, their world of TV will be overrun by imported fare.

In this connection we believe that it would be worthwhile to create a national children's television development fund and foundation whose responsibility it would be to (a) provide the means for the production of good children's programming, and (b) monitor policy, TV content (including advertising) and developments in the media as well as raise public awareness on issues of

PLATE C.1
Advertising: Creating Problems, Offering Solutions

concern. This in turn might encourage more consumer activism with regard to TV and children.

In brief:

1. *Parents should attempt to restrict their child's TV time.*
2. *Teachers and parents can help children to decide what they should watch on TV.*

3. *Adults should look out for things their children seem to be afraid of or do not understand on TV. Parents and teachers should also keep an eye on any other negative effects of TV watching on children such as grogginess, fatigue, strain and a fall in concentration abilities.*

4. *Efforts should be made to discuss 'Bad Programmes' with children and to point out the defects in reasoning, presentation and ideas.*

5. *Children should be encouraged both in their schools and at home to discuss television.*

6. *Greater efforts should be made by parent groups to initiate or activate community activity centres, story-telling groups, and to collectively work to ensure that more and better playgrounds where children can be safe are created so that the growing dependence on TV as a baby-sitter can be reduced.*

7. *Teachers should help students to look for programming that is relevant and has some learning potential and to direct children's attention to the more worthwhile uses of television.*

8. *Since schools are increasingly using television sets both to entertain and to educate children, efforts should be made to create libraries of video tapes suitable for viewing by children.*

9. *Parents and teachers should publicly voice their concern over what they consider negative or harmful programming, especially during prime time or when children are principal users of television.*

10. *Children should be helped to learn that TV violence is not real and that real violence is painful and devastating.*

11. *Efforts should also be made to sensitise children about other people and their lives.*

12. *Sharing with others, caring about the environment and involving children in productive activities helps them to gather valuable human experiences.*

TV POLICY

The government would be advised to appoint a committee to review the policy related to the future of television in India. Such a committee should ideally be supported by experts such as scientists, technologists, telecommunications and computer professionals as

ILLUSTRATION C 2
Looking Beyond the Tube of Plenty

well as involve TV producers, programme makers, advertisers, educationists, journalists, bureaucrats, teachers and parents. The effort to create a well thought-out and workable blueprint for the electronic media can, of course, be successful only if the exercise is conducted with the unquestioned political support of the government and other political parties. The aim presumably would be to articulate a well-defined and comprehensive policy on Indian television—network, cable and satellite TV—treating each separately and together as part of a whole. Currently, changes and developments connected with television are occurring in the absence of such a policy and the results could be extremely damaging for the nation.

The committee must look into the future and on the basis of present and probable developments in technology and software, chart out a course for Indian television well into 2000 A.D. This course should be guided by a vision—a vision of the role television can and should play in such a complex, diverse and variegated society such as ours. Such a vision is not merely desirable but imperative.

Given the pressures on Indian television from transnational networks and the competition arising from their entry, strategies are now required to define (on the basis of the nation's priorities) the expectations we have from terrestrial, satellite and cable TV. Given the diversity of TV services now available, consideration must be given to national, regional and language issues.

Preventing the growth of transnational satellite television seems an absurd proposition today, having allowed it to spread through the nation, unhindered. However, while we may not be able or wish to prevent its future growth, we could exert some influence on transnational TV with regard to programme content. If the political will exists, it is possible, as the Chinese have illustrated, to prevail upon those who run these organisations: in the spring of 1993, the Chinese government complained to STAR TV about BBC's coverage of China, particularly a documentary on Chairman Mao which, it felt, denigrated the memory of the dead leader. STAR TV acted almost immediately and in March 1993, BBC World Service Television was taken off the northern beam of STAR's transmission services which covered China, North Korea, etc. While many satellite TV viewers may lament the fact that BBC (which certainly offers better fare than many other channels) is being unfairly sidelined, the example serves only to indicate that where governments have taken strong positions, the media had been forced to respond. The alternative to transnational media is, of course, high quality programming originating from India becoming a real and worthy option. Such expectations would also hold true for Indian satellite channels such as Zee, Sony, ATN, etc.

As purely commercial ventures, TV services do require the goodwill of governments in order to succeed. While we support the freedom of speech and the press, we do feel that the Indian government could exercise some of the leverage it possesses to help develop Indian television in terms, for example, of training personnel and ensuring access to better programming from private, domestic and foreign media sources.

CABLE TV: IN NEED OF STIMULANTS

All over the world cable TV is more than simply a conduit between satellite TV companies and potential viewers. It offers immense scope for local, community-specific programming as well as educational TV. These are areas almost completely ignored by network and satellite TV; cable TV has the potential to fill the lacunae by locating itself within the context of a community's interests and concerns. It could also provide an opportunity for all those groups and minorities whose points of view are never presented on network and satellite TV. Zee's Zed TV is an example of how cable can be used for educational purposes.

What we are advocating here is the growth of cable TV as an entirely separate entity, one which puts local issues first and is used by the government, non-government organisations, educational institutions and local communities for educational/development purposes.

However, here again there is cause for concern. Any widespread use of cable also requires stringent monitoring by groups of people appointed to the task. Otherwise, there is always the possibility for misue of this very effective form of communication.

In Search of an Indian Character

Policy makers must urgently address the question of new media influences and the cultural implications of foreign programming—especially for children.

As stated elsewhere, the future increasingly seems to belong to media conglomerates. Transnational satellite TV combined with digital and optic computerised compression techniques will offer Indian audiences up to 100 (if not more) channels by the end of this century. Though this suggests that there will be greater choice for the viewer, the truth is somewhat different. For while channel choices and services will no doubt be wideranging and varied, the sources will remain limited.

Already large telecommunications, computer, network and cable TV giants throughout the globe have begun pooling resources with the biggest entertainment companies in the world—Time-Warner, Viacom (MTV), Walt Disney, etc. Such mergers will rule the airwaves simply because they will control both the means of transmission (cable, digital etc.) and the software.

In India, media magnates like Rupert Murdoch and Ted Turner who owns CNN and other media organisations like the BBC have gone in for tie-ups with Indian media groups including Doordarshan and the entertainment industry to gain and then consolidate their hold over the Indian market.

Most of the big telecom and entertainment companies are American. The USA already produces more TV software than any other nation and its programme prices are the most competitive in the world: having recovered production costs in the domestic market, US companies can afford to sell serials/series etc. at low prices to other countries. Whatever they make from such sales is outright profit. Consequently, American serials/series and films dominate cinema halls and TV screens around the world. Nobody has been able to withstand this onslaught successfully. Even in Britain, where BBC and ITV so long dominated the tube, American soap operas and detective serials are increasingly edging out 'institutions' like *Coronation Street* (the most popular soap opera in Britian).

It is nobody's case that American TV programming is intrinsically 'bad'; that it alone is corrupting our children, that it alone is responsible for the continuing loss of values or indeed, that it is the sole reason for the increase of violence in our societies. Nor can it be convincingly argued that our traditions, our culture, our value systems are being eroded by its all-pervasiveness.

For these sins each society must blame itself. Preserving traditions, stimulating and nurturing cultural forces within a country, or a community depends largely on the people themselves. Furthermore, outside influences are beneficial inasmuch as they supply fresh impetus and often regenerate a static or dying culture. The interaction and collision between different cultural forces can also result in new hybrids. Bhangra-reggae and pop star Apache Indian may not appeal to the highest aesthetic standards but they do represent the successful blending of two vastly disparate musical traditions, although some people may regard the new form of music as a subtle cooption into an essentially Western mould serving only to make modern American music more influential.

Having said as much, we do feel it would be naive and wilfully blind to deny or ignore the potency of transnational culture as transmitted through satellite TV. Without being the sole channel of such cultural influences, television is certainly the most influential agent because of its primary audio-visual appeal.

What concerns us here is the impact this will have on the most impressionable members of society: children. Our study has revealed that children are already deeply influenced by what they see on television; if the images they receive largely flow out of Western traditions and value systems, it follows that they are likely to accept, emulate and aspire to those as they grow into adulthood.

Indian television—be it in terms of programming or advertising—has the task of providing an alternative worldview and insofar as it is possible, an Indian one. Therefore, those who are entrusted with the job of guiding the future of Indian TV (be it Doordarshan or satellite channels like Zee TV, Sun etc.,) through the competitive times ahead, should look to providing an Indian character to television.

This is not an impossible task and at the beginning of this chapter we had given the example of *Nukkad*. Other serials/series like *Buniyaad, Tamas, Malgudi Days, Dekh Bhai Dekh* and, of course, the epics *Ramayana* and *Mahabharata* have also shown the way. That they might well represent the counterpoint to transnational culture is supported by two facts: these sponsored serials on Doordarshan were popular with viewers and won strong commercial support too.

In conclusion, this study advocates greater consciousness and less passivity regarding television. It also calls for a long, hard look at the environment and context within which the child is increasingly being presented with the 'television-as-a-solution' to loneliness and lack of other stimulating activities; to boredum and to the need for an ever-present substitute for the parent, the school and other relationships and experiences.

Notes

1. Marguerite Fitch, Aletha C. Huston, and John C. Wright, 'From Television Forms to Genre Schemata: Children's Perceptions of Television Reality' in *Children and Television* edited by Gordon L. Berry and Joy Keiko Asamen, Sage, 1993.
2. W. Leiss, S. Kline and Sat Jhally, *Social Communication in Advertising*, Methuen, New York, 1986.
3. Jerry Mander, *Four Arguments for the Elimination of Television*, Quill, New York, 1978.
4. *Children and Television: Images in a Changing Sociocultural World*. Edited by Gordon L. Berry and Joy Keiko Asamen. Sage, Thousand Oaks, 1993.

ANNEXURES

GENERAL INFORMATION

India—Demographic Features
(1991)

	Population (in millions)		
	Rural	Urban	Total
	629m	217m	846m
	Male	Female	Sex Ratio
	439m	407m	927
	Literacy (%)		
	Urban	Rural	Total
Male	68.7	47.1	52.7
Female	53.8	24.8	32.2
Total	61.7	36.3	42.8

Source: Audience Research Unit (DART), Directorate General, Doordarshan 1994.

ANNEXURE 2

DOORDARSHAN TODAY

1993–94
Primary Service

Transmitters	553	Programme Output	84
High Power	68	Scheduled	
		(hours per week)	
Low Power	380	National	62
Very Low Power	82	Regional	22
Transposers	23	Actual telecast	95
Prog. Prod. Centres	31	ETV	16
(Studios)			
Reg. Networks	12	Total output of	
		all DD Kendras	488
		Commercial Revenue	
Coverage (per cent)		(1992–93 Rs. mil)	3,602
Population	83.6	Budget	
Area	64.5	(1992–93 Rs. mil)	
TV Households (mil)	40.3	Revenue	6,295
Rural	12.0	Capital	1,376
Urban	28.3	Staff	20,201
Community Sets	64,000		

Satellite Channels

Sat. Channels	5	Terrestrial Support	
		Transmitters	
Regional Language Sat.	10	Metro Ent. Channel	5
Channels		(Metros & Lucknow)	
		Other Channels	4
Prog. Output	353	(Delhi)	
(hours per week)			
DD Sat. Ch.	288	Metro Terrestrial	
Regional	125	Reach	
Lang. Satellite		Population (mil)	96.2
Services		Metro Households (mil)	7.0
			(December 1993)

Source: DART, 1994.

ANNEXURE 3

Transmission Hours over Years

	Total telecast in the year* (Hours)	Average per week Hrs.–Min.
1975	339	17–30
1976	1277	24–30
1977	1514	29–10
1978	1458	28–00
1979	1627	31–30
1980	1563	30–20
1981	1643	31–30
1982	2144	40–50
1983	2442	46–40
1984	2729	52–30
1985	2970	57–10
1986	3400	65–20
1987	3579	68–50
1988	3641	78–10
1989	4083	78–30
1990	4135	79–20
1991	4166	79–55
1992	4445	85–10
1993	4938	94–30

Source: DART, 1994.
Note: The figures are from DDK Madras but the pattern is similar for all other places.
    * Includes National Network, Regional but excludes Channel II, UGC, IGNOU and ETV.

ANNEXURE 4

Doordarshan: Major Landmarks

1959:	First TV centre established at Delhi.
1964:	Chanda Committee recommends introduction of commercials on DD.
1965:	Regular service begins from Delhi.
1967:	Government accepts Chanda Committee's recommendations but restricts commercial time to 10 per cent of total broadcasting time.
1976:	First commercial appears on DD.
1982:	Colour transmission begins.
:	National programme introduced.
1984:	Sponsored programmes start.
1987:	Morning transmission commences.
1989:	Afternoon transmission begins.
1993:	National programme duration increased.
1993:	Metro hour launched.

National/Network Programmes
The Evolution

1980 (25 Jan.)
National programme of music and dance from metros.
1982 (15 Aug.)
Daily 90 mts. programme.
1982 (Dec.)
Hindi feature film on network.
1984 (15 Aug.)
Extension up to 11.15 p.m.

1985 (15 Aug.)
Saturday AN transmission.

1987 (15 Oct.)
News bulletin for hearing impaired.
1989 (26 Jan.)
Afternoon transmission.
1989 (1 May)
Extension of morning transmission.
1990 (22 Oct.)
News bulletins in afternoon transmission.
1993 (1 Jan.)
Extension of afternoon transmission and one–hour prime time entertainment programmes.

1987 (23 Feb.)
Morning 45 mts.
transmission.
1987 (7 Apr.)
Late night feature film.

Source: DART, 1994.

ANNEXURE 5

National Network Programme Composition

Fixed Point Chart*

News	Current Affairs	Interview/ Discussion	Music/ Dance	Serial/ Play
16.5	6.5	4.9	5.8	19.6
Features/ Magazines	Women/ Children/ Youth	Sports	Film-based	
14.0	4.5	5.5	22.7	

Actual Telecast in Jan–Oct 1993

DD programmes have often to be changed to accommodate topical events, sports etc. The composition of the programme actually telecast during Jan–Oct 1993:

News	Current Affairs	Interview/ Discussion	Music/ Dance	Serial/ Play
13.4	8.7	4.7	4.9	16.2
Feature/ Magazine	Women/ Children/ Youth	Sports	Film-based	Others
9.8	4.3	17.4	18.3	2.3

Source: DART, 1994.

Note: All figures are percentages. For News, the total telecast time has remained as scheduled but because of the larger base which included extended transmission hours the percentage has come down.

* Weekly Programme Schedule.

ANNEXURE 6

Revenue

Year	(Rs. in million) Gross
1976–77	7.7
1977–78	20.7
1978–79	49.7
1979–80	61.6
1980–81	80.8
1981–82	112.7
1982–83	158.9
1983–84	179.9
1984–85	314.3
1985–86	602.0
1986–87	933.1
1987–88	1363.0
1988–89	1612.6
1989–90	2101.3
1990–91	2538.5
1991–92	3006.1
1992–93	3602.3

Source: DART, 1994.

ANNEXURE 7

The Commercial Earnings by Kendras

(1992–93 Gross)

Kendra/Service	Rs. Millions	Share (%)
National/Network	2059.63	55.6
Delhi + LPTs	392.60	10.5
Bombay	214.47	5.8
Madras	357.84	9.7
Calcutta	138.71	3.7
Bangalore	114.16	3.1
Hyderabad	184.59	5.0
Thiruvananthapuram	83.49	2.3
Guwahati	0.53	0.02
Lucknow	28.15	0.8
Jalandhar	31.28	0.9
Ahmedabad	35.61	1.0
Bhopal	0.40	0.01
Channel II		
Delhi	15.73	0.4
Bombay	16.29	0.4
Madras	25.27	0.7
Calcutta	4.16	0.1
	3702.91*	100.0

Source: AR, 1994.
* Difference between the figure in the previous table is because of late collection in some places.

ANNEXURE 8

Commercial Tariff Spots

(Rs. in thousands for 10 seconds)

Kendra	Super 'A' Special	Super 'A'	'A' Special	'A'	'B'	Time Check before News
National Network	120 (Chitrahaar) 100 (HFF–Sat)	90	50	30	15	25
Delhi	50 (HFF–Sun) 35	22.5	–	10	3	6
Bombay	24	18	–	7	2	5
Madras	24	14	–	4	1.5	4
Hyderabad	16	11	7	4	1.5	4
Calcutta	15	11	6	4	1.5	4
Bangalore	12	11	6	4	1.5	4
Thiruvanantha-puram/ Ahmedabad	10	9	6	3.5	1.25	3
Lucknow/ Jalandhar/ Bhopal/Jaipur	6	6	–	3	1	2
Srinagar/ Guwahati	–	1.5	–	1	0.5	1
Channel II	–	5	–	3.5	1.5	1.5

Source: DART, 1994.

Note: For Chitrahaar (National) 130 for last two spots.

HFF = Hindi Feature Film.

ANNEXURE 8a

Tariff for Sponsorship
National Network
(Programmes of 30 mts including Free Commercial Time or FCT)

Time Category	Doordarshan Programmes		Outside New	Programmes Repeat
Super A Special	600 (40 sec.) (Chitrahaar)	650 (40 sec.) (HFF)	500 (60 sec.)	–
Super A	580 (60 sec.)	380 (40 sec.)	260 (90 sec.)	380 (90 sec.)
A Special	310 (60 sec.)	210 (40 sec.)	170 (90 sec.)	210 (60 sec.)
A	180 (60 sec.)	120 (40 sec.)	80 (120 sec.)	120 (60 sec.)
B		40 (40 sec.)	25 (150 sec.)	70 (90 sec.)

Source: DART, 1994.
Notes: With banking of 30 sec.
   For DD Programmes in Super A, A Spec, A
   Two options with different FCT.
   (Figures in brackets indicate FCT allowed.)

ANNEXURE 8b

Tariff for Doordarshan Satellite Channels

(Rs. in thousands)

Channel	Spots (10 sec.)	DD Programme Sponsorship (for 30 mts)	Outside Prog. Sponsorship (for 30 mts)
Metro Entertainment Prime Time (7.50 to 9.45 p.m.)			
a. Film based	30	500	300
b. Non-film based	25	315	75

Source: DART, 1994.

Note: FCT = 3½ minutes on Metro Entertainment Channel and 4½ minutes for other channels.

ANNEXURE 9

Advertising Overview

ADVERTISING EXPENDITURE

1991–92	*Per cent to GNP*	*1987–89*	*Per cent to GNP*
Rs. 20,000 m	0.37	Rs. 9,300 m	0.32

MEDIA SPEND SHARE

	Press	*Television*	*Radio*	*Cinema*	*Outdoor*
1985	75	12	4	3	6
1992	67	20*	2.5	0.5	10

(* Includes video/cable 1%, STV 1%)

TV ADVERTISING
1992

Top Product Categories	Rs. m	*Top Advertisers*	Rs. m
Soaps	354	Hindustan Lever	422
Detergent		Proctor & Gamble	189
Powders	251		
Toothpastes	184	Godrej	100
Tea	137	Nestle	94
Textiles	104	Colgate	91
(25%, others 75%)		(21%, others 79%)	

Source: DART, 1994.

ANNEXURE 10

Television Sets

*TV Households-Estimates**

1985	6,750,00	1990	27,820,00
1986	11,000,000	1991	30,803,000
1987	13,256,000	1992	34,858,000
1988	17,339,000	1993	40,337,000
1989	22,539,000		

Source: DART, 1994.

* Estimates made by various agencies. According to Electronics Industry, 8.5 million colour TV sets were sold between January and September 1993 and the projected sales for the whole year was 11.5 million. After allowing for replacement, upgradation, etc., the total TV HHS could be higher than 40 million.

ANNEXURE 11

Cable Television

Advent—1984:	To fill the time gaps when DD was not on the air.
Initial Growth:	Mainly by local entrepreneurship and specially in Gujarat and Maharashtra.
Satellite TV:	Big impetus for growth—though viewing was mainly for local VCR channel, STV giving 'respectability' and status.

GROWTH
(Networks)

1984	—	100
1985	—	450
1986	—	800
1988	—	1200
1989	—	2000
1991	—	6000
1992	—	15000

Source: DART, 1994.

ANNEXURE 12

Foreign Satellite Channels

C.N.N.	The Gulf War January 1991	The advent in five star hotels and a few other places.
STAR	May 1991	English Service: STAR Plus, Prime Sports, MTV, BBC.
ATN	15 August 1992	Hindi Service
ZEE TV	20 October 1992	Hindi Service available with STAR programmes.

(Sun TV (Tamil), Asia Net (Malayalam) and PTV also available from some operators.)

GROWTH
STV* HHS

January 92	0.41 m
June 92	1.28 m
February 93	3.30 m
August 93	6.20 m

Source: DART, 1994.
* Estimates of STV:
  IMRB–FSA.
  MRAS–Burke.

ANNEXURE 13

List of Schools/Areas
Covered by the CTA Study in Delhi*

1. Kerala School
2. Mother's International School
3. Mirambika
4. Central School
5. Adarsh Vidya Bhavan
6. Sardar Patel School
7. J.D. Tytler School
8. Mahavir Senior Model School
9. Modern School
10. Govt. Sr. Sec. School for Girls
11. Air Force Bal Bharati School
12. Vasant Valley School
13. St. Columbus School
14. Anglo Arabic Sr. Sec. School
15. NBCC, Bhogal
16. Quetta D.A.V.
17. Friends Colony.
18. Pandara Park
19. Rajender Nagar
20. Defence Colony
21. Punjabi Bagh
22. J.P. Colony
23. Motiya Khan
24. Haiderpur Waterworks
25. Gujearwala Town
26. Babpu Dham
27. Okhla Tent Area
28. Dakshinpuri
29. Ambedkar Nagar
30. Aurangzeb Road
31. Dakshinpuri
32. Chetna Appts., Trans Yamuna
33. Patparganj
34. Model Town
35. Saket
36. Gautampuri

Annexure 13 (Continued)

37. Chanakyapuri
38. Mobile Creches
39. Jagriti
40. Lodhi Colony
41. Madangir
42. Mayur Vihar
43. West Vinod Nagar
44. Munirka

---

* This Annexure provides a list of the areas/institutions/visited during our fieldwork in Delhi, 1992–93, for the Children¸Television and Advertising Survey (CTA).

ANNEXURE 14

Statistical Analysis of DD Advertisements
6 April–3 May 1992

Total	=	1,166
Week One	=	267
Week Two	=	288
Week Three	=	318
Week Four	=	293

CHILD

Week	Direct Appeal	Indirect Appeal	Child Used
One	92	175	95
Two	92	196	99
Three	97	221	109
Four	75	218	109
Total	356	810	412

Annexure 14 (Continued)

LANGUAGE USED

Week	English	Hindi	Eng/Hin	None
One	68	193	6	–
Two	88	191	9	–
Three	108	189	20	1
Four	76	201	13	3
Total	340	774	48	4

MUSIC

Week	Western	Indian	West/Ind	None
One	187	72	8	–
Two	180	83	18	7
Three	202	82	30	4
Four	189	73	20	11
Total	758	310	76	22

CULTURE

Week	Indian	Western	Indian/Western	None
One	80	127	60	–
Two	93	159	36	–
Three	76	179	60	3
Four	86	138	62	7
Total	335	603	218	10

Week	Durable	Non-Durable	Public Service	Corporate Sector	Service Sector	Invest-ment
One	45	204	18	–	–	–
Two	56	209	21	–	2	–
Three	56	242	12	5	1	2
Four	47	220	21	3	–	2
Total	204	875	72	8	3	4

Annexure 14 (Continued)

CLASS

Week	Upper Class	Middle Class	Lower Class	Cut Across	None
One	132	98	5	30	2
Two	184	87	7	10	–
Three	198	91	12	17	–
Four	156	88	14	35	–
Total	670	364	38	92	2

Source: CTA.

ANNEXURE 15

Description of Advertisements Shown to Respondents During Fieldwork for CTA Study

The following is a description of Doordarshan advertisements shown to children during the course of our fieldwork in Delhi. These commercials were screened wherever possible. The ads were shown to children after they had answered the questionnaires and before the group discussion was initiated with them.

The selection represents a cross-section of advertising on Doordarshan in 1992 and includes (*a*) ads targeting children; (*b*) ads using children; (*c*) ads in Hindi, in English or a combination of languages; and (*d*) ads presenting different styles and contextual themes. (It should be noted that although many Indian advertisements have more than one language version, they remain essentially the same.)

THE COMMERCIALS

1. *Lehar Pepsi*: The advertisement for Lehar Pepsi follows a global format and features Indian rock star, Remo Fernandes, along with child

star, Penny Vaz. The ad uses a combination of English and Hindi and is best known for its slogan, 'Yehi hai right choice, baby!' In the version shown to respondents, the lyrics are: 'You hold it, you taste it, you know that it's right. You drink it, you feel good, you know it's the choice . . . .' The visuals focus on Remo and Penny, flashing past a group of women in bright red dresses dancing to the music. The strains of an Indian classical raag intersect briefly as the fizz bubbles out of the bottle.

2. Eveready: The Eveready commercial is in English. Its slogan 'Give me red!' is its only verbal communication. The ad seeks to identify the battery with the elixir of life—available across a bar counter. The ad, which is highly visible on satellite TV (STAR Plus) aims at an international audience and models itself on popular conceptions of a bar room scene (commonly seen on film and TV screens in America). There is no child in the advertisement.

3. BSA SLR: This ad belongs to that set of Indian advertisements which take their inspiration from Hindi films. It uses both Hindi and English in its lyrics: 'ILU, ILU, BSA SLR/Yeh BSA kya hai/Yeh SLR kya hai/Jo halki chale/Style mein chale/BSA SLR—I love you, ILU ILU . . . .' It shows middle class teenagers riding their BSA cycles and enjoying an outing.

4. Bomb Blast: This is one of the many public service advertisements on Indian television. Bomb blasts in Delhi and other states like Punjab prompted the Government to run a series of ads warning the public against potential dangers.

The advertisement is in Hindi and depicts a blast which takes place at the railway station—where suitcases/ briefcases left unattended explode, causing death and damage. In one scene the camera focuses on the remains of a doll blown to smithers in such a blast. The ad employs a woman police officer to outline the dangers, and the safety measures and precautions that the public should follow.

5. Ariel Microsystem: Based on the international campaign for the product, this advertisement is in Hindi, though it ends up with the pun: 'To bahu, aj se, is ghar mein, tumhara hi system hai.' Children are attracted to the advertisement despite the fact that it does not portray a child. It is the humourous portrayal of the well-known domestic conflict between mother-in-law and daughter-in-law that makes it a favourite.

6. Vicco Vajaradanti Toothpaste: The ad uses the radio jingle (heard for many years) which instantly rings a bell with Indian audiences. The ad, rooted in a traditional Indian milieu, emphasises the ayurvedic properties of the toothpaste. In keeping with this, it employs chaste Hindi.

7. Nirma Bath Soap: This advertisement is one of the few that shows ordinary, working people at a construction site and offers then redemption from dirt, sweat and fatigue. The ad is in Hindi (except for the use of the

word 'bath' which it cannot get away from) and does not use or target children.

8. *Godrej PUF Refrigerator*: This commercial is an excellent example of the use of magic by advertisers to attract attention, (especially of children) to a material product. By focusing on a little girl, the ad seeks to appeal to children who might influence parental purchasing choices. The home environment depicted by the ad is sophisticated as is the Hindi used for communicating the special qualities of the product. The ad has been repeatedly described in the main text of this book.

9. *Lehar 7 Up*: Set in Goa, the ad plays on a mix of languages—Portuguese with English subtitles—which gives it a touch of the exotic, and presents an animated Fido Dido as the principle character being wooed by a flirtatious, beautiful woman. The interaction is interesting:

She: 'It's hot isn't it? Waiter, two soft drinks.'

He changes the English subtitle to read: 'Two Lehar 7 Ups'.

She: 'Do you always get what you want? You're so cool'.

He adds: 'Witty, smart, handsome.'

The jingle sums it up with: 'Just cool, light and easy—Lehar 7 Up'. Although the ad uses no children, its appeal to them is obvious.

10. *Barbie Doll*: The English version of this ad moves from dream to reality and its jingle suggests that Barbie is 'a dream come true', and that every 'doll deserves a Barbie'. The ad features only young girls.

11. *Leo Toy Gun*: This ad, primarily in Hindi, features a boy and appeals to the male child. It puts the toy gun into the hands of the 'young master' of the house. The conversation:

Boy: *'Yeh dono andar ghus aiye'*.

Guard: *'Par, yeh bandook kahan se laye, chhote maalik?'*

Boy: *'Leo ki hai.'* And the slogan adds, 'Leo toy gun, Leo fun!'

12. *Glucon D Energy Drink*: This English ad has created the figure of Superhero on almost identical lines as the well-known comic strip character, Superman—cape, insignia and all. The slogan tells us: 'Glucon D—watch how its instant energy makes him perform like a superhero should.' The accent is of course, on the word 'should'. In the ad, the boy turns into 'Superhero' upon consuming a glass of Glucon D and goes on to single-handedly win the cricket match for the losing team.

13. *G.I. Joe*: '5–4–3–2–1! Go G.I. Joe, go Joe . . .!' This ad, in English, promotes 'A new adventure. Every time!' and urges children to 'start collecting now' as it presents toys in battle and young boys playing war games.

14. *Cadbury's Gems*: This English animation ad recreates the James Bond character and his wonderful exploits, telling children, 'This new pack will freak you out.' Very much like the cartoon serial He Man.

15. *Maggi Noodles*: 'Mummy, *bhook lagee hai.' 'Bas do* minute' *'Dekho* Maggi *kare kamaal, peela* packet *ho ya lal, bachchon ko jab bhook lage to,*

MAGGI, MAGGI, MAGGI!' This is considered a successful advertise-ment and one that has introduced a time-saving meal snack for children, convenient for all mothers. The ad depicts a calm and cheerful mother and her happy children.

16. *LML Vespa Scooter*: The slogan, 'It's got the power, it's got the style,' is lifted from a Black American song: 'I've got the power'. The ad is in English, does not use children but focuses on the image of the young man, his woman and his machine. This image especially appeals to young boys.

17. *Hajmola Sweets*: '*Jo bhi khaye, dost ban jaye.*' This humorous ad in Hindi uses a child and an old man to target as wide an audience as possible. It depicts the start of a new friendship—all thanks to Hajmola.

18. *Ivana Perfume Spray*: The Hindi version of this ad (shot in black and white) is extremely sophisticated. The Hindi lyrics set to jazz are splayed and indistinct enough to make language identification virtually impossible. No child is used by the ad. However, the visuals of the commercial could belong to any small screen in the West—a woman dressing with care for her partner, her choice of clothes and jewellery straight out of Vogue while the young man steps out of the shade of a lamp-post as he traipses up to the waiting lady.

19. *Breeze Soap*: Straight out of Hindi film lore, the ad uses a 'hero–heroine' context to suggest that Breeze Beauty soap is responsible for the young woman's good looks. The men are stunned by the good looks of the woman who walks into the party '*Kisne banaya tumhein itna hasine?*' The ad does not feature any children.

20. *Dabur Red Toothpaste Powder*: An ad set in a typically Indian school, it is one of the few which steps away from the glamourous world that advertising normally promotes. The interaction is between 'Masterji' and a pupil and reminds us that toothpowder was once very popular in India. The old man, a funny character, enquires how the young boy has managed to take such good care of his teeth.

21. *Thums Up*: Hindi film star Salman Khan rescues two disappointed children (who could not get tickets to a film starring Khan himself) as the English jingle plays: 'Some days never seem to work out/Suddenly there's someone to brighten up your day/Bring the sun out from the clouds/In a very special way—Thums Up, Taste the Thunder.'

22. *Emami Fairness Cream*: The ad promotes the Indian obsession with fair skin by promising in its Hindi lyrics that if you use Emami Fairness cream, '*kuchh hi din mein rang tera, nikhhar, nikkhar jaye*', suggesting that the cream could change even skin colouring.

23. *Atlas Rebel Bicycle*: This English language commercial has as its central character a teenage boy to whom it carries its message of rebellion in the song: 'Now, the rebel/Hit the road/Turn on the juice/Let the rebel

in you break loose.' The slogan hammers home this message while completely ignoring the actual product—the cycle—except at the very end: 'The Rebel, from Atlas—BREAK LOOSE.'

ANNEXURE 16

CODE FOR COMMERCIAL ADVERTISING, DOORDARSHAN

Doordarshan's Code for Commercial Advertising is fairly comprehensive and exhaustive in its do's and don'ts. Indeed if it were to be interpreted both in letter and spirit there would be no grounds for complaints of any kind whatsoever—particularly moral misgivings. The key, therefore, lies in the interpretation and enforcement of the code rather than its credentials, which are unimpeachable.

Primarily the code reflects the government's anxiety to, at least on paper, uphold the basic tenets of the Constitution. Secularism and equality in terms of sex, race, caste and nationality are cornerstones of the policy, which stresses that advertising must not offend the morality or sense of decency of the people.

Suggesting a number of high-minded principles involving respect for other countries and India's relations with them, the Code specifically targets violence, crime or the incitement of either as one of its main shibboleths.

It also bans advertising for liquor, tobacco or any advertisements linked to money lending, chit funds, saving schemes or lotteries (outside of central or state governments, nationalised or recognised banks and PSUs), matrimonial agencies, fortune-tellers, magic or hypnotism. (These are, however, largely ignored by cable and satellite TV.

The Code emphasises that particular attention must be paid to advertising related to specially vulnerable groups such as women and children and spells out what it considers undesirable in their portrayal.

It seeks to protect the consumer/viewer from unfair advertising such as ads which promise amongst other things, miracle transformations or miracle cures; misrepresent the qualities of a product—either to its advantage or disadvantage; derogatory references to other products or services; misuse of technical or scientific data, incorrect pricing and misleading testimonials. Above all, no advertisement must violate Doordarshan and AIR's Broadcast Code.

The Commercial Code stresses that 'advertising shall be truthful, avoid distorting facts and misleading the public by means of implications and omissions'. Very salutary but very difficult to enforce.

The Code focuses on two important areas of advertising and devotes separate sections to them: Children and Medicines. It is relevant to quote both these sections in their entirety since individual injunctions are either being completely ignored or being so loosely interpreted as to leave the door wide open for any manner of promotion or any kind of product.

ADVERTISING AND CHILDREN

- No advertisement for a product or service shall be accepted if it suggests in any way that unless the children themselves buy or encourage other people to buy the products or services, they will be failing in their duty or lacking in loyalty to any person or organisation.
- No advertisement shall be accepted which leads children to believe that if they do not own or use the product advertised they will be inferior in some way to other children or that they are liable to be condemned or ridiculed for not owning or using it.
- Any advertisement which endangers the safety of the children or creates in them any interest in unhealthy practices, shall not be accepted, e.g. playing in the middle of the road, leaning dangerously out of a window, playing with match boxes and other goods which can cause accidents.
- Children shall not be shown begging or in an undignified or indecent manner.
- No advertisement likely to bring advertising into contempt or disrepute shall be permitted. Advertising shall not take advantage of the superstition or ignorance of the general public.
- No advertisements of talismans, charms and character reading from photographs or such other matter as well as those which trade on the superstition of the general public shall be permitted.
- Advertising shall be truthful, avoid distorting facts and misleading the public by means of implications and omissions. For instance, it shall not mislead the consumer by false statements, as to:

  i) The character of the merchandise, i.e. its utility, materials, ingredients, origin etc.
  ii) the price of the merchandise, its value, its suitability or terms of purchase.
  iii) the services accompanying purchase, including delivery, exchange, return, repair, upkeep, etc.

iv) personal recommendations of the article or service. The quality of the value of competing goods or the trustworthiness of statements made by others.

- Testimonials of any kind from experts etc. other than government-recognised standardisation agencies shall not be permitted.
- No advertisement shall be permitted to contain any claim so exaggerated as to lead inevitably to disappointment in the minds of the public.
- Methods of advertising designed to create confusion in the mind of the consumer as between goods by one maker and another maker are unfair and shall not be used. Such methods may consist of:

    i) the imitation of the trademark or name of competition or the packaging or labelling of goods; or
    ii) the imitation of advertising devices, copy, layout or slogans.

- Indecent, vulgar, suggestive, repulsive or offensive themes or treatment shall be avoided in all advertisements. This also applies to such advertisements which in themselves are not objectionable as defined above, but which advertise objectionable books, photographs or other matter and thereby lead to their sale and circulation.
- No advertisement in respect of medicines and treatments shall be accepted which is in contravention of the Code relating to Standards for advertising of medicines and treatments as per Annexure 1.

CODE OF STANDARDS IN RELATION TO THE ADVERTISING OF MEDICINES AND TREATMENTS

This code has been drafted for the guidance of advertisers, manufacturers, distributors, advertising agents, publishers and suppliers and various advertising media. The harm to the individual that may result from exaggerated, misleading or unguaranteed claims justified the adoption of a very high standard and the inclusion of considerable detail in a code to guide those who are concerned with this form of advertising. Newspaper and other advertising media are urged not to accept advertisements in respect of any product or treatment from any product or treatment from any advertiser or advertising or publicity relating to that product or treatment. The provisions of this Code do not apply to an advertisement published by or under the authority of a Government, Ministry or Department, nor to an advertisement published in journals circulated to Registered Medical Practitioners, Registered Dentists, Registered Pharmacists or Registered Nurses.

GENERAL PRINCIPLES

1. *Cure*: No advertisement should contain a claim to cure any ailment or symptoms of ill-health, nor should any advertisement contain a word or expression used in such a form or context as to mean in the positive sense the extirpation of any ailment, illness or disease.

2. *Illness etc. properly requiring medical attention*: No advertisement should contain any matter which can be regarded as an offer of medicine or product for, or advice relating to, the treatment of serious diseases, complaints, conditions, indications or symptoms which should rightly receive the attention of a registered medical practitioner.

3. *Misleading or exaggerated claims*: No advertisement should contain any matter which directly or by implication misleads or departs from the truth as to the composition, character or action of the medicine or treatment advertised or as to its suitability for the purpose for which it is recommended.

4. *Appeals to fear*: No advertisement should be calculated to induce fear on the part of the reader that he is suffering, or may without treatment suffer from an ailment, illness or disease.

5. *Diagnosis or treatment by correspondence*: No advertisement should offer to diagnose by correspondence disease, conditions or any symptoms of ill-health in a human being or request from any person or a treatment of his or any other person's symptoms of ill-health with a view to advertising as to or providing for treatment of such conditions of ill-health by correspondence. Nor should any advertisement offer to treat by correspondence any ailment, illness, disease or symptoms thereof in a human being.

6. *Disparaging references*: No advertisement should directly or by implication disparage the products, medicines or treatments of another advertiser or manufacturer or registered medical practitioner or the medical profession.

7. *College, clinic, institute, laboratory*: No advertisement should contain these or similar terms unless an establishment corresponding with the description used does in fact exist.

8. *Doctors, hospitals, etc.*: No advertisement should contain any reference to doctors or hospitals, whether Indian or foreign, unless such reference can be substantiated by independent evidence and can properly be used in the manner proposed.

9. *Products offered particularly to women*: No advertisement of products, medicines or treatments of disorders or irregularities peculiar to women should contain any expression which may imply that the product, medicine or treatment advertised can be effective in inducing miscarriage.

10. *Family planning*: Advertisement for measures or apparatus concerning family planning would be permissible insofar as they conform to the generally accepted national policy in this behalf.

11. *Illustrations*: No advertisement should contain any illustration which by itself or in combination with words used in connection therewith is likely to convey a misleading impression, or if the reasonable inference to be drawn from such advertisement infringes any of the provisions of this Code.

12. *Exaggerated copy*: No advertisement should contain copy which is exaggerated by reason of improper use of words, phrases or methods of presentation, e.g., the use of words 'magic, magical, miracle, miraculous'.

13. *Natural remedies*: No advertisement should claim or suggest contrary to the fact, that the article advertised is in the form in which it occurs in nature or that its values lies in its being a 'natural' product.

14. *Special claims*: No advertisement should contain any reference which is calculated to lead the public to assume that the article, product, medicine or treatment advertised has some special property or quality which is in fact unknown or unrecognised.

15. *Sexual weakness, premature ageing, loss of virility*: No advertisement should claim that the product, medicine or treatment advertised will promote sexual virility or be effective in treating sexual weakness or habits associated with sexual excess or indulgence or any ailment, illness or disease associated with those habits. In particular such terms as 'premature ageing' and 'loss of virility' will be regarded as conditions for which medicines, products, appliances or treatment may not be advertised.

16. *Slimming, weight reduction or limitation or figure control*: No advertisement should offer any medical product for the purpose of slimming, weight reduction or limitation or figure control. Medical products intended to reduce appetite will usually be regarded as being for slimming purposes.

17. *Tonics*: The use of this expression in advertisements should not imply that the product or medicine can be used in the treatment of sexual weakness.

18. *Hypnosis*: No advertisements should contain any offer to diagnose or treat complaints or conditions by hypnosis.

19. *Materials to students*: Materials meant for distribution in educational institutions must not carry advertisements of anything other than those of value to students.

ANNEXURE 17

TV ADVERTISING STANDARDS COUNCIL OF INDIA

CODE FOR SELF-REGULATION IN ADVERTISING

Adopted by The Advertising Standards Council of India under Article 2 (ii)f of its Articles of Association at the first meeting of the Board of Governors held on 20 November 1985.

The purpose of the Code is to control the content of advertisements, not to hamper the sale of products which may be found offensive, for whatever reason, by some people. Provided, therefore, that advertisements for such products are not themselves offensive, there will normally be no ground for objection to them in terms of this section of the Code.

DECLARATION OF FUNDAMENTAL PRINCIPLES

This Code for Self-regulation has been drawn up by people in professions and industries in or connected with advertising, in consultation with representatives of people affected by advertising. It has been accepted by individuals, corporate bodies and associations engaged in or otherwise concerned with the practice of advertising with the following as basic guidelines with a view to achieve the acceptance of fair advertising practices in the best interest of the ultimate consumer:

i) To ensure the truthfulness and honesty of representations and claims made by advertisements and to safeguard against misleading advertisements.

ii) To ensure that advertisements are not offensive to generally accepted standards of public decency.

iii) To safeguard against the indiscriminate use of advertising for the promotion of products which are regarded as hazardous to society or to individuals to a degree or of a type which is unacceptable to society at large.

iv) To ensure that advertisements observe fairness in competition so that the consumer's need to be informed on choices in the marketplace and the canons of generally accepted competitive behaviour in business are both served.

The Code's rules form the basis for judgement whenever there may be conflicting views about the acceptability of an advertisement, whether it is challenged from within or from outside the advertising business. Both the general public and an advertiser's competitors have an equal right to expect the content of advertisements to be presented fairly, intelligibly and responsibly. The Code binds the advertisers, the advertising agency and the media owner.

RESPONSIBILITY FOR THE OBSERVANCE OF THIS CODE

As the advertiser originates the advertising brief and sanctions its placement, the advertiser carries full responsibility for the observance of this Code. This responsibility embraces the advertisement in its entire content and form (including testimonials and statements or visual presentations originating from other sources). The fact that the content or form, wholly or in part, originates from other sources is not an excuse for non-observance of this Code.

As creators and expert advisors, the advertising agency has full responsibility to ensure the observance of this Code inasmuch as the facts are known to them: To advise their clients in accordance with this Code; and if clients are not amenable to their advice, to refer the matter to the Advertising Standards Council of India. If the agency view is upheld by the Advertising Standards Council of India and the client is determined to persist with the unacceptable advertisement, under this Code it is the agency's responsibility to refuse to release or in any way assist the release of such advertisement, and the requirement of such refusal is applicable to all other agencies and to media.

Any media owner must view each advertisement offered for publication to them from the point of view of the Code. If any advertisement is considered by the media owner to be in contravention of the Code, the media owner should refer the matter to the Advertising Standards Council of India. All advertisements found by the Advertising Standards Council of India to be in violation of this Code shall be refused publication by all media owners.

This Code does not apply to advertisements in media published abroad and Indian media whose circulation is predominantly overseas.

THE CODE AND THE LAW

The Code's rules are not the only ones to affect advertising. There are many provisions, both in the common law and in the statutes, which can determine the form or the content of an advertisement. The Code is not in competition with law. Its rules and the machinery through which they are enforced are designed to complement legal controls, not to usurp or replace them.

DEFINITIONS

For the purpose of this Code:

- an advertisement is defined as paid-for communication, addressed to the public or a section of it, the purpose of which is to influence the opinions or behaviour of those to whom it is addressed.
- a product is anything which forms the subject of an advertisement, and includes goods, services and facilities.
- a consumer is any person or corporate body who is likely to be reached by an advertisement whether as an ultimate consumer, in the way of trade or otherwise.
- an advertiser is an individual or partnership or corporate body or association on whose brief the advertisement is designed and on whose account the advertisement is released.
- advertising agency includes all individuals, partnerships, corporate bodies or associations who or which work for planning, research, creation or placement of advertisements or the creation of material for advertisements for advertisers or for other advertising agencies.
- media owners include individuals in effective control of the management of media or their agents; media are any means used for the propagation of advertisements and include the press, cinema, radio, television, hoardings, hand bills, direct mail, posters and the like.
- to publish is to carry the advertisement in any media whether it be by printing, exhibiting, broadcasting, displaying or distributing etc.

STANDARDS OF CONDUCT

'Advertising is an important and legitimate means for the seller to awaken interest in his products. The success of advertising depends on pubic confidence. Hence no practice should be permitted which tends to impair this confidence.' The standards laid down here should be taken as minimum standards of acceptability which would be liable to be reviewed from time to time in relation to the prevailing norm of consumers' susceptibilities.

THE CODE OF ADVERTISING PRACTICE

To ensure the truthfulness and honesty of representations and claims made by advertisements and to safeguard against misleading advertisements:

1. Advertisements must be truthful. All descriptions, claims and comparisons which relate to matters of objectively ascertainable facts should be capable of substantiation. Advertisers and advertising agencies are required to produce such substantiation as and when called upon to do so by the Advertising Standards Council of India.

2. Where advertising claims are expressly stated to be based on or supported by independent research or assessment, the source and date of this should be indicated in the advertisement.

3. Advertisements should not contain any reference to any person, firm or institution without due permission; nor should a picture of any generally identifiable person be used in advertising without due permission.

4. Advertisements shall not distort facts nor mislead the consumer by means of implications or omissions. Advertisements shall not contain statements or visual presentations which directly or by implication or by omission or by ambiguity or by exaggeration are likely to mislead the consumer about the product advertised or the advertiser or about any other product or advertiser.

5. Advertisements shall not be so framed as to abuse the trust of consumers or exploit their lack of experience or knowledge. No advertisement shall be permitted to contain any claim so exaggerated as to lead to grave or widespread disappointment in the minds of consumers. For example:

   (*a*) Products shall not be described as 'free' where there is any direct cost to the consumer other than the actual cost of any delivery, freight or postage. Where such costs are payable by the consumer, a clear statement that this is the case shall be made in the advertisement.

   (*b*) Where a claim is made that if one product is purchased another product will be provided 'free', the advertiser is required to show as an when called upon by The Advertising Standards Council of India that the price paid by the consumer for the product which is offered for purchase with the advertised incentive is no more than the prevalent price of the product without the advertised incentive.

   (*c*) Claims which use expressions such as 'Up to five years guarantee' or 'Prices from as low as Y' are not acceptable if there is a likelihood of the consumer being misled either as to the extent of the availability or as to the applicability of the benefits offered.

   (*d*) Special care and restraint has to be exercised in advertisements addressed to those suffering from weakness, any real or perceived inadequacy of any physical attributes such as height or bust development, obesity, illness, impotence, infertility, baldness and the like to ensure that claims or representations directly or by implication, do not exceed what is considered prudent by generally accepted standards or medical practice and the actual efficacy of the product.

(e) Advertisements inviting the public to invest money shall not contain statements which may mislead the consumer in respect of the security offered, rates of return or terms of amortisation; where any of the foregoing elements are contingent upon the continuance of or change in existing conditions, or any other assumptions, such conditions or assumptions must be clearly indicated in the advertisement.

(f) Advertisements inviting the public to take part in lotteries or prize competitions permitted under law or which hold out the prospect of gifts shall state clearly all material conditions as to enable the consumer to obtain a true and fair view of their prospects shall make adequate provisions for the judging of such competitions, announcement of the results and the fair distribution of prizes or gifts according to the advertised terms and conditions within a reasonable period of time. With regard to the announcement of results, it is clarified that the advertiser's responsibility under this section of the Code is discharged adequately if the advertiser publicises the main results in the media used to announce the competition as far as is practicable and advises the individual winners by post.

6. Obvious untruths or exaggerations intended to amuse or to catch the eye of the consumer are permissible provided that they are clearly to be seen as humourous or hyperbolic and not likely to be understood as making literal or misleading claims for the advertised product.

To ensure that advertisements are not offensive to generally accepted standards of public decency:

Advertisements should contain nothing indecent, vulgar or repulsive which is likely in the light of generally prevailing standards of decency and propriety, to cause grave or widespread offence.

To safeguard against the indiscriminate use of advertising in situations or for the promotion of products which are regarded as hazardous to society or to individuals to a degree or of a type which is unacceptable to society at large:

1. No advertisement shall be permitted which:

(a) Tends to incite people to crime or to promote disorder and violence or intolerance.

(b) Derides any race, caste, colour, creed or nationality.

(c) Presents criminality as desirable or directly or indirectly encourages people—particularly children—to emulate it or conveys the modus operandi of any crime.

(d) Adversely affects friendly relations with a foreign state.

2. Advertisements addressed to children shall not contain anything, whether in illustration or otherwise, which might result in their physical, mental or moral harm or which exploits their vulnerability. For example, no advertisement:

(a) Shall encourage children to enter strange places or to converse with strangers in an effort to collect coupons, wrappers, labels or the like.

(b) Should depict children leaning dangerously outside windows, overbridges or climbing dangerous cliffs and the like.

(c) Should show children climbing or reaching dangerously to reach products for any other purpose.

(d) Should show children using or playing with matches or any inflammable or explosive substance; or playing with or using sharp knives, guns or mechanical or electrical appliances, the careless use of which could lead to their suffering cuts, burns, shocks or other injury.

(e) Shall feature minors for tobacco or alchohol-based products.

3. Advertisements shall not, without justifiable reason, show or refer to dangerous practices or manifest a disregard for safety or encourage negligence.

4. Advertisements should contain nothing which is in breach of the law nor omit anything which the law requires.

5. Advertisements shall not propagate products the use of which is banned under the law.

To ensure that advertisements observe fairness in competition such that the consumer's need to be informed on choices in the marketplace and the canons of generally accepted competitive behaviour in business are both served:

1. Advertisements containing comparisons with other manufacturers or suppliers or with other products including those where a competitor is named, are permissible in the interests of vigorous competition and public enlightenment, provided:

(a) It is clear what aspects of the advertiser's product are being compared with what aspects of the competitor's product.

(b) The subject matter of comparison is not chosen in such a way as to confer an artificial advantage upon the advertiser or so as to suggest that a better bargain is offered than is truly the case.

(c) The comparisons are factual, accurate and capable of substantiation.

(d) There is no likelihood of the consumer being misled as a result of the comparison, whether about the product advertised or that with which it is compared.

(e) The advertisement does not unfairly denigrate, attach or discredit other products, advertisers or advertisements directly or by implication.

2. Advertisements shall not make unjustifiable use of the name or initials of any other firm, company or institution, nor take unfair advantage of the goodwill attached to the trade mark or symbol of another firm or its product or the goodwill acquired by its advertising campaign.

3. Advertisements shall not be so similar to other advertisements in general layout, copy, slogans, visual presentations, music or sound effects as to be likely to mislead or confuse consumers.

IS YOUR ADVERTISING LOSING ITS CREDIBILITY?
THE THREAT
THE CONSUMER'S POINT OF VIEW

An unfortunate fact of life in marketing is the quantity of false, misleading and offensive advertising. This has resulted in consumers having an increasing disbelief in advertising and a growing resentment of it. This can affect all advertising—including yours.

This is one aspect of the threat.

THE THREAT IN A COMPETITIVE FRAME

Misleading, false advertising also constitutes unfair competition. If you play by the rules and your competition overpromises, it could lead to marketplace disaster, even litigation. Is that something you want to face?

This is the second aspect of the threat.

THE THREAT
IMPOSED REGULATION

If this kind of advertising continues, it won't be long before statutory regulatory bodies step in. And impose rules, regulations and procedures that make even fair, truthful, decent advertising cumbersome if not impossible. That will certainly affect your ability to compete and grow.

This is the third and possibly the most uncomfortable aspect of the threat.

IF AN ADVERTISEMENT IS WRONG
HERE'S WHAT YOU DO

1. If an advertisement offends you, write to us enclosing a cutting or photographs or detailed description of the advertisement and stating your complaint.
2. Your complaint will be passed to an independent Consumer Complaints Council made up of 14 members.

HOW WILL JUDGEMENTS BE IMPLEMENTED?

If a complaint is upheld, The Advertising Standards Council of India will try its best to ensure that the offending advertisement is either suitably modified or withdrawn.

Pressures that The Advertising Standards Council of India can exert are primarily ethical. But that doesn't make it a toothless lion. Because the media is likely to refuse to carry advertisements judged to be against the Code, preventing the pollution of advertising space and time. And, the Council will issue releases declaring offending advertisements unethical. That alone may be enough.

If an advertisement is wrong,

We'll fight to put it right.

ANNEXURE 18

Doordarshan Commercial Service: Rate Card for Commercial Advertisement and Sponsorship (Effective from 21–3–1994)

1. Annexures I, II and III indicate rates for spot buys and sponsorship.
2. The categorisations are as under:
    (a) *NATIONAL NETWORK (DD-1)*
    - (i) Super 'A' Special
        - (i) Hindi Feature Film (Saturday).
        - (ii) Chitrahaar (Wednesday).
        - (iii) Rangoli (Sunday).
    - (ii) Super 'A'
        - (i) 9.00 p.m. slot on all days (Hindi/English).
        - (ii) 9.30 p.m. to 10.00 p.m. Hindi serials.

	(*iii*) Live coverage/highlights of special international sports (to be intimated in advance).
	(*iv*) Before 'Samachar' at 8.30 p.m.
	(*v*) Any other programme intimated in advance.
(*iii*) 'A' Special	(*i*) Various programmes/slots on Sunday morning (9.00 a.m.-12.00 noon).
	(*ii*) 9.30 p.m. to 10.00 p.m. (except Hindi serials).
	(*iii*) Live coverage/highlights of international sports events.
	(*iv*) Before 'The News' at 10.00 p.m.
	(*v*) Any other programme intimated in advance.
(*iv*) 'A'	(*i*) 10.30 p.m. slot on all days.
	(*ii*) Late night/Tuesday afternoon films.
	(*iii*) Live coverage of national events (on Sundays, holidays and finals).
	(*iv*) Highlights/recorded international sports events telecast after 10.30 p.m.
	(*v*) After 9.00 a.m. on Saturdays only.
	(*vi*) Any other programme intimated in advance.
(*v*) 'B'	(*i*) Morning and afternoon transmission.
	(*ii*) From 11.00 p.m. onwards.
	(*iii*) Regional feature film on national network (Sunday).
	(*iv*) Live national sports events on weekdays and matches up to semi-final.
	(*v*) World of sports/sponsored sports programmes in the afternoon transmission.
	(*vi*) Any other programme intimated in advance.

Metro Entertainment Channel (DD-II)
(Effective from: 21-3-94)

1. Super 'A'	(*i*) 8.00 p.m.-10.00 p.m. (Film-based programmes and serials)

	(*ii*)	Any other programme intimated in advance.
2. 'A' Special	(*i*)	8.00 p.m.–10.00 p.m. (talkshows, quiz, games show, English serials, other non-film based and non-serial programmes).
	(*ii*)	8.00 a.m.–12.00 noon (Sundays only). (All programmes regardless of the format and language.)
	(*iii*)	7.30 p.m.–8.00 p.m. 10.30 p.m.–11.00 p.m.
	(*iv*)	Any other programme intimated in advance.
3. 'A'	(*i*)	7.00 p.m.–7.30 p.m.
	(*ii*)	Any other programme intimated in advance.
4. 'B'	(*i*)	Morning (on all days)
	(*ii*)	Afternoon and programmes up to 7.00 p.m.
	(*iii*)	After 11.00 p.m.
	(*iv*)	Any other programme intimated in advance.

Rate Card—Spot Buy
National Network
Rate for Spot Buy (10 Seconds in Rupees)

Kendra (1)	Super A Spl (2)	Super A (3)	A Spl. (4)	'A' (5)	'B' (6)
National Network	Chitrahaar 1,20,000 1,30,000 (for last two spots) 1,50,000 (in-between) Hindi Feature Film 1,00,000	60,000	40,000	25,000	15,000

1. Before Samachar
   70,000
2. The News
   40,000

Rangoli
Spot Buy
75,000
80,000
(last two spots)
1,00,000
(in-between)

In-between Samachar: 80,000
The News: 60,000

Rate for Sponsorship of Doordarshan Programmes
Produced/Commissioned and Acquired
(in Rupees—30 mts.)

Time Categories

Kendra (1)	Super A Spl (2)	Super A (3)	A Spl. (4)	'A' (5)	'B' (6)
National Network	Hindi Feature Film				
	6,50,000 40 sec.	3,50,000 60 sec.	2,20,000 60 sec.	1,30,000 60 sec.	
	Sponsored Hindi Film 5,00,000 60 sec.	2,40,000 40 sec.	1,60,000 40 sec.	1,00,000 40 sec.	40,000 40 sec.

40 sec. FCT is common to all regional programmes in all categories.

Rate for Sponsorship along with Details of FCT for
Programmes Produced by Outside Producers
(in Rupees—30 mts. programme)

Super A	A Spl.	'A'	'B'	Telefilm/ Teleplay
National Network				
1,40,000 (90 sec.)	1,00,000 (120 sec.)	50,000 (120 sec.)	New prog. 25,000 with (150 sec.)	
Mega Serials 1,80,000 (120 sec.)	Mega Serials 1,00,000 (150 sec.)		(with banking of 30 sec.)	
			Repeat prog. 70,000 (90 sec.)	50,000 (90 mts) 35,000 (60 mts)

Rate Card Doordarshan-II Metro Channel

	Super A		A Special		A Category *	B Category *
	F/	SS	F	SS/ C/I/G/Q		
Spot Buy Rate (10 sec.)	30,000	30,000	22,000	22,000	15,000	10,000
FCT (In sec.)	150	180	150	180	210	210
Sponsorship Fee	2,00,000	1,40,000	1,00,000	50,000 (SS) 1,00,000 (C/I/G/Q)	35,000	20,000

F = Film-based   I = Interviews
SS = Sponsored Serial   G = Game Shows
C = Chat Shows   Q = Quiz

Rate for Satellite Channels

DOORDARSHAN III   *SPONSORSHIP FEE*

Spot Buy (10″)	*DD Programme*	*Outside Programme*
Rs. 5,000	Rs. 20,000	Rs. 5,000
	(60″ FCT)	(270″ FCT)

(For outside produced programme at least 120″ FCT or more will have to be utilised and the balance with any programme on the same day.)

SATELLITE LANGUAGE: REGIONAL SERVICE

I *Tamil/Telugu/Kannada/Malayalam*

SPONSORSHIP FEE

Spot Buy (10″)	*DD Programme*	*Outside Programme*
Rs. 5,000	Rs. 20,000	Rs. 5,000
	(60″ FCT)	(240″ FCT)
		Rs. 5,000
		(210″ FCT: film-based programme)

II. *Bengali/Marathi/Punjabi/Gujarati*

SPONSORSHIP FEE

Spot Buy (10″)	*DD Programme*	*Outside Programme*
Rs. 4,000	Rs. 16,000	Rs. 4,000
	(60″ FCT)	(270″ FCT)
		Rs. 4,000
		(240″ FCT: Film-based programme)

III. *Assameese/Oriya/Kashmiri*

SPONSORSHIP FEE

Spot Buy (10″)	*DD Programme*	*Outside Programme*
Rs. 3,000	Rs. 10,000	Rs. 3,000
	(60″ FCT).	(270″ FCT)
		All Programmes)

Note: For outside produced programme at least 120″ or more will be utilised with the programme and the balance can be utilised with the same language channel one week from the date of telecast.

ANNEXURE 19

Classification Module Used by the CTA Study
Classification of TV Advertisements

Type of Adv.					Frequency/Insertions				Language			Cultural/Class Image												Music		Child Consumer		
CD	ND	SR	SER	CORP	M	A	E	Total No.	E	H	E/H	SR	W	I	UC	W	I	MC	W	I	LC	W	I	W	I	DA	CS	IA

CD : Consumer Durable
ND : Nondurable
SR : Socially Relevant
SER : Services
CORP : Corporate Selling
M : Morning
A : Afternoon
E : Evening

SR : Super Rich (Western/Indian)
W : Western
I : Indian
UC : Upper Class
MC : Middle Class
LC : Lower Class
DA : Direct Appeal
CS : Child is Used as Subject to Appeal to Adult Consumer
IA : Indirect Appeal

Total No. of Screenings
E : English
H : Hindi
E/H : English and Hindi

BIBLIOGRAPHY

AGARWAL, BINOD C. and MIRA B. AGHI (eds.). 1987. *Television and the Indian Child—A Handbook*. UNICEF, New Delhi.

ALLEN, ROBERT C. (ed.). 1992. *Channels of Discourse—Television and Contemporary Criticism*. University of North Carolina Press, USA.

ANG, IEN. 1991. *Desperately Seeking the Audience*. Routledge, London, New York.

ATKIN, CHARLES K. 1981. 'Effects of Television Advertising on Children' in *Children and the Faces of Television: Teaching Violence, Selling*, edited by E. Palmer and A. Dorr. Academic Press, Inc.

BARCUS, F.E. and RACHEL WOLKIN. 1980. *Children's Television*. Praeger Special Studies, New York.

BARNOUW, E. 1978. *The Sponsor: Notes on a Modern Potentate*. Oxford University Press, New York.

———. 1975. *The Tube of Plenty: The Evolution of American Television*. Oxford University Press, New York.

———. 1970. *The Image Empire: A History of Broadcasting in the United States from 1953*. Oxford University Press, New York.

BERGER, J. 1972. *Ways of Seeing*. Penguin, Harmondsworth.

CHAUDRI, MANMOHAN. 1986. *India from SITE to INSAT—Media in Education and Development*, edited by Binod C. Agarwal and Arvind K. Sinha. Concept Publishing Company, New Delhi.

CHOAT, ERNEST and HARRY GRIFFIN. 1989. *Using Television in the Primary School*. Routledge, London.

COPPA, FRANK. J. (ed.). 1979. *Screen and Society*. Nelson Hall, Chicago.

DEODHAR, P.S. 1991. *The Third Parent: Growth and Development of Indian Electronics Media*. Vikas, New Delhi.

DORR, AIMEE. 1986. *Television and Children: A Special Medium for a Special Audience*. Sage, Thousand Oaks.

DOWNING, J., ALI MOHAMMADI and ANNABELLE SREBERNY-MOHAMMADI (eds.). 1990. *Questioning the Media*. Sage, Thousand Oaks.

ENRIGHT, D.J. 1988. *Fields of Vision*. Oxford University Press, New York.

EWENS, S. 1976. *Captains of Consciousness*. McGraw-Hill, New York.

FISKE, JOHN. 1989. *Television Culture*. Routledge, New York.

FISKE, J. and J. HARTLEY. 1978. *Reading Television*. Methuen & Co. Ltd., London.

FITCH, MARGUERITE, ALETHA C. HUSTON and JOHN C. WRIGHT. 1993. *From Television Forms to Genre Schemata: Children's Perceptions of Television Reality*. Children and Television. Editors: Gordon L. Berry, Joy Keiko Asamen. Sage. Quill, New York.

GREENFIELD, PATRICIA MARKS. 1984. *Mind and Media—The Effects of Television, Computers and Video Games*. Fontana Paperbacks, William Collins Sons and Co. Ltd., Glasgow.

GALBRAITH, JOHN KENNETH. 1958. *The Affluent Society*. Houghton Mifflin, Boston.

GERBNER, G. (ed.). 1977. *Mass Media in Changing Culture*. Wili, New York.

HACKMAN, SUE and WINK HACKMAN. *Constructing Vision*. Hodder and Stoughton, London, Sydney, Auckland, Toronto.

HALBERSTAM, DAVID. 1979. *The Powers That Be*. Dell Publishing Co., Inc., New York.

HALL, S. 1986. *Cultural Studies: Two Paradigms*. Media Culture and Society, A Critical Reader. Sage, Thousand Oaks.

HALL, STUART. 1982. As quoted by Joli Jenson in *Redeeming Modernity*. 1990. Sage, Thousand Oaks.

HAMELINK, CEES. 1990. 'Information Imbalance: Core and Periphery' in *Questioning The Media*, edited by John Downing, Ali Mohammadi, Annabelle Sreberny-Mohammadi. Sage, Thousand Oaks.

HENRY, JULES. 1966. *Culture against Man*. Random House, Great Britain.

INGLIS, FRED. 1972. *The Imagery of Power: A Critique of Advertising*. Heinemann, London.

JENSEN, JOLI. 1990. 'Remote Control TV, Audiences and Cultural Power' in *Redeeming Modernity*. Sage, Thousand Oaks.

KELLNER, DOUGLAS. 1990. 'Advertising and Consumer Culture' in *Questioning the Media*, edited by J. Downing, A. Mohammadi and A. Sreberny-Mohammadi. Sage, USA.

KUMAR, KRISHNA. 1989. *Social Character of Learning*. Sage, New Delhi.

LASCH, CHRISTOPHER. *The Culture of Narcissism*. 1979. Warner Books, New York.

LEISS, W., S. KLINE and SAT JHALLY. 1986. *Social Communication in Advertising*. Methuen, New York.

LITTLEJOHN, DAVID. 1975. 'Communicating Ideas by Television' in *Television as a Social Force—New Approaches to TV Criticism*, edited by Richard Adler. Praeger Publishers, New York.

LULL, JAMES. 1990. *Inside Family Viewing—Ethnographic Research on Television's Audiences*. Routledge, London.

MANDER, JERRY. 1978. *Four Arguments for the Elimination of Television.* Quill, New York.

———. 1978. 'The Replacement of Human Images by Television' in *Four Arguments for the Elimination of Television.*

McLUHAN, MARSHALL. 1987. *Understanding Media.* ARK Paperbacks, Routledge and Kegan Paul Ltd.,

McQUAIL, DENIS. (ed.) 1972. *Sociology of Mass Communications*, Penguin, Harmondsworth.

McQUAIL, DENIS. 1975. *Communication.* Longman, London.

———. 1986. 'Commercialisation' in *New Media Politics.* Euromedia Research Group. Sage, London.

MILLS, C. WRIGHT. 1956. *The Power Elite.* Oxford University Press, New York.

MITRA, ANAND. 1993. 'Television and Popular Culture' in *India: A Study of the Mahabharat.* Sage, New Delhi.

MURRAY, LAWRENCE L. 1979. 'Universality and Uniformity in the Popular Arts: The Impact of Television on Popular Culture' in *Screen and Society—The Impact of Television upon Aspects of Contemporary Civilization*, edited by Frank J Coppa. Nelson-Hall Publishers, Chicago.

National Council of Applied Economic Research (NCAER). 1993. *Socio–Economic Effects of Advertising in India.* NCAER, New Delhi.

NIMMO, DAN and JAMES E. COMBS. 1983. *Mediated Political Realities.* Longman, New York and London.

PACKARD, VANCE. 1981. *The Hidden Persuaders.* Penguin, Harmondsworth.

RISSOVER, FREDRIC and DAVID C. BIRCH (eds.). 1977. *Mass Media and the Popular Arts.* McGraw-Hill, New York.

ROGGE, JAN-UWE. 1989. 'The Media in Everyday Family Life' in *Remote Control TV, Audiences and Cultural Power*, edited by E. Seiter, H. Borchers, G. Kreutzner and E.M. Worth. Routledge, London.

SCHILLER, H. 1969. *Mass Communications and American Empire.* Kelly, New York.

SCHUDSON, MICHAEL. *Advertising, the Uneasy Persuasion.* 1984. Basic Books, New York.

SENGUPTA, SUBROTO. 1990. *Brand Positioning.* Tata-McGraw-Hill Company Limited, New Delhi.

WARD, SCOTT, DANIEL WACKMAN and ELLEN WARTELLA. 1977. *Children Learning to Buy: The Development of Consumer Information Processing Skills.* Sage, Beverly Hills.

WILLIAMS, F., R. LAROSE and FREDERICA FROST. 1981. *Children, TV, and Sex-Role Stereotyping.* Praeger Publishers, New York.

WILLIAMS, RAYMOND. 1961. *Culture and Society*. Penguin, Harmondsworth.
————. 1981. *Culture*. Fontana, London.
————. 1990. *Television Technology and Cultural Form*. Routledge, London.
WINN, MARIE. 1977. *The Plug-in Drug*. Viking, New York.
WINICK, MARIANN PEZELLA and CHARLES WINICK. 1979. *The Television Experience—What Children See*. Sage, Thousand Oaks.

PERIODICALS/RESEARCH MATERIALS

A&M (Advertising and Marketing) 1991–1994.
A&M Pathfinder's Study. *Inside the Child's Mind*, July 1989.
American Academy of Pediatricians Task Force Report on *Children and Television*. 1984.
American Academy of Pediatrics: Committee on Communications. 'Children, Adolescence, and Television.' 1990. *Pediatrics Volume 85 No. 6.*; Taskforce on 'Children and Television', 1984.
American Psychological Association. Testimony of Leonard D. Eron before the U.S. Senate Committee on Governmental Affairs.
ANDERSON, DANIEL R. 1985. 'The Influence of Television on Children's Attentional Abilities'. (Paper commissioned by Children's Television Workshop.) University of Massachusetts, Amherst, MA., U.S.A.
BANERJEE, SUBRATA. 'Socially Relevant Advertising and the Developing World'. *Communicator*, September 1989.
Beveridge Committee Report on the BBC.
Brand Equity. IMRB Study on 'Gambling on the Rural Roulette'. 8 April 1992.
Brand Equity. 'Consumerism in the 90s', *The Economic Times*, 5 January 1994.
Brand Equity. 'Nostradamus'. *The Economic Times*, 5 January 1994.
CHAWLA, N.L. 'Disturbing Trends in Child TV Viewing', *The Times of India*, 18 September 1989.
Centre for Science in the Public Interest (CSPI). July 1992. *News Release*, July 1992.
Committee for Children's Television (CCTV). *Strategies for Change*, a booklet produced by the Committee for Children's Television, Metro Detroit, U.S.A.

Doordarshan. *Facts and Figures 1993*. Audience Research Unit. Door-darshan. *Facts and Figures 1994*. Audience Research Unit.

FROME-PAGET, K., D. KRITT, and L. BERGEMANN. 'Understanding Strategic Interactions in Television Commercials: A Developmental Study', *Journal of Applied Developmental Psychology 5*. (145–61), 1984.

HOLMAN, J. and V.A. BRAITHWAITE. 'Parental lifestyles and Children's Television Viewing', *Australian Journal of Psychology*, Volume 34, No. 3, 1982.

HUSTON-STEIN, ALETHA and JOHN C. WRIGHT. 'Children and Television: Effects of the Medium, its Content and its Form', *Journal of Research and Development in Education*, Volume 13, Number 1, 1979.

Indian Market Research Bureau (IMRB). Indian Society of Advertisers Survey, June 1993.

International Commission for the Study of Communication Problems. 1980. UNESCO, Paris.

JHALLY, SAT. 'Probing the Blindspot: The Audience Commodity'. *Canadian Journal of Political and Social Theory/Revue Canadienne de theorie politique et sociale*, Vol. 6, Nos. 1–2, 1982.

JOSHI, P.C. Committee on Software for Doordarshan. 1984.

Many Voices, One World: The MacBride Commission Report, UNESCO, 1980. London: Kogan Page, Paris: *UNESCO*.

Ministry of Information and Broadcasting. Mahalik Committee Report on Doordarshan's Commercial Services, January 1992.

Mallik, Suresh. 1993. Creative Director, Ogilvy and Mather Advertising Agency. 'A Review of Indian Television Commercials: Production Values or Ideas'.

National Coalition on TV Violence (NCTV). *NCTV News*, 1991–1993.

National Commission on the Causes and Prevention of Violence, U.S.A. 1968.

National Institute of Public Cooperation and Child Development. 'Report on the National Seminar on TV and Child Development', 1987.

National Institute of Mental Health's Report (1982); and the U.S. Attorney General's Task Force on Family Violence (1984).

Newsweek, 17 October 1988. Harry F. Waters: The Future of Television (Article).

The Pioneer. April 1993.

Pilkington Committee on British Broadcasting. 1960.

ROBERTS. D., W. GIBSON and P. CHRISTENSON. 'Inoculating Children against Television Commercials'. Paper presented at the annual meeting of the Pacific Association of Public Opinion Research, March 1978. Asilomar, California.

ROY, RAGHU. 'Consumerism in the 90s'. Brand Equity, *The Economic Times*, 5 January 1994.

SAINATH, P. 'Information, Economics and Power—A Journalist's Perspective in One-way Traffic of Ideas between America and India. Informatics/Development.

Star TV Commercial Rate Card, 1993.

TV Guide. 'Violence in the Media. A Debate on TV and Violence', U.S.A., August 1992.

University Grants Commission (UGC) Task Force Report. 'Mass Communication and Educational Technology—An Approach to Educational Software'; 'An Approach to Hardware', 1983.

U.S. Surgeon General's Report, 1972.

WARTELLA, ELLEN. 'Cognitive and Affective Factors of TV Advertising's Influence on Children', *Western Journal of Speech Communication*, Spring 1984.

YADAVA, J.S. 'Does Television Advertising Harm Children?' *Communicator*, December 1989.

INDEX

academic pressure, on children, TV as target and, 72
access, to satellite TV, 99
Action for Children's Television, 58
Adams, Bryan, 175
addiction, to TV, 94
adult issues on TV and children viewing, 69, 74–75
advertisement(s), television, for adult consumers, 190; for children, 190; as entertainers, 151; favourites, 241–46; film-makers, 193; impact of, on children, 166, 243; and promotion of values, 358–59; ranking of, by children of different classes, 313; 'stars', 185; support to Doordarshan, 199; support to television, 138; types appealing to children, 241; understanding, 159ff
advertising, 122, 146; business in Delhi, 146, 233; child in, 190ff; children's response to, 239ff; code for, 100; and consumerism, 126 (*see also* consumerism, criticism of, 130–31); on Doordarshan, 171–89; elements of, 169ff; ethics, 156–57, 297; indifference of, 131–32; industry in US, 129; influence of, on children, 164, 165; patterns of, 171; programming and, 84–85; rates, 85, 128; relevance of, 225; revenue from, 114; and television, 137ff; vehicle of change, 231, 232
affluent children, and advertisements, consumerism, 316–17, 319, 321;

favourite advertisements of, 243, 245; TV at meal time for, 66; TV viewing by, 73
Aiyer, Swaminathan, 341, 342
alien culture, TV advertisements reinforcing, 333
All India Radio, 85
ambitions, of children, 322–23
Americans, time spent on watching TV, 109–10
Amul chocolate advertisement, favourite among children, 147, 194
Anderson, Daniel R., 58
Ann-Mary School, 289
Apache Indian, 175, 176, 369
Ariel advertisement, impact on children, 302, 312, 316
Aryton, Zena, 275
ASIASAT II, 110
ASIANET, 100
Atkin, Charles K., 144, 232, 250
Atlas cycle advertisement, impact on children, 181, 313, 316
Audience Research Unit, at Doordarshan, 42, 97, 237

baby sitter, and TV watching, 67–69
Bakke, Marit, 337
Banerjee, Subrata, 142, 225
Barbie doll advertisement, favourite of children, 186, 278, 284, 285, 286, 290
Barnow, Eric, 54, 125, 126, 133
Bedi, Kabir, 356
Beveridge Committee on BBC, 230
books, children spending money on, 296
Braithwaite, V.A., 70

brand images, and class choice, 265; on TV, 301
Brando, Marlon, 123
brevity and repetitiveness, of advertisements, 170
British Broadcasting Corporation (BBC), 89, 97, 368; discontinuation of service to China, 366; no advertisements in, 137; programme for children, 76
broadcasting, 89; objectives of, 337–38
Byrd, Robert, 108

Cable News Network (CNN), American, 96, 368
cable TV, 38, 97, 98, 385–86; legislation on, 114; programming through, 367; and satellite TV, 94ff; use by political parties, 86; in USA, 109; viewing by children, 64
cartoons, in advertisements, 186; and advertisements for children on Doordarshan, 200, 204; and child-specific advertisements, 85; for children on STAR TV, effect of, 65; violence in, 329–31; watching, 80
CBS, revenue through advertisements, 138
censorship, on Doordarshan and All India Radio by government, 85
Center for Science in Public Interest survey, USA, 253
Channel V, 176; India-specific programmes on, 212
Charren, Peggy, 331
chat shows, 74
Chaudhary, Kavita, 323
child/children, advertising, 146ff, 252ff; in advertising, 190ff, 388; advertising, and consumerism, 155, 226–30; aggressive reactions by, impact of TV and cinema on, 69–70; attitudes to, in India, 246–49; –oriented programmes, and toy advertisements, 278–79;

pocket money for, 293–94; programmes, imbalance in, 359; ranking of advertisements, by different classes, 313; response to advertisements, 239ff; response to music TV advertisements, 173; -specific advertising, 254; -specific programming, 92–93, 104; and television, 49ff; children's television and children's advertising, 202–5
Chitrahaar, advertising during, 85, 88, 197, 199; children watching, 78, 79, 81; drop in viewership, 206; sponsoring of, 208
chocolate advertisements, children's response to, 255, 258
cinema, and TV, 36. See also films
class(es), depicted on Doordarshan, 390; imposition on TV commercials, 319; programme preference by, 80; and relevance of advertised goods, 247; and satellite TV viewing, 99, 102–4
classical music, in advertisements, 176
Code for Commercial Advertising, on Doordarshan, 157–58, 250, 353–58, 394–98
coffee advertisements, children's response to, 269–70
cold drink advertisements, 259–70, 302–4
colour factor, in advertisements for children, 170, 255
colour television, 42, 47, 208
commercials, on Doordarshan, 390–94; earnings by DD Kendras, 379; as information capsules, 159; jingles, children learning, 55; TV, and children, 50, 146ff. See also advertising
commercialisation, of Doordarshan, 88–93; of television, 54, 55, 339
Committee for Children's Television, USA, 70, 360
community television, 113

comprehension, of advertisements, 182

concentration effect, shorter, of children viewing television, 58

concepts and ideas, of television advertisements on Doordarshan, 178–83

consumer, -conscious, advertisements impact of, on children, 178; culture, TV advertisements and, 132, 348–49; ideology, 226

Consumer Education and Research Centre (CERD), Ahmedabad, 124

consumerism, 18–20, 29, 68, 126, 127, 221, 336; children, advertising and, 226–30; impact of, 230–32; spread of, in Delhi, 232–33; in urban India, 56

consumption, ideology, 130; pattern, 18, 20, 265; -related values, 229

Contract advertising agency, 146

corporate advertisements, 238

cosmetic advertisements, impact on girls, 180–81, 184, 304

Couch Potatoes, California, 53

culture (cultural), depiction on Doordarshan, 389; element of, in advertising, 309, 311, 312; identity, 96, 337; 'imperialism', 337, 342; integration, 343; and television, 29

cycles, commercials for, 271–75

demographic features, of India, 373

De Silva, Bruce, 280

detergent advertisements, popularity of, 302

Dev, Kapil, 180, 186, 275

developing countries, television advertising in, 42–43

dominant images, created and sustained by television, 301ff

Doordarshan, 37; additional channels of, 38; advertising on, 171–89; advertisement policy, 197, 210;

afternoon programmes, 79; Channel 2 of, 91–92, 206; classwise children watching, 84; commercials on, 137–38, 140, 390–94, 406, 408; commercial earnings of, 379; commercial services of, 88–93; commercialisation of, 88–90; earnings for, from advertisements, 205–11

Doordarshan, educational programmes of, 77; expansion of services, 87–88; films and film-based programmes on, 93; and gender factor, 102; national network programmes of, 376, 377; primary services of, 374; product advertising on, 383; public service advertisements on, 213–16; revenue of, 378; satellite channels of, and responses to, 91–93, 210, 374, 411; sponsored serials on, 370; tariffs on sponsorship, 380–82, 406–11; transmission hours of, 375; and Zee TV, 207

Dorr, Aimee, 55, 162

durable and non-durable goods, advertisements on, and children's impact on, 234–38, 244

Dylan, Bob, 134

economic liberalisation, and consumer culture, 89, 90; impact of, 336; multinationals' entry into India, 224; and satellite broadcasting, 112

educational programmes, 76; on Doordarshan, 87, 88, 203

emotional manipulation, of advertisements, 70–71

English language, commercials, 306–8; programmes, 81, 95

entertainment programmes, on television, 76, 88; TV as, 40, 46

Eron, Leonard, 329

ethics, of TV advertising, 353–59

Eveready Batteries' advertisements, popularity of, 147, 174–75

family life, TV and, 71
Fanon, Franz, 308
Federal Commission on Communication, 282
films, and film-based programmes, on Doordarshan, 93. *See also* Hindi films
film stars, as role models, 36
film style music, for Indian advertisements, 176–78
financial standings, of satellite TVs, 114
food items, children spending pocket money on, 294, 296
foreign programmes, impact on children, 368
France, objectives of broadcasting in, 337–38
Francis, Vince, 281
free market economy, 337

GATT negotiations, 90, 338
Gavaskar, Sunil, 180, 186
gender, bias, in TV viewing, 73; differential, 274–75; preference of channels, 102; preference of programmes, 84
Gerbner, George, 25, 331
Gill, S.S., 139
girls, display on cosmetics advertisements, 184; parents choosing programmes for, 73–74; viewing TV advertisements, 150
Glucon D advertisement, impact on children, 178, 180, 357
The Godfather, 123
Godrej Puf advertisement, impact on children, 178, 179, 316
'good life' formula, of television advertising, 168
government control, over Doordarshan and All India Radio, 85–86
Greenfield, Patricia Marks, 53, 56
Gulf War, and satellite television, 96

Hajmola advertisement, impact on children, 191
Halberstam, David, 138

Hall, Stuart, 144
Hamelink, Cees, 343
health products, children's preference for, 276; commercials on, 275–77, 357; promotion of, 275
Hindi films, 37, 78, 103, 142; and advertising, 85, 88, 201; -based programmes, 37, 103
Hindi language, commercials, 306, 308; news, 81
Hindustan Levers, 237
Hindustan Thomson, 146
Holman, J., 70
Human Development Index, 321
humour, in commercial advertisements, 184, 194
hyperbole, use of, in advertisements, 178

ice-cream advertisements, children's response to, 258–59
images, and attitudes, 328ff
imported programmes, for children, on Doordarshan, 204; on STAR Plus, 204
independent TV stations, in USA, 109–10
India, television advertising in, 196ff
Indian Market Research Bureau, 245
'informative' advertisements, 128
informative programmes, 76, 88
information technology, 37
Inglis, Fred, 133
international advertising, 191; formats of, 333

Jackson, Michael, 175–76
JAIN TV, religious and political programmes on, 86
Jenson, Joli, 50, 53
Jhally, Sat, 24, 357
joint families, and owning TVs, 48
Joshi Working Group on Software for Doordarshan, 142

Kambli, Vinod, 180
Kellner, Douglas, 129, 142, 342, 343
Khan, Salman, 163, 354

Klein, Stephen, 24
Kumar, Krishna, 46, 342

language, barrier in advertisements, 18, 182; factor, and programme watching, 81; in Indian advertisements, 306; role of, in Doordarshan, 96; of satellite TV, 98–100, 103; and social status, 305; used in Doordarshan, 389
Leiss, William, 24, 357
Leo Toys advertisements, children's response to, 278, 284–87, 290, 305, 356
Leonard, John, 331
license fee, 89
linguistic patterns, 81
Lintas, 146
literacy, 373
Littlejohn, David, 54, 139
LML Vespa advertisement, impact on boys, 186
Loomis, Bernie, 281; on children's TV in the US, 281
Loomis, Mattel, 282
lower classes, impact of TV advertisements on children, 317; and soft drink consumption by children of, 268
Lull, James, 47

MacBride report, 339
Madonna, 175
Maggi advertisements, popularity of, 124, 147
Mahabharat, 42
Mahalik Committee on Doordarshan's Commercial Services, 91; Report of, 89, 210
Maharashtra, Shiva Sena's use of cable operations in, 86
Mander, Jerry, 50, 59, 62, 127, 137, 155, 335, 350
Marg–Eyewitness survey, 242
market(s), decision by children, 229; forces, 29; forces, commercial hype by, 227; information, 24;

niche, satellite TV, and among children, 96; marketplace, Indian, 142, 143, 223, 224, 254; research data, on ownership pattern, 98
meal-time, and TV watching, 66
media, dependent on advertisements, 340; transnationalisation of, 339, 341
Media Advocacy Group, 157
Metro Entertainment (DD2), 197; rates for advertisements on, 407–11. *See also* Doordarshan
middle class children, and culture of TV advertisements, 317, 319; and soft drink consumption by, 268
Miller, Clyde, 228
Mills, C. Wright, 229
models, 183–88
money, children's access to, 293ff
movie mania, 78–80
MRAS–Burke National Television Survey, 87
MTV, 97, 102, 176; impact on children, 107–8; influence of, 183–84
Mudra, 146
multinationals, markets for, and advertisements, 127, 128, 146, 336, 340
multi-network terrestrial TV, 38
Murdoch, Rupert, 110, 114, 211, 368
music, in TV advertisements, 170, 172–78, 307, 389; types of, 173; Western, in Indian advertisements, 312
music video industry, 108

national integration advertisements, 177
National Literacy Mission advertisements, on Doordarshan, 214
national network programmes, of Doordarshan, 376, 377; rates of advertisements for, 406–7
Nukkad, popularity of, 352
nutritional learning, by children from TV advertisements, 144

Ogilvy, David, 183
ownership, of TVs, 42, 47, 48

Packard, Vance, 58, 124, 125, 233
PACRIM study, on India, 143
parents (parental), attitude, to children, 249; choice and child consumerism, 254; concern/intervention on children watching television, 69–73; report on children TV viewing, 56; response to children's demands, 249–51; role in shaping children's attitude to TV, ;52; view of TV watching by children, 59–60; vigilance, 75
passive viewing, by children, 51, 53, 58
Pathfinders, survey on children viewing television, 155, 233, 252, 323
pay channels, 114
peer group pressure, on children, 227; and child consumerism, 254
Pepsi advertisement, children's favourite, 147, 186, 259–64, 307
personal image, 183–88
persuasive techniques, of television advertisements, 128, 132, 160–64, 194
population, of India, 373
'positioning' of advertisements, 154
Prime Sports, 97, 102, 104, 106
Proctor and Gamble, 237
product categories, advertised, 234, 235
programme, on television, contents, 72, 366; preferences, 104, 106–8; preferences by class, 80; selection by parents, 73–74
programming, and advertising, 84–85
protectionism, 336
'protective' education, 50
psychographics, and advertisements, 125
Public Accounts Committee, 210
public service advertisements, 235

quality, of television advertisements, 140; of television programmes, 41, 204, 352

Ramayana, 42
Rangoli, children watching, 78
ratings, for sponsored serials, 206
reading and writing, TV viewing affecting, 20
recommendations, 361–67
regional language programmes, 81
Remo, 176
revenue, of Doordarshan, 378
Rock Machine, 176
role models, 94, 170, 183–88
Roy, Raghu, 143

Satellite Television Asia Region (STAR) TV, 37, 38, 91, 114, 366, 367; children's preference of advertisements on, 166; commercial revenue for, 211–12; impact on children, 332; India-specific programmes on, 212; socially relavant advertisements on, 214, 215; viewing by children, 65
satellite television, 37, 38; cable and, 94ff; children watching, 64, 65, 96–100, 100–104; Doordarshan's response to, 91–93; growth of, 96–98; rates for sponsorship, 102, 411
satellite transmission, 89, 337
school work, TV watching and, 101, 361
Search India, 155
Seghal, Baba, 176
Seldin, Joseph, 225
sexual stereotypes, 301
Sinatra, Frank, 352
Siyaram suiting advertisement, 187, 307
soap advertisements, popularity of, 236–37, 301
soap serials, 92, 106
social bias, 202
social commitments, TV programmes and advertisements, 135

social communication, 343
social interaction, TV and, 61
socially relevant advertisements, on Doordarshan, 213–16
Sophiya, 183
Spock, Benjamin, 161, 330
sponsored programmes, 85, 140, 142, 199–201, 204, 208; rates for advertisements on Doordarshan, 409
sports personalities, in advertisements, 180
STAR Movies, 112
STAR Plus, 97, 102, 104; children's programmes on, 204
status symbol, 265, 269
SUN TV, 100
super rich advertisements, 332
Superhit Muqabala, popularity of, 92; earnings from advertisements, 207
Surf ultra advertisement, popularity of, 179

Tagore, Rabindranath, 95
target group, for advertisements, 196, 200
tariff, for sponsorship on Doordarshan, 380, 381, 382, 406–11
technical superiority, of TV commercials, 170
television (TV), advertising and, 137ff; advertising in India, 196ff; advertising, selling, 234ff; advertisements and consumer ethics, 213; advertisements, impact on society, 25; advertisements, influence on children, 19, 26, 252, 342, 347; advertisements, for middle class, 318, 319; advertisements, role of, in economy, 126; and children, 49ff; and child's attention, 55–58; effects of, 58–60; as entertainment, 40, 71; experience, 39–40; and family life, 61ff, 71, 347; hours, 81–84; as 'image-creator', 164;

informative role of, 159; as magic box, 35ff; as mass media, 28, 37; no discrimination in programme viewing, 74–75; ownership and exposure, 42ff; policy, 364, 366–67; replacing reading, 56, 58; role and meanings of, in India, 47; side effects of, 58–60; technology, 19, 27, 348; text preparation, 47; transmitters of Doordarshan, and reach, 208; video games for children, 284, 286, 287, 291; viewing habits, 72, 73
Television Advertising Standards Council of India, 399–406
Tendulkar, Sachin, 180, 275
Thums Up advertisement, impact on children, 163, 354
time spent, by children watching television, 49
TNT channel, cartoons for children on, 204
toy advertisements, on television and children's impact, 278, 305; in the US, 279, 282
transnational network, 37, 38, 366; embargo on, 112
Turner, Ted, 368

United States, advertisements on television in, 154; cable and network channels in, 351–52; children's advertising in, 253, 279, 282; cultural export by, 338; culture and violence in, 331; domination of films and serials of, 368–69; media domination by, 338, 339; television in, 38
United States National Coalition on Television Violence (NCTV), 107, 329–30
University Grants Commission, educational programme of, 77, 87
urban population, and consumerism, 223
urbanisation, problems of, 68

value system, changing, 336ff; television viewing and, 20
video cassette recorders, viewing by children, 42, 64, 109
viewing habits, of television, 54, 64–65, 98
Vimal advertisement, popularity of, 187
violence, on television, and impact on children, 70, 328–35, 359; Doordarshan's code on, 356
violent games, 289

Wartella, Ellen, 49, 164
Waters, Harry F., 109
Western culture, on television and class bias, 316–17
Western-oriented advertisements, 22, 175, 176, 308, 309, 312, 316
Winick, Charles, 172
Winick, Marianna Pezzella, 172
Winn, Marie, 58
women, Doordarshan's code on advertising of, 355–59
World Wrestling Federation (WWF), impact on children, 70, 106, 107, 291–92

Yadava, J.S., 165

Zee TV, 91, 97, 102, 103; children's programme on, 100, 204; commercial earnings of, 205, 212; popularity of, 206
Zee Movies, 112